CULTURAL THEORY

Praise for the first edition:

"Thorough, well-written and accessible, this text should be an indispensable part of every library."

Douglas Kellner, University of California at Los Angeles

Now in its second edition, *Cultural Theory: The Key Concepts* is an up-to-date and comprehensive survey of over 350 of the key terms central to cultural theory today.

This second edition includes new entries on:

- colonialism
- cyberculture
- globalisation
- terrorism
- visual studies

Providing clear and succinct introductions to a wide range of subjects from feminism to postmodernism, *Cultural Theory: The Key Concepts* continues to be an essential resource for students of literature, sociology, philosophy and media, and for anyone wrestling with contemporary cultural theory.

Andrew Edgar and **Peter Sedgwick** are both lecturers at the University of Wales, Cardiff. They are the authors of *Cultural Theory: The Key Thinkers*, also published by Routledge.

ALSO AVAILABLE FROM ROUTLEDGE

Cultural Theory: The Key Thinkers
Andrew Edgar and Peter Sedgwick
978-0-415-23281-4

Communication, Culture and Media Studies: The Key Concepts (Third edition)
John Hartley
978-0-415-26889-9

Habermas: The Key Concepts
Andrew Edgar
978-0-415-30379-8

The Routledge Companion to Feminism and Postfeminism
Edited by Sarah Gamble
978-0-415-24310-0

The Routledge Companion to Postmodernism
Edited by Stuart Sim
978-0-415-24308-7

CULTURAL THEORY

The Key Concepts

Second Edition

Edited by
Andrew Edgar
and
Peter Sedgwick

Routledge
Taylor & Francis Group

LONDON AND NEW YORK

First published as *Key Concepts in Cultural Theory* 1999

This edition published in 2008
by Routledge
2 Park Square, Milton Park, Abingdon, Oxfordshire OX14 4RN

Simultaneously published in the USA and Canada
by Routledge
270 Madison Avenue, New York NY10016

Routledge is an imprint of the Taylor & Francis Group, an informa business

Typeset in Bembo by Taylor & Francis Books
Printed and bound in Great Britain by
MPG Books Ltd, Bodmin

British Library Cataloguing in Publication Data
A catalogue record for this book is available from the British Library

Library of Congress Cataloging in Publication Data
A catalog record for this book has been requested

ISBN 978-0-415-39938-8 (hbk)
ISBN 978-0-415-39939-5 (pbk)
ISBN 978-0-203-93394-7 (ebk)

CONTENTS

LIST OF KEY CONCEPTS

Absence
Action theory
Aesthetics
Agency and structure
Agriculture
Alienation
Allegory
Analytic philosophy
L'année sociologique
anomie
Archaeology
Architecture
Articulation
Artworld
Author
Authority
Avant-garde
Base and superstructure
Behaviourism
Binary opposition
Birmingham Centre for
    Contemporary Cultural
    Studies
Body
Bourgeoisie
Bricolage
Bureaucracy
Canon
Capital
Capitalism
Cartesianism
Cinema

Citizenship
Civic humanism
Civil society
Class
Class consciousness
Code
Colonialism
Comics
Commodity
Commodity fetishism
Communication
Communitarianism
Conflict theory
conscience collective
Consciousness
Conservatism
Consumption
Content analysis
Contextualism
Continental philosophy
Contradiction
Conversation analysis
Counterculture
Critical theory
Cultural anthropology
Cultural capital
Cultural relativism
Cultural reproduction
Cultural studies
Culture
Culture industry
Cyberculture

KEY TO CONTRIBUTORS

GC Gideon Calder

RC Richard Cochrane

SH Stephen Horton

GH Gordon Hughes

CK Christa Knellwolf

KM Kevin Mills

CN Christopher Norris

JO Jessica Osborne

SKS Shiva Kumar Srinivassan

RW Robin Wackerbarth

CW Christopher Wraight

INTRODUCTION

The world has changed greatly since we published the first edition of *Cultural Theory: The Key Concepts* in 1999. Perhaps the most obvious change has happened in global politics, following **9/11** and the initiation of the 'war on terror'. Yet there have also been other, perhaps deeper and more slowly moving cultural changes that have become unavoidable with the dawn of the new century. These include the increasing impact that new **technologies** are having upon our lives. Biotechnology and especially **genetics** promises to fundamentally change our understanding of what it is to be human. The expansion of the internet and the integration of our lives with the diverse virtual worlds that constitute **cyberculture** similarly promise enormous changes to our self-identity and to our interactions with other people. Even environmental problems of global warming and pollution cannot be ignored by cultural theorists. Environmental change will impact upon our cultures, and our cultures nurture the resources upon which we will draw to cope with and check environmental degradation. Cultural theory therefore has to engage with all these phenomena. This new edition attempts to take account of some of these more pressing developments in theory and culture.

We have also taken the opportunity of a new edition to shift the focus of our book somewhat. Concepts that perhaps should have been in the original edition, such as **education**, **sport** and **leisure**, now have entries. We have also expanded our coverage of the cultural theory offered by humanities subjects, so that we now have entries on **archaeology** and **history**, for example, as well as recognising the emergence of **visual studies** as a discipline in its own right. This has come at the expense of entries on art movements, although substantial entries on **aesthetics** and **architecture** are retained, as are the entries on various genres of music.

In such a rapidly changing cultural and political world, the creativity of cultural theorists in thinking about that world, in imagining possible futures, and beginning to outline the moral, political and

aesthetic arguments that will shape that future, is increasingly important. We hope that this new edition provides a resource appropriate
to the new and exciting cultures of the twenty-first century.

Andrew Edgar and Peter Sedgwick
March 2007

CULTURAL THEORY

The Key Concepts

Second Edition

ABSENCE

In **semiotics**, a term is absent from a meaningful sequence of **signs** if it could potentially occupy a position in the sequence, and if its exclusion affects the meaning of the signs which are present.

AE

ACTION THEORY

In social theory, a distinction is usually made between action and behaviour. While behaviour is purely physical (or instinctual) movement on the part of the agent, action is intentional and meaningful, and more precisely, social action is oriented to the behaviour and action of others. Weber (1978) distinguishes four **ideal types** of action. Traditional actions are performed because they have always been performed so, and thus provide a limiting case of action, being little better than behaviour. Affectual actions are expressive of an emotion. More significantly, *zweckrational* (goal rational or instrumental) action entails the choice of that which is perceived to be the most instrumentally efficient means to the achievement of a goal. (The goal itself may be assessed in terms of the desirability of the consequences of pursuing and achieving it.) An instrumental action is comprehensible in so far as one recognises or shares the agent's view of instrumental or causal relationships in the world. In *wertrational* (value rational) action, the action is oriented to the achievement of a positively valued, and thus taken for granted, goal. Such actions are understood through recognising the importance of the appropriate values to the agent.

Two broad responses to Weber's account may be identified. On the one hand, emphasis may be placed upon the meaningfulness of the action, and the generation of meaning within the community and within the process of social interaction. For Schutz (1962, 1964), the attributing of motivations to actions (and thus the explication of goals, means or values) is the exception rather than the rule. Mundane social interaction is grounded in taken-for-granted responses to the actions of others, and of others' responses to one's own actions. (In effect, most action is unreflective, habitual behaviour.) Should this taken-for-granted **life–world** breakdown, motivation can be attributed, either retrospectively (with 'because motives', explicating the immediate motives of past actions), or prospectively (with 'in-order-to motives', that work effectively to explicate the goals of a forthcoming action), for example, in order to defend one's actions, or orient the actions of others. The meaning of an action ultimately rests upon its negotiation by all participating agents, rather than by an unproblematic appeal to the intentions of the original agent. This approach was developed, to something of an extreme, by **ethnomethodology**.

On the other hand, within a **positivist** tradition, the actions of individual agents are subordinated to an overarching social order. Thus, for Parsons (1937, 1951), the complexity of social interaction, in which there is such a range of interpretations (in terms of intentions, motives or goals) that one will never be able to predict with any certainty how another may react, entails that some prior social mechanism must exist in order to reduce complexity and increase predictability. Thus, interacting agents appeal to **norms** that are **institutionalised** in society, and internalised by individual agents in the process of **socialisation**. Norms do not merely codify the rules pursued by each agent and their evaluation of potential goals, but rather serve to direct their actions. In Parsons's system, the social action of the individual is thereby integrated into the social system as a whole. While Schutz's agents actively draw upon cultural resources to make sense of action as necessary, Parsons's agents more or less passively follow determining rules of conduct.

Further reading: Habermas 1984; Joas 1996.

AE

AESTHETICS

Aesthetics is that subdiscipline within philosophy that deals with questions of art and beauty. While it is in many respects an ill-defined and highly disputed area of philosophy, its principal concerns can be seen as those of defining the concept of 'art', or at least, providing an account of how we come to recognise artworks as artworks; questioning the relationship of art to the non-art or 'real' world (and thereby raising questions about the role of representation (or mimesis) and expression in art, and also of art's relationship to moral and political activity); and providing a philosophy of criticism (that explores how works of art are interpreted and evaluated).

The discussion of judgements of taste occurs throughout the history of philosophy, from the ancient Greeks. Plato's *Hippias Major* contains a discussion of the concept of beauty, and Aristotle's analysis of the structure of drama (and particularly tragedy) had a prolonged, if at times stultifying, influence on art and art criticism. While diverse reflections on art occur throughout the history of philosophy, it is not until the eighteenth century that aesthetics begins to emerge as a well-defined, and self-confident, division within the discipline. It is not coincidental that this follows on, and may thus be seen to respond to, the separation of works of art from craft works. There is little need to justify or explain the existence of craft works. In contrast, art works, increasingly divorced from political, ceremonial or religious uses, are problematic. In 1746, Charles Batteux coined the term fine art (*beaux arts*), arguing that such works shared the common property of beauty. The term 'aesthetics' is coined by Alexander Gottlieb Baumgarten, publishing his *Aesthetica* in 1750. However, Hume's essay 'Of the Standard of Taste' (1757) raises a fundamental problem that serves, periodically, to undermine confidence in aesthetics. The problem is whether or not a judgement of taste is purely **subjective**, for if it is, then rational debate about aesthetic objects is rendered pointless. Kant's *Critique of Judgement* (1790) provides a complex and masterful response to initial doubts about the viability of aesthetics. By appealing to the resources developed in his theory of knowledge and in his moral philosophy, he is able to provide an account of aesthetic judgement that is grounded in the universal structure of the human mind (so that a genuine judgement of beauty is such that all ought to agree with it); and he separates aesthetic experiences from experiences of merely sensual pleasure, principally in terms of the disinterestedness with which the spectator engages with the aesthetic object, and the lack of any practical purpose that can be attributed to the object. Hegel and Schopenhauer are able to build aesthetics confidently into their grand philosophical systems largely on the back of Kant's achievement.

If the nineteenth century saw aesthetics flourish, the twentieth century saw a renewal of doubts and assaults. In lectures delivered in 1907, Edward Bullough confronted doubts as to the utility of aesthetics (1957). Aesthetics does not obviously help either the artist create new work (and indeed the definition of general and universal rules defining 'art' or 'beauty' actual hamper the artist), or the audience to make sense of art (philosophical accounts being too general to illuminate the particular artefact that is before the audience). More bluntly, in the 1960s, the American artist Barnett Newman declared that: 'Aesthetics is for art what ornithology is for the birds', meaning that birds have coped perfectly well in ignorance of ornithology, and artists have coped just as well in ignorance of aesthetics.

The sociological criticisms of aesthetics are perhaps more damning than those arising from within philosophy, and it may be suggested that cultural studies grows out of a reaction to the implicit **elitism** of aesthetics (and more particularly, of the approach to literary criticism defended by Leavis). The development of the **sociology of culture**, for example in the work of Pierre Bourdieu (1984, 1993), throws into question, not merely the **ideological** basis of art (i.e. the distinction between high and **popular culture** that is taken for granted by so much writing in aesthetics), but also the role of aesthetics in perpetuating that ideology, and thus in failing to explore its own cultural and political roots. This is to say that aesthetics may be little more than the illusory justification and glorification of a middle-class leisure pursuit. The main purpose of aesthetics would be that of sustaining the economic (and not the mysterious 'aesthetic') **value** of artworks.

Within philosophy, recent developments within aesthetics have demonstrated a greater sensitivity to the social and cultural contexts within which art is produced and consumed. The American philosopher Arthur C. Danto has suggested that with the rise of **modern** and **postmodern** art, and thus of art forms which self-consciously reflect upon their status as art (and which are most dramatically exemplified by Duchamp's exhibition of a urinal as a work of art (*Fountain*) in 1917), that art itself now poses philosophical questions. Art asks exactly what art is and what the limits and purposes of art might be. Danto therefore recognises that what art is, and the way in which a particular work of art is interpreted, will depend heavily upon the particular historical, cultural and even political conditions within which it is created (Danto 1981). The institutional theory of art, through its key term **artworld**, has brought about a recent convergence with the sociological account of art, albeit without the political criticism implied by Bourdieu and others. Thus, for example, Dickie (1984), in recognising the diversity of art forms that have proliferated in the twentieth century (and not least in the development of conceptual art), argues that the criteria for defining and recognising an object or activity as art emerge within those **institutions**, such as galleries and the journals, which deal with art. An artwork is an artwork because it has been 'baptised' as such through its recognition in the artworld of critics, connoisseurs, gallery proprietors, artists and audiences.

In Germany, the paradox and strength of Adorno's *Aesthetic Theory* (1984), perhaps the last grand theory of art following in the tradition of Kant and Hegel, is that it vehemently embraces the criticisms of aesthetics and art posed by sociology and **Marxism**, while maintaining that art (and especially the **avant-garde** art of the twentieth century) still has a role in resisting ideology. Adorno accepts that art is a product of a particular society (and thus that the production and consumption of art will be intimately bound up with the production of any other artefact and commodity within that society). But art, for Adorno, can still have a moment of autonomy or freedom from that social determinism. It can therefore allow the artist and audience to think in ways that are not condoned by the dominant culture of the day. As such, art keeps alive the hope of resistance to ideology and political oppression.

Further reading: Cooper 1992, 1997; Eagleton 1999; Graham 1997; Maynard and Feagin 1997.

AE

AGENCY AND STRUCTURE

A central problem in social theory is the relationship between the apparently autonomous actions of individuals, and an overarching and stable social order. Durkheim provides a graphic presentation of the problem in his study of suicide (1952), by observing that while the act of suicide must typically occurs in isolation from society and is an action that cannot be repeated, the number of suicides that do occur in a particular society are highly predictable from one year to the next. The problem may be seen in terms of the questions as to whether (or how) structures can determine the actions of individuals; and as to how such structures are created. The most successful and generally accepted solution to these problems may exist in economics, in Adam Smith's account of the free market. The self-interested action of many individual agents, each acting independently of all others, results in the co-ordination of the quantity of goods supplied with the quantity of goods demanded. Superficially the market appears to be the result of some guiding 'invisible hand', akin to the actions of a puppet master perhaps. Smith's analysis of the role of the price mechanism dispels this illusion. (The success of Smith's analysis in economics has misled certain political philosophers, especially in the **social contract** tradition, to apply it beyond its true scope.)

In social theory, attempts to resolve the tension between agency and **social structure** have involved various approaches. At one extreme, structural **functionalists** (following in a tradition from Durkheim) and structural Marxists have tended to belittle the freedom of the individual, reducing social agents to (what Garfinkel called) 'judgemental dopes', or mere bearers of a structure, who passively follow rules that they have internalised during **socialisation**. At the other extreme, the reality of the social structure is denied altogether by ethnomethodologists, or at best, for methodological individualists, is acknowledged as a heuristic, providing a shorthand for what are ultimately multiple individual actions, and thus as having no determining power over the individual. Between these extremes various attempts have been made to understand social structures as the sedimented products of competent human agency, that in turn must be both actively (if unwittingly) sustained or reproduced by such agency, and that provide delimiting (rather than determining) conditions within which action is understood, given meaning, and pursued. In this light, the tension between agency and structure may be seen in Habermas's (1987) analysis of system and **life–world**, and in Anthony Giddens's (1984) theory of **structuration**.

Further reading: Callinicos 1983; Giddens 1979; Sztompka 1993.

AE

AGRICULTURE

Given its central concern with urban life in industrial societies, and with everyday life as experienced by large proportions of the population, cultural studies have relatively little to say about agriculture (in contrast, say, to **cultural anthropology**). However, it is worth noting that agriculture is a fundamental form of **culture** (as its name suggests), and as such a key site at which humanity confronts and transforms **nature** to its own ends. Agriculture is therefore relevant as the subject matter of much high and **popular culture** (from Virgil's *Georgics* of the first century BC, through Thomas Hardy's Wessex, to that quintessentially English (radio) soap opera, *The Archers* ('an everyday story of country folk')). Yet also, it continues to be a boundary where the interrelationship of culture and nature is negotiated—as is indicated, for example, by contemporary concerns about the genetic manipulation of crops and farm animals. Such concerns may conceal the fact that existing agricultural products are themselves already the outcome of centuries of cultural manipulation.

Further reading: Newby 1988.

AE

ALIENATION

Theory developed in the early writings of Marx, that seeks to characterise and to explain the estrangement of humanity from its society,
and its essential or potential nature. In the *Economic and Philosophical
Manuscripts* of 1844 (1975), Marx attributes alienation (a term that
had previously been current in philosophical and theological writings, and most significantly in Hegel) to the **division of labour**
under **capitalism**. For Marx, humanity is distinguished from all
other animal species by its ability, not merely to transform its environment, but to transform the environment through conscious (rather
than merely instinctual) activity. The resultant conscious re-engage-
ment with an environment that is no longer merely natural, but is
itself the product of the labour of previous generations of humans,
gives humanity, uniquely, the ability to shape not only its environment, but also itself. **Production** is, in summary, a process of
objectification, such that subjective human creativity is given objective form in the product. This in turn allows a new self-consciousness
on the part of the subject. Alienation is the corruption of this
objectivity, and the stifling of humanity's self-understanding.

The capitalist division of labour is characterised, not merely by the
specialisation of labourers in manufacturing, so that no individual
works on the whole product but only upon an isolated fragment, but
further by divisions between manufacture and distribution, manual
and mental labour, and labourer and capitalist. These structural features lead to four manifestations of alienation (Lukes 1969). First, the
worker is alienated from the product, in so far as he or she has no
control over its subsequent fate. Second, the worker is alienated from
the act of production, so that it ceases to have any intrinsic satisfaction. The ability to labour itself becomes no more than one more
commodity, having **value** only in so far as it can be exchanged for
any other. Third, the worker is alienated from other workers and
from society as a whole. The worker is treated as an isolated individual, and is judged by his or her ability to fulfil a pre-existing function within the production process. Production therefore ceases to be
a genuinely co-operative or communal process. Finally, the worker is
alienated from humanity's 'species being'. The term 'species being'
was developed by philosopher Ludwig Feuerbach (1804–72), and is
developed by Marx to refer to humanity's potential to determine,
collectively and freely, its own destiny.

In **sociology** and social psychology, alienation has more recently
been taken to apply to the subjective experience of modern life

(particularly in the urban environment and in work). Thus, Robert Blauner (1964) identified four empirically measurable forms of experience of alienation: powerlessness (the experience of being unable to influence one's environment), meaninglessness (from the inability to identify one's contribution to the product), isolation (the lack of any sense of belonging to the work organisation) and self-estrangement (the lack of any psychological reward from the work). This differs from Marx's analysis precisely in so far as Marx's account of alienation was an analysis of the structure of capitalism and the labourer's position within that structure, independent of any subjective perception of it.

A less precisely defined use of 'alienation', albeit one that makes full use of the metaphorical association of being a foreigner, outsider or stranger in one's own land, occurs in much philosophical and cultural commentary on the condition of modern society. Alienation may readily be associated with the experience of exile as in some sense paradigmatic of the experience of the twentieth century. Thus existentialism may tempt parallels to be drawn between alienation and such ideas as anxiety and inauthenticity. Similarly, alienation may be associated with Durkheim's concept of **anomie**, or with Weber's confrontation of the modern individual with the iron cage of **bureaucracy**.

Further reading: Mészáros 1986; Rotenstreich 1989.

AE

ALLEGORY

A drama, poem, picture or other work of art in which characters and events portrayed are used to represent or personify a deeper or veiled meaning, typically a moral or spiritual meaning. Abstract qualities are thus given human or other concrete shape. Monteverdi's opera *Orfeo* (1607), for example, is introduced by a soprano as 'La musica'. Allegory is fundamental to medieval morality plays, where virtues, vices and temptations are personified in the depiction of the struggle for a human soul, as in William Langland's *Piers Plowman* (second half of the fourteenth century). In Edmund Spenser's *The Faerie Queene* (1590–96) the Queen is an allegory of both Glory and Elizabeth I, her knights are allegories of specific virtues, such as Holiness, Temperance and Justice, Prince Arthur is Magnificence, and so on. John Bunyan's *The Pilgrim's Progress* (1678 and 1684) is populated by such characters as Christian and Christiana, Mr Worldly Wiseman, Faithful and Mercy, and allegorical places such as the Slough of Despond, Vanity Fair and the Delectable Mountains. Similarly, allegory provides a key to the interpretation of much Renaissance painting, state imagery and pageantry (see Yates 1975), albeit that the allegorical relationships may be obscure and highly disputable. The exact interpretation of images (and acknowledgement or otherwise that they are indeed allegorical images) within Jan van Eyck's *Arnolfini and his Wife* (1434) fundamentally affects the understanding of the painting as a whole. Albrecht Dürer's engraving *Melencolia I* (1514) provides a particularly intense example of the use of allegorical images. The role of allegory in Baroque music has been explored by Bukofzer (1939), indicating how a conventional meaning can be attributed to specific musical figures (so that, for example, in a Bach cantata reference to the 'cross' in a text may be linked to a sharpened note in the accompanying music, 'sharp' being 'Kreuz' in German). Walter Benjamin's *Origin of German Tragic Drama* (1977) provides an extensive analysis of the role of allegory in Baroque drama. Allegory is understood in terms of conventional and thus interchangeable images, having little or no relationship to their hidden meanings. A parallel is thereby implied with **commodity** exchange. More specifically, allegory is implicated in the encoding, reproduction and exposure of political **power** (manifest, not least, in the image of the melancholy prince). Allegory is cryptically summarised as the authority of power and the power of authority (Benjamin 1977).

Further reading: Kelley 1997.

AE

ANALYTIC PHILOSOPHY

As a school of philosophy, it is typically characterised by its interest in the logical analysis of **language**. The purpose of this analysis is to enhance our understanding of how language maps on to the natural world. The assumption behind this project is that the primary use of language is to communicate facts about that world. This assumption also explains the interest of analytic philosophers in questions relating to the referential relationship between language and reality (see **reference**) and how it is that words mean what they do (see **meaning**).

This tradition of philosophy has been particularly influential in Britain and North America. Its roots can be traced back to the work of Gottlob Frege, through the works of Bertrand Russell (see **meaning**), Ludwig Wittgenstein, the 'Vienna Circle' (see **meaning** and **metaphysics**), Peter Strawson (see **reference**), W.V.O. Quine and through to the present day in the works of Saul Kripke (see **reference**) and Donald Davidson.

As a result of the work of Quine, Davidson and the later Wittgenstein in particular, the assumption that the primary function of language is to refer to or communicate about the natural world has come into question. Indeed, Davidson ultimately rejects this notion of reference altogether (Davidson 1984a). However, there are still many analytic philosophers who support the project of analytic philosophy in its original guise (Kripke 1980).

SH

L'ANNÉE SOCIOLOGIQUE

Journal, edited by Durkheim between 1896 and 1913, that became the main publishing outlet of the research of Durkheimian sociologists, significantly contributing to the dominance of that group in French sociology.

AE

ANOMIE

Key term in Durkheimian sociology referring to the loss, on the part of an individual or group, of **norms** to guide social interaction. The concept serves to illuminate the relationship of individual behaviour and experience to the social structure. Norms mundanely constitute a framework that restricts the aspirations and goals of individual members of a society, so that they are coherent with the means available for their realisation. For Durkheim (1952, 1984) this coherence is a precondition of human happiness. The collapse or erosion of this framework (for example through increasing individualism), or the expansion of available means (for example through rapid economic growth and prosperity), lead to a discrepancy between means and goals. 'The scale is upset; but a new scale cannot be immediately improvised. Time is required for the public conscience to reclassify men and things' (Haralambos 1985:238, citing Durkheim). The term was further developed by R.K. Merton (1968), as a general theory of **deviancy**. Certain groups may experience a conflict between the goals positively valued by a wider society, and the means available within their particular group. The dominant normative framework of the wider society is therefore abandoned, and theft, for example, is adopted as a deviant means to achieve normal goals.

Further reading: Lukes 1969; Orrù 1987.

AE

ARCHAEOLOGY

The study of the human past, through the recovery, analysis and interpretation of its material remains. It is thus the study of material culture, which is to say the physical remains of human activity. The term 'archaeology' can also be used to refer to the very material culture that is studied, as well as to the discipline itself. While initially concern with the distance past or 'prehistory', modern archaeology now complements **history** (and indeed **sociology**) by applying its methods to all historical periods.

The relationship between archaeology and cultural theory is instructive. Archaeology itself tends to borrow theory from other social (and natural) sciences, rather than to generate theory of its own. Yet this borrowing and novel application serves to throw new light on that theory, not least by bringing cultural theory into association with methods derived from the natural sciences (such as radiocarbon dating and geophysical surveys). 'Archaeology' has also been taken up as a useful metaphor for their methodology by some cultural theorists, not least Foucault (1970, 1972).

Archaeology developed out of a Renaissance interest in antiquities and the collection of curiosities. Systematic study of ancient sites began in the early eighteenth century, with the likes of William Stukely surveying ancient monuments such as Avebury, in the English county of Wiltshire. Stukely demonstrated that these monuments were created by ancient humans, and not by giants or devils, as folklore suggested. In America, Thomas Jefferson (the Welsh-speaking third president) systematically excavated burial mounts in Virginia, cutting trenches into them in 1784. Like Stukely, Jefferson recognised that excavation unveiled temporally successive layers of human activity. Jefferson could thus establish the fact that burial mounds had been reused at distinct periods. The discovery of Pompeii and Herculaneum in the early eighteenth century stimulated **Enlightenment** interest in classical antiquity (manifest not least in the work of the art historian, and for many the founder of classical archaeology, Johann Joachim Wincklemann (2001)). Systematic and well-recorded excavations of the site were not begun until 1860. The crucial shift from an interest in antiquities to archaeological research proper lies in the move from a concern with isolated (but no doubt aesthetically pleasing) artefacts to attempts to understand the broader **contexts** within which those artefacts are found, and thus to recognise that the artefact itself can only properly inform the inquirer about human life and social practice if its relationship to the context is fully documented and analysed.

The nineteenth century saw a significant shift in thinking about historical time that inevitably had a major impact on archaeology. The development of geology and Darwin's theory of **evolution** challenged biblical accounts of time and human history. Human history was recognised to unfold in a timescale far greater than the 5,000 or so years suggested by a literal interpretation of the Christian scriptures. That humans had a 'prehistory' came to be accepted in the mid-nineteenth century. John Lubbock's *Prehistoric Times* became a best-seller upon its publication in 1865.

The Danish scholar Christian Thomsen's *A Guide to Northern Antiquities* (published in Danish in 1836 and in English in 1848) proposed the classification of artefacts, and thus of human history, in terms of the technology available within each period: hence the three periods of the Stone Age, Bronze Age and Iron Age. Excavations in Greece and Turkey (by the likes of Heinrich Schliemann) demonstrated the existence of Bronze Age cultures predating the classical Greece known from literature.

The late nineteenth and early twentieth centuries saw the refining of excavation techniques, and large-scale excavations of sites in the Middle East (inspired by a desire to explore the historical reality of events recounted in both Greek text, such as Homer, and the Christian Old Testament), and Europe and North America. This was a period largely devoted to describing and documenting sites. The broader theoretical questions that concerned these early scientific archaeologists tended to focus on the nature of cultural change. Assumptions about the central role that Egypt and Greece must have played in the development of Western culture pushed theorists to diffusionist models of cultural change. That is to say, that the dominant assumption was that ideas and cultural innovations defused out core areas of civilisation such as Egypt to peripheries, or were carried in waves of migration, rather than developing independently in geographically diverse areas.

The most important archaeological theorist in the early twentieth century was V. Gordon Childe. While still drawing on diffusionist theory, he adopted a **Marxist** approach to historical change in order to explore the development of farming and civilisation, based upon comparative studies of prehistoric changes across Europe and the Middle East (Childe 1927). These innovations are seen as revolutions, akin to the industrial revolution. Childe coins the terms 'Neolithic Revolution' and 'Urban Revolution' respectively for these events (see Childe 1956 and 1964). Unlike more orthodox Marxist theory, Childe worked with a consensual rather than a conflict model, in that he saw innovation occurring through the progressive managing role of early secular **elites**, with **religion** acting as a conservative force, inhibiting technological change.

The post-war period saw a significant development of the theoretical sophistication of archaeology, as well as in the scientific methods available to archaeologists. Not least of the latter was the introduction of more reliable methods for dating artefacts, and in particular radiocarbon dating, although collaborations with other specialist scientists also became increasingly important. Botanists could shed light on the plants used and eaten by societies; anatomists could identify animal bones, and so on. The evidence of human activity studied by archaeologists could now expand beyond material artefacts, such as buildings or pottery shards. The first theoretical advance that may be seen to take advantage of this new range of material was 'cultural **ecology**', championed by Julian Stewart and Gordon Willey in the USA and Graham Clark in the United Kingdom. Their work focused on the way in which cultures interact with their environments, and Clark in particular looked for evidence of organic remains that would be indicative of the way in which a site was inhabited and used.

The introduction of 'processual' archaeology (or the New Archaeology) marked a major theoretical step forward, albeit one that drew upon and incorporated the ecological approach. This development was given decisive focus in the work of Lewis Binford (Binford and Binford 1968) and David Clark (1968). Processual archaeologists criticised previous approaches to archaeology for being unscientific. Earlier archaeology had not, they argued, provided explanations of cultural change, but mere descriptions or narratives of particular sites. Explanation required hypotheses that could be empirically tested (typically through appeal to quantifiable data), and generalised beyond a single or few sites. The processual approach is highly indebted to **positivist** understandings of scientific method. In practice, it drew heavily on **systems theory** and the sort of **functionalist** explanations dominant in sociology and **cultural anthropology**. A society is seen as a system, interacting with its environment. More precisely, human behaviour is seen as the articulation of different subsystems of cultural and non-cultural phenomena. These might include the natural subsystems of animal movements, or geological and meteorological processes, as well as the cultural subsystems of population dynamics, the differentiation of economic, political and other subsystems within a society, as well as the existence of other societies (and thus the processes such as economic and ritual exchange or conflict that may exist between societies). Comparative studies allowed the generation of generalised accounts of cultural change (and thus the development of a global archaeology).

Post-processual archaeology emerged in the 1980s as a criticism of processual archaeology (Hodder 1986). The key focus of the criticism lay in what was perceived to be an over-reliance of processual archaeology on a model of explanation derived from the natural sciences, as well as an overemphasis upon the subsistence or economic productivity of societies. These two points are linked. By focusing on a society's function of adapting to its environment, processual archaeology is seen to neglect much of the **culture** of that society. Crucially, processual archaeologists fail to recognise the **symbolic** processes through which cultures give **meaning** to material artefacts. Post-processual archaeology thus drew upon **hermeneutics**, **phenomenology** and **structuralism** (as well as Marxism, **feminism** and social theories such as Giddens's theory of **structuration**), to provide it with the theoretical tools necessary to explore the way in which inhabitants of a culture would experience their environment as a meaningful one, with that experience shaping their practice within the environment. This leads also to a shift away from generalisable hypotheses, and towards accounts of the particularity and distinctiveness of different cultures. To illustrate briefly, while processual or functionalist approaches to the large megalithic stone monuments (such as tombs, burial mounds and henges, which is to say, megaliths) would stress the function that these monuments played in the maintenance and reproduction of the society (for example in legitimating power structures), post-processual approaches would stress the symbolic associations of the monuments (and thus, for example, the link between the tomb and the house, and thus their part in articulating the culture's understanding of death).

Cognitive-processual archaeology represents the processual archaeologists' attempt to incorporate the post-processual criticisms, by giving greater emphasis to the symbolic. An extreme positivist approach to explanation is abandoned, although suspicion is expressed about the dangers of relativism inherent in the post-processual approach, and the assumption that the modern archaeologist can reliably recreate the experiences and understandings of an individual from the past. Cognitive-processual archaeologists thus continue to demand the testability of their hypotheses, while abandoning the aspiration to construct universal cultural laws. Insights from Marxism and feminism as to the significance of **ideology** and political conflict within societies are readily incorporated, as well as more sophisticated philosophical reflections about the nature of theory, borrowed from or stimulated by sociology and the other social sciences. Not least, archaeologists recognise that in engaging with the past, archaeological accounts reveal as much about the present (and our understanding of ourselves) as they do the past. The archaeologist is not a disengaged observer, but a product of their own society, and the preconceptions and cultural biases of that society will shape their engagement with the past.

Further reading: Renfrew 2003; Renfrew and Bahn 2004; Shanks and Tilley 1992.

AE

ARCHITECTURE

The concept of architecture can cover all types of construction (housing, temples, office blocks, and so on), or it may be used in opposition to building, in order to focus upon construction that is intended to be more prestigious or impressive. In its more inclusive sense, it may be argued that an understanding and engagement with architecture is fundamental to any comprehensive understanding of culture. One of the most extreme explorations of this idea may be found in Heidegger's reflections of the relationship between Being and dwelling (1993). By relating dwelling to building, Heidegger presents dwelling as the fundamental form of human existence. Buildings express the human capacity to organise the environment within which they live, in terms of locations that are meaningful, and thus to articulate and bound their cultural world. It may then be suggested that it is through architecture that particular **cultures**, as well as humanity as a whole, come to express and understand themselves. It is through confrontation with the buildings of another culture that we can recognise their otherness. The narrower definition, however, highlights the important point that the built environment is the product of political hierarchies and is expressive of these hierarchies. The environment one encounters is typically one reflecting the differential power of groups to build as they please. Taken further, as the work of Foucault and Deleuze, for example, has shown, architecture can also be understood as a means of controlling populations.

Despite architecture's importance, **cultural studies** have perhaps dealt only obliquely with it. On the one hand, architectural theory and practice has influenced cultural studies as an early source of the concept of **postmodernism**. On the other hand, cultural studies renew the response to architectural space that is fundamental to modernist experience, either through consideration of **urban** existence and the city in general, or through specific spaces, such as those of the hotel lobby and the shopping mall.

The concept of postmodernism has been developed in architectural theory to mark a response, in both theory and practice, to the perceived crisis and failure of the modernist architecture that had dominated twentieth-century building (represented for example by the work of the Bauhaus, Le Corbusier, Mies van der Rohe and, at a slight tangent, Frank Lloyd Wright). The history of modern architecture can, perhaps all too easily, be summarised in series of slogans. Le Corbusier's 'the house is a machine for living in', or that architecture is 'the masterly, correct and magnificent play of masses brought together in light' are indeed well worth quoting. Yet of all these, the first and most fundamental is Louis Sullivan's maxim that 'form follows function' (coined in 1896). Like most architectural slogans, including Le Corbusier's, it has been as influential by being misunderstood as it has by being understood. It does, however, mark Sullivan's position in founding modern functionalism. Any part of a building is to be so designed as to express the function that it performs within a building. A weight-bearing beam is to look like a weight-bearing beam. This expresses a shift in architectural thinking, away from ornament (at its most dramatic in Adolf Loos's association of ornament and crime (1966)) and towards a renewed rationalism.

Architectural rationalism, especially in its European form, tended to articulate an explicit political (and typically socialist) programme, and thus to reflect upon the relationship between architecture and society. Crucially, this development, for all its actual diversity, represents what may be understood as an **Enlightenment** appeal to a universal reason, for the solution of all social problems. Rationalism thus led to an emphasis upon the technical possibilities of building (exploited in the use of steel, concrete and glass in high-rise building) and mass production. Partly in response to the need for cheap housing in the interwar years, architects explored the possibilities of prefabrication. However, underpinning this is a tendency to sunder the building, planned according to a universal rationality, from the particular environment or habitat within which it was erected. Beyond this, reason was also applied to the design, not simply of individual buildings, but of the housing estate and even the city as a whole in urban planning. The Athens Charter, published after the fourth Congrès Internationaux d'Architecture Moderne in 1933, and deeply indebted to Le Corbusier's thinking at the time, presented a rational approach to the 'functional city'. Despite its benign intent, the inhabitants of a city are reduced to little more than the passive occupants of a plurality of rationally administered functional spaces. Robert Jan van Pelt's argument that Auschwitz fulfilled the classical functions of a city (veneration of the dead, celebration of the future, government, dwelling, sustenance and trade) provides an ironic and disturbing comment on this conception of urban planning.

Robert Venturi may be placed as at least one of the first key critics of modernism. More polemically, the likes of Christopher Jencks and Tom Wolfe popularised the resultant alternative conception of architecture. Postmodernism emphasises a restoration of meaning to the built environment, through the use of a plurality of conventional design elements. Ornament is most emphatically reinstated in Venturi's analysis of the place of commercial signs (not least in Las Vegas casinos) as expressive of modern American culture. Postmodernism is thus 'multivalent', rejecting the idea of a single universal and ahistorical reason. An increased playfulness and ambiguity, alongside the use of metaphor or the pastiche of historical styles (used without reflection upon their historical specificity), challenges the most severe modernist structures. Michael Graves's Public Services Building in Portland, Oregon (1980–2), with its diverse lines and textures, is as typical of postmodernism as the monumental steel and glass of Mies's Seagram Building, New York City (1954–8) is of modernism. Similarly, urban planning comes to be challenged by a community architecture that would seek to involve residents in the planning process and uses vernacular styles that are sensitive to a local environment.

Outside the confines of architectural theory, the urban experience, as a characteristically modern experience, has had a central place in the development of the social sciences. In the work of authors such as Simmel, Weber and Benjamin, the nineteenth- and early twentieth-century experience of the city came under scrutiny, either directly, as, for example, in Simmel's account of the metropolis (1950b), or indirectly through reflection of the place of the city in literature, as in

Benjamin's study of Baudelaire and Paris (1973a). Williams's seminal study of the tension between the urban and the rural was published in 1973. Again, the debate over postmodernism has renewed interest in the urban, not least in the work of Berman, Baudrillard and Jameson, Cixous and Virilio. Despite the diversity of this writing, a common concern may be that of how to make sense of and to articulate the urban experience, and the plurality of its meanings. This may further mark the neglect of the issue of meaning by modernist architectural theory, thanks to its over-emphasis on a technologically oriented functionalism. In addition, the development of the city in the late twentieth century exemplifies a number of core postmodernist themes, for example in terms of the shift from production to consumption, increased gentrification, and the role of tourism in defining and reshaping the city. Leach has expertly brought together key representative texts in the cultural theory of architecture in his *Rethinking Architecture* (1997).

Further reading: Kolb 1990; Watkin 1977, 1992.

AE

ARTICULATION

The joining together of two social forces in a structured and hierarchical relationship. The term emerges in Marxist, and particularly Althusserian, analyses of the **mode of production**. At any given historical moment, one mode of production is dominant. It does not, however, exclude other modes, but rather forces their adaptation to its own needs. Thus, the **feudal** monarchy may survive in **capitalism**, but only in so far as it is adapted to the needs of capitalism (see Anderson 1979). The concept has been developed in analyses of **race**, **gender** and **nationalism**.

AE

ARTWORLD

Term in **aesthetics**, originally coined by Arthur Danto (1964), but developed by George Dickie as the key concept within the institutional theory of art. Certain modern works, notably by Duchamp (especially *The Fountain*), and conceptual art, pose problems for traditional approaches to aesthetics, in so far as they claim the status of works of art, yet seemingly have none of the characteristics traditionally attributed to art. Institutional theory attempts to resolve this problem by arguing that there are no properties inherent to an object which serve to determine it as art. Rather, the status of artwork will be conferred upon the object by the artworld. The artworld is defined, by Dickie, as 'a loosely organised, but nevertheless related, set of persons including artists ..., producers, museum directors, museum-goers ..., critics ..., philosophers of art, and others' (Dickie 1974:35–6). In summary, it is a largely self-defined group of people, who express an interest in art, and thus negotiate the current status of particular artefacts. According to institutional theory, artefacts that were not originally created as works of art (e.g. medieval or antique works created before the modern concept of 'art' had been formulated) may be accorded the status of art now, and similarly, objects once considered to be art may have that status removed from them. The question may legitimately be asked as to whether institutional theory may not more properly be understood as an approach within the **sociology of culture** than within aesthetics.

AE

AUTHOR

The author is superficially understood to be the creative, and individual, source of a written **text**. The idea that there is a unique creator of a text, and that the task of reading is, in consequence, a more or less passive process of recovering his or her intentions and meanings, has been variously challenged. Nineteenth-century **hermeneuticians**, notably Wilhelm Dilthey, challenged the assumption that the author had any privileged insight into the meaning of his or her text by critically examining the active process entailed in reading, and thus the need to construct rather than merely to recover meaning from a text. In effect, the author's self-understandings are exposed as merely one more interpretation of the text amongst many others. In **aesthetics**, criticism of the 'intentional fallacy' holds that interpretation of a work of art cannot claim to be definitive or authoritative by having recovered the author's intentions. (Within **post-structuralism**, Barthes most spectacularly declared the 'death of the author' (1977c).) Challenging the author's status thereby pushes aesthetic reflection towards the intrinsic qualities of the artwork or text, and at the extreme undermines the possibility of there being a single, definitive or correct reading.

It may be noted that only certain texts typically have authors attributed to them. Thus private and functional texts, such as shopping lists, exercises, advertising copy and much journalism, are not credited to an author, or the authorship is not perceived as significant to the understanding of the work. Similarly, many texts (such as folk songs, jokes, urban myths) emerge in an oral tradition, where again, conventional ideas of authorship are inappropriate. Conversely, any text (such as provisional drafts, letters and diaries) written by someone considered to be an author (such as an established novelist) may acquire additional significance precisely because of this authorship. Individual authorship may also, paradoxically, be attributed to products of co-operative work, so that a film may be attributed to the director (or possibly the producer), although rarely to the writer of the screenplay.

Further reading: Biriotti and Miller 1993; Burke 1992.

AE

AUTHORITY

Concept in **sociology** and political philosophy indicating the **legitimate** use of **power**. An agent thus submits willingly to, or is obedient to, the commands of another agent if that agent is perceived to be in authority. Obedience to authority is not induced through coercion and the threat of violence. In social theory, the analysis of authority is first developed by Weber. He focuses on the question of why certain agents have authority. He offers three **ideal types** in explanation. Authority may be legal-rational, in which case authority is bestowed on rules or laws, typically through some regular and public process of law formation or a demonstration of the necessity and efficiency of the rules (as in the case of **bureaucracies**). Traditional authority again follows more or less well-defined rules, but such rules are grounded in traditional practices, customs and cosmologies, rather than in recent, public processes of formation. Charismatic authority rests, not in rules, but in the personality (and sanctity or heroism) of a particular leader, and thus in that person's teaching and example.

In political philosophy, the question of authority may be seen to receive a crucial modern formulation in the work of Hobbes. Hobbes effectively addresses the question of the need for authority (contingently in the face of the social disorder of civil war) and the grounds upon which individuals should submit to it. In Weberian terms, Hobbes's account is a legal-rational one. It is, for Hobbes, rational to form a free **social contract** with a sovereign, providing that the sovereign maintains the social order and delivers peace. This approach is developed in the **liberal** tradition. A state is perceived to have authority in so far as its rules and laws would be acceptable to all rational citizens, independently of any particular interests they may wish to pursue. John Rawls's (1972) thought experiment of an 'original position', in which potential citizens plan a society in ignorance of their own talents and interests, is the most sophisticated contemporary version of such social contract accounts. In contrast, **communitarian** political philosophy suggests the primacy of traditional authority. In contradistinction to liberalism, agents are understood as already embedded in a particular community and culture. The agent's judgement of authority will thus depend upon values taken for granted in their community.

Political 'realists', such as Vilfredo Pareto and Gaetano Mosca, reject the distinction between authority and power, arguing that all submission and obedience is ultimately imposed upon the mass of social members. The distinction between authority and power is questioned more subtly by certain accounts of **ideology**. Within **Marxism** particularly, the possibility that agents may be coerced, not merely by the use or threat of physical violence, but also by the control that a dominant group or class can exercise over ideas (for example, through control over **education, mass media** and **religion**), is broached. A state may have authority in the eyes of its citizens, only because those citizens are denied the relevant cultural resources and information necessary to recognise that it is not acting in their best interests. The increasing difficulty that states find in maintaining authority has been analysed by Habermas (1976b) within the theory of a legitimation crisis.

Further reading: Barry 1989; Hampton 1997.

AE

AVANT-GARDE

Metaphorical term used in art theory and political philosophy. The French 'avant-garde', or English 'vanguard', literally refers to the foremost part of an army. Metaphorically, since the beginning of the twentieth century, it has been taken to refer to the political or cultural leadership by an elite. Implicit in this idea are assumptions of political or cultural progress, which the avant-garde pursues. The mass of society will be more or less indifferent to, or ignorant of, their interest in this progress, and will resist or be hostile to the avant-garde. As a key aspect of cultural modernism, the avant-garde typically expresses itself through obscure and innovative techniques, deliberately resisting easy assimilation into popular or mass culture (see Adorno 1984). In political theory, the avant-garde is seen as a necessary intellectual elite, leading a mass that remains afflicted by **ideology** and thus by a **false consciousness** that blinds it to its own best interests (see Lukács 1971). With the increasing questioning of modernism, and indeed of **Marxism**, the validity of the avant-garde has itself come into question (see Bürger 1984).

AE

BASE AND SUPERSTRUCTURE

Metaphor (from architecture) used in **Marxism** to indicate the relationship between the economy and the rest of society. Just as the size and shape of the superstructure of a building will depend upon the extent and depth of its foundations, so the characteristics of the non-economic spheres of human social life will depend upon the nature of economic activity. For Marxism, the economic base is composed of the **forces of production** and the **relations of production** (crudely, the application of technology and the relationships established between those who carry out the productive work and those who control the process of production). The **capitalist** base will therefore encompass industrial production techniques and the markets in **labour** and **commodities**, and the **feudal** economic base will encompass pre-industrial production and serfdom. The superstructure is most simply defined as referring to all other spheres of society, but specifically including the state, law, the family and cultural or ideological spheres such as **religion**, the arts and the **mass media**.

The model of base and superstructure leaves open two questions, the response to which depends upon the precise way in which Marxist social theory is interpreted. The first and more pressing question focuses on the nature of the determinism involved. The explanatory mechanism that relates the base to the superstructure centres on the manifestation of **class** conflict and power. The promotion and exploitation of a given set of forces of production is held to be in the interests of one class (e.g. early industrial production and the **bourgeoisie**). The economic power of the dominant class (manifest as political power in the state) will allow it to influence the development and shaping of superstructural institutions so that they provide the most advantageous conditions for the exploitation of the forces of production. Legal systems will therefore facilitate the refinement of the relations of production (e.g. by allowing a free labour force for capitalism), while other superstructural institutions will tend to legitimate the existing economic and political order (as natural, God-given or just), and carry out the socialisation of new members of society. A strict determinist model would grant the superstructure little or no autonomy from the base. This would allow, in principle, a Marxist social science to generate strict, deterministic laws that would facilitate the prediction of the structure and the historical development of a society from knowledge of its economy. More flexible models suggest that superstructural institutions will have a greater or lesser degree of autonomy from the base, and thus will be able to develop independently of the immediate or overt interests of the dominant class. The relationship of causality need not then be one-way, giving scope for superstructural developments to influence economic development. The economic base may then merely be determinant in the last instance, or may set broad limits within which the superstructure may take shape.

The second question asks for a precise definition of the boundary between the base and superstructure. This is not easily given, because of the ambiguous status of the legal system. Superficially, the legal system is confined to the superstructure, yet the labour law, or any form of commercial law, serves in large part to define the relations of production. As such it is part of the economic base. It is not clear whether or not the relations of production can be defined in non-legal terms. The ambiguity does, however, serve to emphasise the dangers of placing too much theoretical weight on an unconsidered metaphor. The base–superstructure model is a useful image, but it cannot serve as a substitute for rigorous theorisation of the relationship between the economy and the rest of society.

AE

BEHAVIOURISM

An approach to psychology that argues that the discipline can only be genuinely scientific if it concerns itself with publicly measurable phenomena, such as muscular and glandular responses. The approach may therefore be seen as a response to the problems inherent in a dualist account of the human being (where the human being is understood as a mind or soul within a body) and with the status of any claim to knowledge of the mental states of another human being.

The introduction of behaviourism into psychology is usually credited to J.B. Watson in the 1910s. Watson reacted against introspection as a technique in psychology, ridiculing the demands that were put upon psychologists to be trained supposedly to distinguish and classify their own mental states. Influenced by the research that Pavlov had carried out on the reflexes of animals (demonstrating that if a dog was presented with the sound of a bell prior to food, it could be conditioned to salivate upon the sound of the bell alone). From this, Watson was able to argue that an appeal to mental states in the explanation of human action was unnecessary. Explanation could proceed, on positivist lines, by identifying law-like associations between external stimuli and the subject's observable response to them. Thus, a mental state, such as 'being hungry', could be understood, or operationalised, purely in terms of the behaviour that one expects of the person or animal in that state. (Crudely, 'being hungry' is manifest in, or in stricter forms of behaviourism, exhausted by, the behaviour of seeking food.) A subject's behaviour will not then depend upon (inwardly and privately experienced) mental states (such as intentions, purposes and emotions), but rather upon the 'recency' and frequency with which particular stimuli have been encountered. In line with this, Watson adopted a position of strict environmentalism, to the effect that little if anything is innate (or genetically determined) in human behaviour. Humans learn in response to the stimuli provided by their environments.

Watson was forced to retire from academic life in 1920 (after his scandalous divorce), but behaviourism became a dominant force in American psychology up to the 1960s, being developed most significantly by Edward Guthrie, Clark Hull and B.F. Skinner. Guthrie remained close to Watson's concept of behaviourism, although he dropped frequency as a significant determinant of behaviour. Hull aspired to a systematic and mathematically expressed account of human behaviour. Skinner's behaviourism moved away from Watson's, and particularly from the centrality given to the concept of the reflex, in order to focus on the effect that behaviour has upon the environment. What matters about behaviour, for Skinner, is that it strives to adapt to the animal's environment. For example, a laboratory animal changes the position of a switch, and thereby causes food to become available. Crucially, Skinner argues that the animal's behaviour cannot be explained in terms of its intention or purpose to acquire food. Rather, the intention or purpose of the action lies not in some anticipation of the future, but rather because this was the effect of the behaviour in the past. Thus, animals (including humans) are argued not to act because they have a purpose, but rather because of past consequences.

Skinner distinguishes between 'methodological behaviourism' and his own 'radical behaviourism' (again marking a break from Watson). The methodological behaviourist simply accepts that mental events are publicly unobservable and so cannot play a legitimate part in a publicly verifiable scientific explanation. The radical behaviourist recognises the existence and role of mental events, and attempts to come to terms with (rather than merely sidestep) their privacy, by arguing that they are governed by the same forms of (stimulus–response) conditioning that govern public behaviour and that they lie in discoverable causal relations to overt behaviour. Skinner's behaviourism therefore attempts to embrace even mathematical and logical reasoning and introspection within the same explanatory framework as that applied to the conditioned behaviour of laboratory animals.

The controversial nature of behaviourism rests not merely upon what may appear to be an excessively mechanistic account of human being, and the challenges it poses to the supposed dignity of human freedom, but also in the fact that, at least in the hands of Watson and Skinner, it was intended to have a practical application in mundane social life. The extreme prospect of this is given by Skinner in his novel *Waldon Two* (1976), describing the community where behaviourist techniques are used to condition a population into co-operation, love and even creativity. More mundanely, behaviourist psychology lies behind behaviour therapy and various techniques that allow individuals successfully to overcome phobias or neuroses.

Further reading: Skinner 1973, 1974; Zuriff 1985.

AE

BINARY OPPOSITION

Concept in **structuralism**, rooted in Saussure's linguistics but also Radcliffe-Brown's (1977) **cultural anthropology**, serving to explain the generation of meaning in one term or **sign** by reference to another mutually exclusive term. The two terms may be seen to describe a complete system, by reference to two basic states in which the elements in that system can exist (e.g. culture/nature; dark/light; male/female; birth/death). One side of the binary opposition can be meaningful only in relation to the other side. Each side has the meaning of not being its opposite. A term may therefore appear in more than one binary opposition, with its meaning being modified accordingly. (Thus, death may be understood as an event as 'not birth'; or as a state as 'not life'.) Binary oppositions structure perception and interpretation of the natural and social world.

In any system of signs, certain binary oppositions may be seen to stand in determinate relationships to each other. One binary opposition may be open to transformation into another, therefore enriching the meaning of all the terms concerned. Thus, for example, in Western cultures, the opposition between birth and death may be transformed into an opposition between white and black (for example manifest in white christening robes and black hearses). Put differently, white is to black, as birth is to death. In addition, the binary opposition may contain an implicit evaluation, so that, for example, birth and white are associated with good, and death and black with bad. The analysis of such series of oppositions provides a crucial insight into the working of **ideology**. Consider, for example, the following series: male/female; public/private; culture/nature; reason/emotion. Ideology may therefore work precisely to the degree that such series of binary oppositions are taken for granted, appearing to reflect rather than to structure the world. The critique of ideology entails the explication of a series of binary oppositions as a culturally specific interpretation, selection and privileging of elements from the ambient world.

A further implication of the theorisation of binary oppositions focuses upon the status of ambiguous categories. Anything that shares characteristics of both sides of the opposition is suspect or otherwise problematic. Anthropologists have therefore suggested that the importance given to human hair or nail clippings in magic and folklore rests in their ambiguous status. They are at once part of the body, for they grow from the body, but have no feeling and are easily cut from the body without pain or damage. Similarly, *rites de passage* mark ambiguous stages in a human's development between childhood and adulthood. Magic, ceremony and the sacred are thus seen to be concerned with ambiguous categories.

AE

BIRMINGHAM CENTRE FOR CONTEMPORARY CULTURAL STUDIES

Founded in 1964, as a postgraduate research centre at the University of Birmingham, UK, the Centre for Contemporary Cultural

Studies has had a pivotal role in the development of cultural studies in the United Kingdom. (A significant number of the leading figures in British cultural studies have passed through the Centre at some stage in their careers.) Initially under the directorship of Richard Hoggart and Stuart Hall from 1968 to 1979, the Centre developed much that is now typical of the subject matter of cultural studies and the techniques of analysis. Under Hall, research topics developed from an initial interest in the 'lived' culture of different classes (stemming from Hoggart's own work in *Uses of Literacy* (1957)), to the centrality of the **mass media**, and associated areas of youth and **subcultures**, education, and **race** and **gender**. The Centre was interdisciplinary from its inception, drawing most notably on **sociology** and **literary criticism**, but also importantly on history (for example through the influence of E.P. Thompson (1963)). The Centre's theoretical development may be seen in part as a response to American approaches to the study of mass media. Drawing on the intellectual resources of contemporary Europe, including both Althusser's and Barthes's **structuralism**, the Centre approached the media as ideological and hegemonic institutions. **Popular culture** is therefore understood as the site of the resistance and negotiation of marginal and disempowered groups within **society**. The Centre's work may also be characterised by the collaborative nature of its research. The Centre's series of working papers became a key medium of publication, both for its staff and its postgraduate students. Under the directorship of Richard Johnson and then Jorge Lorrain, some shift in the focus of the Centre's research away from textual analysis of the media and towards the history of everyday life has been identified by some commentators. In 1988, the Centre became the Department of Cultural Studies, offering undergraduate courses in addition to postgraduate research. The University of Birmingham closed the Centre in 2002.

Further reading: Turner 1996.

AE

BODY

Until recently, the body has been either ignored or made marginal in philosophical, political and cultural theory. Thus, in philosophy, human agency and the **identity** of the person were traditionally seen to lie in the mind. The mind (or soul) was permanent and, in its rationality, was the source of all our knowledge. A key philosophical problem (for example from the writings of Descartes in the seventeenth century onwards) was the relationship of the mind to the body. A few thinkers, especially within the seventeenth- and eighteenth-century empiricist tradition of British philosophy (such as David Hume), could be seen to be making something of the human body by recognising that our experience of the world entirely depends upon our bodily sense organs. However, even this potential was stifled by emphasising sight and hearing as the sources of knowledge. The more obviously bodily senses of smell, taste and touch are sidelined, and so too are the implications that they have for our practical engagement with the world through our bodies. At the end of the eighteenth century, Kant demonstrates the problematic status of the senses in his *Critique of Judgement* (1987). On the one hand he argues that it is only as both rational and sensual (or embodied) creatures that we can experience the pleasure of beauty (as opposed to the purely rational delight in the morally good, or the purely physical agreeableness of food and drink). On the other hand, beauty rests in sight and hearing, not in touch, smell and taste.

In the mid-nineteenth century, Marx's view of human beings as fundamentally beings that transform and create their own environment through **labour** offers some awareness of embodiment. It is perhaps only in American **pragmatism**, at the end of the nineteenth century, that the importance of the embodied, practical experience of the world is given thorough and rigorous treatment in philosophy. It is here that the importance of taken-for-granted knowledge of the world, carried in the habitual skill and competence with which we use our bodies to manipulate and test the world, comes to the fore. In the twentieth century, this perspective is developed in Heidegger's work, for example in his concepts of 'ready–to–hand' and 'present–at–hand' (1962:102–7). Normally, objects are used unthinkingly. While a tool works, we do not worry about it. When it fails, we step back and question and examine it. Thus, we acquire conscious, theoretical knowledge of the world, only when the world trips us up practically. Against Descartes's assumptions, we cannot gain knowledge through merely reflecting on the world. We need a reason to reflect upon it, and that reason comes only through a bodily engagement. Thus Heidegger, like the pragmatists and even David Hume, introduces the body into philosophical thought by directly criticising the way in which Descartes does philosophy. Heidegger further emphasises the necessity of the body—along with all its contingencies—to our self-understanding as human beings in the demand that we must accept that we are mortal. The Heideggerian approach was influential on the development of French **phenomenology**, particularly in the analysis of 'flesh' by Maurice Merleau-Ponty (again beginning from the argument that consciousness is embodied in a particular world) (1962), and Jean-Paul Sartre (not least in his spectacular analysis of torture, as the attempt to capture and possess the freedom of the victim within his or her flesh) (1958:303–59).

In Western political theory, the body is again ignored until recently. **Liberalism**, for example, adopts a model of human being that stresses rationality. As such, it is the human intellect that matters. Indeed, the unrestrained pursuit of bodily desires may be theorised as a threat to political order. In addition, liberalism tends to assume a series of more or less implicit dichotomies. Reason is set against unreason, mind against body, and male against female. Liberalism's traditional blindness to gender difference, and to the exclusion of women from politics, may in part be understood through this association of reason, mind and masculinity

In the late 1970s and early 1980s, with the revival of liberal theory through the work of John Rawls (1972), there also came a new criticism of liberalism from the **communitarians**. In this line of argument, Michael Sandel (1982) is critical of Rawls (and thus contemporary liberalism) precisely because the Rawlsian model of human beings is disembodied and disembedded. That is to say that Rawls artificially abstracts human beings from the bodily and cultural experiences that form them as the particular beings they are. In effect, Rawls is accused of assuming that the human being, as a rational personality capable of choice, exists prior to its embodied life in a particular community. Sandel argues that the very ability to choose and to hold **values**, and to be aware of ourselves as individuals, comes only from bodily experience, and cannot exist prior to it.

In cultural theory, there is a significant literature on the nude as a core subject matter of Western art. In part, this literature comes from the orthodox approach of a cultural historian, such as Clarke's analysis of the idealisation of the body according to historically varying cultural norms (1956). More recently **feminists** and others (such as John Berger (1972)) have placed the nude in a political context, in order to question the ascription of intrinsic **aesthetic** value to it as part of the **patriarchal** or **ideological** structure of power in Western culture (Diprose 1994; Grosz 1994; Irigaray 1985a).

The understanding of the body develops in cultural studies through the recognition of the body as a site of meaning. A **semiotic** approach may be taken to the body Umberto Eco's characterisation of the body as a 'communication machine' is telling (1986). The body is not simply there, as a brute fact of nature, but is incorporated into culture. The body is indeed a key site at which culture and cultural **identity** is expressed and articulated, through clothing, jewellery and other decoration and through the shaping of the body itself (through tattoos, hair styles, body-building and dieting, for example). It is through the body that individuals can conform to or resist the cultural expectations imposed upon them. Sociology has thus been able to turn to the analysis of 'body-centred practices' (see Turner 1984). Foucault's analysis of the development of the prison system and state punishment focuses on the body as the subject of discipline (1977a). Crucially, the body is shaped and disciplined through systems of surveillance, either actual surveillance or surveillance that is imagined to be occurring. Analysis of the body can therefore increasingly see it as a product of social constraint and construction (which is a theme also found in Goffman's work), or of the languages and **discourses** within which it is discussed and analysed (as, for example, in the languages of medical science, psychiatry and criminology).

AE

BOURGEOISIE

Much used, but often poorly understood term, referring to the dominant **class** in capitalist society. In Marxist theory, it is most strictly employed in opposition to '**proletariat**', where it refers to the owners of productive **capital** (and thus to mercantile, industrial and financial entrepreneurs). What distinguishes the bourgeoisie is that they have no need to sell their labour in order to survive. While such a bold contrast may be effective in the analysis of early **capitalism**, it fails to grasp the role and status of the administrative and managerial classes that have emerged with the development of high and late capitalism. Thus, 'bourgeoisie' is frequently used to refer to the 'middle classes' of contemporary capitalism. While such classes may still need to sell their labour (as does the working class), their higher financial reward, and higher status, entails that the continuation of capitalism is as much in their interests as in the interests of any class of owners. The role that the middle classes have in shaping culture has led to the frequent use of the adjective 'bourgeois' as a derogatory term.

Further reading: Gay 1984, 1986; Habermas 1989a.

AE

BRICOLAGE

Engaging metaphor developed from Lévi-Strauss's structural anthropology. The French word 'bricoleur' refers literally to the sort of worker capable of mending or maintaining any machinery and installation by reusing items from elsewhere, typically improvising new uses for these items. So, in cultural theory, and especially the analysis of **subcultures**, the term refers to the processes by which elements are appropriated from the dominant culture, and their meaning transformed, for example through ironic juxtapositions, to challenge and subvert that culture.

Further reading: Lévi-Strauss 1966.

AE

BUREAUCRACY

As the term is understood in contemporary **sociology**, bureaucracy is that form of administration in which decision-making power is invested in offices, rather than in identifiable individuals. While bureaucracies have existed in pre-industrial societies (including feudal China), it is the fundamental role that bureaucracy plays in the organisation and control of twentieth-century **capitalism** that has received greatest theoretical and empirical study

The classic source for the theory of bureaucracy is Max Weber, published in the 1920s. Weber proposed a six-part model (or **ideal type**) of bureaucracy, that served to specify its distinctive characteristics (even if these characteristics need not all be present in any particular empirical example of a bureaucracy) (Weber 1946b). Weber's characteristics are as follows: a high degree of specialisation, with complex tasks broken down and clearly allocated to separate offices; a hierarchy, with chains of **authority** and responsibility clearly defined; activity is governed by a consistent system of abstract rules; officials work impersonally, without emotional or personal attachment either to colleagues or clients; personnel are recruited and promoted on the grounds of technical knowledge, ability and expertise; the official's activities as an official are wholly separate from his or her private activities (so that a professional position cannot be used for personal advantage). For Weber, this structure is the most efficient (and therefore most instrumentally rational) way in which to organise the complex activities of a modern industrial society. As such, bureaucracy is an unavoidable feature of advanced society, not merely in industry, but in almost every area of social life. Mommsen has thus written of the total bureaucratisation of life (1974). Weber himself predicted, not just the growing influence of bureaucracy in capitalism, but also a convergence between capitalist and Soviet communist societies, in terms of the dominant role played by bureaucracy in both.

While bureaucracy is technically efficient, for Weber, it also has undesirable consequences for democracy. Innovative activity, which is to say activity that does not make sense within the narrow parameters of the bureaucracy, is inhibited. This is because nearly all social activities must proceed through stages that are predetermined by bureaucracies, and those bureaucratic structures are themselves inflexible and possibly unresponsive to change. Further, technical expertise is concentrated within the democratically unaccountable offices of the bureaucracy, so that bureaucratic decisions and procedures are not easily challenged. Bureaucracy thereby becomes a 'steel-hard cage' that encloses us all.

Marxism has perhaps contributed little to the theory of bureaucracy. Bureaucracies were less extensive when Marx and Engels were writing, and they may be seen to be generally antipathetic to bureaucracy. The classic Marxist writings notably underestimate the significance that administrative structures have in capitalism (and thus have little to say on the significance of the managerial **classes**). The Marxists who have had most to say about bureaucracy tend to be those who seek to fuse Marxist and Weberian theories. In *History and Class Consciousness* (1971), the Hungarian Marxist Lukács began to use Weberian accounts of bureaucracy and rationalisation to extend Marx's theory of **commodity fetishism** into an account of the reification of the social totality (and thus to explain the distinctive **ideological** forms of contemporary capitalism, in so far as society confronts the individual as an autonomous, quasi-natural object rather than as a product of human agency and choice). This in turn influenced the **Frankfurt School**, and especially T.W. Adorno, in developing a characterisation of late capitalism as a totally administered society.

Further reading: Beetham 1996.

AE

CANON

Typically the term is used to encompass what are generally recognised as the most important works in a particular artistic tradition (most usually of literature or music). It is derived from its original use, dating from the fourth century, to refer to the authoritative and definitive books of the Christian Bible. Defenders of the notion of a canon would argue from the position that there are universal **aesthetic** values (albeit that these values may unfold over time, with the development of the tradition). Individual works are therefore included in the canon on the grounds that they best express these universal values. The canonical works are therefore the finest expression of a particular language, and may indeed be taken as the expression of a culture's or a nation's identity. The idea of a canon has come under increasing criticism, not least with the emergence of Marxist and feminist criticism in the 1960s, and **post-struc-turalist** and **post-colonial** accounts of culture. With increased sensitivity to cultural **pluralism** and to the economic and political conditions of artistic production, the canon appears less as an expression of universal values than as an expression of power relations. The canon may be seen to exclude subordinated groups at a number of levels. First, the canonical works may represent certain groups (non-whites, the poor, women) according to culturally dominant **stereotypes**. Second, the canon may exclude works produced by those groups, or not recognise the media within which those groups have traditionally expressed themselves. Finally, the manner of expression celebrated within the canon (including preconceptions of the nature of human subjectivity and creativity) may be inappropriate in articulating the experience of subordinated groups.

Further reading: Eagleton 1984; Kermode 1975.

AE

CAPITAL

Concept from economics, referring most obviously and intuitively to the machines, plant and buildings used in the industrial manufacturing process. More technically, capital is one of four factors of production. A factor of production is a resource that is valued, not for its own sake, but for its function in the production of other goods or services that are of intrinsic value. The other factors of production are land (including all natural resources prior to their extraction, the land surface, sea and space), **labour** (being the ability of human beings to engage in productive work) and entrepreneurship (being the ability to organise together the other three factors in the production process). Capital is any resource or item used in the production process that has already been subject to some form of productive labour.

AE

CAPITALISM

A form of social and economic organisation, typified by the predominant role played by **capital** in the economic production process, and by the existence of extensive markets by which the production, distribution and consumption of goods and services (including **labour**) is organised. The development of capitalism may most readily be linked to industrialisation, and thus has its purest manifestation in nineteenth-century Britain and USA. However, a more limited form of (mercantile) capitalism, characterised by limited markets in commodities, and thus by the existence of a small capitalist class of merchants, but without industrial production or free labour markets, existed in medieval Europe.

Different theories of capitalism exist, especially within social theory, providing different explanatory models of the origin of capitalism and of its predominant features. In **Marxism**, capitalism is theorised in terms of the organisation of production and the resultant relationship between economic **classes**. The emergence of capitalism is thus explained in terms of the development of industrial technology (or the **forces of production**). A capitalist society is structured through the antagonism of two dominant classes: the **bourgeoisie** which owns and controls the means of production, and the **proletariat** that owns only its ability to work (and therefore survives by selling its labour power). At the surface, there appears to be a fair and free exchange of commodities, including labour power, through the market mechanism. In Marx's analysis, beneath this surface lies a systematic exploitation of the proletariat, in so far as the price of labour set on the free market is less than the value of labour's product. The bourgeoisie are therefore seen to appropriate **surplus value** akin to the discrepancy between the costs of producing a commodity and the total revenue received from its sale. While Max Weber's analysis of capitalism shares much in common with Marx's, Weber places greater emphasis on the surface organisation of capitalism, and thus on capitalism as a system of exchange and **consumption** (1964 and 1979). The link between capitalism and rationalisation is central to this account. For Weber, a precondition of capitalist development is the development of double-entry bookkeeping (and thus the possibility of rational control and prediction of the capitalists' resources).

At the beginning of the twentieth century, European and American capitalism developed in a number of key areas. Weber's analysis of rationality responded to the increasing **bureaucracy** of capitalism, as more complex production required ever more sophisticated forms of administration and control. This in turn leads to the rise of a white-collar middle class that is distinct in its interests and allegiances from either the working-class proletariat or the bourgeoisie. Furthermore, banks and other financial organisations became more significant, as the day-to-day control of production was increasingly separated from ownership. A distinctive form of finance capital was identified, for example, by the Austro-Marxist Rudolf Hilferding (1981) around 1910. Linked to this development is both the increasing concentration of capital, so that production is controlled by fewer, larger corporations (leading to monopoly capitalism), and the expansion of capitalism into colonial markets. Increasing state intervention, not merely in the regulation of capitalist production, but also in the ownership of the means of production, leads to a further deviation from the 'pure' model of free-market capitalism. A period of organised capitalism thus begins to emerge after the First World War, and continues, with the increasing multinational consumption and production bases of major corporations, under the rise of welfare-state capitalism and Keynesian economic policies, at least into the 1970s. All these developments may be seen to obscure the basic lines of class conflict identified by Marx. The proletariat is increasingly differentiated within itself, and through greater job security and real income, is more integrated into the capitalist system. The economic crises predicted by Marx are at worst managed and at best avoided by interventionist governments.

There have been developments over the post-war period in technology (with the decline of traditional manufacturing industries and the rise of communications and knowledge-based industries) and in consumerism (with increasingly affluent working and middle classes); as well as there being political shifts in the 1980s away from state intervention in the economy. All these demand new theories to explain the organisation of contemporary societies. Thus theories of late capitalism (Jameson 1991), post-industrial **society** (Bell 1973), disorganised capitalism (Lash and Urry 1987) and various accounts of **postmodernism** suggest a more or less radical break from capitalist modes of organisation.

Further reading: Bottomore 1985; Giddens 1973; Mandel 1972; Sayer 1991.

AE

CARTESIANISM

A term which, strictly speaking, means 'of, or bearing some relation to, the thought of philosopher René Descartes' (1596–1650). However, 'Cartesianism' has also come to signify a **metaphysical** viewpoint that bears upon issues of personal **identity**, the nature of the **self**, and also questions in **epistemology**.

In reply to the writings of contemporary sceptics who questioned whether we can have any certain knowledge, Descartes's writings seek to show that there is at least one certain piece of knowledge we are in possession of. Arriving at this view, he argues, involves employing what is termed the 'sceptical method'. Thus, Descartes resolves to 'demolish' all his beliefs, and afterwards attempts to construct the foundations of knowledge as stable and lasting science. In order to do this, it is sufficient merely to bring into question all one's opinions, i.e. to show that they are *not certain*, rather than that they are false. For instance, what we often accept as true are beliefs derived from experience (from the senses). But, the senses can deceive us, so many beliefs derived from them can be doubted. But some beliefs cannot be doubted: 'for example, that I am here, sitting by the fire, wearing a winter dressing gown holding this piece of paper in my hands, and so on'. However, taking his scepticism one step further, Descartes asks how can we distinguish between being awake and asleep? Having sensations could be a product of the imagination; nevertheless, even if the sensation of having a body is merely a dream, there are some things ('simpler and universal', of which bodies are made up) which are real, i.e. notions of quantity, shape, size and number.

Thus, we can distinguish between the physical sciences (physics, astronomy, etc.) which depend upon composite notions (they conceive of objects as having specific sizes, shapes, etc.), and other forms of knowledge (e.g. geometry, mathematics) which do not. Whether we are asleep or awake $2 + 3 = 5$ and a square has four sides. Some might argue that the existence of an omnipotent God guarantees that these beliefs are true. But suppose that 'I am so imperfect as to be deceived all the time'. Then, even these beliefs are doubtful. Suppose that 'not God [...] but rather some malicious demon of the utmost power and cunning has employed all his energies to deceive me'. I might think $2 + 3 = 5$, but I am being fooled. What then?

According to Descartes, one thing remains true: even if I am being deceived, I am still thinking: 'I must conclude that this proposition, *I am, I exist*, is necessarily true whenever it is put forward or conceived by me in my mind'. This is most famously expressed in the phrase 'I think, therefore I am' (*cogito, ergo sum*). But, what is this 'I' that thinks? (i) There is the mechanical structure of the human body. (ii) There are the activities which humans pursue: they walk about, eat, have perceptions from their senses, etc. On Descartes's view, these activities are the actions of a 'soul' or 'mind', which is a different kind of substance from physical stuff.

The properties of a body are physical: it can be seen, moved, occupies a particular space, etc. The 'power of self-movement', however, is not a property we can attribute to a physical body. Given the presence of his malicious demon, Descartes thinks that the existence even of the body can be doubted. But the self that thinks cannot: 'At present I am not admitting anything except what is necessarily true; that is, I am a mind, or intelligence, or intellect, or reason [. . .] a thinking thing'. Descartes thus holds that he is a mind, 'not that structure of limbs which is called a human body'. In this way Descartes's mind–body (or 'Cartesian') dualism is thereby set firmly in place. What is essential about him, he contends, is that he is a mind, not a body. In other words, he is essentially a thinking thing, and mind is essentially different from body.

From the standpoint of epistemology, what is notable about Descartes's argument is that it is **subjectivity** (the 'I think') that forms the foundation of knowledge. Moreover, the conception of subjectivity that Descartes proposes is thus one that is not constrained by the social world. Indeed, it is (at least purportedly) derived independently of any assumptions about the nature of society or even material reality. Hence, the relationship between the human subject and the external world which it experiences is accounted for by way of a model which places the subject 'outside' the world, as a kind of observer who is not implicated in it. There have been a number of criticisms of this view. For instance, the German philosopher, Martin Heidegger (1889–1976), offers an account of the subject that is directly opposed to this central presupposition of Cartesianism. For Heidegger, the subject (or, more properly *Dasein*) is not a passive observer of experience, but is actively engaged in its own world. Thus, on Heidegger's view, human subjects are not 'in' the world in the same sense that a match might be said to be 'in a match box'. Rather, we are 'in the world' in a concrete sense that cannot be divorced from our actual Being. Hence, our world cannot be viewed from an 'objective' perspective that is external to it, as a spectator sitting in the stalls of a theatre might be said to view the events that unfold in a play. Rather, we actively relate to our world, and this relationship is constitutive of that world. Thus, for example, in addition to our ability to conceptualise objects we can also relate to them as things we can grasp in a practical sense (in Heidegger's parlance, they are not merely 'present-at-hand' but 'ready-to-hand'). On Heidegger's view, Cartesianism cannot provide us with an adequate account of how this latter form of relationship to the objects in our world is possible because it has driven an irreconcilable wedge between cognition and what is conceived.

The Cartesian thesis has important cultural ramifications, in so far as traditional scientific forms of **discourse** presuppose a notion of subjectivity which has much in common with this model (i.e. the notion of a passive or neutral observer). Equally, the history of modern philosophy (by which is usually meant philosophy after Descartes) is marked by a critical (and sometimes not so critical) engagement with many of the central tenets of Cartesianism.

Further reading: Descartes 1986; Heidegger 1993; Mulhall 1996.

PS

CINEMA

Motion pictures emerged from slide shows displayed at fair grounds and vaudeville theatres in the late nineteenth century. By the beginning of the First World War, films had developed from shorts of a few minutes to performances of 90 minutes or more. The period after the war saw, at once, the establishing of Hollywood as a global centre for film production, and the development of a more sophisticated means of narration, not least through the work of German expressionists and of Soviet film-makers such as Eisenstein and Pudovkin. In the late 1920s the first sound films were produced and Technicolor was introduced in the 1930s. During this early period, writing about film focused on the status of film as an art form, and thus the aesthetic experience associated with film, and on the development of cinematic techniques, such as the handling of the camera, the length and nature of shots, and the process of editing (not least in the role of montage). Such technical and aesthetic analyses were complemented by reflections on the social function of cinema. The neo-Marxists of the **Frankfurt School**, along with Walter Benjamin, focused on the relationship of cinema to **ideology** (for example in the theorisation of the **culture industry**), and the impact that art forms based in mechanical reproduction have on traditional conceptions of art and the aesthetic experience.

In the 1940s and 1950s, German Marxist analyses of cinema continued, most notably in the work of Siegfried Kracauer (1947). The French review *Cahiers du Cinéma*, founded in 1951, began to develop a new and distinctive approach to film criticism, not least through the writings of the review's editor, André Bazin (1967). The group associated with *Cahiers* developed an account of the film director as **author**, in part by recognising how Hollywood directors, who were otherwise part of a highly controlled production process, could mark a film with signs of their authorship through the distinctive style with which they constructed scenes. Bazin further developed an account of the role of the spectator as an active interpreter of the film. He argued that realist cinema, that eschewed Eisenstein's emphasis on montage in favour of what is termed 'deep-focus' editing, gave greater scope for ambiguity of expression, thereby at once reproducing the ambiguity of real life, and requiring a greater interpretative effort from the spectator.

The 1960s saw a fundamental challenge to the *Cahiers* group, crucially in its celebration of the director as author. This challenge came through the application of **structuralist** and **semiological** approaches to cinema. Within structuralism, the film is treated as a text. The task of the structuralist critic, exemplified by the work of Christian Metz (1974), is to expose the hidden meaning of the text and the grammatical structure that underpins it by determining the range of meaningful combinations of the significant cinematic elements (treated as **syntagm**). Will Wright (1975) analysed westerns, for example, in terms of the way in which a series of **binary oppositions** (inside society/outside society; good/bad; strong/weak; civilisation/wilderness) common to all westerns are variously articulated, principally through the positioning of the hero in relation to society. In a classic Western of the 1930s to 1950s, the hero is aligned with a good society, against a threat from the wilderness. In westerns of the late 1950s, this opposition is reversed, with an all-powerful society now being set in opposition to the good hero.

While structuralist accounts disrupted the preconception about the author, and thus the interpretation of the film through the author's intentions and style, they still tended to assume that there was a single fixed meaning to be extracted from the film. At worst, the film was also considered as a text in isolation from the historical and material conditions of its production. Structuralism was thus itself challenged by the rise of **post-structuralism**, and its associated plurality of approaches (not least through the influence of Derrida and

deconstruction, of Lacanian **psychoanalysis** and of **feminism**). The film ceases to be seen as a text in isolation from others, but in terms of a plurality of possible relations to other texts (including material production processes). The meaning of the film is therefore fluid, being a result of the interaction of texts. At its core, the post-structuralist approach may be seen to raise the question of the construction of both the author and the spectator by the film text. The spectator's gaze, and the voyeuristic pleasure gained from viewing, become crucial to this analysis. Cinema presupposes, or constructs, a certain viewing subject. Initially, for example in the work of Metz, this spectator is assumed to be male. Women display 'to-be-looked-at-ness', both to the hero within the film and to the male spectator in the audience. The pleasure from viewing is thus seemingly constrained within male fantasies (and hence the 'Oedipal trajectory', in which a male protagonist overcomes difficulties in order to find, and settle down with, a woman). Laura Mulvey (1975 and 1993) explores this further. The male gaze leaves no obvious scope for female pleasure. Mulvey argues that the female spectator must therefore either identify with the passive position of the women on screen (a position of unpleasure), or adopt a male position. The possibility of a non-patriarchal cinema would, in consequence, demand a radical challenge to traditional cinematic forms.

A final, important, component in a cultural studies approach to cinema rests in the use of **ethnographic** studies. The post-structuralist reduction of the audience to products of the cinema's textuality, so that the nature of the spectator can be deduced from the text, is challenged by empirical questioning of cinema goers about their experience of and attitudes to film. Thus, Jackie Stacey's (1994) work is grounded in the interviewing of women who identified themselves as keen cinema goers in the 1940s and 1950s. Through categories of 'escapism', 'identification' and 'consumerism', she explores the utopian aspect of cinema going (not least, following Dyer (1985) in so far as the cinematic text provides solutions for real social problems experienced by the audience, but also in recognising the real luxury experienced within the cinema as a building), but thereby emphasises the self-consciousness which the audience has of its relationship to the film, the film star and the products associated with films.

Further reading: Cavell 1971; Deleuze 1991; Dyer 1979; Kracauer 1960; Metz 1982.

AE

CITIZENSHIP

A human agent who is endowed with particular social characteristics which have a legally codified political significance (such as rights, duties and obligations, the freedom to make decisions which are a matter of their own private interests and to participate in matters of public interest, to participate in the life of **civil society**) is generally said to have citizenship. Such citizenship is sometimes termed 'substantive citizenship', in contrast to the possession of 'formal citizenship', which is now usually taken to signify merely the fact of being a member of a nation state. The possession of citizenship in the first of these senses implies that an individual is part of a socio-political body, and that the rights, duties, and so forth which that individual has are possessed both concretely and in virtue of their being a member of that body. Thus, for instance, a French citizen is granted a particular political status (citizenship) as a result of being both (i) subject to and (ii) able to appeal to the rule of French law. Whether the possession of a particular right necessarily entails obligations is, however, unclear. Such a view would be disputed by, for instance, advocates of **libertarianism**, who tend to conceive of rights as being the fundamental issue accompanying questions of political freedom. Likewise, whether the legal codification of rights is commensurable with the satisfactory articulation of the interests a subject may have, has been questioned by the philosopher Jean-François Lyotard.

Further reading: Marshall 1950; Mead 1986; Turner 1986; Turner and Hamilton 1994.

PS

CIVIC HUMANISM

An approach to questions of political **authority** and **power** which can be traced back to the writings of the Ancient Greek philosopher Aristotle (384–322 BC), civic humanism has a conception of power, authority and the civil agent which is markedly different from those of either **liberalism** or **Marxism**. Most famous amongst exponents of civic humanism is Niccolò Machiavelli (1469–1527), although other thinkers have offered accounts of political power which embrace civic humanist thought (e.g. James Harrington (seventeenth century) and, in the twentieth century, the exponent of 'Guild Socialism' G.D.H. Cole, while certain elements of

Enlightenment thinker J.-J. Rousseau's *The Social Contract* could be said to exhibit attitudes in common with this tradition). Both Machiavelli's *The Discourses* (a work that in many ways stands in stark contrast to his *The Prince*) and Harrington's *The Commonwealth of Oceana* (influenced by Machiavelli) give a good idea of the civic humanist attitude to politics. They advocate a politically active citizenry which is endowed with a strong sense of civic duty (Machiavelli terms this sense 'civic virtue'). Central to civic humanism is the contention that the legislature which governs a community must consist of laws that ensure the reproduction of the conditions necessary to the survival of that community, namely civic virtue (hence Harrington's maxim that 'good laws make good men'). The civic humanist thus conceives of the political agent not, as with liberalism, in terms of an individualism which expresses its identity by making choices unhindered except by the minimum of justifiable state interference, but as an extension of the identity and governing principles underlying the community itself. There is, in other words, no rigid distinction between the so-called 'public' and 'private' spheres. In turn, the citizen is conceived of as an autonomous being to the extent that he or she performs an active role in the political and cultural life of the community (the model here being that of the Ancient Roman Republic). Both Machiavelli and Harrington sought to produce a 'balanced' political legislature, i.e. one in which both the interests and talents of the wealthy few (nobles) and the plebeian majority were exploited and played off against each other in order to arrive at a model of government that prevented the worst political consequences of the three different forms of government (i.e. absolute monarchy, aristocratic rule or democratic rule—deemed capable of degenerating into tyranny, oligarchy or anarchy, respectively).

Further reading: Harrington 1992; Machiavelli 1983; Pocock 1975.

PS

CIVIL SOCIETY

Before the work of the philosopher Hegel, the term 'civil society' was roughly equivalent in meaning to the term 'state' (see Allen Wood's introduction to Hegel's *Elements of the Philosophy of Right*: xviii). Hegel, in using this term, was alluding to the social domain of market exchange (the market economy—a notion derived from such texts as

Adam Smith's *Wealth of Nations*) in which individual civil agents freely engage in the pursuit of financial wealth, and the ownership and exchange of goods. Civil society is contrasted by Hegel with the realm of the family, in which the ties between members are based on mutual affection (the bonds of love). In contrast to the family, civil society is defined as a realm of engagement in which an individual pursues their own private ends, and in so doing encounters others primarily as means for the satisfaction of subjective needs (in other words, the relationship between individuals is an instrumental one). In civil society the individual thereby gains a sense of identity derived from his or her relative independence from others. Yet, for Hegel, this independence contains within it a shared characteristic, for through the active pursuit of their subjective ends individuals also develop a sense of mutual interdependence. Civil society, therefore, is not for Hegel merely to be understood as the outcome of individuals engaged in the free pursuit of their own desires (a domain purely of the market economy in Adam Smith's sense), but as bringing with it a sense of shared interests in which individuals recognise both the duty they have to support themselves *and* their duties towards one another (for instance, within civil society, Hegel argues, individuals can claim certain entitlements such as the right to job security, the right to education and to protection from such social hardships as poverty). Because of this, civil society is characterised by Hegel as constituting a 'universal family', which is composed of groups or 'corporations' of individuals who are affiliated by means of a common craft or profession. On Hegel's account civil society is contrasted with the state, which is ultimately concerned with the ethical good of the whole and takes the principle of the universal family to its logical fruition by functioning as a means of mediating between the competing claims of differing interests (both of individuals and corporations) with the aim of achieving the well-being of the whole of society (in Hegel's terms, the 'ethical life').

The young Karl Marx inherited Hegel's conception of civil society, and displayed a more or less uncritical attitude towards it. In his later writings, however, Marx came to adopt the view that civil society and the state are intimately connected, contending that the apparent freedom of individual association and pursuits in civil society is in fact a masked manifestation of an underlying structure of state power, the latter being in the hands of a wealthy capitalist minority whose aim is the exploitation of the majority in the interests of enhanced profit. On a Marxian view, therefore, the realm of civil society is intimately connected with issues of **power** and **ideology**. Some recent commentators (see Keane 1988) tend to adhere to the Hegelian view, namely that civil society is a sphere of individual association which may be contrasted with the domain of state power. The meaning of the term has not, therefore, been exhausted by Marx's attempted revaluation of it.

Further reading: Hegel 1991; Keane 1988; Smith 1986.

PS

CLASS

Classes may primarily be understood as economic groupings, although the relevant economic factors that serve to identify a class may be disputed. Thus, in the Marxist tradition, classes are defined in terms of the ownership of productive wealth, while other traditions look to differences in income or occupation. Class divisions are typically seen as fundamental to the stratification of society, and as such may be associated with differences in power and culture. Crucially, classes are not typically understood as aggregates of individuals, where class analysis would be concerned with classifying some common attribute shared by these individuals. Rather, classes are understood as social entities that have a reality that is independent of the individuals that make them up. As such, class may be a crucial causal factor in explaining the constitution of the individual human subject.

Marx and Engels's famous, if slightly glib, comment that all preceding history has been the history of class conflict (1985), expresses much that is fundamental to the Marxist approach to class. The analysis of any given society, at any moment of history, can focus on the latent or explicit conflict that exists between two major classes. The subordinate class will be active economic producers in the society. However, the members of that class will not have control over the production process, and thus will not be able to retain the full value of what they produce, or otherwise determine the allocation and distribution of that product. This is because the dominant class will own and control the society's stock of economic resources (or **means of production**), and will thereby control the fate of whatever is produced with these resources. The relationship between the dominant class and the subordinate classes will therefore be one of exploitation, although the precise nature of exploitation will depend upon the particular historical stage, or **mode of production**, in which it occurs. In **capitalism**, for example, the dominant class is the **bourgeoisie**, which owns **capital**, while the subordinate class is the **proletariat** (the members of which have only their ability to labour, which they must sell in order to survive). Exploitation occurs through the appropriation of **surplus value**, which is to say that the proletariat's reward for selling its labour is worth less than the **exchange-value** of the product when it is sold. While the bourgeoisie and proletariat are recognised as the major historical players within capitalism, Marx recognised that other classes will exist. At any moment in history, these classes can be the remnants of earlier historical stages (so that, for example, a **feudal** aristocracy survived into capitalism), or may be the early form of a class that will subsequently become significant (such as the mercantile capitalists who existed in late feudalism). Other groups may have ambiguous class positions, such as the small, petit-bourgeois producer (including the shop keeper or independent entrepreneur) in capitalism, who own insufficient productive property to free themselves from the necessity of labour (see Marx 1976).

Class conflict, within **Marxism**, is understood in terms of the conflicting interests of classes. It is in the interests of the dominant class for the existing economic relations to continue. It is in the interests of the subordinate classes to see the ending of those relations. Overt class conflict, in the form of revolution, is however inhibited, at least in large part, through **ideological** mechanisms (such as educational institutions, **religion** and the **mass media**) existing in the society. A theory of ideology suggests that the dominant class does not maintain its position purely through the exercise of physical force (or control of the means of violence). Rather, the threat of violence is complemented, and possibly, in the short term, rendered redundant, by structures of belief that appear to give legitimacy to the dominance of the ruling class. Thus, under the influence of ideology, the subordinate classes will hold beliefs that are against their own objective long-term interests. The issue of ideology becomes a core issue for cultural studies when more sophisticated theories of ideology (not least those centring around the concept of **hegemony**) suggest that the subordinate classes do not simply accept, passively, an account of the world that is in the interests of the dominant class, but rather more or less successfully negotiate and resist that account, in the light of their own experience. **Culture** thereby comes to be seen as fundamentally structured in terms of class inequalities.

While the Marxist tradition tends to explain all social inequalities through reference to economic differences (so that the dominant economic class is also expected to be dominant politically and culturally), in the tradition of sociological analysis that arises from the work of Max Weber, a more layered account of social inequality is favoured (1946c). Weber complements an economic analysis of class by analyses of differences in **power** and social **status**. Weber's approach to the economic determinants of class is itself more varied than that of Marx. First, Weber does not presuppose that all social differences can be collapsed on to economic differences (noting, for example, that the aristocratic Junta in late nineteenth-century Germany held political power, in spite of the existence of an economically powerful bourgeoisie). Further, for Weber, at least with respect to contemporary capitalism, an individual's class position does not depend exclusively upon his or her relationship to the means of production, but is realised through the market. Weber thus talks of market opportunities, such that an individual brings various resources, including ownership of stocks of capital, the ability to labour and, crucially, high levels of skill, to the labour and capital markets. Different resources will earn different levels and kinds of material and symbolic reward (or **life-chances**). This allows the Weberian to make differentiations within Marxism's proletariat class, in order to explain the higher levels of material reward and status accorded to intellectuals and managers or administrators over those of manual workers. This in turn throws light on the ambiguous class position of those groups, in that while they are to be strictly defined as labourers, their short-term or apparent class interests, self-understanding and cultural identity may accord more closely with those of the property-owning bourgeoisie. (Analyses of these groups have been a key part of E.O. Wright's (1985) class theory, for example.) In addition, analysis of differences in the social status, or the prestige and respect, that is associated with different social positions, can lead to an analysis of the distinctive lifestyles that are associated with different classes (so that class is again seen as a cultural, rather than purely economic, phenomenon).

There is a danger that the Weberian approach to class analysis can be reduced to an account of class purely in terms of occupational difference and thus to something akin to the registrar general's classification of socio-economic groups (professional; employers and managers; intermediate non-manual; skilled manual and self-employed non-manual; semi-skilled manual; unskilled manual) found in the United Kingdom. Without a rigorous underpinning in class theory, such classifications tend to do little more than label, for administrative purposes, aggregates of diverse individuals, rather than to describe and account for classes as real social entities and to explain the constitutive role that they have in our lives. A further problem with all class analysis, that its reduction to socio-economic groups serves to exemplify, is its failure to take account of the position of women. Precisely because class analysis is conducted predominantly in terms of economic activity, women have either remained invisible or been allocated to the class of their male partner, on the grounds that they were not active as wage earners, or if they were wage earners, their wage (and associated economic position) was secondary to that of their partner. Socialist feminists have attempted to analyse the relationship between men and women as itself analogous to a class relationship, by focusing on the male expropriation of female labour (for example in unpaid housework, or in the differential that continues to exist between male and female wages) (Barrett 1980).

See also: **social mobility**.

Further reading: Bennett *et al.* 1981; Eagleton 1991; Edgell 1993; Giddens 1973; Giddens and Held 1982.

AE

CLASS CONSCIOUSNESS

Within Marxist theory, class consciousness refers to the self-understanding that members of the **proletariat**, in particular, have of themselves as members of a **class**. Marx distinguishes between a class in itself and a class for itself. A class in itself is a social group that is determined by a common economic position. A class for itself is collectively aware of that determination, of its place within the economic and social structure, and in consequence of its real interests in social change. A class for itself, and thus a group in possession of genuine class consciousness, will have thrown off the illusions of **ideology** and **false consciousness**. For Marx, this transformation was to be achieved through the increasing collectivisation of production under capitalism, so that dominant ideas of individualism would no longer make sense to an oppressed proletariat.

In non-Marxist sociology, the term 'class consciousness' may be used, but is less well defined or focused. It may refer to the perception that individuals have of their class position and the way in which they articulate that awareness. Thus, for example, elements of class consciousness may include one's self-identification as belonging to a particular class, and thus accepting the label 'working class', or one's awareness of another class (owners and managers) as constitutive of one's opponents.

Further reading: Lukács 1971; Marx 1968; Marx and Engels 1985.

AE

CODE

A signifying code is a set of culturally recognised rules that guide the way in which a **text** may be read. The code will determine the material from which significant units can be selected (see **paradigm**) and the manner in which selected units can be meaningfully combined (see **syntagm**).

AE

COLONIALISM

Although it once brought with it connotations of narrow provincialism and tastelessness, the word 'colonialism' has come in the twentieth century more or less exclusively to signify the forcible invasion, occupation and administration of non-Western cultures and nations by European and North American forces. In this regard, colonialism is most evidently a nineteenth- and twentieth-century phenomenon. However, the roots of this phenomenon can be traced at least as far back as the burgeoning of mercantile capitalism and the accompanying development of the ideology of **liberal** individualism in eighteenth-century Europe. Colonial instincts and possessive individualism go hand in hand, as is witnessed by the philosopher John Locke's (1632–1704) justification of the taking of land in the Americas in his *Two Treatises of Government* (first published in 1690). The central concerns of the *Second Treatise*, the assertion of individual natural rights in a 'State of Nature', the establishment and justification of civil government and the acquisition and protection of property through individual labour, are ultimately used to legitimate not only 'the disproportionate and unequal possession of the earth' (section 50) but the taking into European possession of the 'wild woods and uncultivated waste of America' (37). Locke sees America as a vast tract of unused (because uncultivated) land akin to the common land that is held in kind under British common law. The native inhabitants, in turn, are portrayed as lacking the competence to make of the land what it is truly worth. The difference between an acre of land in Europe and an equivalent acre in America is simple enough to point out: where the former may yield five shillings of 'Benefit' per year the latter is 'possibly not worth a penny, if all the profit an *Indian* received from it were to be valued, and sold here; at least, I may truly say, not 1/1000' (43). Since Native American Indians have not 'joyned with the rest Mankind' in embracing the principle of exchange according to the use of money, the lands they inhabit '*lie waste*' (45) and are ripe for legitimate appropriation through the investment of labour, which is what exclusively confers the '*Right of Property*'. Locke's vision of a primitive America whose 'pattern' conforms to the 'first Ages' of the Asian and European continents (108) expresses the feeling of superiority of Western culture over its non-Western counterparts. In the following two centuries this sense of superiority was compounded by accelerating industrial expansion and the concrete power it afforded. The dominance of the West brought with it the requirement that non-Western cultures live according to an agenda set by the interests of the more powerful West. The establishment of imperial lordship, marked by the militarism that increasingly characterised Europe and the West from the time of Bismarck's establishment of the Second German Reich in 1871 to the outbreak of the First World War in 1914, signalled an age of imperial competition between European powers to establish either total economic or direct governmental control over foreign lands, especially the newly explored African continent. Doubtless, amongst the reasons for this was the desire prompted by free market forces to secure important natural resources coupled with the perceived financial benefits that imperial economic development might be considered to bring with it. The exploitation and suffering that this kind of colonial activity engendered is portrayed tellingly enough by Joseph Conrad in his 1902 novel *Heart of Darkness*, as is the potential cultural desolation that is unleashed on the coloniser (Conrad 2000).

The beginnings of the demise of European colonial power can be dated from the end of the First World War and the destruction of the German and Austro-Hungarian empires. At the same time, the emergence of the communist Soviet Union in Russia in 1917 brought with it a further consolidation of the Western industrial model and its cultural hegemony. As Hobsbawm points out, although illiberal in aspect and opposed to the pursuit of individual wealth, the communist system no less than the West embraced the industrial economic and social model. The ensuing seventy-year struggle between Western liberalism and Eastern communism was hence a struggle for domination between opposed camps situated on common territory that extended the cultural–economic domination of the West. It is in this regard most especially that the 'twentieth century history of the non-Western or more exactly non-north-Western world' was 'essentially determined by its relations with the countries which had established themselves in the nineteenth century as the lords of humankind' (Hobsbawm 1995:200).

In the wake of the Second World War, the great empires of Western Europe decisively receded, in spite of the reluctant attitude of the French and Dutch governments. Britain, facing economic impoverishment in the aftermath of the war, relinquished power over those parts of the Indian and African continents that it had once held in thrall. The French were ultimately forced out of Algeria and their other territories. The demise of this form of colonialism did not, however, signal an end to the colonial story. The United States may have openly favoured the dismantling of Europe's empires, but it did so not least because the demise of these empires represented an opportunity to expand its own influence in a post-war world marked by an intensifying struggle with the Soviet Union. The outcome of this struggle was the collapse of the Soviet empire in 1989 and the inauguration of a period of American world dominance. Such domination has been marked by large lending to those so-called Third-World countries whose elites have sought to emulate the Western model. This has given rise to crippling debts which, in spite of recent pragmatic attempts on the part of Western governments to alleviate the situation, have served to compound the gulf between North and South. In turn, the development of global economic practices signalled by multinational corporations has brought with it a burgeoning American economic and cultural hegemony. Thus, European colonialism has ultimately given way to American neocolonialism. That colonial expression by Western powers on a nineteenth-century scale remains possible is witnessed by the recent Second Gulf War and the American-led and British-sponsored overthrowing of Iraqi dictator Saddam Hussein. Doubtless, these events are connected with the anxieties (and possibly anger) of the Western political class in the wake of the terrorist attacks of 11 September 2001 in New York (**9/11**). Yet, subsequently refuted claims by the American administration that Iraq was connected with these attacks and the (false) assertion by the British government that Iraqi chemical weapons posed an imminent threat to the safety of its citizens have served to substantiate the suspicion that this war is an expression of militarism and colonialism pure and simple. Subsequent protestations by these leaders that the main justification of the invasion is the liberal democratisation of Iraq—even if it must be at the cost of the lives of a few thousand Western servicemen and hundreds of thousands of Iraqi citizens—have also served to fuel suspicions of a cultural colonialism no less invasive and controlling than its nineteenth-century imperial counterparts.

Further reading: Hobsbawm 1987, 1995; Pommeroy 1970, 1974.

PS

COMICS

Cartoons, comic strips and comic books have, perhaps, been relatively neglected, not merely by orthodox **aesthetics** and criticism, as might be expected, but also by cultural studies (especially in comparison to the amount of attention devoted to other aspects of **popular culture**, such as **television** and **popular music**). Apart from the interest in the comic (and its close relative, the cartoon) as a complex **text**, developing its **narrative**, at best, through the interplay of visual image and literary text, the comic and cartoon have played an important role in youth culture, **subcultures**, and political resistance throughout the twentieth century.

The comic may be seen to have an important precursor in the political cartoon. The term 'cartoon' was not transferred from the sphere of high art (where it refers to a preparatory drawing) until the nineteenth century (when the humorous magazine *Punch* parodied designs submitted for House of Commons frescoes—and not a lot of people know that). However, what may be recognised as political cartoons emerged in late eighteenth-century England, notably in the work of Gillray and Rowlandson. Their images commented upon and ridiculed public personalities (including the royal family, military leaders and even Lady Hamilton). The French artist Henri Daumier was imprisoned in 1832 for his caricatured attacks on Louis Philippe. While the political cartoon remains a popular and important feature of mainstream newspapers throughout the world (and as such an important source of political comment, criticism and **ideology** within democracies), the 1960s saw the emergence of the 'underground' comic. Robert Crumb's *Zap* linked the comic to the values of the **counterculture**, articulating the issues of drug use and sexual expression.

The comic strip, as something that is generally amusing rather than politically pointed, became established in America in the last decade of the nineteenth century, with Richard F. Outcault's 'Hogan's Alley' being published (with significant commercial success) in the newspaper *New York World*. The strip cartoon emerged as an attempt to exploit new colour printing techniques, with Outcault's main character (the Yellow Kid) being presented in a bright yellow nightshirt. In 1893, Outcault's separate strips were gathered together into a comic book and published by William Randolph Hearst as a supplement to the *New York Journal*. Original comic books began to appear in the 1930s. Shortly afterwards, the move from purely humorous to adventure- and fantasy-based comics occurred in the USA, most famously with Jerry Siegel and Joe Shuster's *Superman* (published by DC Comics), rapidly followed by *Batman*, *Captain America* and *Captain Marvel*. In the post-war period the subject matter of comic books diversified to include westerns, romance and science fiction. In the 1960s, the comic book image (including its method of printing through Ben Day dots) was appropriated as a core element of pop art by Roy Lichtenstein.

In Britain the development of the comic was quite distinct from, and earlier than, that in America. While the American comic strip is associated with newspapers, in Britain the comic emerged as a separate publication for children. *Ally Sloper's Half-Holiday*, a comic in the modern sense, with regular characters, was first published in 1884. This was followed by *Comic Cuts* and *Chips* in 1890. If American comics were motivated by new technology, British comics were motivated by the rise of mass literacy, as a result of the 1870 Education Act. The late 1930s saw perhaps the most distinctive development in the British comic, with the publication of *Beano* and *Dandy*. The humour of these, and many subsequent comics, was far more anarchic and less respectful to authority than that of their predecessors. Even if authority figures did occasionally get the better of their young tormentors, they expressed their authority through unseemly ferocity.

The British understanding of the comic as a magazine marketed for children also widens the coverage of the term to include a range of magazines marketed for children and adolescents (whether the comic strip is their core component or not). Magazines such as *Jackie* (that significantly retained a variant on the comic strip, in the photo story) were amongst the first cultural artefacts to receive sustained attention within cultural studies (McRobbie 1989, 1991), not least in terms of the part they played in the **articulation** of **gender** and **sexuality** within contemporary **ideology**.

The comic book saw a significant revival in the 1980s, with the emergence of the 'graphic novel'. Typically, these took on the themes of the super-hero comics, but now with a new realism, irony and depth. Thus, Frank Miller's *Batman: The Dark Knight Returns* (1986) reflected on the prospect of a middle-aged Bruce Wayne coming out of retirement. Alan Moore and Dave Gibbons's *Watchmen* (1987) worked through the implications of super heroes being real, and highly fallible men and women in the real world. Art Spiegelman's *Maus: A Survivor's Tale* (1987) and *And Here My Troubles Began* (1992) used the comic strip conventions of anthropomorphic animals to tell the story of a survivor of Auschwitz.

Further reading: Barker 1989; Gravett 2006; McCloud 1993; Pearson and Uricchio 1991; Sabin 1993.

AE

COMMODITY

A commodity is an object (or service) that is produced for exchange (or a market) rather than for **consumption** or use by the producer. 'Commodity' is the most basic category in Marx's economics, for it opens up his analysis of **capitalism**, and specifically of the part that the commodity and commodity exchange play in the exploitation of the **proletariat**. (See **commodity fetishism**.)

AE

COMMODITY FETISHISM

'Commodity fetishism' encapsulates much of Marx's criticism of the **capitalist** economy (which is to say, an economy grounded in the ownership of private property and in the exchange of **commodities** through markets). Marx argues (1976:163–77) that in the exchange of commodities, the social relationships between human beings take on the appearance of relationships between objects. Indeed, this relationship between things takes on a phantasmagorical appearance, such that the things confront us as if they themselves were a strange and obscure crowd of persons. Interpreted slightly differently, properties (such as price) that are ascribed to objects through **cultural** processes, come to appear as if they were natural or inherent properties of the objects.

Commodity fetishism occurs because, in a capitalist economy, producers only come into contact with each other through the market. As such, they relate to each other, not as substantial, complex and unique human beings, but as producers of commodities, and these commodities are made comparable to (and therefore inter-changeable with) any other commodities through the common stan-dard of money. Thus, that which is qualitatively unique and distinctive, both in producers and product, is concealed by transfor-mation into a pure quantity.

The theory of commodity fetishism therefore suggests that capital-ism reproduces itself by concealing its essence beneath a deceptive appearance. Just as quality appears as quantity, so **objects** appear as **subjects** and subjects as objects. Things are personified and persons objectified. Ultimately, market exchange becomes the appearance of the real essence of production, so that humans falsely understand themselves as consumers rather than as producers. This, in turn, conceals the process of exploitation inherent to capitalism (expro-priation of **surplus value**).

The theory of commodity fetishism was fundamental to the development of the theory of **ideology** within Western **Marxism** in the account of reification offered by Lukács and members of the **Frankfurt School**.

Further reading: Burke and Moore 1979; Carver 1975; Dant 1996.

AE

COMMUNICATION

In many respects, communication, as the exchange of information between two or more agents, is the most fundamental concern of cultural studies. A number of different approaches to the analysis of communication may be identified.

In **structuralism** and **semiology**, communication is analysed in terms of the **codes** or rules and conventions that determine the meaningfulness of any message, in terms of the selection and combi-nation of meaningful elements (or **signs**). This approach, in turn, leads to an interest in **texts** (be these written and spoken texts, or other carriers of meaning and significance, such as clothing and social actions) and the process of producing and reading them, as well as problems of how (if at all) the sign can refer to a world that is external to the text. In **hermeneutics**, the processes of reading and interpretation are treated less systematically. Emphasis here rests upon the competence that ordinary people and readers have in developing interpretations by working with the relationship between the particular meaningful unit before them, and the larger whole (or horizon) that provides the context in which the unit makes sense (and crucially, where the meaning of the unit reciprocally modifies the meaning of the context). Within **sociology**, analysis of communication comes to prominence with the rise of those schools of sociological inquiry that emphasise the social skills and competence that members of society possess. Thus, the **symbolic interactionists** and **ethnomethodologists** show an interest in how a meaningful and stable social reality is created and maintained through skilful interaction, and thus through the exercise of forms of communicative competence.

The wider implications of a study of communication, that are suggested by the interest that sociology has in communication, are to be seen through the etymological link between communication and community. For Aristotle, a state is a community held together by the communication of the diverse perspectives within it. Communication is what holds a community together. The political and moral worth of the community can therefore be analysed in terms of the communication that is possible within it. Thus, the philosopher of science, Charles Sanders Peirce, projected an ideal scientific community, in which there would be free and open communication between all participants. Open communication (or democratic participation) is therefore presented as a precondition of good science. Jürgen Habermas has developed this idea in his notion of the 'ideal speech situation' (McCarthy 1978:306–10). This is again a projection of perfect communication, in which all participants are able to question others as to the sincerity, factual accuracy and meaning of what they say, as well as their moral entitlement to say it. Actual communication will fall short of this ideal, as political and **ideological** structures distort it, inhibiting participation or understanding by specific groups or individuals. The degree to which it falls short is a measure of the justice of any particular society.

Further reading: Habermas 1970a, 1970b; Williams 1962.

AE

COMMUNITARIANISM

An approach primarily to questions of ethics and politics (although its ramifications extend also into the domain of **epistemology**) which holds that the norms which function in any particular cultural community are the only sources of what is to count as ethically or politically right. In other words, communitarians reject any stand-point which seeks to provide forms of justification for conceptions of morality or politics which transcend cultural contexts (such as Rawls's formulation of an 'original position' as providing a rational justification for basic principles of political justice—see **liberalism**).

The key thinkers who have been associated with a communitarian approach are Alasdair MacIntyre, Michael Sandel, Charles Taylor and Michael Walzer. MacIntyre's approach to questions of ethics holds that if we are to offer a coherent account of what a human subject (conceived of as a moral being) is, then we must recognise the fact that individuals are embedded in social practices and traditions. This shared (i.e. communal) nature of the meaning of ethical action is, in MacIntyre's view, a necessary precondition of it, and thus an essential property of any conception of what we mean by a 'human good'. Sandel's work has tended to focus on criticising Rawls's conception of the self. Rawls, Sandel argues, constructs a metaphysical account of the self in order to ground his liberal politics, and in turn ignores the social dimension of individual identity in his account of what constitutes a political subject. Likewise, Taylor has adopted a similar approach, taking as his point of focus the shared linguistic precondi-tions which, he holds, are necessary to the articulation of person-hood, morality and reasoning ability. Thus, in Taylor's view, community (understood as being constituted out of a shared structure of linguistic norms) is necessarily presupposed by conceptions such as subjectivity, agency, ethical rightness, etc. Walzer, too, has adopted the position of arguing that the nature of what constitutes a good is dependent upon a shared realm of meanings, and that it must therefore follow that any conception of justice must be dependent upon the communal struc-ture of meanings which a political community has. Communitarians thus take the position of foregrounding the social dimension of ethi-cal language. In light of this, it is possible to claim that the approaches adopted by these thinkers have features in common with those of some advocates of **postmodernism** (e.g. Michel Foucault, Jean-François Lyotard, Richard Rorty), although it is worth noting that, for Charles Taylor at least, the issue of whether we are obliged to adopt a postmodern anti-epistemological attitude (rather than over-coming the transcendental epistemology outlined by Kant in other ways) is one which is far from settled.

Further reading: Avineri and De-Shalit 1992; Bell 1993; MacIntyre 1981, 1988; Mulhall and Swift 1996; Sandel 1982; Taylor 1990, 1997; Walzer 1983.

PS

CONFLICT THEORY

In **sociology**, 'conflict theory' refers to a diverse group of theories that emerged in the 1950s and 1960s to challenge the orthodoxy of structural **functionalism**. Functionalists tended to assume that stable societies are generally harmonious, with conflict being seen as undesirable and aberrant. Functionalism therefore rejected the possibility that societies could be characterised in terms of long-term structural conflict between different groups. The sources of conflict theory may be traced back to the political philosophies of Hegel and Marx and to Simmel, to **social Darwinism** and to **elite** theory. Conflict theories may be broadly classified into two forms. **Marxism** is typical of those theories that see social conflict as occurring along a single, all important axis. In Marxism, this is **class** conflict, and as such is conflict over control of the economy and the means of production. Such accounts suggest that conflict will ultimately undermine social stability (leading according to Marxism to a class-based revolution, and, in elite theory, to the succession of an old and exhausted elite by a new and vital one). In contrast, the version of conflict theory that was developed by Lewis Coser (1956) from Simmel's work suggested that conflict may also occur along a wide range of axes, and that such conflict is advantageous to the stability and growth of an open, pluralistic society. (The precise significance of conflict is therefore seen to depend upon the sorts of social and political structures within which it occurs. Open societies can tolerate and benefit from conflict in a way that closed or authoritarian societies cannot.) Coser's account suggests that all conflicts cannot be mapped onto a single axis, such as class division. Thus, any individual protagonist could be one's ally in one dispute and one's enemy in another. Such pluralistic conflict serves to bind society together, for conflict is typically worked out within commonly accepted and approved social institutions, generating new ideas and motivation for gradual reform.

Further reading: Collins 1975.

AE

CONSCIENCE COLLECTIVE

Term in Durkheim's sociology, indicating the reality of society over and above that of the individual. Individual consciousness and moral conscience is derived from a normative order which coerces social members into thinking, judging and acting according to certain, socially desirable, **norms**.

AE

CONSCIOUSNESS

The notions of 'consciousness' and 'mind' are often taken as interchangeable. Consciousness is the awareness by an individual (human or animal) of its environment and, if self-conscious, of its place in and relationship to that environment. Humans, higher primates and certain other creatures, e.g. dolphins, are usually regarded as self-conscious. Some philosophers, e.g. Jonathan Glover (1990a:46–50), have conjectured that there exists a progressive spectrum of consciousness starting with lower, mere conscious animals and ending with self-conscious human beings.

The stance one adopts regarding the nature of consciousness and on what can possess this property, depends upon one's view of the nature of mind. A dualist such as René Descartes would view 'souls' (minds) and bodies as two radically different substances. **Bodies**, according to Descartes, have shape, mass and location both in time and space. Minds, on the other hand, although containing thoughts that have duration, do not share any other properties with bodies. This radical separation of minds and bodies led to the infamous mind/body problem. This is the problem of how two substances, so totally different in their natures, can causally interact, granted that minds do in fact affect bodies and vice versa. Descartes would not agree that animals are conscious since he held only humans have souls.

In modern philosophy of mind, the attempt to answer the mind/body problem usually results in the adoption of materialism. Materialists attempt to explain the mind in physical and biological terms. Behaviourists suggest that the mind is nothing more than a series of dispositions to behave in various ways given certain sorts of environmental stimuli. Most behaviourists reject all talk of inner psychological processes. Supporters of the mind–brain identity theory take a reductionist approach, holding that the mind is nothing more than the brain. Functionalists argue that mental phenomena or psychological states can be understood in terms of the causal relationships that exist between causal stimuli, other mental states and the behaviour that results. Eliminativists suggest that all our common-sense talk of psychological states, such as beliefs and desires, is wrong. In fact eliminativists, such as Paul Churchland, hold that science will ultimately generate a much better model than the one we have now for explaining consciousness. This new model will result in a wholly different view of what minds are and how they work.

Further reading: Churchland 1988, 1995; Crane 1995; Descartes 1968; Ryle 1949.

SH

CONSERVATISM

Conservatism is perhaps better described as constituting an attitude towards politics and society rather than a political ideology. Its origins can be traced back to Edmund Burke's *Reflections on the Revolution in France* (1790), which was inspired by the events of the French Revolution into articulating the basic characteristics underlying conservative thinking. As such, modern conservatism may well be said to have drawn its first inspiration from a reaction to the rationalist ideals of the **Enlightenment**, which found (albeit rather distorted) expression in the French Revolution. These reactions are: (i) a negative attitude towards social change; (ii) a tenaciously held faith in the moral and political rightness of traditionally held attitudes and beliefs; (iii) a generally bleak and pessimistic view of human nature, i.e. conservatives tend to think that individuals left completely alone to pursue their own goals will generally descend into an at best immoral, and at worst amoral, lifestyle (a view which stands in direct contrast to the more optimistic conception of the individual held by both **liberalism** and **socialism**); and (iv) the view that society is an interconnected structure of relationships constituting a community.

In the twentieth century there have been a number of significant (or at least well-known) exponents of conservatism. Michael Oakeshott has frequently been cited in this connection, although his political thinking, as well as owing a significant debt to such philosophers as Aristotle, Thomas Hobbes and G.W.F. Hegel (the latter two of which display 'conservative' tendencies), also has features which might equally be described as having features in common with the thinking of **communitarianism** and is, in any case, far more complex than such a label might imply. Leo Strauss and, most recently, Roger Scruton, might both be taken as better examples of modern conservative thought.

Latterly, the German philosopher Jürgen Habermas has provided an account of conservatism which links it to the writings of **post-modernism** (e.g. Jacques Derrida, Michel Foucault, Jean-François

Lyotard). Postmodern thinking, Habermas argues, in articulating its criticisms of the Enlightenment (i.e. of the Enlightenment faith in reason and science) is in effect the expression of a resurgent conservatism which takes its inspiration from the writings of those 'darker' thinkers of the bourgeois tradition, Sade and Nietzsche (although it may well be equally germane to connect the thought of a thinker like Lyotard with the liberal tradition, with which his later work shares some common features).

Further reading: Burke 1982; Oakeshott 1975; Scruton 1984.

PS

CONSUMPTION

The idea that **capitalism** had become a 'consumer society' arose, at least in western Europe in the 1950s, in response to increased affluence and changes in the economic and industrial structure (a move away from traditional heavy industry and towards new technologies and service provision) after the Second World War. This awareness gradually led to an increased interest in consumption as a culturally significant activity. However, important theories of consumption can be found from the late nineteenth century onwards.

Social theorists such as Thorstein Veblen and Georg Simmel were amongst the first to begin to articulate the significance of consumption to urban existence. Veblen's (1953) account of the 'conspicuous consumption' of the new **bourgeois** leisure **class** suggested that class identity could rest, not upon occation, but upon patterns of consumption, that served to construct distinctive lifestyles and express **status**. Similarly, Simmel's essays, including those on 'The Metropolis and Mental Life' (1950b) and on 'Fashion' (1957), analyse the manner in which consumption may be used to cultivate what for Simmel is a sham individuality. Such sophisticated, and indeed blasé, consumption allows the consumer to differentiate him or herself. Fashion is thus seen to work through a curious interplay of conformity and dissension, of familiarity and strangeness, in so far as fashion-conscious consumers at once consolidate their membership of the fashionable as they distinguish themselves from the mass. Fashion, for Simmel, represents an attraction to the exotic, strange and new, and yet, thanks to its continual historical change, an opportunity to ridicule the fashions of the past (and thus paradoxically one's own once fashionable self).

Marxists typically demonstrate a similar, or even more pronounced, scepticism as to the value of consumption, not least in so far as Marxist social theory is grounded in the view of human beings as primarily **producers**. An emphasis on humans as consumers suggests an **ideological** distraction from the essence of economic and political struggle, or at best a manifestation of the unfulfilling or **alienating** nature of production within **capitalism**. Perhaps the most sustained Marxist engagement with consumption came from the **Frankfurt School**. The account of the **culture industry** proposed by Horkheimer and Adorno (2002) holds that twentieth-century capitalism is a distinct **mode of production**, at least in comparison with the high capitalism of **Marx**'s own time. For Marx, nineteenth-century consumers could freely choose between **commodities** on the grounds of the utility (or **use value**) that they would derive from them. A useless commodity would be rejected, and thus the consumer retained some vestige of power with high capitalism. Horkheimer and Adorno argue that in late capitalism, use value has been brought within the control of the capitalist producers, thanks to the power of advertising and the mass media. The consumers buy, crudely, what capitalism wants them to buy. The model of the culture industry is, however, more subtle than this. The consumers are not, on Horkheimer and Adorno's account, passive dupes of the capitalist system. Rather, the most efficient way of surviving and gaining some pleasure within the constraints of a highly bureaucratic and instrumental society, is to accept the goods offered, and that consumption may serve to express a deep awareness of the damage that capitalism is inflicting upon them. Adorno imagines a 'shop girl' who visits the cinema, not because she believes that the fantastic events of the cinema could happen to her, but because only in the cinema can she admit that they will not happen to her (Adorno 1992b:49–50). This vignette expresses a side of Frankfurt theory that is often lost to its less-sensitive readers.

More recent approaches to consumption recognise the **utopian** element inherent in shopping. An ideology of shopping may be analysed, where shopping or consumption are perceived as solutions to the discontents of one's life. In Lacanian terms, shopping promises to make us whole again. Yet, as with Freud's analysis of dreams, the pursuit of consumption may be interpreted as an illusory solution to the real problems of social life. In effect, this returns the analysis to the Frankfurt position. The continual round of consumerism is rejected as a short-term and ultimately illusory solution to one's problems. The task of theory would be to expose the real (social and psychological) problems that cause this discontent in the first place. Jacques Attali (1985) has lamented upon this theme, suggesting that when we purchase music (in the form of records), what we do is exchange our own labour (and thus involvement in the pressures and necessities of working life) for a commodity. But, unlike most other commodities, we carry out this exchange only in the utopian expectation of some day having the leisure time to enjoy it. (We work, in effect, for the promise of a work-free future.) This time, of course, never comes, and the use value of the music lies forever unrealised.

More positive accounts of consumption, not least in that they suggested the potential of consumption as a form of political resistance, first emerged in association with **subcultural** theory. Youth subcultures, from the 1950s onwards, were seen as consuming the products of capitalism, but not in a manner that accorded with the expectations of the producers. The consumer is thus credited with the ability to make his or her own use value from the commodity. Michel de Certeau (1984) thus describes consumption as 'secondary production'. While the products may be imposed by capitalism, the ways of using them are not. The shopping centre itself (as well as a number of key contemporary commodities, such as the 'Walkman' (du Gay *et al.* 1997) and 'Barbie' dolls (Rand 1995)) has become the focus of much analysis from cultural studies. Shopping is recognised as a highly popular leisure activity (and not simply the means to other leisure activities). The shopping centre becomes one focus of this activity, not least in so far as the shopping centre may well offer attractions other than shopping (including restaurants, cinemas and other leisure facilities). Yet, again, different groups will consume the centre itself differently. The young, unemployed, elderly and homeless, despite the fact that they are overtly excluded from consumerism due to lack of economic resources, will still find use within the centre (for example as a source of shelter, warmth and entertainment, or as a meeting place) (Morris 1993).

The theoretical issues in the analysis of the political and social significance of consumption perhaps revolve around the conceptualisation and understanding of human autonomy and individuality. Empirical evidence (for example that 80 per cent of all new products are rejected by consumers) is, in itself, of little value in establishing whether or not consumers have exercised active and autonomous choice. Simmel's pseudo-individualism, and even Horkheimer and Adorno's culture industry, are not incompatible with such statistics. Yet, consideration of consumption does indicate much about how humans find scope for self-expression (however glorious or impoverished this expression is ultimately judged to be) within the close restrictions of their everyday life.

Further reading: Bocock 1993; Corrigan 1997; Falk and Campbell 1997; Miller 1995.

AE

CONTENT ANALYSIS

Content analysis is a specific approach to the analysis of **communication**. It strives to avoid subjective bias and to generate quantifiable (statistical) results. Content analysis is most appropriate to the analysis of large samples, rather than to individual **texts**. The statistical occurrence of key units within this sample is of significance. For example, the content analysis of television news reports of strike action might focus on the proportion of reports (or the proportion of all broadcast time devoted to strike action) which cover a particular industry, and compare these to the actual proportion of all industrial action that this industry represents. Thus, if 50 per cent of all strike reports concern the car industry, and yet only 5 per cent of all strikes (or days lost through industrial action) are from the car industry, this would suggest some form of selective reporting. The claim of content analysis to avoid subjective bias rests heavily upon the possibility of using clearly defined and thus unambiguously applicable units of analysis.

Further reading: Weber 1990.

AE

CONTEXTUALISM

The philosophical argument that sentences have no **meaning**, and actions have no moral **value**, independently of the context within which they occur. In the philosophy of language, contextualism responds to the fact that certain words must refer to a specific context in order to have meaning and to be determined to be true or false. Thus, the sentence 'She is a cultural theorist' will vary as to its truth, depending upon who is referred to by 'she'. However, this argument may be taken further, to conclude that meaning and truth of all sentences are context dependent. 'Bourdieu is the cultural theorist' may, superficially, appear to be true and meaningful, independent of its context. However, as a response to the question: 'What is the weather like?' it is utterly meaningless (see MacIntyre 1981:195). A contextualist theory of **meaning** will strive to explicate the rules that competent speakers must master in order to use language appropriately within varying contexts (see, for example, Habermas 1987:120–26).

In ethics, contextualism may be opposed to those moral theories that hold that the moral worth of an action can be derived from certain abstract principles. Such non-contextualist approaches to ethics have been dominant within the Western moral tradition, exemplified by Kant, and, to a lesser degree, utilitarianism. Contextualist approaches have become increasingly important in the late twentieth century. A key development was the 'situational ethics' of Joseph Fletcher (1966), who held that the value of actions cannot be separated from the context or situation within which the action is performed.

The importance of context may be illustrated first by reference to **architecture**, where a sense of context may be crucial to interpreting the meaning of an existing building and the design of a new building (see Gadamer 1975:138–42). Context here may invoke not merely the existence and design of adjacent buildings, but also, in Peter Smithson's words, 'In the context of the patterns of human association, patterns of use, patterns of movement, patterns of stillness, quiet, noise, and so on, patterns of form, in so far as we can uncover them' (1975).

Second, one may refer to **archaeology**, where 'context' is very much a technical term, referring to the conditions within which an artefact is found. The point is that while the artefact on its own may have great beauty, if it is stripped from the context within which it was found, then little can be determined about its age, or about its use and importance, for such information can only be accurately determined by analysing the artefact's relationship to other artefacts and indicators of its manufacturers' and users' lifestyles and practices. The artefact out of context thus has little real significance for the archaeologist (see Renfrew 2003:55–8). Professional archaeologists' long-term suspicion of metal detectorists (and others who plunder 'treasure' from archaeological sites) reflects this recognition of the importance of a knowledge of context to effective interpretation of an artefact.

AE

CONTINENTAL PHILOSOPHY

The term 'continental philosophy' is generally applied to the work of philosophers who come from the mainland of the European continent. However, there is within the range of thinkers who might be thus described such a diversity of approaches to a wide variety of philosophical questions that it is really quite difficult to categorise them in a homogeneous manner as 'continental philosophers'. Nevertheless, it is true that during the last one hundred years or so there has been a split between, on the one hand Anglo-American **analytic philosophy** and, on the other, philosophy as it has been practised by the continental tradition. This might be best described as a division which occurred at an institutional level (i.e. within the university systems of mainland Europe, the United Kingdom and the USA). If there was a key moment which served to define this split, it might be located within the work of philosophers within the analytic tradition rather than the continentals (e.g. that of Bertrand Russell and Gottlob Frege). Thus, for example, Russell, a philosophy student in Britain at a time when Hegel's philosophy was dominant in the university system, and himself a youthful devotee of it, came to regard what he saw as the excesses of metaphysical speculation and idealism in the thought of not only Hegel but also such thinkers as Schopenhauer and Nietzsche, with a distinct air of suspicion (see his *A History of Western Philosophy* (1946) for a good impression of his attitude). In the place of such speculation, Russell and other analytics propounded a rigorous analytical discourse which concentrated upon, for example, elucidating definitions of key philosophical notions (e.g. **meaning**, **reference**, **language**). Above all, one might characterise analytic philosophy's rigour in terms of its commitment to a primarily logical form of **discourse**, and an accompanying commitment to a primarily metaphysical understanding of the meaning of terms such as 'necessity'. Analytics have generally sought to clarify issues of meaning, and have usually avoided what many of them have considered (even until quite recently) to be the vague idealistic speculations characteristic of thinkers within the continental tradition (Gilbert Ryle's famous dismissal of Heidegger's *Being and Time* as not worth reading is perhaps the most notorious expression of this attitude). Continental philosophy, if one indeed ventures to define it, might better be understood by situating it within the context of specific debates about questions of knowledge, rather than characterising it in terms of its purportedly 'speculative' character. Such an approach is especially useful since the question of knowledge is a concern common to both the analytic and continental traditions, and some comparison and contrast is thereby rendered possible. Naturally, there are exceptions to the account offered below, but it is certainly the case that what is discussed under the rubric of a 'continental' approach embodies something markedly different from the analyses of many analytic philosophers.

Where analytic philosophers have tended to treat the investigation of questions about knowledge in what may be called logical-metaphysical terms (see, for example, Ludwig Wittgenstein's early text, *Tractatus Logico-Philosophicus* (1921)), a significant number of continental philosophers have conducted their research with an additional emphasis on the material/temporal factors that may be significant to knowledge. Thus, for example, Nietzsche's account of the generation of knowledge is one which concentrates upon an analysis of the material conditions that are fundamental to its possibility. Indeed, for Nietzsche, 'knowledge' is thereby rendered the consequence of a series of contingent eventualities, while the logical preconditions of thinking are often taken to signify *not* an ontological proof of how the world is (and a criterion, therefore, of objectivity and truth) but an indication merely of a human incapacity to think about the world differently. That we must think logically, on Nietzsche's view, does not entitle us to the further claim that the world itself ought to conform to the strictures of logical form (see Nietzsche's notebooks, as published in *The Will to Power* (1968b), which contain many versions of this kind of argument), but rather pays testimony to the material conditions in which the human species developed.

This point can be further illustrated by the approach of analytic and continental commentators to Kant's project, in the *Critique of Pure Reason* (1964), of elucidating the a priori conditions required for the possibility of knowledge. By the phrase 'a priori' Kant means independent of all empirical experience. Although, for Kant, all knowledge is knowledge about experience, it does not follow that the conditions for the possibility of having experience are themselves derived from experience. Analytic commentators (e.g. Stroud 1984:153ff.) have generally taken this independence to have a metaphysical significance. For Stroud, 'a priori' always means independent of experience, and concerns the subjective conditions (i.e. those features a **subject** must have in order to know something) which are to be found 'in' us. On Stroud's view, such conditions are those properties which a mind must have in order to be capable of knowledge (1984:160). For Stroud, the subjective conditions are 'characteristics' or properties of human beings. They are what must necessarily be true of a mind in order for knowledge to be possible for it. The kind of necessity involved here is metaphysical, i.e. it concerns those conditions in virtue of which knowledge is possible for us. Necessary conditions, taken in this sense, need not exist prior to (i.e. before) what they are conditions for. Hence, the possibility that the sense of 'a priori' might also be taken as meaning preceding experience is ignored within Stroud's account. In contrast, a thinker like Michel Foucault takes a rather different view of the meaning of Kant's notion of the 'a priori', which reflects how it has been articulated within the continental tradition (see Foucault's *The Order of Things* (1970, discussed below, and *The Archaeology of Knowledge* (1972)).

Foucault takes Kant's critical enterprise to constitute a turning point in the history of European philosophy (as initiating the period of modernity), and considers the legacy of Kant in the French and German traditions. He therefore attempts to provide an account of what he believes to be the received (continental) interpretation of this legacy. On Foucault's view, the classical conception of the theory of knowledge can be characterised as taking the search for its conditions as being a matter of the relationship between representations (i.e. the question of how our representations of experience map on to reality). Kant's modern account, in contrast, does not seek to locate these conditions at the level of representation (Foucault 1970:241, 254), but instead sidesteps the issue of representation in order to address the question of those conditions 'on the basis of which all representation, whatever its form, may be posited' (ibid.:242, 254–5). On Foucault's account, such a starting point is equivalent to analysing 'the source and origin [*la source et l'origine*] of representation' (ibid.:243, 256). On this view, Kant's interest in the conditions of knowledge is one which concentrates on the matter of its prior (i.e. preceding) conditions. This point can be highlighted by turning to Foucault's implicit attribution to Kant of a view of the subject as an 'empirico-transcendental doublet' (ibid.:318, 329). This view, Foucault argues, has given rise to two kinds of analysis of human knowledge: (i) a reductivist empiricism, which is interested in the 'anatomo-physiological conditions' of knowledge; and (ii) a form of transcendental, dialectical analysis, which examines the historical conditions of knowledge (ibid.:319, 330). Foucault sees both kinds of analysis as explaining the genesis of knowledge, not its logical/metaphysical conditions of possibility. The first seeks to elucidate the historical development of knowledge after the fact (**positivism**), the second to provide an account of those conditions of knowledge which history must fulfil (**dialectics**) (ibid.: 320, 331). In both cases, what is analysed are the antecedent conditions of knowledge. Thus, Foucault takes the Kantian notion of the necessity which grounds the validity of our knowledge to be a matter of its antecedent conditions. The 'a priori', taken in this sense, is what is prior (in a temporal sense) to experience.

From this comparison, it is evident that the two traditions tend to depart from one another not with regard to the kinds of question they ask (in this case the question concerns the necessary conditions of knowledge), but in terms of how the question is dealt with. The emphasis on the significance of the temporal or material mode is not merely present in Nietzsche and Foucault (both of whom also treat ethical and political questions with an eye on the problem of **power** which is itself generated from an investment in a material analysis of social relations). In Martin Heidegger's *Being and Time*, likewise, temporality is seen as being fundamental to the success of any interpretation of the ontological question of the meaning of Being. Equally for Gilles Deleuze, temporality is taken to form the basis for the construction of an account of an ontology of 'becoming'.

Of course, as already mentioned, there are exceptions to the account offered above, and it is worth emphasising again that it would be incorrect to read 'continental philosophy' as an all-embracing term which indicates a set of doctrines with regard to how philosophical enquiry ought to be conducted. Jacques Derrida, for example, has pursued an approach which does not embrace the material mode, but offers an account of processes of signification which problematises a metaphysical attitude to questions of knowledge whilst at the same time remaining both firmly within the domain demarcated by metaphysical thinking and highly suspicious of the historicised project Foucault engages in (see his criticisms of Foucault in the essay 'Cogito and the History of Madness' in *Writing and Difference* (1978)). Likewise, Jean-François Lyotard should really be described as a thinker who employs a range of strategies common to both the analytic and continental traditions (and indeed constructs his arguments in the light of his knowledge of the works of Russell, Frege and Wittgenstein as well as Hegel, Nietzsche and Heidegger).

Further reading: Foucault 1970; Hylton 1990; Kearney and Rainwater 1996; Silverman and Welton 1988; Stroud 1984; West 1996.

PS

CONTRADICTION

In the case of a proposition (*p*) which makes an assertion (*f*) (for example, concerning a state of affairs) which is denied by another proposition (*q*), the two propositions are said to be in contradiction. The assertion of the truth of one of the propositions (*p*) necessarily implies the falsity of the other (*q*). Thus, in logic, the *principle of non-contradiction* states that two mutually exclusive states of affairs cannot simultaneously be asserted to be the case, e.g. it is impossible for something to exist and at the same time not to exist. The principle of non-contradiction thus serves as a rule for the construction of arguments that have *validity*. In the work of Hegel and Marx, contradiction performs an important function. Hegel's conception of **dialectic**, for instance, is dependent upon the notion of contradiction for its force. For Hegel, contradiction is a principle fundamental to the nature of existence, which is overcome in the dialectical process.

In the social and political spheres, the notion of contradiction has been used to articulate a range of problems basic to the relationships that exist between civil agents. In **civil society**, for example, contradictions may arise from the fact of individual civil agents pursuing their own particular purposes (*x*'s purposes may not be commensurable with *y*'s purposes) or from their having mutually incompatible interests.

PS

CONVERSATION ANALYSIS

Conversation analysis emerged in **sociology**, specifically through **ethnomethodology**. Conversations are highly organised social events, with participants typically able to tell when they must or are able to speak, when they may legitimately interrupt, or when they must respect another participant's silence and not speak. In conversations, participants therefore manifest their competence in managing social interaction. Conversation analysis is primarily concerned with the description of conversations. Class studies have been carried out on the first five seconds of telephone conversations.

Further reading: Atkinson *et al.* 1984; Moerman 1988; Sacks 1992.

AE

COUNTERCULTURE

The term 'counterculture' was coined in the 1960s, largely in response to the emergence of middle-**class** youth movements (such as the hippies), to refer to groups that questioned the **values** of the dominant culture. While centring on an opposition to the Vietnam War, the hippie counterculture also expressed its dissatisfaction with the values and goals of capitalism, such as consumerism, the work ethic and a dependence on technology. In general, the concept of counterculture may now be extended to the values, beliefs and attitudes of any minority group that opposes the dominant culture, but more precisely, does so in a relatively articulate and reflective manner. Thus, at its emergence, the Christian **religion** was a counterculture, in opposition to the dominant Jewish and Roman cultures. In the early period of British **capitalism**, the Quakers and the Methodists represented countercultures in opposition to the dominant values of Anglicanism.

See also: **subculture**, **youth culture**.

Further reading: Hill 1975; Roszak 1968; Yinger 1982.

AE

CRITICAL THEORY

'Critical theory' is something of an umbrella term, and has come to be associated in the Anglo-American academic world with a brand of textual analysis which has taken root predominantly in university English literature departments. The term itself, however, was first linked to the work of the **Frankfurt School** (e.g. Horkheimer, Adorno, Benjamin and Marcuse). In the hands of these thinkers, critical theory was envisaged as a rigorous critical engagement with social and philosophical issues which aimed at the cross-fertilisation of research methods derived from the social sciences with a Marxist theoretical framework for conceptualising social relations. However, as exemplified by Horkheimer and Adorno's book *Dialectic of Enlightenment*, there always existed in the work of the Frankfurt School a tendency to question certain ideas that were central to **Marxism** (for instance, the traditional Marxist confidence in the politicisation of the proletariat leading to revolution, or an unproblematic affirmation of the **Enlightenment** ideal of rationality as providing the key to social progress).

Since the 1980s, the term 'critical theory' has come to be associated with an approach to textual criticism which draws upon the writings of thinkers linked with **structuralism**, **post-structuralism** and **postmodernism** (for example, Foucault, Derrida and Lyotard). Some exponents of critical theory have also found room for the adoption of approaches derived from New **Historicism** or from the writings of psychoanalyst Jacques Lacan. From this it is apparent that any simple or clearly circumscribed definition of 'critical theory' in this sense is not possible. However, a number of characteristics might be cited as a means of arriving at a rather broad description of certain significant features of this form of critical theory.

In the wake of French structuralism, a brand of textual analysis evolved during the 1970s which concentrated on elucidating readings of literary texts in the light of Ferdinand de Saussure's linguistics. Thus, a text was conceived of as a structured network of signs, the meanings of which are determined not by what each sign refers to, but (i) through their differential relationship to one another, and (ii) through a relation of **binary opposition**. Structuralist analysis sought to provide an objective/scientific description of the structural economy of meaning present within texts. Recent critical theory was developed in the wake of the move from structuralism to post-structuralism initiated by the work of such figures as Paul de Man and the French philosopher Jacques Derrida. Derrida's advocacy, in *Of Grammatology* (1976), of a strategy of **deconstruction**, in which the analysis of texts is undertaken with the object of interrogating oppositional structures of meaning so as to allow for the identification and questioning of hierarchically organised conceptual orders, forms the basis of much of the more recent work undertaken in critical theory. Perhaps the most influential of Derridean notions in this context is that of *différance*, which for him represents the continual deferral of the possibility of a closure of meaning within language. Language, on this account, is not merely a system of differences (as with the model of language derived from Saussurean linguistics), but a 'system of *différance*' (Derrida 1981:28), which may be provisionally arrested so as to produce key conceptual orderings (such as those of '**objectivity**' and '**subjectivity**', '**self**' and '**other**') as its effects. In critical theory, this view of language has resulted in the production of readings of literary and philosophical texts which concentrate upon elucidating the hierarchies present within them, and then attempt to suspend or destabilise those hierarchies by way of invoking the *différance* hypothesis. Unfortunately this strategy has been repeated so often that one is inclined to suspect that Derrida's notion of *différance* has, in practical terms, been reduced to a form of 'magic lexicon' by those critics who seem inclined to adopt it uncritically as a key to unlocking the 'hidden' meanings present within texts. Such critics thereby seem content to let the work of critical engagement be reduced to the mere invocation of a meta-rule.

This latter fact is perhaps ironic, given the avowed commitment on the part of many critical theorists to a form of epistemic relativism. The roots of this relativism can be traced to two primary influences. First, to the recuperation of the writings of Michel Foucault, whose analysis of discourses of power has led some to stress the importance of power relations in the construction of meaning within texts (perhaps, in this context, the most productive effect of Foucault's influence is the work of E.W. Said, which has exerted an influence in furthering the critical awareness of colonial and post-colonial issues in contemporary **culture**). Second, Jean-François Lyotard's advocacy of a postmodern pluralism with regard to questions of ethics and knowledge, in works such as *The Postmodern Condition* (1989) has also left its mark upon the work of literary critical theory (although their reading strategies sit less comfortably with Lyotard's more recent work in texts such as *The Differend* (1988) which demonstrates a notably ambivalent relationship to postmodernism). Likewise, Jean Baudrillard's writings have also exerted some influence on the attitudes and ideas of critical theorists (see Norris's account of this in his *Uncritical Theory* (1992)). To this extent, and in spite of the fact of its frequently having been practised by academics ensconced within literature departments, critical theory of this type has, in effect, ceased to be a primarily literary discourse—if, indeed, it ever was. In its dealings with literature it has exhibited a tendency to question the received literary canon, and at the same time has demonstrated a strong commitment to intervening in issues which have, in general, hitherto been of sole interest to philosophers (something which, indeed, one might expect, given that many of the key influences upon critical theory have been thinkers, like Derrida and Lyotard, who work within the philosophical tradition). Thus, questions about the nature of identity, of meaning and of the relationship between language and experience (i.e. the realism versus antirealism debate) have all been identified as being important to the practice of critical theory by various exponents.

More recently, a number of key problems have been identified within critical theory, most notably by Christopher Norris, whose attitude towards it has undergone some radical revisions since he first espoused it in the early 1980s (see *Deconstruction: Theory and Practice* (1986)), the most recent edition of which contains a postscript which pays ample witness to its author's disillusionment). Whereas, in his earliest work, Norris displayed a confidence in the radical possibilities of a critical theory committed to an ethical and epistemological relativism, in his later writings (i.e. those dating from the late 1980s onwards) he has come to regard critical theory as embodying and embracing a form of uncritical relativism which has divested itself of the possibility for a radical engagement with contemporary political and ethical concerns. For instance, Norris's book *Uncritical Theory* attacks the anti-realism of Baudrillard, citing as a case in point his articles on the Gulf War which appeared in various French and English newspapers just prior to and immediately after the conflict. Baudrillard's claim that the Gulf War would not (and indeed his assertion subsequently that it did not) ever happen, are seen by Norris as the excesses of an anti-realism which has overstepped the boundaries of reason and ethical responsibility. Likewise, the postmodernism espoused by Lyotard's book *The Postmodern Condition*, and taken up by many critical theorists, has been met by Norris with some strong, and often perceptive, passages of criticism.

Whether or not one accepts the tenets of literary critical theory, its development within literature departments must be viewed as significant. Attempts on the part of critical theorists to render all human experience in terms of 'textuality', their criticisms of the realist thesis as it is put forward by some philosophers within, for instance, the analytic tradition, and indeed some of their attacks on philosophy itself, may well come to be viewed primarily as being symptomatic of a bid to debunk and thereby take control of the academic 'high ground' of ontology, metaphysics, ethics and epistemology which has traditionally been the domain of philosophers. Ironically (and, indeed, tellingly), however, one of the figures who has exerted an influence on critical theory, Lyotard, was and remains committed to the view that philosophy does and ought to have some privileged claims with regard to these issues (Lyotard's distinction in *The Differend* and elsewhere between the 'philosopher' and the 'intellectual', for instance, pays ample testimony to this fact). This demonstrates the existence of a deep tension within critical theory, between its avowed aims and its philosophical/theoretical heritage which has, at least as yet, not been resolved. For if the proponents of critical theory follow Lyotard's example and move towards a more Anglo-American philosophical orientation, many of its basic precepts and arguments will require careful scrutiny and, perhaps, radical revision.

Further reading: Derrida 1976; Harland 1987; Norris 1986, 1992.

PS

CULTURAL ANTHROPOLOGY

Anthropology, that literally means the study of man or humankind, is divided into two branches: physical (or biological) and cultural. Physical anthropology is concerned with the physical variation in human form. While in the nineteenth century, this variation was understood in crude evolutionary terms, and was frequently used to justify the superiority of the white European form over other, supposedly more primitive, forms, now physical anthropology stresses only the diversity of human form (as adaptation to diverse environments), not any progress. A similar shift occurred in cultural anthropology as it matured into a respectable (and indeed fundamental) social science at the beginning of the twentieth century. Thus, an initial concern with the progress of human society and culture (still reflected in the occasional use of 'primitive' society) was replaced by a recognition of the diversity of human culture, and the different but none the less equally complex and valid structures and logics that underpinned these cultures.

Perhaps the first great anthropologists, at least in the modern development of the subject, were Marcel Mauss (in France) and Franz Boas (in the United States). Mauss, the nephew and pupil of Emile Durkheim, developed a comparative approach to anthropology. Working with **ethnographic** (which is to say, descriptive) data, compiled by others, from a wide range of pre-industrial and small-scale societies, he sought to find common patterns in the organisation of social and cultural life. In *The Gift* (1966) he analysed the exchange of gifts. Mauss understood that the gift carried with it a reciprocal moral obligation. The gift had to be returned, in some form, at a later date. Gift exchange could therefore be explained as a 'total **social fact**'. That is to say, it is an activity that has implications throughout society, in the economic, legal, political and religious spheres. (Hence, political power might be secured through the potential leader's ability to make gifts, thereby binding the recipients of these gifts to him, for they would repay the gift in political allegiance.) If Mauss developed a theoretical side of anthropology, not least in that he recognised the complexity of other cultures, and the cognitive aspects of a culture (in that one's culture provides the human agent with the resources to make sense of and to classify the natural and social worlds (Durkheim and Mauss 1963)), Franz Boas promoted the empirical side of anthropology. After living amongst the Inuit (during work on a meteorological expedition), Boas stressed the importance of describing the finest detail of everyday life in cultures, and thus the importance of **field work** and ethnographic techniques.

Bronislaw Malinowski's study of the Trobriand Islanders of New Guinea (1922) provided a model for sound anthropological research for many years. It combined meticulous ethnographic descriptions of the society, with a **functionalist** explanatory framework. In effect, Malinowski sought to explain the various features and institutions of the society in terms of the functions they fulfilled, which is to say, the needs they satisfied, in order to maintain and reproduce the culture. The functionalist approach was dominant in anthropology prior to the Second World War, with the British anthropologists E.E. Evans-Pritchard (1951) and A.R. Radcliffe-Brown (1952) pre-eminent. However, in the United States, important work was being carried out by, amongst others, Ruth Benedict and Margaret Mead (1928). Benedict's work (1935) produced remarkably elegant interpretations of cultures in terms of their articulation of a dominant theme (or, in the case of Japanese culture, the clash between two themes: the military (the 'sword') and aesthetic (the 'chrysanthemum') (Benedict 1989)). Benedict's and Mead's work, like that of Mead's teacher, Boas, explicitly focused on the role that culture has in shaping human personality. In the **nature**–nurture debate—that is to say, the debate over the respective influence of cultural acquisition and genetic inheritance in the shaping of human personality and other traits—cultural anthropologists have typically supported the 'nurture' side of the argument. At the extreme, suggested by Benedict's work, the newborn human may be presented as a blank slate upon which culture can write whatever traits it chooses (thus placing great emphasis on the importance of **socialisation**). In practice, this approach may lead to difficulties in explaining the behaviour of those who do not conform (the **deviant**).

The work of Mauss and Radcliffe-Brown had a major influence on Claude Lévi-Strauss, and the development of structuralist anthropology in the immediate post-war period. His *Elementary Structures of Kinship* (1969) treated marriage rules broadly in the manner of Mauss's total social fact. The rules that governed marriage (for example, the widespread custom of preferring first cousins as spouses) were seen to underpin meaningful exchanges between male-dominated clans. Women are the 'messages' transmitted between clans, as they give away daughters and receive wives. The influence of Saussure's **semiology** on Lévi-Strauss was combined with work already done by Radcliffe-Brown on the structures found within **myths**, and especially on the use of **binary oppositions** (such as black–white) to articulate the meaning of the myths. Lévi-Strauss's magnum opus, the four-volume *Mythologies* (1970, 1973, 1978, 1981), along with *The*

Savage Mind (1966), explore not simply the ways in which human cultures organise classificatory systems (and indeed integrate their understanding of the natural world with an articulation of the social world), but rather present these structures, including particular mythological narratives and classificatory systems, as manifestations of a deep structure that is grounded in the working of the human mind as such. The diversity of particular mythologies and beliefs is seen to employ a relatively limited set of meaningful units (or symbols). The combination of these elements is determined by rules that are akin to grammatical transformations. (In effect, particular mythologies are akin to Saussure's **parole**, while the underlying structure is **langue**.)

If Radcliffe-Brown's work influenced **structuralism**, Evans-Pritchard's work was instrumental in stimulating debate over **cultural relativism**. The British, Wittgensteinian philosopher Peter Winch took up Evans-Pritchard's accounts of witchcraft practices amongst the Azande in order to explore the incommensurability of different cultures (Winch 1958). That is to say, Winch developed the relativist position that all **values** and all knowledge claims were valid and meaningful only relative to the particular culture (or, in Wittgenstein's terminology, 'form of life') within which they emerged. If so, this entails that one cannot understand these values and beliefs except in their own terms. The anthropologist was therefore required to immerse him or herself in the culture studied, and not to try to translate their findings into the values and beliefs of his or her own western European culture. The Winchian approach works against the type of comparative and explanatory work carried out by Mauss or Lévi-Strauss, for that would be seen to violate the uniqueness of each culture, and the requirement to understand and interpret it in its own terms (not those of an alien scientific culture, such as that of functionalism or structuralism). At a less extreme position, cultural anthropology continues to celebrate the diversity and validity of other cultures as cognitive systems, leading to the rise of series of subdisciplines within cultural anthropology, concerning the way in which cultures organise their knowledge of various phenomena—hence 'ethnomedicine' is concerned with the way in which non-Western cultures articulate their knowledge of medicine; or 'ethnobotany' with the knowledge and classification of plants.

Further reading: Ingold 1996; James *et al.* 1997; Leach 1982; Strathern 1995.

AE

CULTURAL CAPITAL

Class membership is defined, at least within the Marxist tradition, in terms of the individual's access to and control of economic **capital** (such as industrial machinery, raw materials and also finance). Pierre Bourdieu (1973) drew an analogy to an individual's access to cultural resources in order to explain the workings of the educational system in a class-divided capitalist society. Children will have differing degrees of cultural competence (including information and skills), acquired prior to school within the family. The education system will not then overtly discriminate in favour of the children of the dominant class. Rather, all children will be assessed 'neutrally', in terms of their ability to perform according to the same criteria of excellence. These criteria will, however, be derived from the dominant culture. The children of the dominant class will do better, so yielding interest (in terms of 'symbolic power') on their parents' investment in cultural capital.

AE

CULTURAL RELATIVISM

The view that fundamentally different standards of morality, practices and belief systems operate in different cultures and cannot be judged with regard to their worth from a standpoint exterior to them. Cultural relativism thus holds that there is a fundamental incommensurability between the value systems of different cultures. Whether or not such a view commits one to a relativism with regard to questions of knowledge (see **epistemology**) is a further issue which depends upon whether or not one is inclined to hold that the rules of validity which apply with regard to the construction of knowledge claims (for example, the principle of non-**contradiction**) are culturally constructed. However, it is difficult to see how a cultural relativist can defend any notion of epistemic validity from the charge of being likewise culturally produced, and therefore incommensurable with conceptions of validity that are generated within different cultures or contexts. It is possible to define more recent cultural relativism in terms of its commitment to a particular model of language and meaning derived from (or having strong parallels with) the work of the later Wittgenstein. Thus, Richard Rorty's espousal of a **liberalism** and **postmodernism** which is relativistic about the practices and procedures that constitute interpretative communities owes a debt to the Wittgensteinean 'meaning is use' thesis. Although it has often been claimed that the cultural relativist is interested in giving voice to the perspectives of marginalised interests and cultures, it is by no means clear that this is the case. Some have argued (cf. Christopher Norris, *The Contest of Faculties* (1985)) that Rorty's espousal of cultural and epistemic relativism brings with it the spectre of cultural imperialism.

See also: **cultural anthropology**.

Further reading: Hollis and Lukes 1982; Margolis 1991; Norris 1985; Rorty 1991.

PS

CULTURAL REPRODUCTION

The term 'cultural reproduction' was coined by Pierre Bourdieu (1973) to refer to the process by which the **culture**, and thus political power, of the dominant **class** is maintained from one generation to the next, through the education system. More generally, the term may be seen to highlight the problem of how societies continue to exist and remain relatively stable over long periods of time. This continued existence requires more than just physical reproduction, in the sense of sufficient births to replace those who have died or left the society. The culture of that society must be transmitted to the new generation. Cultural reproduction is thus intimately linked to the role that **socialisation**, or the process through which individuals internalise the culture of their societies, plays in this stability. As Bourdieu's definition highlights, part of this problem of cultural transmission is not simply the stability of the manner in which society is organised, or the stability of the key values and beliefs of its culture, but rather the stability of the political structures and the structures of domination and exploitation within the society. As such, it may be seen as a process by which political structures are given legitimacy or **authority**.

In the Marxist tradition, social reproduction refers to conditions necessary for the renewal of **labour**. Again, this is not simply a matter of physically replacing labourers, but more centrally involves the place of social and cultural institutions, such as housing, **education** and health care in that process.

Further reading: Jenks 1993b.

AE

CULTURAL STUDIES

While the term 'cultural studies' may be used, broadly, to refer to all aspects of the study of **culture**, and as such may be taken to encompass the diverse ways in which culture is understood and analysed, for example, in sociology, history, **ethnography** and **literary criticism**, and even **sociobiology**, it may also, more precisely, be taken to refer to a distinctive field of academic enquiry. In this second use, its historical roots can be traced back to the work of Raymond Williams and Richard Hoggart in the late 1950s and early 1960s, and thus to the formation of the **Birmingham Centre for Contemporary Cultural Studies** in 1964, originally under the directorship of Hoggart and then of Stuart Hall. From this body of work there emerged a multi-disciplinary approach to culture, drawing not merely on the orthodox approaches derived from the social sciences, but also on more radical approaches suggested by, for example, **feminism**, **Marxism** and **semiotics**. This miscellany of approaches facilitated the asking of new questions, and thus to a reconceptualisation of exactly what was entailed by the term 'culture'. In particular, cultural studies can be seen to have set itself against the preconceptions about culture found in the traditional critical disciplines, such as literary criticism, **aesthetics** and musicology. While such traditional disciplines predominantly treated cultural products as objects or texts that could be legitimately, or even exhaustively, studied in isolation from the social and historical contexts of their **production** and **consumption**, the exponents of cultural studies sought to situate cultural products explicitly in relation to other social practices, and particularly in relation to political structures and social hierarchies, such as **race**, **class** and **gender**. An implication of this approach was that the cultural products to be studied could not merely be those selected and celebrated by an intellectual and artistic elite, but would rather be the material and symbolic products encountered in all strata and sections of society.

Cultural studies can therefore be seen to be situated between an approach to culture that is explicitly opposed to the celebration of high or elite culture, as represented, for example, in the canonical texts studied in English literature, or the subject matter of traditional musicology, and an approach that is more positively derived from the social sciences, and particularly from **cultural anthropology** and the sociology of culture.

Further reading: Grossberg *et al.* 1992; Hall 1980, 1996; Inglis 1993.

AE

CULTURE

'Culture' is not easily defined, not least because it can have different meanings in different contexts. However, the concept that lies at the core of **cultural studies**, it may be suggested, is very much the concept that is found in **cultural anthropology**. As such, it avoids any exclusive concern with 'high' culture (which is still found, for example, in the writings of Arnold and Leavis, and in **elite** and mass society theories). It entails recognition that all human beings live in a world that is created by human beings, and in which they find meaning. Culture is the complex everyday world we all encounter and through which we all move. Culture begins at the point at which humans surpass whatever is simply given in their **natural** inheritance. The cultivation of the natural world, in **agriculture** and **horticulture**, is thus a fundamental element of a culture. As such, the two most important or general elements of culture may be the ability of human beings to construct and to build, and the ability to use **language** (understood most broadly, to embrace all forms of sign system).

Gillian Rose's use of the Jewish myth of the Tower of Babel is illuminating in this context (1993). At Babel, humans attempted to reach heaven by building a tower. God did not merely destroy the Tower, but in order to prevent a further attempt, he prevented **communication** by imposing a multiplicity of languages. This story is often seen as an **allegory** of language. Rose, however, takes it further, as an allegory of language and **architecture**. It is therefore seen to comment upon key themes of cultural studies, including the community, the conflict of diverse cultures, **power**, law and morality, and knowledge. A few of these themes may be outlined. Rose's argument is that Babel represents, not simply an architectural project, but also the building of a city. Cities are a crucial cultural watershed, for in the city, diverse cultures (customs, beliefs and **values**) come together. In a city, people become aware, perhaps for the first time, that they have a culture, for there is always someone who disagrees with what you have always taken for granted. Our self-awareness as cultural beings is grounded in this confrontation, and thus in the exercise of power (as we struggle to sustain our own values against an assault from **others**). The point of Babel, and perhaps of all human culture, is that in the architectural achievement of the tower-city, humans gained a sort of immortality. While the individual may die, the buildings of his or her generation will live on and become part of the future. Cultures endure even though the individuals who built them die. So, at the very least, our understanding of time is transformed, and our understanding of history created. Yet this 'reach', as Rose calls it, entails the loss of a nai?ve self-certainty. The unity and universality of the isolated, nomadic early Jewish tribe is confronted and questioned by its encounter with a plurality of other cultures and their claims to universality. Paradoxically, at the very moment in which we become aware of ourselves as cultural beings, we are both enabled (we can do new things and, in principle, do anything we like), but can no longer ever be certain what is the right thing to do, and so in doing anything, we fall into conflict with others. Thus, **cultural studies** is necessarily concerned with artificiality, and the political struggle to find and defend meaning.

Further reading: Jenks 1993a; Williams 1986.

AE

CULTURE INDUSTRY

The term '**culture** industry' was coined by the **Frankfurt School** theorists Horkheimer and Adorno in *The Dialectic of Enlightenment* (2002), to refer to the production of mass culture. This deliberately contradictory term (setting the culture against its apparent antithesis in industry) attempts to grasp something of the fate of culture in the highly instrumentally rational and bureaucratic society of late **capitalism**. The account of the culture industry may be seen, at root, as economic, and as such an integral part of the reinterpretation of dialectical materialism that is a central theme of *The Dialectic of Enlightenment*. The culture industry, embracing advertising as much as radio and **cinema**, serves to transform **use value** (the utility that consumers derive from a **commodity**) into something that is produced by the capitalist system. It may be suggested that the combination of advertising and the **mass media** promotes less particular products, and more a capitalist lifestyle.

This account of the absorption of use value into production goes hand in hand with Adorno's analysis of the fate of the relationship between the **forces of production** and the **relations of production** in twentieth-century capitalism. The independence of use value in nineteenth-century capitalism gave the human subject genuine autonomy and thus potential for resistance (thereby destabilising capitalism). This autonomy is now increasingly lost. Similarly, administrative techniques, that developed as part of the forces of production (to increase the efficiency of industry), now become fundamental to the relations of production (so that market exchange and property ownership are subordinated to bureaucratic organisation, and the employed and the unemployed alike become claimants for welfare payments). The contradiction between the forces and relations of production, that for Marx would bring about the fall of capitalism, is removed in this totally administered society.

The account of the culture industry has frequently been trivialised by its critics (not least those within cultural studies). Horkheimer and Adorno do not, for example, obviously assume that human subjects are passive victims of the culture industry, and nor is the culture industry an instrument of **class** rule. The total administration of contemporary capitalism embraces and constrains everyone, so that although the property-owning **bourgeoisie** may continue to benefit materially from the system, they are as powerless before it as the non-property-owning classes. Yet these powerless subjects continue to struggle with the system, and to survive within it. Horkheimer and Adorno hint that **consumption** of culture industry products is diverse. The radio ham, for example, attempts to retain some autonomy and individuality by building and operating his or her own radio, rather than accepting what is given, ready-made. Others use the cover of culture industry institutions, such as the cinema, to admit the unhappiness that would paralyse them in the real world. Even within the culture industry, not all of its products are homogeneous. Orson Welles (and later Michelangelo Antonioni) demonstrate that cinema has the critical and self-reflective potential that Adorno attributes to all autonomous art; Bette Davis keeps alive the tradition of great acting; and, if the nuances of the text are to be believed, Warner Brothers' cartoons do not share the simple minded capitulation to **authority** that is the hallmark of Disney.

Further reading: Adorno 1991a; Cook 1996; Held 1980.

AE

CYBERCULTURE

The cultural space ('cyberia' (Escobar 1994)) that has been created through computer **technology**, and in particular computer-based communications and thus the internet. Cyberculture is thus the vast gathering of information, misinformation, sounds, images and ideas that can be accessed through the internet, along with the set of practices, attitudes, values and ways of thinking that respond to and are a consequence of the 'cyberspace' that has been created through the global interconnection of computers. The interpretation and analysis of cyberspace overlaps significantly with concerns over the relationship between humanity and other forms of technology, not least that of mechanical and genetic enhancement of the human body in the form of the cyborg (see **post-humanism**). Such phenomena have been extensively and critically explored in science fiction. William Gibson's work is particularly important, not least in that Gibson coined the terms 'cyberspace' (in the short story *Burning Chrome* (1986)) and 'cyberpunk' (the latter signifying this particular genre of science fiction) (Gibson 1984).

The internet was originally developed by the American military in the 1960s. The idea of linking many, geographically dispersed computers as nodes in a network was intended to protect the computer system from nuclear attack, precisely because there is no one vulnerable point to be destroyed. Beyond its military uses, the early internet was a tool of academia. The prototype of the internet was the ARPAnet, that first linked computers in four American universities in 1969. Commercial interest in the possibilities of the internet reached a crucial point in the late 1980s and early 1990s, as Tim Berners-Lee developed the hypertext software necessary for the development of the World Wide Web. The internet could then develop beyond the realm of government activity and education, coming to play an increasingly fundamental role in commercial activity, entertainment and many forms of social interaction. It takes on its distinctive form as a rhizome (and Deleuze and Guattari's (1987) theorisation of this term has been highly influential in cultural theory's response to the internet). As such, the internet invites the user to sidestep the linear forms of thought and exploration that have long dominated Western thought. Thought is decentred, allowing the user to explore and negotiate their own overlapping and entwining paths through a seemingly amorphous cornucopia of information.

The internet, like most new technologies, has generated extremes of loving enthusiasm and profound fears. The clash between the two has been, and continues to be, worked out in a series of moral, political and cultural debates. Early concerns over the appropriate use of the internet ('netiquette'), as a wider and at times commercially motivated public began to intrude into the previously academically refined internet, continue, for example in concerns over (and the sheer irritation at) the abuse of email through spam. More profoundly, the internet has generated moral panics over access to pornography and images of violence. These debates echo fears that go back at least as far as

Book 10 of Plato's *Republic*, with its expression of concern over mimetic art, precisely because there is perceived to be something dangerously seductive about the virtual worlds such artefacts conjure (Plato 1998).

However, the politics of the internet remains, possibly, the most enduring concern. At one level, the increasing importance of the internet in everyday life (be this at the level of commercial activity, political involvement or social interaction) exacerbates the significance of having no access to the internet. Questions of justice are then raised as those groups and individuals who do not have internet access are excluded from importance sources of knowledge and social involvement. On another level, fears are raised both about commercial control of the internet and governmental control. The weight of traffic on the internet has recently led certain commercial providers to suggest the possibility of making available a faster, but more expensive, internet 'highway', to those willing and able to pay (thus potentially undermining the openness of the internet). Governments continue to have effective power to censor their citizens' access to the internet (with the activity of the Chinese government frequently being cited as a key example of an unacceptable degree of control) and to monitor email exchanges. The internet is also playing an increasingly significant role in struggles for liberation and in identity politics. The internet has become an increasingly valuable tool for revolutionary and resistance groups to broadcast their ideas and information, avoiding more readily controlled **mass media** (such as **television**). The role that blogging has played in articulating the opinions and experiences of Iraqis (and indeed American combatants) involved in the Gulf War is a case in point.

Precisely because cyberspace allows the user to reinvent or fictionalise their **identity**, it is also a space in which identities can be creatively explored (Turkle 1996, 2005). The question of who I am while in cyberspace is ever present. The user may be understood to fuse (in the style of a cyborg) with the very technology that facilitates the internet. Traditional notions of embodiment are challenged by the experience of cyberspace. Cyberfeminism (following Haraway's (1991) analysis of the cyborg) has explored the way in which cyberspace opens up the possibility of **deconstructing** traditional patriarchal **binary oppositions**, such as those between male and female, and technology and nature (see Kennedy 1999; Plant 1997).

If cyberspace is transforming our understanding of ourselves as individual and embodied beings, then the use of cyberspace and the internet is also, in practice, transforming the ways in which we interact with others. The internet is rapidly, and unpredictably, creating new forms of interaction, from the email, MSN messaging, and blogs, to the development of 'MySpace', 'Second Life' and similar internet sites, where the distinction between 'real' and 'virtual' friendships and social relationships and even economies begins to become blurred (Gefter 2006).

Further reading: Bell and Kennedy 2000; Lévy 2001; Sardar and Ravetz 1996.

AE

DANCE

Dance has perhaps been rather neglected by the social sciences and by **cultural studies**. Dance is nonetheless an important activity across society and in very different societies. At one extreme, there is the apparently elitist classical ballet. Within high **culture**, the conservatism of ballet is challenged by the **avant-garde** of 'modern dance'. While such activity may appear to aspire to an **aesthetic** autonomy that serves to divorce it from social and cultural concerns (although there have been a significant number of ballets with political themes and subject matter produced in the twentieth century), modern dance can be seen as a fundamental exploration of the **body**, and the conventions that govern its movement and presentation in contemporary culture. Ballroom, tap and various other dance forms should not be neglected as widely enjoyed leisure activities. The concept of folk dance suggests that dance can represent a community's expression of its **values**, **identity** or resistance to external pressures, although such folk dance may also be a commercial construction (for example, for a tourist industry).

Angela McRobbie has pointed to dance, not simply as a rich and important part of youth **subculture**, but specifically as a part of feminine youth culture. Its neglect by cultural studies is therefore seen as symptomatic of the general neglect of female involvement in subcultures. McRobbie points to a number of different levels upon which dance can be approached. It is a leisure activity, a source of diffuse erotic pleasure and a form of exercise. Conversely, it may be a form of control of the female body and movement, through its emphasis on grace and beauty. Yet it is also a way in which the dancer can herself take control. For McRobbie, dance can be an extension of the private culture of femininity, into a public space. Dance is a form of evasion and an opportunity for fantasy, as the dancer is both out of control and therefore out of the reach of controlling forces. Dance is 'simultaneously a dramatic display of the self and the body, with an equally dramatic negation of the self and the body' (McRobbie 1991:144).

Further reading: Foster 1996; Thomas 1993.

AE

DECONSTRUCTION

As the term itself implies, deconstruction grew out of **structuralism**. Jacques Derrida coined the term 'deconstruction' and he is the most significant representative of this philosophical and critical movement. As he explains, the project of deconstruction in his vastly influential work *De la grammatologie* (1967), its goal is to dismantle the structures of meaning so as to expose the premises on which they are built and to reveal the concepts of objectivity and linguistic autonomy as constructs. Derrida has always insisted that deconstruction cannot be treated as a clearly defined methodology; the chief reason for this being that deconstruction rejects the idea that there is a controlling intelligence which can recognise and explain the structuring principles of language (especially the system of **binary oppositions** which play such a dominant role in structuralism). In this sense, deconstruction is a development of structuralism which acknowledges that the massively ambitious goals of structuralism could only be envisaged on the grounds of a reductive understanding of language, society, history and cognition.

Because deconstruction is aware of the potential failures of any methodology, it adopts an intensely self-critical stance. First and foremost, it points out that the production of **meaning** at any particular moment is far removed from being a spontaneous expression of ideas and instead involves conventions and preconceptions that are deeply ingrained in language. Meaning is an expression brought forth by an autonomous mind, which explains Derrida's attack on the notion of 'presence', as suggesting control over the full range of meanings of any particular utterance. When deconstruction established itself in the late 1960s, its chief interest was in formulating a critique of language and representation. The contemporaneous claims of a group of intellectuals, notably Roland Barthes and Michel Foucault, concerning the 'death of the **author**' (a catchphrase by means of which they argued for the subject's loss of control over the production of linguistic meaning) also subverted the view that language was a (neutral) form for the expression of ideas.

The American version of deconstruction was oriented towards a practical analysis of literary texts. Its chief representative, Paul de Man, focused on the rhetorical dimension of language and, together with Geoffrey Hartman and J. Hillis Miller, established deconstruction as a literary critical practice that was to be known as the 'Yale School' and flourished in the 1970s and 1980s.

Derrida's insistence on overturning the order of priority between speech and writing showed that there can be no spontaneous linguistic agency. He emphasises that whatever is said is preconditioned by the structural possibilities of what can be said and he uses the term dissemination to suggest that language possesses a self-regulating rationale. But then, language cannot be equated with the *logos* either and there is no metaphysical instance which guarantees linguistic stability. Or rather, language is affected by a negative force which disturbs order. By revealing logical inconsistencies, deconstruction points towards ideological complicities and disrupts the text's explicit claims. Deconstructive critical practices seek to identify power relations; not only as represented within the text itself but also as they precondition certain responses to the text. That is to say, deconstruction studies works of art through an analysis of the structural logic of the representational medium (language) and the tradition of interpretation associated with a particular kind of text as a means of resisting its ideological outlook.

Because deconstruction rejects any categorical distinction between text and context, it has frequently been accused of being apolitical. However, critics like Barbara Johnson, whose involvement with **feminism** and **Marxism** made a political commitment imperative, showed that deconstruction had to rethink its relation to issues of class, gender and race. In recent years, prominent critics such as Gayatri Spivak have referred to themselves as Marxist feminist deconstructionists. Adherents to this line pursue the goal of a critique of ideology when they engage in an analysis of cultural definitions and distinctions (such as those between male and female; black and white; central and marginal). Even though the play of meaning which characterises all language also applies to the language of the critic of ideology, this should not be understood as incapacitating any kind of intervention but rather as a warning that claims made in an authoritarian manner are particularly likely to be dismantled by language's auto-deconstructive potential.

Further reading: de Man 1979; Derrida 1976; Holub 1992; Johnson 1980; Norris 1987; Ryan 1982.

CK

DETERMINISM

In philosophy, determinism has generally been contrasted with free will. The latter holds that humans are able to make choices and act upon them, the former that our choices are determined by other forces, and our actions, therefore, can be accounted for in, for instance, causal terms. On a broader 'cultural' level, the concept of determinism is an analogous one: a determinist would be someone who argues that social and cultural activities are causally derived from more immanent forces (for example, the role of **power** relations in the constitution of **subjectivity**). A determinist may hold (as traditional Marxists do) that **ideology** and its accompanying cultural forms are a direct consequence of the base-structure of economic relations; or, as with **social Darwinism**, that there are basic underlying social laws which, as in the natural world, determine which social types are best according to the dictates of 'the survival of the fittest' principle; or that what language you speak determines what thoughts you can have. It might be added that any extreme causal determinism (such as that advocated by psychologist B.F. Skinner) flounders on an objection presented by Michael Oakeshott: namely, that the determinist, in order to be making a true claim, must also include the theory itself within their account (i.e. be self-reflexive), and thus an all-out theory of determinism is, on its own terms, something determined in advance (a problem linked to **epistemology**). At the social level, this view is mainly significant with regard to the question of how much autonomy **individuals** have.

Further reading: Honderich 1993; Oakeshott 1975; Skinner 1974.

PS

DEVIANCE

The concept of 'deviance' may be understood to develop, within **sociology**, in reaction to orthodox criminology. While criminology studies crime, and thus the breaking of law, the sociology of deviance looks to a broader range of activity. The behaviour of the deviant deviates from some generally accepted, or consensual, **norm** of behaviour. The alcoholic may break no laws, but his or her behaviour deviates from society's normal expectations as to what is a reasonable level of alcohol consumption.

This simple definition is problematic in at least two respects. First, it assumes that there is a pre-existing consensus within society as to what is normal. In reply, it may be suggested that this consensus is, in large part, generated through the pursuit and definition of deviance. Cohen's (1980) analysis of 'moral panics' illustrates this. In a moral panic, a group or individual comes to be defined, particularly through extensive **mass media** coverage, as a threat to the **values** and interests of the society. The public are thereby sensitised, not merely to the apparent threat, but also to the values that are threatened.

The second way in which the initial definition oversimplifies the phenomenon of deviance is that it assumes that deviance occurs simply by breaking some norm. There are two problems with this. First, rules and norms are complex, and the precise application of them often depends upon subtle and contextual interpretation. Under certain circumstances, all rules can legitimately be broken. This entails that there is always scope for negotiation and argument as to whether or not a particular act was deviant. This, for example, is typical of pupils' disobedience of school rules. The second point, that in some respects emerges from this, is that someone only then becomes a deviant through a social process, occurring after the initial violation of a norm. Many members of society break norms, and do so frequently. Only some of these people come to be recognised by others, and by themselves, as deviants. This process is typically theorised as **labelling**. Deviance entails that a person has come to be described according to a value-laden term (so that, for example, the drinker becomes an alcoholic, the gourmet a glutton). Members of certain groups (such as the more affluent and educated **classes**) may have the power and resources to resist such labels (which in turn may partly explain the higher rates of criminality and deviance recorded amongst members of subordinate classes and **ethnic** groups). The public recognition and application of certain labels (such as hooligan, thief, drug taker, child abuser) will serve to isolate the individual from normal society. The individual may therefore take shelter within a deviant subculture, so that the initial, and possibly aberrant act of rule breaking becomes typical of his or her behaviour. Deviance may therefore be seen to be 'amplified' by the very social institutions (such as the police and courts) that exist to control deviance.

See also: **subculture**.

Further reading: Aggleton 1987; Downes and Rock 1982.

AE

DIACHRONIC

See: **synchronic/diachronic**.

DIALECTICAL AND HISTORICAL MATERIALISM

Historical materialism is the theory of social change developed by Karl Marx and Friedrich Engels. History is divided into a series of epochs or **modes of production**. Each is characterised by a distinct economy and a distinct **class** structure. Historical change is fuelled by the progressive expansion of the productive power of the economy (and thus the development of technology, or the **forces of production**) and is manifest in overt class conflict and revolution.

Dialectical materialism encompasses those aspects of Marxist philosophy other than the theory of history, including **epistemology** and ontology. It became the dogmatic official philosophy of the Soviet Union. The term was not used by Marx or Engels, with attempts to develop a coherent dialectical materialist philosophy beginning with Plekhanov and Lenin, building on Engels's *Anti-Dühring* (1947), and *Dialectics of Nature* (1973). Dialectical materialism is characterised by its materialism and its rejection of any form of scepticism. The material world is held to have primacy over the mental, so that the body is the precondition for consciousness. It is held that this material world is, in principle, knowable through the work of the empirical sciences. In addition, the philosophy is **dialectical**, in that it presents reality as in development. This is to argue, not simply that there is change in the material world, but rather that reality is characterised by the emergence of qualitatively new properties.

Further reading: Callinicos 1983; Cohen 1978; Cornforth 1971; Ruben 1979.

AE

DIALECTICS

In philosophy, the term 'dialectics' originally referred to the argumentative style found in Plato's dialogues. Socrates, Plato's main protagonist, would interrogate other philosophers, thinkers and assorted experts, most typically as to what they meant by a particular concept (such as 'justice', or the 'good'). The Socratic method typically worked by exposing the shallow and ultimately incoherent understanding that others had of concepts, but without Socrates necessarily providing an adequate and coherent definition of his own.

The term 'dialectic' took on a related, but distinctive, meaning in German philosophy in the late eighteenth and early nineteenth centuries, in the work of Kant, Fichte and Hegel. It was Fichte who proposed the common characterisation of the structure of a dialectical argument as thesis, antithesis and synthesis. That is to say, one thesis would be proven. An equally good proof would be provided for an alternative and incompatible thesis. The **contradiction** between the thesis and antithesis would then be resolved typically by a leap to a different way of looking at the problem, so that the initial contradiction is explained away by recognising the limits upon one's reasoning and knowledge that taken for granted presuppositions placed upon the original argument.

Hegel's dialectic is rather more subtle and complex than this. The three terms of Hegel's dialectic may best be seen as universal, particular and individual. The universal is a stage of naï?ve self-certainty. A single, all-encompassing entity exists. (For example, the newborn human being knows nothing of the world other than its own existence.) Yet there is no real knowledge here, for that only occurs when there is differentiation or sundering. The entity will come to know itself only if it recognises what it is not (and thus encounters some **other**). The universal is therefore particularised, sundered, or broken up. (The pure subjectivity of the newborn infant encounters an alien object.) This stage of particularisation gives rise to a fruitful period of growth and self-discovery, not merely for the individual human. This is how Hegel characterises human history as a whole. This period ends when the subject recognises itself in the object. The universality of the first stage of the dialectic is then restored, but in a new, profoundly self-conscious form. The subject has returned to itself, but has learnt of itself through the journey. (It is now incidental that many great nineteenth-century novels, such as Goethe's *Wilhelm Meister*, and Dickens's *Great Expectations*, manifest a similar structure (that of the *Bildungsroman*), as the hero discovers him or herself through a series of adventures in a strange and difficult world.)

Hegel's dialectic is not simply a structure of argument, but is the very structure of the cosmos, manifest from the grandest levels (the development of human history, or the movements of the planets) to the humblest (the growth of a plant). **Marx** uses this model to explain the development of human history through a series of epochs or **modes of production**. History begins as humanity breaks out of the nai?ve universality of primitive communism, and is forced into class society. Here humans make history, but not under the conditions of their choosing. Which is to say, the products of subjective human action confront humans as alien objects. In communism, this form of history ends, for then humans will have understood themselves as social beings (and will thus have the self-consciousness of the Hegelian individual), and will make history and society as they choose.

In twentieth-century cultural theory, the **Frankfurt School** philosopher Theodor Adorno and the French psychoanalyst Jacques Lacan have, independently, made remarkably similar reinterpretations of Hegel. By claiming to know the final stage of the dialectic, Hegel presumes to know and be able to describe absolute truth. Both Adorno and Lacan reject this authoritarianism of the presumption to know absolute truth. Adorno therefore proposes a 'negative dialectics'. That is to say, the dialectical process is arrested at the second stage. The best that we can then know is the contradictions and inconsistencies, both in the world and in our knowledge of the world, but we cannot presume to escape them. Similarly, Lacan is concerned to analyse the ways in which we spend our lives struggling to restore an 'imaginary' universality before we were sundered from unity with our mother (and thrown into an empty and incomplete world of selfhood and language). Our lives are the pursuit of substitutes for this lost universality. The idea of a psychoanalytic 'cure', that would restore unity (and thus achieve an Hegelian individual), is rejected.

Further reading: Adorno 1973b; Hegel 1975a; Lacan 1977a; Mepham and Ruben 1979; Rosen 1982.

AE

DICTATORSHIP OF THE PROLETARIAT

In Marxist-Leninism, the dictatorship of the **proletariat** occurs directly after the revolution that brings down **capitalism**, and yet before the achievement of communism. The phrase suggests that state power, that was previously in the hands of the dominant **bourgeoisie**, is transferred to the newly dominant proletariat, in order to manage the transition to communism. Crucially, in communism, there will be no state (for it will have withered away during the preceding period of socialism). The term 'dictatorship' is misleading to a degree. Lenin (1992), in striving to break away from the institutional constraints of the old tsarist state, conceived of a participatory direct democracy, grounded in workers' councils.

Further reading: Draper 1987; Ehrenberg 1992.

AE

DIFFERENCE/*DIFFÉRANCE*

Difference: In terms of the **structuralism** advocated by linguist Ferdinand de Saussure, difference constitutes the basis upon which **signs** have **meaning**. Difference in this sense refers to the structurally related phonetic differences between elements of language as they are situated within the system of signs which constitute *langue* (i.e. the fundamental structure of meanings which must be in place at any given time if a speaker is to be able to speak). Thus, meaning is regarded within this model as a system of differences.

Différance: In the work of French philosopher Jacques Derrida, '*différance*', likewise, constitutes the conditions of possibility for meaning in language. As opposed to Saussure's fixed conception of meaning as a structure of difference, however, Derrida's neologism is meant to capture the ceaseless movement of meaning which is a condition of its production, i.e. that meaning is simultaneously 'differential' and 'deferred'. *Différance* is, when spoken, indistinguishable from 'difference', and thereby supplements the Saussurean sense of difference by indicating a semantic slippage (made apparent here only in writing rather than speech) which operates so as to prevent the meaning of a sign achieving a state of self-presence. In other words, meaning on this view is never entirely present within language at a given moment, but is conceived of as a chain of signification that remains incomplete. As such, *différance* is regarded by Derrida as signifying neither a word nor a concept, but as the condition of the functioning of words and concepts. This notion has been deployed by exponents of literary **critical theory**. Derrida's own elaboration of it, however, is situated within the context of a sustained analysis of the Western metaphysical tradition, and attempts to use the term as a means of decoding the economy of meaning in a whole variety of texts (i.e. as a kind of meta-concept) run counter to much of the spirit of Derrida's own thinking.

Further reading: Derrida 1973, 1987.

PS

DISCOURSE

There is no single meaning to the word discourse, even if one takes it in a technical sense. Of course, a 'discourse' can mean simply a dialogue between speakers; but it has also come, within linguistics for instance, to mean the way in which linguistic elements are conjoined so as to constitute a structure of **meaning** larger than the sum of its parts. A variant on this sense is also, however, present within conceptions of discourse important to cultural studies. Of the various theories that have been put forward, the conceptions of discourse present within the work of Michel Foucault and Jean-François Lyotard are relevant to cultural theory.

On Foucault's view, various social practices and institutions (for example, those of education and politics, religion and the law) are both constituted by and situated within forms of discourse (that is, ways of speaking about the world of social experience). A discourse, on this view, is a means of both producing and organising meaning within a social context. **Language** is thus a key notion within this view, for it is language which embodies discourses. As such, a discourse constitutes a 'discursive formation', i.e. discourses are conceived of as signifying ways of systematically organising human experience of the social world in language and thereby constituting modes of knowledge. A key function of a discursive formation, on this view, is not merely its inclusive role but also its exclusive role: discursive formations provide rules of justification for what counts as (for example) knowledge within a particular context, and at the same time stipulate what does *not* count as knowledge in that context. On Foucault's account, it follows that the realm of discourse can have a repressive function. Accompanying this notion of discourse is the contention that such concepts as subjectivity cannot be understood as they have generally been within, say, the political tradition of **liberalism**. Whereas, for a liberal, a subject is a more or less unproblematic political entity, from the viewpoint of Foucaultean discourse analysis, subjectivity itself must be constituted by discourse, and hence language. It should be added that if this is the case, then it seems strange to seek to characterise any form of discourse as being 'repressive', for if there is no subject that is not constituted by discourse, then one is entitled to ask about who or what is being 'repressed'.

Lyotard's notion of 'genres of discourse' (see *The Differend: Phrases in Dispute* (1983)) has some similarities with Foucault's conception of discursive formations. However, Lyotard came to propound his views in the light of reading a range of texts from the tradition of **analytic philosophy** (e.g. late as well as early Ludwig Wittgenstein, Bertrand Russell, Saul Kripke) as well as writers from the tradition of **continental philosophy**. Lyotard's notion represents a cross-fertilisation between these two traditions. From the analytics he takes such notions as that of 'rigid designation', which is a term used to describe the function of proper names (this is derived from Kripke's *Naming and Necessity* (1980). Thus Kripke argues that a proper name—note that in his view, even 'gold' counts as a proper name in this sense—has as its function the role of fixing and thereby stipulating the same entity in any number of possible worlds, achieved through an act of 'initial baptism'; in analytic philosophy this has led to the adoption by some of *a posteriori* **essentialism**), and Wittgenstein's conception of 'language games'. From the continental tradition, Lyotard takes some of the basic postulates of **post-structuralism** (for instance, the view that the meaning of a term like subjectivity is constituted with language). A (genre of) discourse, on Lyotard's account, is a way of organising reality according to a particular set of rules. These rules tell us how to link together the basic units of language ('phrases'). On this view, genres of discourse have the following distinguishing features: (i) as already mentioned, providing the rules of justification whereby phrases can be linked; and (ii) the stipulation of purposes— i.e. one only links phrases with a view to some particular goal or other. A Lyotardean view, therefore, takes discourse as being fundamental in organising meaning, although the basic linguistic units of language are not of themselves 'discursive' in nature (a phrase must be 'seized' by a genre of discourse in order to be codified and thus given a particular meaning).

What is common to conceptions of discourse in the work of figures like Foucault and Lyotard is the notion that language, understood as discourse, is primary when it comes to the issue of how we are to understand questions of culture and society. Moreover, a rational account of social structures is held to be problematised by this approach. Thus, on a Lyotardean view, the plurality of genres of discourse functions to prevent the assertion of any single genre's primacy with regard to establishing what ought to count as true— since all genres are organised according to particular purposes and there are a multiplicity of purposes, it follows that no single genre could be said to be adequate to the task of establishing a meta-narrative for this purpose. Forms of this attitude have been criticised by Jürgen Habermas, whose approach is markedly different. For Habermas, discourse can be interpreted in terms of its possibility to take on the form of a regulative ideal (an 'ideal speech situation'), which would serve to preserve a critical space for thought which is not subject to the contextualised pressures of particularised interests or **power**.

Further reading: Foucault 1972; Kripke 1980; Lee 1992; Lyotard 1988; Schiffrin 1993; White 1987.

PS

DIVISION OF LABOUR

'Division of labour' refers to the differentiation of tasks and occupations within a society. Three distinct forms of, or at least approaches to, the division of labour may be identified. In economics, the division of labour was recognised, in the eighteenth century, by Adam Smith (1976), to be the source of the increased productivity of the industrial capitalist economies. While within a craft economy, a single worker could spend a day making a pin, in a factory, the production of a pin would be divided into a dozen different tasks, with each worker devoted to a single task. For Marx (1975), the division of labour is a key evil of capitalism, in so far as it results in **alienation** (that is to say, the work process becomes meaningless to the workers). In **sociology**, Durkheim (1984), writing at the end of the nineteenth century, identifies the division of labour as central to explaining the difference between pre-industrial and industrial societies, but now in terms of the way in which the societies are held together as stable units. In industrial society, with an extensive division of labour, each individual is dependent upon everyone else for the provision of the bulk of his or her needs. The undesirable correlate of this is **anomie**, or a loss of moral **value** and meaning in social life. More recently, feminist theorists have addressed the problem of the sexual division of labour. The sexual division refers to an allocation of tasks and occupations between men and women, both within the public economy and within the domestic economy of the household. A 'horizontal' division exists in that certain tasks and occupations within the public economy (which tend to mirror domestic activities, such as cleaning and nursing) are predominantly allocated to women, and equally women are excluded from certain supposedly male occupations (such as engineering). Similarly, a 'vertical' division exists, in that women's occupations themselves typically enjoy lower **status**, lower pay and less power than male occupations, and that women are disproportionately employed only in the lower ranks of any profession or occupation.

Further reading: Gorz 1973; Walby 1986.

AE

DRAMATURGICAL MODEL

The dramaturgical model attempts to explain everyday life by drawing an analogy with theatre. The model therefore emphasises the idea that social actors are playing roles, and that a key part of social interaction is the way in which these actors present those roles to each other. Goffman (1959) provides a justly famous account of the different roles that waiters play in the dining room and the kitchen of a restaurant. The polite and deferential behaviour before the customer is replaced by a more relaxed and indeed cynical behaviour before fellow workers. This approach, in practice, perhaps has less explanatory power than it has power in focusing descriptions of face-to-face social interaction (or 'encounters'). It does, however, raise important questions about the nature of personal **identity** in social interaction. For Goffman, we change not simply roles, but also selves, as we move from one encounter to another.

Further reading: Berger 1963; Burns 1992.

AE

ECOLOGY

The science of the relations between organisms and their environment. Ecology was so defined by one of its first proponents, the German writer Ernst Haeckel, in 1866, although etymologically the term is derived from the Greek for household (*oikos*) and implies something of human nurturing of nature within a homestead. The modern use of the term may thus be seen to have both purely scientific and deeply normative senses.

As a natural science, ecology develops in the mid-nineteenth century, not least under the influence of Darwin's theory of **evolution**. Evolutionary theory argues that a species develops by adapting, through random changes, to its environment. Changes in the environment will weed out those individuals least fitted to cope. Survivors will pass their successful characteristics on to their descendants. The crucial relationship of the organism to both its physical environment, and to other organisms within that environment, is central to ecological study, which began to develop as a distinct scientific subdiscipline in the late nineteenth century with the work of E. Warming and A. Schimmer and others in studying the development and succession of plant communities. As ecological thinking developed, the conception of these relationships moves from one of simple competition over scarce resources, to a recognition of the interdependence of organisms within a 'web of life'. In 1916, Frederic E. Clements proposed the holistic, but highly controversial, idea of a plant community as a superorganism. While this notion was soon challenged, holistic ways of thinking continue, influenced by **systems theory**. Modern ecology may be seen to focus primarily upon the cycling of nutrients through ecosystems.

This model of explanation and analysis was adopted in the **sociology** of the Chicago School in the 1920s. Drawing on Warming and Clements's work on plant ecology, Robert Park, Ernest Burgess and others sought to account for the way in which competition between individuals and groups over scarce resources within the urban environment generated social forces and structures that were not intended by the individual agents. Such competition led to a selective pressure, stimulating specialised responses to the environment that, through concepts such as 'invasion', 'domination' and 'succession' borrowed from plant ecology, served to explain the succession of ethnic groups and **subcultures** between different zones within a city. Perhaps mirroring the development of ecology in the natural sciences, later human ecologists were critical of the emphasis placed by the early Chicago School on competition, not least in so far as pure competition would result in the breakdown of the city as a social unit. Later studies have therefore looked to the role that co-operation, interdependence and the functional differentiation of social groups, alongside competition, play in the adaptation of groups to their environments, and in integrating the city through shared forms of communication, including common **culture**, **mass media** and urban politics.

While the normative dimensions of ecological thinking may have their roots in the eighteenth century, for example in the new appreciation of nature and especially of the garden (see **horticulture**), developed by the European bourgeoisie, the political implications of the science of ecology were already being articulated in the mid-nineteenth century. Precisely in so far as ecology encourages reflection on the relationship between the organism and its environment, it began to suggest models for the most appropriate, morally or politically desirable relationship of humanity to the natural world. As early as 1860s, George Perkins Marsh had responded to the pollution resulting from American urbanisation and industrialisation (in *Man and Nature*), and argued for governmental organisation of natural resources. In 1872 the American National Park System was established. John Muir drew on the tradition of Ralph Waldo Emerson (1803–82) and Henry David Thoreau (1817–62) to defend the parks (*On National Parks* (1901)), again stressing the threat to nature and natural beauty posed by industrialisation and current farming practices. Political thinkers such as the anarchist Peter Kropotkin (in *Fields, Factories and Workshops Tomorrow* (1899)) and the socialist William Morris (*News from Nowhere* (1890)) linked themes of social reform to the human relationship to nature and, in Morris's case, to an appreciation of its beauty.

Politically informed ecological thought re-emerged in the post-war period, as signs of environmental crises became increasing more evident. A litany of high-profile events included the grounding of the oil tanker *Torrey Canyon* off the south coast of England in 1967, the chemical leak at the Union Carbide plant in Bhopal, India, in 1984, and the meltdown of the nuclear reactors at Three Mile Island, Pennsylvania (1979) and at Chernobyl (1986), as well as more general concerns about acid rain, the erosion of the ozone layer and today, most obviously, the phenomenon of global warming. Rachel Carsons's *Silent Spring* (1962) is frequently cited as a key text in stimulating public awareness, although Fairfield Osborn (*Our Plundered Planet* (1948)) and Aldo Leopold (*A Sand County Almanac* (1949)) may be acknowledged as important precursors. The 1960s nonetheless saw a significant expansion of ecological thought and activitism. Writers such as Paul Ehrlich warned of the dangers of human population growth (*The Population Bomb* (1968)), and ecological issues became a theme within hippie and **counterculture** thinking (represented, for example, in the work of Theodor Roszak).

The Limits to Growth, a report published in 1971 by the 'club of Rome', highlighted the threat to the environment posed by industrial growth. It marked the beginning of a fundamental shift in thinking about the economy. The impact that unrestrained economic growth was having on the environment, both in terms of pollution but also through the use (to the point of exhaustion) of non-renewable resources, such as fossil fuels, was recognised. The report advocated population control, more sparing use of natural resources and a check on consumerism. In 1987, *Our Common Future*, a report from the 1987 World Commission on the Environment and Development (known as the 'Brundtland Report'), developed this thinking by articulating and defending the notion of 'sustainable development' as 'development that meets the needs of the present without compromising the ability of future generations to meet their own needs'.

The most radical approach to environmental issues comes from the 'deep ecology' movement. Developed by the philosopher Arne Naess, deep ecology argues that all other approaches to the environment are anthropocentric, which is to say that they implicitly or explicitly put a higher value on human beings than upon any other creature. Deep ecologists strive to place the interests and intrinsic value of non-human animals (and of plants) on a par with those of humans, so that the natural environment ceases to be seen as a mere resource to exploit in the pursuit of human goals.

In 1971, the pressure group Greenpeace was lanched. Environmental issues were gradually beginning to take a higher profile, through the action of groups such as Greenpeace, but also in mainstream politics, with a Green Party (*Die Grünen*) being founded in the then West Germany in 1980, which also drew together **feminist** thinking (represented not least by Petra Kelly) and **Marxism** (with Rudolf Bahro). At this time East Germans such as Robert Havemann and Wolfgang Harich offered models of ecosocialism, not least as a challenge to the capitalist orientation of the Club of Rome. Ecological issues gradually became a legitimate concern of national governments, and a subject for international treaties and international law. 1992 saw the first 'Earth Summit' in Rio de Janeiro, and while it led to no concrete agreements, it did herald a series of summits and agreements, albeit of questionable effect in limiting the environmental impact of industrialisation. Crucially, modern ecological politics poses a fundamental challenge to the industrialised first world, as to how that industrial growth can be sustained in the face of ever-increasing CO_2 emissions and the exhaustion of non-renewable resources, but also in its relations to the developing nations, and thus to questions of global justice.

Further reading: Bahro 1984; Bookchin 1980; Gorz 1980; Naess 1989; Oeslschlager 1995.

AE

ÉCRITURE FEMININE

A number of French **feminist** theorists, notably including Hélène Cixous and Luce Irigaray, have developed the idea and practice of an *écriture feminine,* a form of writing and reading that resists being appropriated by the dominant patriarchal **culture**. It is argued, developing on the **psychoanalysis** of Lacan, that **patriarchal** culture privileges a hierarchical way of thinking, grounded in a series of oppositions (such as male/female; culture/nature; intelligible/sensitive; active/passive), with the male dominant over the female. The male is active and looks, in comparison to the passive female, who is merely observed. Femininity is therefore only present as it is observed by the male, and, crucially, while the feminine is the **other** to the masculine, for Cixous, the male is interested in this other only in order to return to itself—that is to say that the masculine desire for woman is ultimately a self-love (1987). The woman is therefore excluded from patriarchal culture, not least in that she is a non-presence even to herself. The woman is separated from her own body and her own desires. The woman simply cannot make sense of herself in a language that is designed to articulate and conceptualise masculinity. *Écriture feminine* appeals back to the bodily experience that is prior to the separation of the child from the mother, and thus to that which is prior to the imposition of the father's law.

Cixous seeks to recover the feminine in terms of its plurality. The relationship of maternity (the 'm/other relation') serves to subvert the masculine concept of **subjectivity**. While the male subject is unified and autonomous, the experience of child birth and nurturing, for Cixous, suggests a disruption of the self and a genuine encounter with the other. The relation is a 'gift' economy, where everything is given, but nothing is expected in return. A similar relationship is uncovered in bisexuality (which in turn highlights the masculine denial of its own femininity). Bisexuality, that is seen to be characteristic of women, offers a *jouissance* (or ecstasy) that is distinct from male desire and pleasure, for it entails an interplay of difference and the other. This *jouissance* cannot be described in masculine language. Similarly *écriture feminine* cannot be theorised, for it attempts to facilitate the return of that which has been repressed by the imposition of the symbolic and its patriarchal law. In Cixous's own writing, this is expressed in the use of pun and wordplay, and a disruption of traditional oppositions such as those of theory/fiction or theory/autobiography.

Irigaray's writing has explored the possibility of a feminine writing through readings of the philosophical tradition that exposed what is repressed or passed over in silence (including the **body**, and the elements of water, earth, fire and air) (1991), and the exploration of a 'feminine god' (of multiplicity and flow) that is outside the grasp of patriarchal religion and theology but also is 'yet to come' (1986:8).

AE

EDUCATION

The processes through which an individual is inducted into the **culture** and knowledge of their society. Education is thus part of the broader process of **socialisation**. 'Education' may be understood to refer to more formally organised processes of socialisation, and in particular those that are regulated by the state.

Discussions about education may be seen to cluster about two main themes. First, there is a philosophical concern with the nature and goals of education and the ways in which education may be improved. Precursors to contemporary debates may be found in the work of the English philosopher John Locke (1964) in the seventeenth century, and in the eighteenth century by Jean-Jacques Rousseau's *Emile* (1991), although philosophical discussion reaches back, in the Western tradition, at least as far as Plato's *Republic* (1998). Different approaches to education strongly reflect differing assumptions, not merely about the purpose of education, but more importantly about human nature and about childhood. Thus, for Locke, the child is a blank slate, written on by experience. Good education is crucial to ensuring that the child is exposed to appropriate experiences, and thus to well-grounded knowledge. Locke significantly opposed corporal punishment. Rousseau argued for the essential goodness of the child (in defiance of the Christian doctrine of original sin). Culture corrupts that goodness, so education should ideally allow the goodness to flourish, not least by providing the child with an environment through which they can learn for themselves.

With the increase of state involvement in education in the nineteenth century and the development of the welfare state in the twentieth, reflection on education becomes increasingly tied to questions of social policy. Here two core concerns may be identified. On the one hand there are questions as to the part that education plays in the organisation of a just and fair society. In particular, this has come to focus on the contribution that education makes to a **meritocracy**. Education should allow children to discover and develop their talents, regardless of their cultural or economic background. The relationship between justice and education may also be seen in the intimate links that the American **pragmatist** philosopher John Dewey draws between education and democracy (Dewey 1974).

On the other hand, education has been identified as a source of social integration. In the earlier part of the twentieth century, the issue of social integration was largely presented in terms of **class** difference, and thus of the problem of either finding a culture common to all, or to find forms of education appropriate to the different classes within society. As late as the 1970s, G.H. Bantock (1975) could defend a differentiation between an education grounded in a high culture for the elite and a 'folk curriculum' for the working classes. Such approaches to education typically reflect a distinction between mental and manual labour, presupposing that an 'academic' education, grounded in a high culture that is seen to be intrinsically valuable, serves the ruling elite and middle classes. A practically orientated, or vocational, education is tailored to the perceived needs to the working classes. The issue of social integration has become more prominent recently, in a different form, in the face of the increasingly multicultural or pluralistic nature of contemporary societies. Governments' attempts to articulate and impose some form of 'core curriculum' on schools may be seen, in part, to be a response to this phenomenon, alongside desires to teach the skills and attitudes of responsible citizenship.

If one side of the debate over education concerns what it ought to be, then the other side concerns what education is. The two sides are complementary. A social policy can be effective only if one knows how education works, and perhaps more crucially, why it does not. There is thus a long history of sociological studies in education, in no small part concerned with why certain individuals and groups are let down by the educational process. Three broad approaches to the explanation of educational achievement and non-achievement may be identified.

Deterministic approaches presuppose that an individual's educational achievement depends upon some extrinsic factor, such as their biology or their social background. While biological factors, and not least innate levels of intelligence or talent, should not be ignored, a pure determinism that argues that education can have no effect upon achievement has little empirical support and has limited implications for social policy. Social determinism, more critically, raises doubts about the effectiveness of formal education in the face of other processes of socialisation (Halsey *et al.* 1980).

Second, there is a substantial critical literature that explores the role of education as an **ideological** process. Education is seen as giving a false legitimacy to the inequalities of a class society. Louis Althusser (1971) identifies education as part of the **ideological state apparatus**, following the arguments of earlier **Marxists**, not least those of Antonio Gramsci. While the concept of ideology, in this context, may be primarily tied to Marxist approaches to education, the broader issue may be understood in terms of a recognition of the difference between the rhetoric and reality of education, which is to say, between what education officially aspires to achieve and what it actually achieves. The more succinct encapsulation of this difference is expressed in the idea of the 'hidden curriculum' (see Bowles and Gintis (1976)). While the 'overt' curriculum is the subject matter formally and openly defined as that which pupils should be expected to learn and in which they should become competent, the 'hidden' curriculum refers to a gamut of social skills, values and personality traits that serve to integrate the child into society. Crucially, these traits do not bring about a just and homogeneous society. Rather, children learn to accept their place within the class system, and absorb the social competences and attitudes necessary for future occupational positions, for example as factory workers.

This approach to education has also been used to explore critically education's role in the reproduction of **gender** (Stanworth 1983) and **racial** inequalities (Anyon 1980). It has long been argued that teachers have, at times unwittingly, different expectations of male and female pupils, and will assess their work according to different (and gender stereotypical) criteria. Similarly, supposedly integrating national curricula can be seen as promoting the values of a dominant class or ethnic group. The teaching of history provides clear examples, where the histories of minority ethnic groups may be marginalised or excluded, in favour, for example in the United Kingdom, of history that may continue to celebrate the values and achievements associated with an imperial past.

Bourdieu's concepts of **'cultural capital'** and 'habitus' provide powerful explanatory tools for the analysis of these phenomena (Bourdieu 1977). Schools are seen to promote a certain form of social competence and behaviour. Pupils from specific (and typically more economically privileged) backgrounds will be more familiar with the school's expectations, precisely because there is a certain homogeneity between the culture and expectations of the home and the school, and will thus more readily fit into the school environment and so prosper. Pupils lacking a cultural capital that values positive attitudes to academic learning, acceptance of authority, linguistic competence and awareness of elite culture, will struggle. A common curriculum, offered to all on the grounds of equality of access, will thus lead to the reproduction of inequality, precisely because pupils with inappropriate cultural capital will be unable to benefit from the very opportunity presented to them.

Bernstein (1977, 1996) identifies a similar tension between the culture of working-class pupils and that of the school by focusing on language use. He argues that there are two different ways in which a natural language can be used. An utterance made in a 'restricted code' is highly context dependent. Interpretation of the meaning of the utterance will be dependent upon knowledge of a taken-for-granted stock of values and ideas, inherent to a particular community. In contrast, an utterance in an 'elaborated code' seeks to be independent of any particular context, by explicating the meanings, assumptions and values underpinning it. Basically it is argued that working-class families encourage the learning of language only within a restricted code, while elaborated codes are used in schools, thereby placing working-class pupils at a disadvantage.

Approaches to education in terms of ideology can be criticised for tending to treat the pupil as the passive recipient of education, rather than as an agent who actively engages with education, and at times actively rejects the values and possibilities that it offers. Thus a third, 'voluntaristic' approach to education explores this active engagement with the educational process. Thus Giroux (1983), for example, has argued that schools are 'relatively autonomous' institutions. Teachers and pupils alike have scope to engage critically with the curriculum, coming to recognise hidden values and the silencing of certain cultural or political positions. Paul Willis (1977) has argued that working-class pupils may explicitly reject the middle-class values that their teachers represent. The issue here is not one of pupils lacking the necessary cultural capital or linguistic skills to perform well at school, but rather an autonomous decision on the pupils' part to remain within the working-class culture (and occupations) of their families, rather than aspire to the white-collar occupations school promises.

Further reading: Illich 1971; Moore 2004; Robbins 2006.

AE

ELITE

An elite is a small group that has leadership in some sphere of social life (such as a cultural elite), or has leadership of society as a whole. The elite is typically understood to be relatively homogeneous and with a largely closed membership. Modern elite theory developed in the early years of the twentieth century through the work of Vilfredo Pareto (1963), Gaetano Mosca (1939) and others. This theory was opposed to **socialism**, not least in so far as it argued for the inevitability of the division of all societies into an elite (with superior organisational abilities), and an inferior mass. More significantly, at a theoretical level, elite theory suggested, again in contrast to socialism and **Marxism**, that the power of the dominant group in society did not have to be rooted in economic power. In so far as classes are economically defined, elite theory therefore offered an alternative account of **social stratification** and hierarchies to that provided by class theory. In this light, the work of C. Wright Mills (1956) on the 'power elite' is significant. Mills argued that contemporary America was dominated by an elite that unified three key spheres of society: industry, politics and the military. Unlike earlier elite theorists, Mills's concern was to expose the elite and the adverse effects that it had on democracy, rather than to celebrate its inevitability.

In the study of **culture**, elite theory has had its greatest impact through mass society theory and in the assumption that there is an inherently superior elite culture. This culture is seen, at worst, to be threatened and eroded by the contemporary **mass media**, or at best, that the mass media are incapable of serving elite culture. As such, elite theory explicitly or implicitly judges **popular culture** by the standards of elite culture, and finds it wanting. It is therefore typically insensitive to the subtleties and complexities of popular culture.

Further reading: Bottomore 1993; Scott 1990.

AE

EMPIRICISM

A philosophical approach which stresses the primacy of experience in all human understanding. Empiricism is usually dated from the works of philosopher John Locke, whose *An Essay Concerning Human Understanding* (1690) argued that all of our ideas and concepts ultimately derive from our experience of the world. Locke famously stated that the human mind is something akin to a blank sheet of paper, which is subsequently 'written upon' by experience. Bishop Berkeley and Scottish **Enlightenment** philosopher David Hume are also regarded as key exponents of empiricism, although their approaches differ in some ways from Locke's. The works of Locke and Hume inspired Immanuel Kant (especially in response to the latter's scepticism concerning the possibility of universally valid knowledge) to produce the *Critique of Pure Reason* (1781). Hume's *A Treatise of Human Nature* (1739) (later recast as *An Enquiry Concerning*

Human Understanding) famously deployed the empiricist approach to argue that the basis of all human reasoning resides in custom or habit (in other words, that social structures exert a determining effect with regard to our conceptual abilities).

Further reading: Hume 1990; Locke 1975; Priest 1990; Woolhouse 1988.

PS

THE ENLIGHTENMENT

An intellectual movement which occurred in France (but also in Britain in the form of the 'Scottish Enlightenment') during the latter part of the eighteenth century. Key thinkers associated with the Enlightenment were d'Alembert, Diderot, Hume, Kant, Rousseau, Smith and Voltaire. The maxim propounded by Kant, 'Dare to understand!', sums up well the underlying optimism which spurred much Enlightenment thinking. This thinking was characterised by a number of significant attitudes: a faith in the ability of reason to solve social as well as intellectual and scientific problems, an aggressively critical perspective on what were perceived as the regressive influences of tradition and institutional religion (the latter expressed in Voltaire's famous declaration concerning the Christian religion: 'Crush the infamy!'), a faith in humanism and the ideal of progress, and the espousal of a politics of toleration and free thinking. In spite of the generally critical stance towards religion, not all Enlightenment thinkers were, like Diderot, avowed atheists; Voltaire espoused a passionately held belief in a non-Christian deity, whilst Hume was phlegmatically agnostic with regard to such matters, although his famous criticism of the belief in miracles demonstrates a typical Enlightenment commitment to a sceptical view of metaphysical beliefs in the light of advances in the physical sciences after Newton's *Principia*. That said, Hume's thought often cuts against the grain of the Enlightenment faith in reason, while Rousseau's writings are often associated with the development of **romanticism**.

Commentators such as Habermas continue to adhere to the basic project of Enlightenment as set out by Kant, i.e. an adherence to a critical project of modernity which has as its aim the articulation of a rational basis for discourses of knowledge, and political and social criticism. Lyotard (most notorious for his early (1979) espousal of **postmodernism**) also takes the Enlightenment to signify a key moment in the development of critical reason, namely the initiation of post-modernity (found in the writings of Kant—principally the *Critique of Judgement*). Other thinkers in the nineteenth and twentieth centuries have either reacted against the Enlightenment project, or attempted to rearticulate it in diverse ways. For example: (i) Nietzsche's thinking (in spite of his current association with postmodern anti-Enlightenment thought) without doubt owes a significant debt to the Enlightenment tradition, especially his books of the late 1870s and early 1880s (*Human, All-Too-Human* (1878–80), for instance, was dedicated to the memory of Voltaire when it was first published, and adopts a methodological scepticism which shows the influence of Enlightenment thought); and (ii) Horkheimer and Adorno's work (cf. *Dialectic of Enlightenment* (2002)), which seeks to unpack the key methodological presuppositions underlying the Enlightenment conception of rationality while adhering to its critical ideals.

Further reading: Berlin 1979; Gay 1988a; Habermas 1988.

PS

EPISTEME

A term in the work of Michel Foucault (see *The Order of Things* (1970)). An episteme is a form of knowledge. In modernity, particular forms of **discourse**, Foucault argues, have provided the basic, and limited, concepts which ground the sciences (for example, a particular **epistemological** conception of the **subject**). Together, these constitute the modern episteme.

Further reading: Foucault 1970; Habermas 1988; Smart 1984.

PS

EPISTEMOLOGY

A philosophical term meaning 'theory of knowledge'. Epistemology concerns itself with the analysis of what is meant by the term 'knowledge' itself, and with questions about (i) what we can be said to know (the limits and scope of knowledge) and (ii) its reliability, and what constitutes justification or warrant for holding a belief and thereby deeming that belief to be 'knowledge'. Thus, philosophers may ask: 'Is there any difference between knowing and believing something to be the case?', or 'To what extent does the acquisition of knowledge depend upon reason or the senses?' There have been a wide variety of approaches to this issue. Plato (*c.* 428–348 BC) held that our rational capabilities are an intrinsic property of our minds and are the sole source of knowledge (a view usually placed under the rubric of 'rationalism'). The exponents of **empiricism**, in contrast, argue that human understanding and hence knowledge is a result of sense experience alone. Hence, according to empiricism, what we know is the consequence of our ability to have perceptions of the world via our senses (this view is primarily associated with thinkers such as Locke, Berkeley and Hume).

Against the empiricists, the German philosopher Immanuel Kant argued that there are necessary conditions of knowing that cannot be reduced to mere experience. Thus, Kant offered an account of the 'a priori' conditions of the possibility of experience. A priori judgements can be arrived at independently of experience. On this view, we have a form of knowledge (a priori knowledge) which exists prior to, and independently of, any empirical knowledge. Indeed, according to Kant such knowledge (for example, the 'pure intuitions' of time and space) is the precondition of the possibility of our having any knowledge of experience at all. One can best understand Kant's point by way of a comparison with Locke's empiricist conception of the mind. According to Locke, the human mind is like a 'blank sheet' which is then 'written' upon by sensory experience. This view, however, is open to the objection that if the mind is capable of having experiences then this must be so in virtue of some structure that it has prior to having any particular experience. If our minds were simply 'blank sheets' then how would we be able to recognise any experience as an experience in the first place? The ability to have experiences, Kant argues, cannot therefore be derived from any particular experience, hence there must be a priori judgements which constitute the conditions of the possibility of experience. Kant holds that there are two kinds of a priori knowledge, one based upon 'analytic' judgements, the other upon 'synthetic' judgements. Analytic a priori knowledge would include such propositions as 'all triangles have three sides' (i.e. it is true by definition, and we need no experiential data to establish its truth). Thus, in thinking a subject, A, and a predicate, B, the predicate is contained within A as part of it. In contrast, in synthetic judgements the predicate, B, is external to the subject, A (*Critique of Pure Reason*: A7/B11). A synthetic judgement thus involves an act of inference which goes beyond the scope of the analytically derived concepts one has at one's disposal independently of experience (i.e. such judgements involve the empirical or external world). All judgements concerning experience are, for Kant, synthetic, and all knowledge that has any genuine value is knowledge about experience.

In addition to such debates as those listed above concerning where our knowledge comes from, it is worth noting that philosophers also tend to draw distinctions between *kinds* of knowing. For example: (i) 'knowing that ... ', which involves knowledge claims that are factual and capable of being established by way of reference to evidence; (ii) 'knowing how ... ', the kind of knowledge required to do certain kinds of things (such as riding a bicycle); (iii) 'knowledge by acquaintance', which includes such things as knowledge gained through individual experience or personal knowledge (e.g. memories) and is not necessarily verifiable in the way that the kind of knowledge mentioned in (i) is; and (iv) 'knowledge by description', which involves knowledge that is derived from our being informed about certain relevant facts, characteristics, etc., that pertain to something or someone (e.g. 'Shakespeare' is the person who wrote *Hamlet, King Lear* and other plays, was married to Anne Hathaway, and so on). As is often the case with philosophers, there is some considerable disagreement as to the usefulness of these definitions.

Significant amongst other perspectives on knowledge are the views put forward by thinkers such as Friedrich Nietzsche (1844–1900) and, following him, Michel Foucault (1926–84). There are many possible interpretations of Nietzsche's attitude to questions of knowledge (his work has, for instance, certain parallels with some of the ideas central to **pragmatism**). However, one dominant interpretation of knowledge that has exerted an influence upon views associated with **postmodernism** and **post-structuralism** is derived from the manner in which Foucault interpreted Nietzsche's work. For Nietzsche, 'knowledge' is not something which can be analysed properly in the absence of considerations of relations of **power**. This is because, on Nietzsche's view, what we deem 'knowledge' is in fact the expression of an assemblage of drives and interests (see for instance the posthumously published notes which go to make up *The Will to Power*). This attitude parallels Nietzsche's interpretation of the meaning of morality, offered in *On the Genealogy of Morals* (1887). Here, Nietzsche offers an account of ethical systems which identifies the values they espouse with their genealogical heritage: 'slave' morals valorise the 'meek' because the slave is a victim; 'noble' morality, in contrast, values what is powerful. Both slave and master, in short, in one way or another affirm themselves through their moralities. Foucault developed an argument on the basis of this account which sought to analyse knowledge forms as expressions of determinate social interests (see **discourse** and **genealogy**). Whatever the respective merits and problems with their views, one thing is clear: neither Nietzsche (as represented in this way) nor Foucault have an 'epistemology' in the way in which other thinkers, such as Kant, have had. Indeed, if we are persuaded by them, then it is a short step to abandoning epistemology in favour of an intricate analysis of social relations (although what the status of such analyses would be as forms of knowledge is perhaps an awkward issue, especially for Foucault).

However, it is not clear that one can abandon epistemology so easily. Thus, as Nietzsche himself noted at the beginning of *Human, All-Too-Human* (1878–80), providing an analysis of something's origins does not necessarily count as an exhaustive explanation of it. Thus, whatever the conditions or intentions that gave rise to a discourse, it may not be a straightforward matter to reduce its meaning merely to those conditions. Equally, although he certainly did not construct a formal 'theory of knowledge', Nietzsche did not entirely abandon the temptation to pose epistemic questions. Thus, many of his observations remain relevant to the study of epistemology (for instance, it is arguable that from the *Genealogy* one could derive a normative account of justification which could be situated comfortably within the domain of epistemological enquiry). Equally, the genealogical method developed by Foucault can be subjected to various criticisms derived from alternative readings of Nietzsche (a good example is offered by Peter Dews, in Krell and Wood 1988). What is offered by this kind of perspective that is perhaps most significant is its inherently critical attitude to **Cartesian** epistemology, for in so far as power is constitutive of modes of knowledge it is also constitutive of the knower.

Further reading: Dancy 1985; Dancy and Sosa 1992; Foucault 1970, 1972, 1977b; Krell and Wood 1988; Nietzsche 1968a, 1968b.

PS

ESSENTIALISM

The view that there are essential properties which define what something is, and without which it could not be what it is. One form of essentialism ascribes these properties in virtue of a definition being given. For example, an essentialist of this kind would hold that there are certain essential properties which define what the term 'gold' refers to (a particular atomic weight, colour, properties of hardness, malleability, etc.). In turn, any piece of gold must have those properties which are included within the definition of 'gold' in order to be designated as real gold. Whether or not adoption of this view commits one to holding that these properties must exist in reality *prior to* the act of naming an object, so that a definition, if it is true is a priori true (see Lyotard's criticism of essentialism in *The Differend: Phrases in Dispute* (1988), section 88) is perhaps an open question.

Note also that there is a difference between this form of essentialism and the view which holds that objects must possess a hidden, concrete or 'real' essence which in turn causes us to attribute to them their observable properties (i.e. their 'nominal essence'). This position was first elaborated by empiricist philosopher John Locke. A variant of this view was revived in the 1980s in the wake of American philosopher Saul Kripke's arguments about the nature of proper names. Simply put, Kripke's account implies that since language succeeds in referring to things by means of proper names (Kripke calls such names 'rigid designators', it should be noted that, for him, instances such as 'gold' are proper names), what it refers to must possess properties which make the referent of the name what it is independently of that language. This position is often referred to as '*a posteriori* [i.e. after the fact] essentialism'. This is because on Kripke's account it is only the act of naming and thereby fixing a reference that is necessary a priori (i.e. before the fact), whereas the particular properties selected when one names something may be 'accidental' to what is referred to, and it could turn out that what is named does not have all or some of these properties.

Further reading: Kripke 1980.

PS

ETHNIC/ETHNICITY

Generally a word used to refer to different racial or national groups which identifies them in virtue of their shared practices, **norms** and systems of belief. By terming groups 'ethnic' they are usually implicitly identified as being in a **minority**, and as possessing a different range of attitudes or traditions to the ones held and adhered to by the majority of a society's members. In turn, 'ethnicity' denotes the self-awareness on the part of a particular group of its own cultural distinctiveness. As is self-evident, the assertion of ethnic identity can be unifying or divisive in equal measure—often depending upon who is asserting it, of whom, and in which context. In some situations the self-aware possession of an ethnic identity could be a unifying experience (for instance, a point of focus for a given community). In other instances, the attribution of 'ethnicity' might well be regarded as a provocative and injuring form of **stereotyping** embodying **racism**. Thus, the issue turns upon *who* actively designates one particular social grouping as 'ethnic': for to be defined as 'ethnic' and to assert one's own 'ethnicity' are two very different things. In both cases, what is at stake may well be an issue of **power**. However, in the former case the affirmation of ethnicity can be understood as an assertion of one's own identity in the face of a social status quo. In the latter, one's ethnicity is being defined by the 'majority opinion' of others, and as such may well be an oppressive manifestation of the power of the more dominant forces and interests within a society.

Further reading: Foster 1960.

PS

ETHNOCENTRISM

The tendency to refer exclusively to one's own cultural **values** and practices, even if engaged with others who may not share those values. Likewise, the tendency to describe and judge the systems of value and dominant practices of other **cultures** from the standpoint of one's own. Such an attitude has connections with the **stereotyping** of others and can be a feature of **racism** and **prejudice**.

Further reading: Allport 1980.

PS

ETHNOGRAPHY

Ethnography is the approach to research most closely associated with **cultural anthropology**, although it has played a central part in the development of **cultural studies**, for example, in the work of Richard Hoggart (1957), Phil Cohen (1980), Paul Willis (1977, 1978) and Angela McRobbie (1991). Ethnography entails the close and prolonged observation of a particular social group. The ethnographer is not concerned to describe the behaviour of the members of the group, but rather to understand the **culture** of that group from within. The anthropologist Clifford Geertz characterises this as recognising the difference between a twitch and a wink. A wink and a twitch may look the same as a physical movement, so that photography could not distinguish between them. However, the wink is governed by a social convention, and is therefore meaningful (although this does not prevent twitches being embarrassingly mistaken for winks, and vice versa). As Geertz puts it: 'That's all there is to it: a speck of behaviour, a fleck of culture, and—*voilà!*—a gesture' (1973:6). Obviously, the ethnographer is not concerned just with isolated gestures, although a crucial part of the ethnographer's task is to record in detail particular events and actions from the everyday life of the group. From this particular material, the ethnographer is ultimately concerned to explicate the whole gamut of **norms**, **values** and **rules** that govern and give meaning to behaviour within the group. The central problem confronting the ethnographer is then that of overcoming the barriers that exist to understanding and interpretation. These will be associated with the difficulty of coming to terms with values and meanings that may be radically divergent from the ethnographer's own, and recognising the danger of imposing one's own values on the culture. (McRobbie (1981), for example, is critical of the exclusion of women from much, male-dominated, ethnographic description of youth **subcultures**.)

See also: **field work**, **participant observation**.

Further reading: Stanley and Roland 1988.

AE

ETHNOMETHODOLOGY

The term 'ethnomethodology' was coined by Harold Garfinkel, supposing it to mean 'people's methods', to refer to an approach to the **sociology** of everyday life, that became popular in the 1960s. Ethnomethodology is concerned with the way in which members of society create the ordered social world in which they live. As such, it is opposed to those approaches to sociology (such as **functionalism** and **Marxism)** that presuppose a social reality that is independent of the social agent and that has some quasi-causal influence over him or her. Ethnomethodology claims that members of society in fact have a great deal of skill (or competence) to recognise and continually produce significant and ordered social events, through co-operation with each other. The ethnomethodologist therefore refuses to take for granted any social order. It is never just there, but is always continually maintained in existence by those involved. The competence these lay members of society have is grounded in a recognition of the **indexicality** of all actions and utterances; which is to say, that social actions have unique meaning in unique contexts. The skill of the lay member lies in being able to draw on rather approximate shared, and thus general, understandings and procedures, in order to be able to create these unique meanings and draw on the particular characteristics of the social event. The true sociologist is then not the scientific expert who provides an account of social activity and social structure in a language that is largely incomprehensible to that spoken and understood by society's members. The true sociologist, in the sense of the person who has expertise as to how society works, is the lay member him or herself. Ethnomethodology seeks merely to make us conscious of the competence that we already have, but take for granted.

The two core approaches that ethnomethodologists use to study society are the 'breaching' experiment and **conversation analysis**. In a breaching experiment, the experimenter deliberately defies a convention taken for granted by other members of society. In a now classic experiment, Garfinkel instructed a class of students to return to their parental homes and to act as lodgers. To the parents, the behaviour of their children was bizarre and disturbing, as the taken-for-granted (and unnoticed) conventions of how children behave in their home (and thus how parents behave to their children) were unravelled. Conversation analysis seeks to document how particular examples of social interaction are sustained. Classic studies sought to explicate the taken-for-granted rules that determined the ordering of a telephone conversation, not merely as to turn taking (the person who answers the telephone speaks first—so try answering the telephone, say nothing and see what happens), but also as to who controls the topics raised in the conversation and when the conversation is acceptably ended.

Ethnomethodology was originally criticised for ignoring many of the traditional issues of sociology and, not least, problems of power. However, in the hands of feminist sociologists, ethnomethodological techniques have offered an attractive alternative to increasing statistics-based and positivistic sociological approaches. Issues of power can begin to be incorporated into ethnomethodology, in conversation analysis for example, by simply recognising that men have more power to control a conversation than women.

Further reading: Garfinkel 1967; Heritage 1984; Hilbert and Collins 1992; Turner 1974.

AE

EUGENICS

A term coined in 1883 by the nineteenth-century British scientist Sir Francis Galton. The eugenics theory holds that the physical and character traits of an individual or race can be modified and controlled by way of cultivating practices that encourage positive ones and discourage negative ones. Such practices might include physical exercise, or the combating through various treatments of drug dependence or sexually transmitted diseases, and, more disturbingly, sterilisation. The notion of human perfectibility is central to the theory of eugenics, as is that of 'degeneration' (a notion that was given popular appeal in the 1890s by Max Nordau's polemical work of the same name (see Nordau 1894)). Eugenics represents a mixture of influences, central amongst which is that of **social Darwinism**. The earliest supporters of eugenics were in Britain and America. In America, in the first years of the twentieth century, eugenics principles were enshrined in state law. As a result, the 'treatment' of thousands of people deemed to be mentally retarded or to exemplify 'moral degeneracy' resulted in the forced sterilisation of over 60,000 people. In spite of the appalling nature of this example, much worse was to follow in Nazi Germany where, unsurprisingly given the inherent racism of Nazi ideology, a racial genetic fostered the development of an aggressive eugenics. Their adoption of eugenics policies led to the mass sterilisation of over 500,000 people deemed to be retarded, suffering from mental illness, or born with deformities. A notorious figure within Nazi eugenics was Dr Josef Mengele, who from a young age exhibited proto-Nazi sympathies and was awarded his PhD at Munich and made a medical doctor at Frankfurt for dissertations in eugenics (see Gutman and Berenbaum 1994:317ff.). From May 1943, Mengele conducted experiments on gypsy and, later, Jewish children incarcerated at Auschwitz-Birkenau, where he had been appointed to the medical staff after a severe battle wound removed him from active service in the Waffen SS. Mengele was never caught and died of a stroke while swimming on holiday in 1979. The horrific excesses of Nazi eugenics quickly led to its decline in the post-war era. However, modern developments in genetic engineering and recent practices, such as the genetic screening of pregnant women, means that many of the issues genetics raises remain with us. The key ethical question posed by the instrumentalist dreams that eugenics and genetics seek to tempt us with has been well framed by Habermas (2003:115): 'Would not the first human being to determine, *at his own discretion*, the natural essence of another human being at the same time destroy the equal freedoms that exist among persons of equal birth in order to ensure their difference?'

Further reading: Galton 1907; Gutman and Berenbaum 1994; Kevles 1985; Osborn 1951.

PS

EVOLUTION

The long-term process wherein a species, social group or social form undergoes changes. Early evolutionary theorists included the eighteenth-century figures Chevalier de Lamarck and Erasmus Darwin. Lamarck's concept of evolution holds that the evolution of living beings occurs by way of a principle of use and disuse, which in turn allows for the cultivation of specific features that can then be transmitted by an individual to its offspring. Lamarck's use/disuse principle is straightforward enough: the more an individual uses a specific anatomical feature the more that feature develops. Thus, if an animal is obliged to run a great deal in order to avoid predators it will, if successful in its quest to avoid being eaten, perhaps develop longer, muscular legs. The animal's offspring are in turn endowed with an enhanced propensity for this newly exaggerated limb feature. Over time, subsequent generations of the animal's descendants slowly pass on this propensity to an ever-greater degree until, eventually, they are born with muscular, long legs. One can see why Lamarckian evolution might have an appeal for those who like to think that human perfectibility is possible through acts of will and discipline. The modern notion of evolution was formulated by Charles Darwin (1809–82—Erasmus Darwin's grandson) in his book *The Origin of Species* (1859). What is important about Darwin's account of evolution is the notion of 'natural selection'. The notion was deeply influenced by Thomas Malthus's (1766–1834) *Essay on the Principle of Population* (1797) which argued that the ratio of population increase in cities always outstrips the ratio of possible increases in food production. Plague, famine and war act as natural checks on population, which is why populations never actually exceed specified natural restrictions for long. Darwin applied this insight to the survival of species in nature. The natural world is dominated, he argues, by a 'struggle for life' in which animals compete with one another for limited resources. Evolutionary change is provoked in living forms by forces present in the environment. Such environmental forces can include both physical conditions and the influence of other life forms. Thus an organism interacts with its environment, negotiating with it in the struggle for life in the attempt to reproduce itself. The reproduction of all organisms involves the generation of random variations. This notion of randomness is crucial to Darwin's theory and has a specific nuance of meaning. When applied to living beings, 'randomness', as Darwin means it, is guided in one very limited sense: it does not imply that any conceivable variation is possible for any organism. No degree of randomness can lead to a species of bird suddenly developing a genetic variation for gills, or people suddenly having a propensity for growing beaks. However, random variation is 'random' in the sense that the variations which spontaneously occur between generations of animals cannot be predicted in advance because there is no internal predisposition to vary in one specific way rather than another of those possibilities available. Variation cannot, it follows, be understood as a 'response' to environmental conditions any more than it represents some kind of inbuilt tendency to change in one way rather than another. Natural selection works when random variations (the basic material, so to speak) come up against environmental conditions which have the effect of selecting one rather than another randomly generated individual for survival simply because the variations that individual has happen to enhance its ability to survive in those particular conditions. Change the conditions sufficiently, as can happen (e.g. the environment gets warmer or colder, one species intrudes into another's habitat), and a variation that once was useful becomes fatal. The struggle for life occurs because, over vast expanses of time, living beings have developed which exploit all the available space of the environment. To use Darwin's own metaphor, the world can be thought of as a log with 10,000 wedges hammered into it along its entire length. Each wedge represents a species. If a new species arises it must, in order to survive, drive itself into an available crack somewhere between the rest of the wedges and thereby force another out. Each available position on the log represents a niche. From this it follows that diversity is underwritten into the mechanism of natural selection. All diversity of life, it follows, can be explained as the multifarious outcome of an original ancestral form. Thus, the tree of life can be envisioned as looking like something akin to a tree, starting from a basic unified and simple form and branching outward into diversity. One thing that this does not imply, however, is something long associated with the popular understanding of Darwinism: no teleological necessity is involved in evolution. Consequently, there is nothing about the forms of life as they exist today that has arisen as the result of some purpose. To put it another way, the kind of self-consciousness which we, as humans, value so highly is in no way to be taken as an inherent property of the development of species. It might be the case that the conditions for life have arisen elsewhere in the universe, but it would not follow from this that life like 'us' exists there or ever would. As this point implies, one of the central impacts of Darwin's theory of evolution is best assessed by way of its cultural importance for the secularisation that marks European social changes in the past 200 years. The social and cultural appeal of the theory should not, it follows, be underestimated. Witness, in this connection, the example of **social Darwinism**. Perhaps more interesting is the influence of Darwinian evolution on **pragmatist** thinkers such as John Dewey and on other aspects of recent philosophy (see Dennett 1996). Others have sought to either use or criticise evolutionary theory. Thus, right **liberal** thinker F.A. Hayek sought to articulate economic change in terms of a rhetoric of evolutionary processes (Hayek 1973) that justifies minimal state intervention in market economies. Against this, religious adherents who favour a creationist account of life have both argued against evolution and for the view that an evolutionary science is possible which leaves room for belief in God. The latter advocates the view that living beings are evidence for the existence of a (divine) designer. Such an approach lacks persuasive evidence and dangerously confuses theological and teleological concerns with scientific ones (something that the history of **eugenics** might provoke reservations about).

Further reading: Darwin 1976; Dawkins 1991; Dennett 1996; Dewey 1997; Gould 1980; Laszlo 1987.

PS

EXCHANGE-VALUE

Exchange-value is one of the key concepts in Marxist economics. Marx identifies two forms of **value** in **commodities**. **Use value** is grounded in the possibility of the object satisfying some identifiable human need or desire. The 'value' of the object, however, lies in the fact that it is a product of human **labour**. According to Marx's version of the **labour theory of value**, the value of a commodity depends upon the amount of labour time that has been spent in its production. Marx qualifies this simple observation by noting that the actual labour time expended is not relevant (so that the products of a slow, lazy or unskilled worker will not be worth more than those of a fast and efficient worker simply because the slow worker took longer to produce anything). Rather, Marx refers to 'socially necessary labour time', which is that required to produce a given amount of a useful commodity 'under the conditions of production normal for a given society and with the average degree of skill and intensity of labour prevalent in that society' (1976:129). This value is understood as exchange-value when different sorts of commodities (that is, commodities with different use values) are exchanged. Thus, if it takes 5 hours to produce 10 yards of linen, and 20 hours to produce a coat, then 40 yards of linen are equivalent to (or have the same exchange-value as) 1 coat. Exchange-value is expressed in (although is not strictly identical to) a monetary price.

Further reading: Cunningham-Wood 1988.

AE

FALSE CONSCIOUSNESS

In **Marxism**, false **consciousness** occurs when a **class** fails to recognise the course of political action and allegiances that are in its real interests. Such a class is under the sway of an **ideology**.

See also: **class consciousness**.

AE

FASCISM

Fascism is not a homogeneous political doctrine, but a collection of unrelated, sometimes contradictory, ideas derived from a number of cultures. Fascist ideology resists definition, exhibiting itself instead as an umbrella term for a collection of reactionary drives, united only by historical circumstance. Nonetheless, by utilising *via negativa*, one may approach a reasonably coherent impression of the main tendencies active within fascism: in opposition to **liberalism**, fascism upholds a totalitarian state and a claim to socialist principles; whilst in opposition to communism, fascism places emphasis on the importance of nationhood, racial purity and the idea of the elite. Along with these distinguishing criteria, fascist regimes are marked by an identification of the national will with the person of the national leader, militarism and a vague appeal to natural law in order to justify these claims. 'Fascist' also serves as a pejorative term in a more general sense, denoting an institution or authority deemed to exhibit any of the above features; a fact which may serve to illustrate the ill-defined nature of the ideology from which it is derived.

Ernst Nolte has identified six different theories to account for the fascist phenomenon: a Christian account whereby fascism is the result of a secular society; a conservative approach which blames the rejection of the old order; a liberal theory which sees the roots of fascism in totalitarian government; a nationalist theory which identifies fascism with aggressive nationalism; a Marxist interpretation which places emphasis on the contradictory nature of modern industrial capitalism; and Nolte's own, 'non-partisan', theory which stresses the uniqueness of fascism to its particular epoch, independent of sociological trends. Many theorists see the rise of fascism as a direct consequence of the alienation produced by modern industrial societies, while others prefer to emphasise the independence of fascist thought from social conditions. These contrasting approaches have respectively been labelled 'heteronomic' and 'autonomic' theories by Martin Kitchen, who argues that a proper understanding of the fascist urge must take account of both types of theory. Nonetheless, a consensus on the precise origins and nature of fascism remains elusive; Marxist critics tend to identify fascism with capitalism run riot, while liberal theorists may make little distinction between fascist Nazi Germany and Stalinist state communism.

The extent to which fascism remains a potent force in contemporary societies is a source of contention. Although eminent scholars, such as Hannah Arendt and Carl Friedrich, have argued that fascism is rooted in a specific cultural and historical context, current scholarship often highlights the continuing influence of fascist ideology within modern societies. This may be demonstrated by the proliferation of revisionist histories circulating in Europe denying the severity of the Holocaust and playing down the unpalatable, racially selective nature of fascism, together with the presence of fascist parties such as the British National Party and the Italian National Alliance within Western democracies. There is, however, agreement within mainstream academia on the fundamental character of fascism: an internally inconsistent, vague and inchoate set of prejudices, distinguished only by a historically proven ability to degrade and destroy the moral and rational character of any culture willing to adopt it.

Further reading: Laqueur 1988.

CW

FEMINISM

The core of feminism is the belief that women are subordinated to men in Western culture. Feminism seeks to liberate women from this subordination and to reconstruct society in such a way that **patriarchy** is eliminated and a culture created that is fully inclusive of women's desires and purposes. There are many different kinds of feminist theory but they all have these goals in common. Where they differ is in the particular visions of what such a reconstructed society would look like and in the strategies they employ to achieve it.

The first well-documented feminist theorist in the Anglo-American tradition is Mary Wollstonecraft who produced a social theory of the subordination of women in her tract *A Vindication of the Rights of Woman* in 1792. Wollstonecraft engendered a political activism that has remained at the core of Western feminism.

Initially, feminism was primarily concerned with women's political and economic equality with men. It gathered pace in the nineteenth century with political publications cataloguing the injustice of sexual inequality, for example *The Subjection of Women* (co-authored by J.S. Mill and Harriet Taylor Mill in 1869), and through activist organisation of women's suffrage groups such as the Women's Social and Political Union (WSPU) (founded in 1903). The twentieth century saw the proliferation of civil rights movements and groups campaigning for economic equality who focused on the issues of state welfare for mothers, equal education and equal pay. These early feminist issues continue to be a priority for all feminists and are a vital prop for later feminist theory in their emphasis on the importance of economic and political equality as a prerequisite for women's emancipation. They are especially prominent in liberal feminism, which has its roots in the civil rights movement and which maintains that equal opportunities and equal rights are the key to full social equality.

Whereas early feminism emphasised political and economic equality with men, the feminism that had its beginnings in the decades after the Second World War aimed to achieve a fuller and more sophisticated understanding of the cultural nature of oppression. To this end 'second wave' feminists look at the ways in which cultural institutions themselves underpin and perpetuate women's subordination. In particular, feminists reject the assumed universality of male values. Instead, they argue, in order to fully emancipate themselves from patriarchy, women must look to their own experience to create their own values and their own identities.

As feminism has developed, different areas of theory have concentrated on different aspects of oppression: Marxist feminism claims all oppression to be a product of social and economic structures; radical feminism locates sexual oppression in the male manipulation of women's sexuality; psychoanalytic feminism looks at the construction of women's subjectivity in a sexist culture; socialist feminism combines many of these insights in a theory of the systematic oppression and exploitation of women in a patriarchal society, where women's procreative role is co-opted in the service of capitalism.

Moreover, theorists argue that women's oppression is deeply rooted in the very structures of our cultural norms. A particular feature is the existence of **binary oppositions** predicated on the assumed polarity of the sexes which work to undermine the feminine in a variety of instances. For example: in politics the distinction between the public (male) and the private (female) serves to exclude women from positions of social importance and authority; in language, Hélène Cixous (*The Newly Born Woman* (1987)) has argued that gendered binary oppositions are an intrinsic part of grammar and syntax and so affect the possibilities of knowledge; and in ethics, Carol Gilligan (*In A Different Voice* (1982)) has argued that care, traditionally the province of the female, is devalued in opposition to a male idea of justice.

Recently, Western feminism has come to the realisation that it is itself a product of a particular cultural tradition, that belonging to the white European/American, rather than a universal expression of women's struggle for emancipation. For black women and women of colour the fight for liberation is as much a racial as a gender issue. They criticise the ethnocentricity of the Western feminist tradition at the same time as endorsing the common fight against oppression.

Partly as a reaction to the charge of ethnocentricity, so-called 'third wave' feminism seeks to overcome the difficulties surrounding the question of what or who exactly 'woman' is, and who it is that the feminist movement claims to represent. In common with **post-structuralism**, third-wave feminism abandons the concept of a single collective identity. Instead it offers ideas of ambiguity and difference as a means of understanding the unique issues and interests of each woman. This development is a controversial issue within feminism. Its critics argue that the notion of identity is itself fundamental to the analysis of oppression. Its dissolution undercuts the possibility of resistance and change, thus compromising feminism's political commitment.

Further reading: Cudd and Andreasen 2005; Howie *et al.* 2004; Saul 2003.

JO

FEUDALISM

In Marxist theory, feudalism is the **mode of production** (or historical epoch) that precedes capitalism within western Europe. Feudalism may be characterised by its decentralised structure of authority, and its pattern of landholding. A feudal lord was linked to a politically subordinated vassal through an oath of fealty. The vassal swore loyalty to the lord, and expressed this loyalty typically through the willingness to supply military services. The vassal would fund this army through large land holdings divided amongst his own subordinates. (This lord–vassal relationship would occur through several levels of the aristocratic hierarchy, with knights at the bottom, in a process called 'sub-infeudation'.) At the base of the feudal economy, serfs were legally tied to work the land owned by their lords. The serf (or peasant) did have some control over the **means of production**, although without any legal ownership (in contrast to the **proletariat** in **capitalism**). Exploitation within feudalism occurred through the payment of rent. Serfs were legally obliged to transfer a portion of their product to the lord, either in kind, in money, or through working on the lord's land. (The Marxist model of feudalism inevitably oversimplifies the actual structure, focusing as it does on the two most significant **classes**, the aristocracy and the serfs or peasants. In practice, from the twelfth century onwards, significant numbers of serfs were able to buy their freedom, and move to the growing towns. The scope of feudal authority was thus increasingly restricted.) The dominant **culture** of feudalism, particularly in so far as culture is understood as an **ideology** that legitimates the existing political order, centred on the role of the church in offering a morality of obedience and acceptance of one's place in the social order.

Further reading: Bloch 1961; Hindess and Hirst 1975.

AE

FIELD WORK

Field work may broadly be understood as the collecting of empirical sociological or cultural data, generally through participation in a social activity or **culture** (hence **participant observation**) or merely through close observation of that culture ('field observation'), as in the field work associated with **cultural anthropology**. Lévi-Strauss likened the cultural anthropologist's long and intimate association with a particular culture during his or her field work to a would-be psychoanalyst him or herself undergoing analysis. It exposes the taken-for-granted assumptions that one has inherited from one's own culture, and that might otherwise make you insensitive to other cultures.

Further reading: Lareau and Shultz 1996.

AE

FOLK MUSIC

The simplest definition of folk music is music that is orally transmitted between generations, within a culturally homogeneous community. It is typically thought to be of unknown origin. The idea of 'folk' also suggests a rural community, and thus that folk music represents a survival of pre-industrial culture. This simple definition turns out, however, to be somewhat problematic.

The key period in the collecting of folk song is, perhaps, the end of the nineteenth century and the beginning of the twentieth (although an interest in folk culture had been a characteristic of European **romanticism**, with Herder being an early advocate of the study of folk cultures). The exploration of folk song had several motivations. First, there was a concern to preserve what was perceived to be a rapidly vanishing **culture** (hence, for example, the work of Cecil Sharp in England and in the Appalachian mountains). The collection of folk song rapidly threw into question a number of assumptions about this music. Folk song was discovered not to be a discrete entity, like an art song or a popular song. It will change between performances (even consecutive performances by the same singer). Further, it is not necessarily of anonymous origin. Commercial popular songs were being incorporated in the 'folk' tradition even in the nineteenth century.

A second motivation for folk-song study was the recognition, within a number of European societies, that the recovery of a folk tradition could be important to the articulation of a national **identity** (hence, for example, the use of folk song material by Czech, Hungarian, Welsh and English composers in the early twentieth century). These two motivations indicate something of the way in which the very idea of 'folk' is a construction, owing more to political and social dissatisfactions than to the **cultural anthropologist**'s concern to understand pre-industrial society. The aspiration to recover a folk community suggests a critical response to the industrial present, or a way of articulating political tensions. The pioneering work by A.L. Lloyd in the mid-twentieth century extended this response by questioning the association of 'folk' with a more or less mythical rural past. Lloyd looked at the folk music of urban communities (1967), revealing a rich musical tradition within working-class culture. In certain respects this approach could itself lead to a new myth (of a working-class culture untouched by the corrupting hand of commercial mass culture).

A third motivation for the interest in folk music was as a source of renewal for composers of Western art music. The tonal system of Western music, that had been dominant since the early seventeenth century, was widely seen to be exhausted. While, for most listeners, this system (or musical language) might seem natural, it was in fact very much a product of convention and codification. Much folk music was written in pentatonic or modal scales, and so can sound very different to art and **popular music**. It usefully served to disrupt taken-for-granted expectations of how music should sound. It therefore provided a number of composers (such as Vaughan Williams and Holst in England) with the resources for the revitalisation of their own high art tradition.

The concept of 'folk music', be it in the original sense of the oral tradition of the 'people' or in the more recent sense of a certain **genre** of popular music (albeit one grounded in the styles of anonymous folk music, as is manifest in the tradition of Woody Guthrie, Pete Seeger and Bob Dylan), is a complex construction. It must be treated as much as an expression of political aspiration as a description of the way the cultural world really is.

Further reading: Harker 1985; Lloyd 1967; Vaughan Williams 1963.

AE

FORCES OF PRODUCTION

In **Marxism**, forces of production are the productive capacities available to a society. As such, they include material technology (such as machines, tools and sources of power), and the physical and intellectual skills and capacities of the population. Marx (1971) suggests that forces of production continue to develop, in terms of their productive capacity, throughout history. Social change occurs through the growing conflict between the developing forces of production and the essentially static economic, political and legal organisation of a society (the **relations of production**). Exploitation of a new technology will therefore require the overthrow of the existing social order. (See **mode of production**.)

Further reading: Balibar 1970; Cohen 1978; Cutler *et al.* 1977.

AE

FRANKFURT SCHOOL

The term 'Frankfurt School' refers to the work of those philosophers, cultural critics and social scientists who belonged to, or were associated with, the Frankfurt Institute for Social Research. (The figures most readily associated with the School are Max Horkheimer, Theodor Adorno, Herbert Marcuse, Erich Fromm and Walter Benjamin, and in the School's post-war 'second generation', Jürgen Habermas.) The Institute was opened in 1924, but began to develop the distinctive approach to **Marxism** with which it is now associated only when the philosopher Max Horkheimer became its director, in 1930. The Frankfurt School approach can be characterised as an attempt to develop an Hegelian-Marxism that is appropriate to the conditions of twentieth-century **capitalism**. A major influence on the Frankfurt School is thus found in the work of the Hungarian Marxist Georg Lukács, not least in so far as his *History and Class Consciousness* (1923) offered a reading of Marx that was grounded in the German philosophical tradition of Kant and Hegel, but also in that it sought to modify Marx's account of capitalism by recognising the importance of the work of the sociologist Max Weber (not least in his analysis of the increasing role that **bureaucracy** and administration play in contemporary industry and government). To this, the Frankfurt School added an interest in **psychoanalysis**, and thus the project of fusing the work of Marx and Freud. Overall, the Frankfurt School, especially under Horkheimer's guidance, sought to pursue multidisciplinary research projects, in which the empirical social science research would be directed and its results analysed by Marxist theory.

Horkheimer characterised the approach of the Frankfurt School as **'critical theory'**. He drew a distinction between critical theory and what he called traditional theory (1972a). The latter, which had dominated Western scientific enquiry since the early seventeenth century (and thus the **Enlightenment**), assumed that the scientist was independent of the object of his or her study. A sound scientific methodology would allow the scientist to observe and describe the world as it really was, and to generate hypotheses and laws to explain it. For Horkheimer, this ignored the fact that the scientist (and thus the whole **institution** of science) was a product of social and historical forces. The scientist is not independent of the society and culture within which he or she lives. Scientists are shaped by that culture. Thus, for Horkheimer, the very way in which a scientist sees the world, and the way in which he or she makes sense of what is seen, will be conditioned by society. In addition, at least for the social sciences, the object that the scientist observes is also itself a product of historical change. Critical theory acknowledges these points, and incorporates them in its approach to empirical enquiry and analysis. Crucially, the critical theorist is aware that the way in which he or she sees the world is conditioned, not least by the political and **ideological** structures of society. Critical theory is therefore self-**reflective**. Its enquiry encompasses not just the society that is 'out there', seemingly independent of the observer, but also the way that society shapes and distorts the perception of society. Critical theory is therefore a form of 'ideology-critique'—that is to say that it is not simply an analysis of the social conditioning of knowledge (as is found in the **sociology of knowledge**), but also a recognition of the power structures inherent in that conditioning. Knowledge is therefore seen to play a central role in the **reproduction** of a politically unequal and **class**-divided society.

The complexities of this approach become clear if it is compared to the work of Lukács. He was equally aware of the historical development and conditioning of both the knowing **subject** and known **object** in scientific and philosophical enquiry. However, Lukács believed that he had found, in the **proletariat**, and more precisely in the vanguard of the Communist Party, a perspective that was finally free of ideological distortion. The Frankfurt School never made such an assumption, for both empirical and political reasons. Empirically, by the late 1930s most members of the School had abandoned any hope in the revolutionary potential of the working classes in advanced capitalism. The working class was seen to be as highly integrated into capitalism as any other class. Developing Weber's account of bureaucracy, it was argued that all groups within society were equally subordinated to the administrative systems of government and industry, and the classes were to be distinguished not by **power**, but material affluence. The proletariat therefore did not represent a privileged perspective on capitalism. In addition, the developmental view of history that Lukács defended (derived from Marx's historical materialism) was also abandoned. History, for the Frankfurt School, was not a gradual emancipation of humanity, but a tightening of the grip of technical and administrative control of all humanity. Politically, the Frankfurt School associated truth claims, be they the truth claims of Enlightenment science or of political leaders, with **authoritarianism**. Those who claim knowledge of (absolute) truth, either ignoring the social conditioning of their position or claiming to have surpassed it, are politically dangerous, whether they are Stalinists, Nazis, or the bureaucratic administrators of the Western democracies. This, in effect, is the key thesis of Horkheimer and Adorno's study, *Dialectic of Enlightenment* (written during their wartime exile in the United States (2002)). The Enlightenment emerged as a critical exercise, dispelling **myth** and superstition. As it developed, this critical faculty was blunted, so that in ceasing to be self-critical, it makes its own principles absolute (and thus they become a new myth, accepted without reason). In becoming dogmatic, the Enlightenment itself becomes authoritarian (and finds itself manifest in the brutal but efficient administration of the Nazi extermination camps).

It is worth noting, especially in comparison to recent **postmodernist** criticisms of the Enlightenment, that Horkheimer and Adorno do not simply abandon the Enlightenment. The problem is, as Adorno puts it, that there has been too little Enlightenment (i.e. critical self-reflection), not too much. The Frankfurt School position is thus a delicate (and at times perplexing) balance between a self-critical avoidance of dogmatic truth claims, and a desire to remain politically committed and not to relapse into what is, for them, the equally undesirable position of **cultural relativism**. A relativist, in arguing that not just knowledge but also judgements of moral goodness and political justice are culturally conditioned, is left unable to challenge the political system within which he or she lives (Adorno 1967). (For the Frankfurt School, the prime example of this is Martin Heidegger's capitulation to Nazism.) It is in the work of the philosopher T.W. Adorno that this problem is most dramatically worked out. Adorno's notion of 'negative dialectics' (1973b) or non-identity thinking is a reworking of Hegel's **dialectics**. The Hegelian dialectic is in three stages, the last of which is the achievement of absolute truth.

Adorno abandons this stage, leaving all thought and reflection at the preceding stage. Here there is a yearning for the truth, and thus for a final state of security and stability. However, that is merely the reaction to a fragmented, particularised or contradictory condition. In order to express and deal with this condition, Adorno argues in contradictions. For Adorno, the only way to grasp contemporary reality is to a describe it always in two contradictory propositions, and to hold both to be simultaneously true and false. For example, contemporary society is both a product of human action and understood by its members (as Weber argued), and yet also something that stands against its human members as natural and objective (as the French sociologist Durkheim argued). Adorno may therefore be seen to approach the truth critically or 'negatively'. By identifying contradictions in contemporary thought and contemporary society, he identifies the limits of his understanding (and thus the point at which his understanding is conditioned by a contradictory and 'false' society). His grim vision is expressed in the aphorism he borrows from the philosopher Bradley: 'When everything is bad, it is good to know the worst' (1978a).

As theorists of **culture**, the Frankfurt School leave a rich and diverse heritage. There is, for example, the sociology of literature of Leo Lowenthal (1989). Lowenthal was concerned to develop a Marxist reading of literature, explaining how economic and class structures find expression in the form and content of literary works. Horkheimer (1972b) and, in a wide range of writings on music, literature and **popular culture**, Adorno (1991a, 1991b, 1992a, 1992b) attempt to integrate a Marxist sociology of art with more orthodox **aesthetics**. Crucially, they see art (and especially the art of the modernist **avant-garde**) as one of the few sources of resistance that remain in contemporary capitalism (and thus as something from which critical theory can learn—art is a source of political insight). To explain this, recourse is once again needed to one of Adorno's endeavours to think in contradictions: art is at once a **social fact** and autonomous. That is to say that on the one hand, Adorno and Horkheimer acknowledge the validity of sociological explanations of art, that see it as a product of social and economic forces (and especially note the influence that the rise of **bourgeois** markets for art have on its development). On the other, they argue that art can still have aesthetic **value**. The point is that the very material which art uses (be this physical material like paint and sound, or the forms and **genres** that the artist inherits from previous generations) have a social history attached to them. They have a sedimented social content, precisely because, as the sociologist argues, they are socially conditioned.

However, the artist, thanks paradoxically to the workings of the art market, has a freedom that other economic producers do not have. The artwork is not meant to be useful. It is not produced solely in order to make a profit (or **surplus value**) like any other **commodity**. Rather, the artist has the freedom to pursue purely artistic problems and to create to artistic ends (not economic ones). This is the key, for while the artist is a producer, just like any other producer within capitalism, and he or she is working with the materials given by his or her society, again, just like any other producer, the artist has a unique freedom to play with those materials. The artist can then break out of the taken-for-granted, ideological ways of using materials and thus ways of seeing the world. The importance of avant-garde art, for Adorno and Horkheimer, is therefore that it shatters the illusions of our everyday understanding of the world. (Good art, in its innovation and invention, is also good politics.) As Horkheimer puts it, art breaks away from the usual forms of communication that dominate and deaden social life, so that the **natural** (i.e. what is taken for granted) becomes unnatural (i.e. is exposed as problematic and cultural) (1972b:279). However, both Horkheimer and Adorno readily acknowledge the great problem of contemporary art: the majority of people shun it as it fails to say anything to them. In this respect, popular culture is superior to high art. Again, the reader is left with contradictions, rather than solutions and, for Horkheimer and Adorno especially, a political paralysis. While they may be able to theorise what is wrong with contemporary society, and see this expressed in high culture, they are ultimately unable to act or to communicate this knowledge to any popular political movement.

See also: **culture industry**.

Further reading: Arato and Gebhardt 1978; Bronner and Kellner 1989; Connerton 1976; Jay 1973; Wiggershaus 1994.

AE

FUNCTIONALISM

Functionalism was the dominant **paradigm** within **cultural anthropology** and **sociology** throughout the first half of the twentieth century. At its most basic, it attempts to explain any given social or cultural **institution** in terms of the consequences which that particular institution has for the **society** as a whole.

(Functionalism is therefore an alternative to historical accounts of the emergence of institutions or societies.) Functionalist explanation assumes that all institutions ideally participate in maintaining the stability of the society, and thus in reproducing the society from one generation to the next. Society, in accord with a frequently used analogy to a biological organism, is assumed to have the property of homeostasis, which is to say the various parts of the society work to maintaining the society as a whole. Thus, for example, the functions of the modern family are those of physically nurturing and **socialising** the young. The culture (including the morality, or **norms** and **values** of the society) is thus transmitted, largely unchanged, from one generation to the next, and the economy is provided with a supply of individuals who are capable of playing useful **roles**.

The American sociologist Robert K. Merton (1968) proposed the distinction between manifest and latent functions. Latent functions of social institutions are those functions of which the social actors are not conscious. Such functions then go beyond any deliberate intentions that the actors may have in carrying out their own particular activities. Thus, the priests or shamans, who initiate at a rain dance, may regard themselves as attempting to control the weather. The functionalist sociologist or anthropologist will rather say that the ceremony serves to raise the morale of the group, and thus stabilise and integrate it, perhaps in the face of stresses caused by sustained bad weather.

The most complex version of functionalism was developed largely by Talcott Parsons (1951). He used a systems theory approach borrowed from cybernetics. A system is theorised as maintaining its integrity in relation to an external environment. If a society is treated as a system, then there would be a set of four 'functional prerequisites' that the social system, like any system, would have to perform in order to maintain integrity and so survive. The first functional prerequisite that needs to be satisfied is the adaptation to the external environment. This, in effect, is the task of the economy in any society (to make the resources of the external environment available to the society). The second prerequisite is goal-attainment. Certain institutions in society (such as the political institutions) must be capable of directing the society. Integration, the third prerequisite, maintains internal order (so can be seen as the work of the police and education). The final prerequisite, pattern-maintenance, entails the motivation of the members of the system to perform the functions required of them. This prerequisite is met by the cultural subsystem. Culture is thus, for Parsons, itself to be understood as a system (and thus it will have the four prerequisites of any system). In principle, Parsons's analysis of subsystems within systems can be carried on *ad infinitum*, or at least down to the individual social agent, who is, him or herself, also a system.

Functionalism has been criticised for its inability to deal with social conflict and social change. Functionalists tend to assume that society is a largely homogeneous whole, with a substantial consensus over the core norms and values. In terms of its analysis of **culture**, functionalism gives no scope for a theory of **ideology**, with the implication that a consensus could be manufactured or contested. There is, in addition, little scope to recognise conflict between subgroups within the society, either as suggested by the Marxist model of **class** conflict, or in terms of the **conflict theorist**'s account of conflict as a sign of a politically vibrant, open society. **Deviance** from the consensual norm is condemned as 'dysfunctional', which is to say disruptive to the social whole. The conservatism inherent in this account of conflict is also seen in the treatment of social change. Societies are seen to change not through revolutionary convulsions, as suggested by the Marxists, but rather through an ever-finer differentiation of social functions (and thus, creation of subsystems). As societies become more sophisticated, new specialist institutions will arise to fulfil functions previously carried out less satisfactorily elsewhere. Thus, the pre-industrial family was largely responsible for a child's education. In industrial society, the school emerges as a specialist educational institution.

Functionalism's greatest fault was perhaps its inability to deal with **meaning**, and to be able to recognise the capacity of social actors actively to recognise and construct a meaningful social world in which they could live and move. For this reason, the first significant challenge to functionalism's supremacy in the social sciences came from **symbolic interactionism**. The more sophisticated versions of functionalism, linked to **systems theory**, have seen a revival in recent years, not least in the work of the German social theorist Niklaus Luhmann (1982). This version of functionalist theory has also been influential on the work of Jürgen Habermas (1984, 1987).

Further reading: Giddens 1977; Radcliffe-Brown 1952.

AE

FUNDAMENTALISM

A highly conservative approach to religious belief, characterised by a return to the supposed fundamentals of the **religion**, and a rejection of modern theories of scriptural interpretation.

The term was originally applied to conservative Protestants in North America in the 1920s. Between 1910 and 1915 two California oil millionaires funded the publication and distribution of *The Fundamentals*, a twelve-volume work that sought to restate the fundamental tenets of the Christian religion. At the core of this restatement lay the 'five fundamentals' adopted by the general assembly of the (northern) Presbyterian Church in 1910: the absolute and literal truth of the Bible as a work inspired by God; Christ's virgin birth; Christ's supernatural atonement for human sins; his physical resurrection; and the authenticity of the gospel miracles. This return to fundamentals can readily be understood as a reaction against more liberal theologies and approaches to scriptural interpretation, and not least to those approaches to interpretation that reject the possibility of any notion of 'literal' interpretation (see **hermeneutics**).

Beyond an approach to scriptural interpretation, Christian fundamentalism also has important consequences for the social and cultural practices of the believer. Typically, precisely because the fundamentalist holds to the absolute truth of their own position, as one that is divinely inspired, their moral and political values may be characterised by an opposition to liberal values of pluralism, individualism, and free speech, but also to the equality of women. Such attitudes may be seen to reflect a nostalgia for a supposed period of perfect religious faith and practice, for example to an Arcadian early Christian church, but also a millennialist focus on the imminent end of the world and last judgement.

Opposition to other religious and secular belief systems may entail a commitment to taking violent action against them, in the need to fight the evil of non-belief or heresy. Examples of violent action by Christian fundamentalists are relatively rare. This may be because Christian values typically already have a place in the broader Western society to which the fundamentalist belongs, and if the fundamentalist does not retreat from the secular world, then he or she may effectively exploit existing democratic structures to exert pressure on policy-makers. The mobilisation of conservative Christians by the Republican Party prior to the 1980 and 1984 presidential elections, as well as the role of Jerry Falwell's Moral Majority as a pressure group, are illustrative of this. However, violence has been associated with fundamentalists' opposition to abortion.

In so far as the fundamentalist holds the truth of the religion to be immutable to the changes of tradition, custom and scientific advances in the world, fundamentalism may be seen to intervene strongly, and sometimes again violently, in **education** and other cultural institutions. Perhaps the most famous example of this intervention is the 'Scopes Monkey Trial'. Given a literalist interpretation of the Bible, and particularly the opening chapters of Genesis that describe the creation, Darwinian theories of **evolution** are a common target of fundamentalist ire. In 1925, a Presbyterian layman, William Jennings Bryan, attempted to stop the teaching of evolution in public schools in Tennessee. In more recent cases, creationism has been successfully proposed to be taught alongside Darwinism in schools in Kansas. Currently a debate is active in the United Kingdom and the USA as to the scientific status of the doctrine of intelligent design, and thus again its legitimacy as an alternative to Darwinism.

Sociologically, fundamentalism is seen to arise typically amongst marginalised or socially ambivalent groups. The fundamentalist need not therefore come from a traditionally powerless and oppressed strata of society. Rather, he or she is more likely to come from a group whose social fortunes have recently been reversed, or whose aspirations to social mobility (and thus to enjoy the benefits of modernisation) have been thwarted. The original Protestant fundamentalists came from groups recently excluded from power due to economic crisis. While the term 'fundamentalist' is readily transferred to certain adherents of non-Christian religions (and in particular to Muslims), this transfer can be problematic. In particular, belief in the literal and divinely inspired truth of the Qur'an is characteristic of the faith of all Muslims. Similarly, the Christian acceptance of a separation of religious and secular life is far less evident in Islam, so that a demand to ground social and educational policies on religious tenets is more typical of Islamic belief and practice. The variety of alternatives to the term 'fundamentalism' that have been proposed indicate something of its scope of what is encompassed by 'fundamentalism' (both within and outside Christianity) and of the manner in which it is perceived: revivalist, radical, militant, extremist (Bruce 2000:12).

Something akin to fundamentalism may be identified in various religions, including Hinduism, Judaism and Buddhism, where there are violent attacks on the adherents of other faiths (as Hindus have attacked Muslims in India, or in the conflict between fundamentalist Sinhala-Buddhists and Tamils in Sri Lanka), or demands to replace secular law by religious law (and hence, for example, in Israel, the demand from Jewish fundamentalists that all public transportation be closed down on the Sabbath).

In Islam, the terms 'traditionalist' or, more precisely, 'Islamist' tend to be preferred to 'fundamentalist'. The Islamist movement began in the nineteenth century and was pursued into the twentieth (by Jamal al Din al-Afghani (1837–97), Muhammad Abduh (1849–1905), and Rashid Rida (1865–1935)), as an attempt to reform Islamic society by combining Western science and technology with a return to early Islamic practices (so that all developments after the *salaf* of 610–855 CE were rejected). In the twentieth century, the Muslim Brotherhood (founded in Egypt in 1927) once more looked for inspiration in the early Islamic society, but rejected the integrationist approach of the earlier Islamists, in order to counter Western **colonialism** and the threat of secularisation. The Brotherhood pursued its goals, in part, through violent attacks on both property and individuals (including the assassination of two Egyptian prime ministers). Escalating tensions in the Middle East in the 1960s (including the defeat of Arabic forces by Israel in the 'Six Day' war of 1967) are seen to have shifted the political concerns of radical Islam away from notions of Arab nationalism, and towards a more radically Islamic approach. The deposition of the Shah of Iran in 1979 appeared to mark a crucial shift of Islamic politics away from Western secular models grounded in notions of nationalism, and towards the pursuit of a 'fundamentalist' theocracy. The subsequent decades saw the rise of a more militant Islam, expressed in political movements (such as the Taliban's control of Afghanistan) and the terrorism associated with al-Qaeda, but also in the protests over the publication of Salman Rushdie's novel *Satanic Verses* in 1988 (and the subsequent legal judgement or *fatwa* issued by the Iranian spiritual leader Ayatollah Khomeini). The events leading up to and following **9/11** are almost inevitably read in the light of this supposed conflict between Islamic fundamentalism and a secular or Christian West. The assumption of a simple opposition however overlooks the support that Western nations have given to supposedly fundamentalist movements when it has been perceived to be in the West's interests.

While fundamentalism may be understood as a reaction to modernisation, this is problematic. Perhaps because the fundamentalist typically occupies a socially and politically ambiguous position (rather than being simply disempowered), the rejection of modernity is rarely wholesale. While cultural and moral practices associated with modernism may be subject to searing criticism by the fundamentalist –

not least by characterising Western culture in terms of its **alienation**, selfish individualism and hedonism, as well as its imperialism – fundamentalists have continued to embrace key forms of Western technology, as the example of the Islamists suggests. The fundamentalists of the late twentieth and early twenty-first centuries demonstrate a creative and powerful engagement most significantly with modern communications technology. Christian fundamentalists in America and elsewhere have quickly found ways of exploiting **television** and the internet; and outside the West, Muslim groups have used audio cassettes and more recently CDs and DVDs to propagate their message, avoiding more heavily regulated communication media.

Further reading: Antoun 2001; Brasher 2001; Bruce 2000; Ruthven 2004.

AE

GENDER

The concept of 'gender' is typically placed in opposition to the concept of 'sex'. While our sex (female/male) is a matter of biology, our gender (feminine/masculine) is a matter of **culture**. Gender may therefore be taken to refer to learned patterns of behaviour and action, as opposed to that which is biologically determined. Crucially, biology need not be assumed to determine gender. This is to suggest that, while what makes a person male or female is universal and grounded in laws of nature, the precise ways in which women express their femininity and men express their masculinity will vary from culture to culture. Thus, qualities that are stereotypically attributed to women and men in contemporary Western culture (such as greater emotional expression in women; greater tendencies to violence and aggression in men) are seen as gender, which entails that they could be changed. The literature of **cultural anthropology** gives many examples of different expressions of gender in non-Western societies (with the work of Margaret Mead being exemplary in this respect). The reduction of gender to sex (which would be to see gender differences as themselves biologically determined) may be understood as a key move in the **ideological** justification of **patriarchy**.

Further reading: Butler 1990; Walby 1990.

AE

GENEALOGY

A method of analysis of forms of ethical (Nietzsche) or epistemological (Foucault) discourse. Nietzsche, in *On the Genealogy of Morals* (1887), was the first to outline this approach, and Foucault's work owes much to him. Nietzsche's text argues that the basis of morality and the meaning of value-attributions such as 'good', 'evil' and 'bad' are not derived, as is often supposed to be the case, from either altruistic or utilitarian modes of valuing (nor, it might be added, from any divine sanction). Rather, ethical systems can be understood in terms of their 'genealogy', that is, as being produced by social and historical processes. Above all, morality for Nietzsche, represents *not* a disinterested conception of what constitutes the 'good', but is rather an expression of the interests of particular social groups. Thus, the notion of 'good' has, he argues, two modes of derivation which signify two very different social perspectives and hence systems of valuing. First, the 'good', in its original sense, expressed the viewpoint of the noble classes who inhabited the ancient world. 'Good', taken in this sense, meant 'beloved of God', and was the expression of the nobles' affirmation of their own identity. 'Bad', in turn, expressed a secondary phenomenon, i.e. the nobles' reaction to those who were their social inferiors ('common', 'plebeian', etc.). Noble (or master) morality was thus premised on an affirmation of the identity of the noble as a bestower of values. Second, 'good' in the second sense Nietzsche outlines was a secondary mode of valuing derived from the appellation 'evil' ascribed by slaves to describe their oppressors (the nobles). Slave morality, as Nietzsche terms it, therefore derived its notion of 'good' as a secondary consequence of the negative valuation 'evil'. In this way, negation is the 'creative deed' of the slave. Slave morality, Nietzsche argues, is the morality of both the Hebraic tradition and of Christianity, and is a '*resentiment*' morality, i.e. one whose genealogy is that of the slave's resentment of the noble's/master's power over them. It is, in Gilles Deleuze's phrase, a 'reactive' morality, rather than an active or affirmative one.

Nietzsche's genealogical method is in fact a variant on a project outlined in one of his earlier works, *Human, All-Too-Human* (1878–80). In the opening sections of that work he argues for the construction of a 'chemistry' of the religious and moral sensations and values. In other words, Nietzsche takes the view that values (and, indeed, feelings/sensations) can be revealingly understood by producing a causal and historical account of them which seeks to unearth their origins. To this extent, the genealogical approach fits in with much of Nietzsche's philosophical thinking, which often expresses the view that what has hitherto been regarded as valuable (or even sacred) can be adequately accounted for within a materialist methodology of explanation. Foucault's genealogical method of investigation, likewise, takes as its point of departure the historical conditions which constitute **discourses** of knowledge. His analysis of, for example, the clinical definitions and treatments of madness since the seventeenth century emphasises the importance of social relations (above all, relations of **power**) in the construction of knowledge, and seeks to reveal through painstaking historical analysis the influences and interests which underlie and are concealed by discourses which claim to articulate objective knowledge. A key problem, at least with Foucault's application of the genealogical method, is that in applying it to forms of knowledge he opens himself to the criticism that his own discourse is itself a production of historical factors and an expression of interests (see Peter Dews's criticisms listed in the readings below, which provides a Nietzschean criticism of Foucault's methodology).

Further reading: Dews 1988; Foucault 1977b; Minson 1985; Nietzsche 1968a, 1986.

PS

GENETICS

The scientific study of the inheritance of, and variations in, the traits and characteristics of individuals and populations. Advances in this science are having major consequences for medical and other technical interventions on the human body and on human populations, and thus upon the way in which humans live. The ethical implications of genetic medicine are being extensively debated, with contributions from cultural theorists such as Baudrillard (2000a), Habermas (2003) and Derrida (2002). The pursuit of research in genetics has also raised new questions for the philosophy of science, not least as to the nature of the gene itself and the form that explanation and argument takes in the genetic sciences (Graham 2002).

Like all **technologies**, the appropriation, application and understanding of genetics and genetic technology is shaped by expectations and the interpretative resources made available by **culture**. 'Gene' and 'genetics' will not necessarily mean the same to the scientific community as they do to lay communities (Nelkin and Lindee 1995), and from the point of view of cultural theory, it is not at all self-evident which, if any, understanding should be privileged. Lay understandings of genetic research will shape the way in which that research is absorbed into everyday practices, and the way in which it might shift lay understandings of what it is to be human. Yet, equally, the cultural presuppositions of scientists will shape their research, and thus what is discovered about the gene and the manner in which those discoveries are communicated. While genetic technology, and in particular the scope that this may give for the modification of human capacities and human nature, has received extensive attention from **post-humanists**, genetics has nonetheless suffered from a relative neglect from cultural theorists in comparison to other technologies, such as computing (see **cyberculture**).

Study of the science of genetics has been largely and most fruitfully conducted from within a feminist framework. The key figure here is perhaps Sandra Harding and her account of 'strong objectivity' (1992, 2003). She strives to avoid two extreme interpretations of scientific practice. Scientists would typically favour a view of science as a purely objective activity, detached from the influences of its ambient culture. In contrast, cultural theorists might want to reduce science to one more cultural practice, with its results having no stronger claim to objectivity or truth than any other cultural practice (such as **religion**, or art and literature). Harding's notion of strong objectivity recognises that scientific practice is shaped by its cultural context, but that none the less it is a disciplined activity that yields objective analyses of natural phenomena. Cultural biases can then lead to bad science. In the light of this argument, Haraway (1997), herself trained as a biologist, has proposed that contemporary research in genetics cannot avoid the cultural-religious milieu created by the rest of society. She thus finds something reminiscent of Christian **theology** in Richard Dawkins's account of the gene (Dawkins 1976). Similarly, American biologists retreat into a culture of 'scientific creationism' as they strive to avoid coming into conflict with the dominant belief in a biblical creation that characterises much contemporary American culture.

Spanier and Fox Keller have, within a similar framework, explored the impact that a patriarchal culture has had in shaping genetic research and the presentation of its results. In particular, presuppositions about the nature of heterosexual reproduction and the need for an 'active' male and 'passive' female lead to the inappropriate gendering of certain forms of the single-celled bacterium *E. coli*, and to misrepresentations of the process of fertilisation (Spanier 1995). Fox Keller explores the history of genetics, and again the influence that patriarchal assumptions have had upon it. For example, she argues that the assumption made by geneticists in the 1960s that the mechanism triggering genes into action is located in the nucleus is based on nothing more than a preconceived notion of the passivity of the egg's cytoplasm (Keller 2000).

The work of the molecular biologist Robert Pollack might also be noted, for he recognises the contribution that literary theory might have to explanations within genetics. He argues that the comparison between the genetic code and a literary text is more than a mere metaphor. 'The letters of a human genome do encode more information than the Britannica, and both genome and encyclopaedia carry their information in a single string of letters' (Pollack 1994:21). Literary theory should thus structure the approach biologists take to understanding genes, not least in recognising the multiplicity of readings that a gene sequence might yield.

Pollack's arguments make clear that the gene, just like any other natural phenomenon, does not interpret itself. The gene is rather represented, to scientists as much as to lay people, in images. These images have been explored extensively by theorists such as Van Dijck (1998) and Turney (1998). Van Dijck explores the metaphors that surround discussions of the gene (such as 'code', 'message' and 'medium') whereby DNA is represented as a communication system. Yet, while Pollack might take these on-board as opening up genetic research to literary theory, Van Dijck is more cautious, suggesting a link between these metaphors and wartime practices of code breaking (1998:37). Van Dijck also offers a history of the representation of the gene since the 1960s. The profound threat that is popularly perceived to be posed by genetic technology, results, she argues, from the challenge that genetics poses to our usual notions of bodily integrity, and the boundaries that exist between nature and culture, science and society, and fact and image. Yet, this disruption occurs, paradoxically, against a reinforcement of traditional ideas of hereditary determinism.

If cultural theorists have examined the representation of the gene, then artists have already begun to develop that representation. Perhaps foremost amongst artists interested in genetics is Eduardo Kac. Kac's most notorious work of art is Alba, a rabbit who was genetically modified (through the insertion of genetic material from a jellyfish) so that she glows green when exposed to blue light. In other 'transgenetic artworks' Kac has explored the nature of DNA as a code. By linking the four bases of DNA (A, C, G and T) to the computer code ASCII (so that A = 00; C = 01; G = 10; T = 11), the statement 'cogito ergo sum' could be translated into a DNA sequence and this sequence used to genetically modify a plant (see Kac 2007).

Cultural anthropologists, such as Rabinow (1992) and Franklin (1993, 1995, 2003), have begun to explore the impact that genetics will have on everyday practices. As early as 1992, Rabinow was suggesting that genetic technology will be embedded in our social fabric at the micro level, leading to a new 'biosociality', where 'nature will be modelled on culture understood as a practice'. In effect, Rabinow, in line with other thinkers such as Rheinberger (2000), sees the enormous potential of genetics to allow humanity to rebuild nature and human nature, changing the very laws of biology. Franklin is more resistant to this fusing or blurring of the boundaries between nature and culture. Yet she suggests that the meaning of the biological has changed. It is now a category in which nature is both unavoidably present, and yet increasingly absent, in mixtures of the biological and the technical (Franklin 2003).

If cultural theorists foresee a breakdown, or even **deconstruction**, of the **binary opposition** of nature–culture, many are equally fearful of the threat of a resurgent essentialism, whereby knowledge of genetics is taken to define the essence of humanity (or any other species). This is, in effect, to respond to the paradox identified by Van Dijck, such that genetics at once breaks down traditional categorical structures and reinforces ideas of hereditary determinism. The notion of 'genetisation' has been coined to encapsulate this new essentialism (see Hedgecoe 1998). Paralleling the older idea of 'medicalisation', whereby more and more behavioural traits and ways of being are (illegitimately) interpreted as medical problems (see **health**), so 'genetisation' refers to the (inappropriate) interpretation of behaviour and human capacities and properties in genetic terms (Lippman 1993:178). Genes come to be seen as the 'essence of life', in what Haraway has seen as 'instances of barely secularized Christian realism' (Haraway 1997:10). The appeal of genetisation is precisely that it appears to reassert fixed and immutable boundaries in the face of the flux and disruption of a **postmodern** culture.

A final link between genetics and cultural theory may be noted. Genetic investigations are increasingly becoming an important methodological tool of the cultural and social sciences. Tracing genetic inheritance is a means of uncovering population movements, and thus historical events, that may have gone unrecorded in written documents or other material artefacts. Recent years have, for example, witnessed a substantial number of genetic studies dealing with the origin of various Jewish groups. Perhaps the most widely publicised of these were the various studies carried out on the *Cohanim* (Jewish priests), and those on the origins of a small African Judaising tribe called the Lemba and on the Bene-Israel Indian Jewish community (Zolloth 2003). Priestly status is transmitted from father to son. Hence, if tradition is correct, all Jewish priests should demonstrate some genetic similarities on their Y-chromosomes. Research into the Lemba Judaising group in southern Africa and on the Bene-Israel Indian Jewish community (groups belonging to what sometimes is described as 'newly discovered' Jewish communities, as their early history is not adequately documented and their Jewishness has been questioned), demonstrate that both groups have what is known as the 'Cohen modal haplotype', and thus that their traditions of inherited priesthood were borne out in their molecular biology. The research has attracted a lot of media attention, as well as the attention of historians and anthropologists, who, as in the case with the tests on African-Americans, raised questions about the impact of population-specific genetic research on the **identity** of the tested and the ethical implications of genetic anthropology (Parfitt 2003a, 2003b).

Further reading: Burley and Harris 2002; Condit 1999; Cooke and Turner 1999.

AE

GENRE

A mode of categorisation. A genre denotes a set of shared character-istics which allows for the grouping together of different forms of artistic expression or cultural production. For example, the genre of the novel denotes a body of texts which all conform to the basic defini-tion of what constitutes a novel (i.e. texts which contain fictional characters, a narrative structure, etc.). Likewise, in the medium of **television**, 'soap operas', 'documentaries', or 'situation comedies' all signify particular genres. That said, it is frequently very difficult to provide an exhaustive list of the features which define a particular genre, since any given work that may be situated within a particular genre may well possess features which are not normally shared by other instances of that genre, or lack features common to others. The term 'genre', taken in this sense, might thus be best viewed as a rather loose means of lumping sometimes more or less diverse instances toge-ther. Moreover, works ostensibly situated within a genre can express an ironic relationship to the genre itself (for example, a soap opera which sends up the soap opera genre, and is therefore a situation comedy).

Amongst philosophers, Jean-François Lyotard's conception of 'genres of discourse' perhaps offers a more rigorous account. On his view, a genre is a way of linking incommensurable linguistic elements together (i.e. a set of rules of linking) and is characterised by its purpose.

See also: **discourse**.

PS

GLOBALISATION

The notion of globalisation can be traced at least as far back as Marshal McLuhan's invocation of a 'global village' in the early 1960s (see **mass media**). Following on from his conception, one can say that the term 'globalisation' denotes the simultaneous internationalisation and formalisation of forms of thought and communication as a consequence of the standardisation of methods of production, presentation, marketing, distribution and branding. In this sense, globalisation is explicitly tied to the realm of economics. From its earliest manifestation these characteristics appeared in large and powerful international companies with an eye on the expansion of existing markets. Companies like the Coca-Cola Corporation sought to maximise standardised production methods by subtly adapting them so as to retain overall continuity while at the same time fitting the specific market requirements (primarily linguistic) of different cultural milieus. The aim, it follows, was to exploit the enhanced market potential offered by being able to reach out to a culturally diverse customer base through a single, where necessary minimally flexible but ultimately rigidly managed, system of production, distribution and consumption. Multinational corporations such as McDonalds are amongst those who most famously perfected and thereby exploited this possibility. One immediate and obvious consequence is a certain uniformity of product within a vast geographical range. A multinational burger served in New York does not differ significantly in the essentials from one served on other continents, and nor is it desirable for it to do so. Another necessary accompanying consequence is, it follows, the standardisation of practices. In other words, globalisation brings with it cultural conformity and the shrinking of diversity in so far as the production of goods in one locality must accord with the same standards as in all others. Another consequence of globalisation is an increased general public awareness of the influence of foreign economic and cultural interests upon domestic life. This is manifest not merely by the fact that the provision of certain industries and services can, due to financial considerations, be moved from domestic markets and situated elsewhere. It is also apparent in the political rhetoric that has dominated since the collapse of the Soviet Union in 1989. The end of the Cold War brought with it the proclamation of a 'New World Order' whereby it was presupposed that the triumph of free-market liberal capitalism (specifically on the American model) would herald a new era of global economic development. Thus, Fukuyama (1992) prematurely celebrated the demise of history itself as a consequence of the victory of the West over the Soviet system. As should be clear from McLuhan's thesis, globalisation is unthinkable without the technological backdrop against which social change has occurred. In the first years of the twenty-first century, the potential of specifically global technologies has been made most manifest in the burgeoning of communications, not least in the internet and the growth of online businesses. Other technologies, including air travel, have likewise a central role in the globalisation process.

The by now common acceptance of globalisation as an unavoidable fact of modern life has had the effect of inclining politicians in the West to emphasise the inescapable nature of the conditions that abide in the world market place (as was the case with the Clinton administration in the USA). Politics is thereby rendered susceptible to being reduced to a matter of aping the management techniques that are diagnosed as being at work in the international social arena. With this comes the perceived requirement that all nations accede to the competitive ethos which global markets imply. This explains the perceived need to adhere to strict and methodologically standardised monetary policies (witness the British Labour government's handing over of the power to set interest rates to the Bank of England in 1997). Ethical language is thereby rendered prone to being fused with and compromised by a pragmatic rhetoric of the market place, as is witnessed by the address to the 2006 Labour Party conference of British prime minister Tony Blair (Blair 2006). The values of the Labour Party, Blair begins, are non-negotiable: they 'don't change'. These values are currently represented by words like 'democracy', 'solidarity', 'social justice', 'choice', 'opportunity', 'tolerance', 'respect', 'reform', 'modernisation' and 'community'. Such words, the audience is assured, faithfully encapsulate the ideals espoused by the socialist founders of the Labour Movement, but they have the 'value-added' feature of contemporary significance: in the wake of global transformations 'our values have to be applied anew'. The speech thus urges us to accept the idea of political leadership as embodying unchanging values, but simultaneously seeking to harmonise the eternal with current demands. The politician's self-image here is of a questing being caught in a 'battle ... to secure the future'. As the speech progresses it becomes increasingly clear what talking about securing the future means. It means facing economic realities and embracing the 'change' that these realities force upon us. The world we inhabit is increasingly transient and resistance to the forces that make it so is useless. The manner in which the situation is then summarised is striking: 'The character of this changing world is indifferent to tradition. Unforgiving of frailty, no respecter of past traditions, it has no custom and practice.' Thus, the speech moves from the rhetorical invocation of a world that embraces timeless principles of morality to a world devoid of such principles. It turns out that the unchanging moral tenets celebrated at the speech's outset are situated in the context of a Darwinian struggle for existence. The world of global economics, like the world of nature, is a sphere in which weakness, tradition, custom and even 'practice' count for nothing. The ways of doing things that defined earlier generations and which were endowed to the present in the form of that web of practices that make up its history and traditions are in this way rendered meaningless hindrances to future success. *Plasticity* is now the prime virtue without which there would be no hope of survival in the economic jungle of the future. Britain's competitors (specifically China and India) cannot be ignored, they 'can only be beaten' – there is, to recall a well-worn phrase, no middle way here.

The vision of globalisation that this speech presents celebrates instrumentalism. Instrumentalism is the view that means and ends can be neatly differentiated and the speech is reassuringly confident of the speaker's ability to do so: 'New Labour was first and foremost about disentangling means and ends'. If we know what we want, the instrumentalist thinks, then it is simply a matter of finding the right method to get what we want. The problem with instrumentalism is that it ignores the subtle but profound relationships that exist in cultures between values and traditions. Practices, customs and traditions embody values, they are not neutral structures that exist independently of ethical standards. In public conduct generally, whether international or local, customs and practices enshrine standards and it is for this reason that values are strictly speaking unthinkable without practices: without the customary ways of acting that embody and thereby communicate them, values are drained of meaning. For example, doing something in a manner acknowledged to be 'just' – no less than acting in a way that is deemed 'neighbourly', 'honourable', 'polite' or 'professional' – means to subscribe to the practices and customs that constitute justice: it is the very subscription to the conventions that makes these things concrete and meaningful. Of course, such things are not immune to change. But the very fact that practices and customs change indicates that they are at the same time retained and developing. Globalisation, if properly understood, must be grasped with this in mind, for it allows us to address the cultural realities that the instrumentalist account necessarily obliterates.

An implication of the above account offered of the relation between practices, traditions and global economic change (or 'modernisation') is that the cultural dimension (the realm of traditions, conventions and practices) cannot be ignored without peril. As Habermas has noted (2003), the accelerating process of modernisation in the non-occidental world has brought with it resentments and violent outbursts that pose important questions for the self-understanding of the West (see **9/11**). A critical re-examination would need to bring with it a more circumspect attitude towards the methodological standardisation that is celebrated by instrumentalist rhetoric.

Further reading: Featherstone, 1990; Lechner and Boli 2004; Scholte 2000.

PS

GRAMMATOLOGY

The first edition of I.J. Gelb's *The Study of Writing,* carried the subtitle: *The Foundations of Grammatology* (dropped from the second edition, 1963). Defining the term, and his project, Gelb wrote: 'The aim of this book is to lay a foundation for a full science of writing. ... To the new science we could give the name "grammatology"'.

The linguist Ferdinand de Saussure had already argued that the study of language in general should be undertaken on a scientific basis (see his *Course in General Linguistics*; French original published in 1916). Rejecting the historical method of previous approaches in order to focus on the state of a language at any given time, Saussure sought to uncover the unchanging principles which form the structural basis of all language. The resultant theory construed language, in the abstract, as a sign system in which meaning is produced by the contrast between different sound combinations.

Despite his achievement in the field of general linguistics, Saussure did not deem it necessary to explore writing as a human phenomenon in its own right. He was content to view it as a derived, secondary and instrumental form of language, fraught with various kinds of difficulty and danger.

Gelb's grammatology has been judged a failure precisely because he made no attempt to propound a theory of writing which could rescue its study from the shadow of general linguistics. His approach remained historical and did not break with older, pre-Saussurian, models of study. He simply classified writing systems as belonging to one of three evolutionary forms: logographic (word-based systems), syllabic (syllable-based systems), alphabetic (systems based on units of sound, or phonemes).

In more recent times, Roy Harris has attempted to do for grammatology what Saussure did for general linguistics. In his *Signs of Writing* (1995) he outlines a theoretical framework for the systematic analysis of writing as a 'uniquely complex form of communication'. Unlike Gelb, he does not restrict his analysis to speech-based forms; he includes in the field of study the notation systems of mathematics and music.

In *Of Grammatology* (French original published in 1967), Jacques Derrida takes a very different, more philosophical tack. He exposes the tendentious privileging of speech over writing in Western thought, from Plato (who denounced it as thrice removed from truth, presence and origins) to Saussure (who characterised it as a disease of language). Acknowledging the evolutionary priority of speech, Derrida argues that this historical contingency has been worked up, illegitimately, into a 'metaphysics of presence'. A whole network of evaluative contrasts (presence/absence, interior/exterior, body/spirit, etc.), of fundamental importance to Western metaphysics, is seen to cluster around the speech/writing hierarchy.

In order to disrupt this tradition of thought, Derrida highlights what he calls *arche-writing*. This refers to the prevenient structures or systems which underlie every human practice, including speech, and which can only be represented by means of inscriptional metaphors such as *prescript*, *programme*, or various words with the suffix *-graphy* (choreography, cinematography, etc.). He observes that even denigrators of writing like Plato, Rousseau and Saussure are continually forced to use such metaphors in order to describe language.

Further reading: Derrida 1976.

KM

GRAND NARRATIVE

A term associated with Jean-François Lyotard's account of **post-modernism**. A grand narrative (or meta-narrative) is a narrative form which seeks to provide a definitive account of reality (e.g. the analysis of history as a sequence of developments culminating in a workers' revolution offered by classical **Marxism**). In terms of Lyotard's later work, meta-narratives (or meta-**genre**s of discourse) founded on the logical aporia (or 'double bind') of class as discussed by **analytic** philosopher Bertrand Russell: 'either this genre is part of the set of the genres, and what is at stake in it is but one among others, and therefore its answer is not supreme. Or else, it is not part of the set of genres, and it does not therefore encompass all that is at stake, since it excepts what is at stake in itself' (*The Differend: Phrases in Dispute,* section 189).

Further reading: Lyotard 1988, 1989.

PS

HEALTH

All societies may be seen to interpret and evaluate the physical and mental condition of human beings, and in particular to articulate boundaries between 'normal' (or healthy) and abnormal (unhealthy) states. Cultural theorists, philosophers and sociologists have all devoted attention to the cultural construction of health and illness, and to the medical professions that have the **power** to define, diagnose and treat the unhealthy.

The question of the nature of health and disease may be seen to be at the core of philosophical inquiry into health and the meaning of such terms as 'illness' and 'disease' (Seedhouse 2001). Broadly, 'illness' is usually taken to refer to the experience of being unwell; 'disease' to its objective and bodily manifestation. Yet theories of disease are highly contested. The model of disease that is dominant in Western health care provision is the biomedical model. This emerged in nineteenth-century Europe. It understands health to be a property of the body, or more specifically as the failure of the body, for whatever reason, to function optimally. Disease is thus approached as a predominantly physiological phenomenon. The doctor's task is to remove the disease or abnormality, not least in so far as 'health' is understood purely negatively as the absence of disease. Following this biomedical model, the doctor's relationship to the patient is primarily to the diseased body, and not to the patient as a social, psychological or cultural person. The philosopher David Seedhouse has interpreted this as seeing health as a **commodity** (Seedhouse 2001). Health is something I possess. If I lose it, I can have it replaced, through medical intervention, and like any other commodity I can insure against its loss or damage. This model legitimates an interventionist health care system, and not least one that relies upon the development and application of new **technology** (and not least that provided by the pharmaceutical industry) to cure patients.

The biomedical model accepts that there may be multiple causes of the loss of health, including infection and injury. It could therefore exist alongside a commitment to public health, that also arose in the nineteenth century. However, a public health approach already places the phenomenon of disease in a wider perspective. A person's vulnerability to disease is seen to be dependent upon the sort of environment within which he or she lives and works. This approach shifts the emphasis of medical practice away from cure and towards prevention, not least by improving housing conditions and hygiene, and reducing pollution. In the twentieth century, this led more or less directly to the importance of epidemiology, which is to say the **statistical** analysis of the distribution of disease and the exploration of statistical links between disease and other environmental and lifestyle factors. The association between **class** and health status is well documented (see Townsend 1982). As a recognition that one's chance of suffering disease is related to sociological and cultural factors, increasing emphasis may also be placed upon the individual to avoid dangerous or high-**risk** activities (such as smoking, eating high-fat diets, and so on). Such approaches are in danger of overestimating the autonomy that individuals have over their lifestyle choices.

The biomedical model has come under increasing attack in the twentieth-century philosophy of medicine. More 'holistic' positions approach disease not simply as a phenomenon of the body, but linked to the mental well-being and lifestyle of the patient. This is encapsulated in the World Health Organisation's definition of health (offered in its 1946 *Constitution*): 'a state of complete physical, mental and social well-being, not merely the absence of disease or infirmity'. While this definition is frequently criticised for being overly idealistic, it does stress that health is a positive achievement. One becomes diseased not simply by losing the optimal functioning of one's body, but also through the attitude that one takes to the potentials that are present in one's body (and one's mental and perhaps spiritual capacities). Thus, it might be argued that a person who has no physical impairment, yet lives a sedentary and 'unhealthy' lifestyle is more unhealthy than a person confined to a wheelchair who none the less lives an active and fulfilled life (Seedhouse 2001). Such approaches may be seen to be highly prescriptive, privileging certain lifestyles over others.

This leads philosophical analysis to another important question: How is the normality of the healthy state determined? Debate has run between those who have tried to ground the norm of good health in natural (or physiological) factors (such as the normal functioning of the species (Boorse 1975, 1977)), and those who have emphasised the cultural construction of normality (see Canguilhem 1978). In this context, the early work of Michel Foucault has played an important role in the development of a critical and historical discussion of illness and medicine. His studies of mental illness (1971) and the hospital (1976) explored the historical construction of modern notions of illness and its treatment. With respect to mental illness, Foucault holds that it is a construction of the **Enlightenment**. Mental illness represented an 'unreasonableness', in opposition to which the 'reason' celebrated by the Enlightenment could be defined. The mentally ill are effectively the '**other**' of the Enlightened. Substantial work has been carried out in **history** and **sociology** on the construction of other 'diseases', and not least those relating to supposedly abnormal sexual practices (see Porter 1996; 1997:258–62 and 702–4).

The sociology of health and medicine has pursued two dominant areas of inquiry: the nature of the medical profession and the practice of being ill. The medical profession was approached in large part as a paradigm example of a profession in modern societies (Freidson 1970). While much of this work was done in the United States (by **functionalist** sociologists, such as Talcott Parsons, from the perspective of cultural theory), it is again the early work of Foucault that stands out. In his study of hospitals, *The Birth of the Clinic* (1976), he attended to both the rise of the hospital as an institution (as he had earlier explored the history of the asylum), and on the relationship between the medical professional and the patient. In particular, Foucault explored the power exercised by the doctor, not least through the 'medical gaze' through which the patient is objectified as a body inhabited by pathologies. Explorations of the power of the medical professional, both over the patient and in respect to other professions (and not least the policing of the boundary between legitimate medical practice and 'alternative' medicines), continues (Armstong 1983; Starr 1982).

Within this tradition one may situate critical discussions of the over-medicalisation of contemporary society. The term 'medicalisation' is most closely associated with Ivan Illich (1976). Illich argued that contemporary society was increasing characterised by the illegitimate intrusion of medicine into more aspects of life, so that more phenomena and practices come to be defined as medical problems (such that they submit to treatment within the parameters of the biomedical model). Ann Oakley's study of childbirth offers a telling illustration of this. She argues that while increased medical intervention in childbirth may have reduced the risks involved, much is unnecessary, and the use of high-tech interventions serves to alienate the mother from an all-important emotional experience. Increasingly the mother's experience is defined by the technology and medical expertise that surrounds her, and her personal responses are discounted (to the point of being told that she cannot be in pain, for pain killers have been administered) (Oakley 1984).

There is a sociological concern with the practice of being ill. Talcott Parsons's concept of the 'sick role' was central to this inquiry (1975). Parsons's argument was that falling ill exempts a person from the norms and obligations typically associated with their social **role** (so that, for example, they are no longer expected to go to work nor to look after their family). The sick role none the less places new obligations on the patient, primarily one of complying with doctors' instructions and thus recovering as soon as possible. Parsons's work has been criticised for its presupposition of the biomedical model. The sick role works only for acute illnesses that are amenable to rapid technological treatment. However, as the sociologist Arthur W. Frank has argued, in contemporary society the incidence of chronic illness is rising (1995). It is becoming more typical to fall ill, and then either to remain ill or to move to a state of remission. The sick role is inappropriate in such states. More significantly for cultural theory, Frank recognises that the response to chronic disease is therefore not the technological fix advised by the biomedical model, but rather the search, on the part of the sufferers, for the cultural resources through which they can make sense of their illnesses and restore the narrative integrity of their lives. Only by being able to tell an appropriate story about themselves as an ill person will they be able to find orientation for their future lives.

Frank's work may be seen to fit into a growing literature on illness and narrative (see Charon 2004) and the cultural construction of the experience of illness. Amongst the most significant essays within cultural theory is Susan Sontag's *Illness as Metaphor* (1979). Responding to her own experience of breast cancer, Sontag explores the manner in which aesthetic images shaped perception of medical reality. She explores connections between the twentieth-century interpretations of cancer and the culture of tuberculosis (TB) in the nineteenth century. The Romantic construction of TB allowed the appearance of the TB sufferer to become fashionable (albeit that it is a selective image, ignoring, for example, the foul smell of the sufferer's breath). The consumptive is a key romantic figure, a wanderer and Bohemian. The consumptive confronts death, and thereby explores their very individuality. Subsequently Sontag extended this analysis to AIDS (1989).

Further reading: Bury and Gabe 2006; Lupton 2003; Purdy and Banks 2001.

AE

HEGEMONY

The term 'hegemony' is derived from the Greek *hegemon*, meaning leader, guide or ruler. In general usage it refers to the rule or influence of one country over others, and to a principle about which a group of elements are organised. In twentieth-century **Marxism**, it has been developed by the Italian theorist Antonio Gramsci (1891–1937) to explain the control of the dominant **class** in contemporary **capitalism**. He argues that the dominant class cannot maintain control simply through the use of violence or force. Due to the rise of trade unions and other pressure groups, the expansion of civil rights (including the right to vote) and higher levels of educational achievement, rule must be based in consent. The intellectuals sympathetic to the ruling class will therefore work to present the ideas and justifications of the class's domination coherently and persuasively. This work will inform the presentation of ideas through such institutions as the **mass media**, the church, school and family. However, precisely because this hegemonic account of political control entails consent, ideas cannot simply be imposed upon the subordinate classes. On the one hand, the ruling class will have to make concessions to the interests and needs of the subordinate classes. On the other hand, the subordinate classes will not accept hegemony passively. The ideas of the dominant class will have to be negotiated and modified, in order to make them fit the everyday experience of the subordinate classes. (Members of the subordinate classes may therefore have a dual consciousness. They will simultaneously hold contradictory or incompatible beliefs, one set grounded in hegemony, the other in everyday experience.) The theory of hegemony was of central importance to the development of British cultural studies (not least in the work of the **Birmingham Centre for Contemporary Cultural Studies**). It facilitated analysis of the ways in which subordinate groups actively respond to and resist political and economic domination. The subordinate groups need not then be seen merely as the passive dupes of the dominant class and its **ideology**.

Further reading: Bocock 1986; Fontana 1993; Gramsci 1971; Sassoon 1987.

AE

HERMENEUTICS

The theory of textual interpretation and analysis. The roots of hermeneutics lie in biblical and legal practices of exegesis. However, modern hermeneutics is generally taken as beginning with the work of Friedrich Schleiermacher (1768–1834). Amongst other things, Schleiermacher contended that: (i) hermeneutics is an art of interpretation; (ii) the meaning of a text is a matter of the original readership for which it was intended; (iii) interpretation is a circular process, since the parts of a text depend for their meaning upon the whole and vice versa; and (iv) misunderstanding is a precondition of understanding texts (against the view associated with the **Enlightenment**, which foregrounded the primacy of reason, and thus the clarity of understanding, in interpretation). The most influential aspect of the work of Wilhelm Dilthey (1833–1911) was his postulation of a difference between 'understanding' and 'explanation' as underlying the distinction between the human sciences and the natural sciences. This view, along with Schleiermacher's identification of meaning with authorial intention, was questioned by the later work of Martin Heidegger (1889–1976) and Hans-Georg Gadamer (1900–).

Heidegger's conception of *Dasein* is one which, by implication, questions the role and, indeed, the traditional humanist conception of the subject in interpretation and meaning. *Dasein* is an entity which can, for example, ask questions about its own existence. In turn, Heidegger conceives of *Dasein* as constituting a temporal structure of interpretative understanding, which is thus always already engaged in the activity of interpretation. Since this is the case, meaning and interpretation are fundamental to *Dasein*'s being-in-the-world, and cannot be properly described in terms of an exterior vantage point (the 'hermeneutic circle'). All interpretation, on this view, always concerns what is already 'understood'. Hence, there is no transcendental **subject** in the Kantian sense, functioning to ground meaning according to principles which draw a distinction between the 'form' of the understanding and its interpretative 'content'. That said, it is not clear that Heidegger is a straightforward anti-realist (either at this stage in his development, i.e. the writing of *Being and Time*, or even later) as critics such as Richard Rorty have claimed.

Heidegger's pupil, Gadamer, is perhaps the most famous recent exponent of hermeneutic theory, in the shape of 'philosophical hermeneutics'. Gadamer takes from Heidegger the contention that the understanding is realised through the activity of interpretation. Interpretation, in this account, is grounded in 'fore-having', 'fore-sight' and 'preconception'. Principal among Gadamer's claims is that interpretation does not proceed, as with the Enlightenment model, on the basis of free and rational criteria, but is in fact grounded in 'prejudice' (a view derived from Schleiermacher). In contrast to Schleiermacher, however, on Gadamer's conception the meaning of texts is not dependent upon their original or intended sense, but on such factors as the language, norms and traditions in and through which subjectivity finds itself constituted. The intersubjective conditions which go to make up a tradition, according to Gadamer, provide the standpoint from which interpretation precedes (hence, we always begin with 'prejudice'), but do not determine it completely. This is because interpretation, in his view, is an engagement which takes the form of a reciprocal relationship between reader and text. Hence, although one starts with prejudgements in order to engage in interpreting, a text has the ability to transform one's preconceptions, for example, by resisting a reading that is being imposed upon it. Thus, one may move, through the activity of interpretation, to an engagement with the **other**, which is able to re-structure the interpreter's preconceptions, and thereby the basis of his or her understanding. Interpretation, therefore, is an unlimited, open-ended process.

Critics of Gadamer include Jürgen Habermas, who has sought to argue that there are in fact limits to the scope of hermeneutic analysis. Habermas notes that it is a theory which considers interpretation only in terms of everyday language, and not all forms of social life and the products thereof are a matter of everyday language; rather, they may be constituted by conditions which are independent of this language.

Further reading: Gadamer 1975; Habermas 1971; Heidegger 1962; Hirsch 1967; Llewelyn 1985.

PS

HISTORICISM

A theory which holds that an historical analysis of human beliefs, concepts, moralities and ways of living is the only tenable means of explaining such phenomena. Thus, an historicist rejects the belief that, for example, there are any a-historical, necessary truths concerning the construction of human **identity** (see also **essentialism**), on the grounds that such concepts are the result of historical processes particular to specific **cultures** and cultural forms. Historicism therefore extols a **cultural relativism**. Thinkers associated with the historicist approach include sociologist Karl Mannheim, who (combining an epistemological relativism and a cultural relativism) argued that all knowledge of history is a matter of relations, and that the perspective of the observer cannot be excised from historical analysis. Michel Foucault's work, in turn, argues for the belief that the **self** is historically constructed, rather than a naturally produced and universal structure common to all times and cultures. This position has led to arguments about the construction of aspects of identity in relation to issues of **race** and **gender**.

In the United States, Foucault's work (as well as that of Raymond Williams) has had an influence in initiating New Historicism, which takes as its point of departure a cross-fertilisation between theories associated with **post-structuralism** and **Marxism**. New Historicists are interested in the social and **ideological** effects of **meaning** and its construction. They offer readings of primarily literary texts which, in contrast to the non-historical, text-based approach of traditional criticism, seek to interpret them in the cultural context of their production by way of an historical methodology, and yet spurn the development of **grand narratives** of history or knowledge. Writers who have adopted this approach include Stephen Greenblatt, who provided a first elaboration of New Historicism in his *The Forms of Power and the Power of Forms in the Renaissance* (1980).

Further reading: Greenblatt 1980; Hamilton 1996; Mannheim 1972; Veeser 1989.

PS

HISTORY

The historian E.H. Carr published what is probably the most famous reflection on history by an active historian, *What is History?*, in 1961.

According to Carr, history is not what most people think it is. It is not, for example, a construction of a narrative about the past that is rooted only in documented facts. This view gives rise to the false idea that the historian always begins by collecting 'facts' and only then plunging into the maelstrom of interpretative activity. The common-sense view, according to Carr, smacks of a questionable **empiricism** and may be doubted. For instance, the notion that facts exist in a unified sense, such that the fact that X has a headache is of the same kind as an 'historical fact' is by no means certain. Of course, Carr tells us, the historian must be as sure of his or her facts as possible. It is essential, for example, to get the dates of events correct. But praising an historian for doing what is merely a duty is pointless— something as akin and absurd, Carr says, to praising architects for using good building materials. What makes a fact or past event an historical fact is the historian's interpretation (which is not to say that the interpretation is all that makes it what it is). When Caesar crossed the Rubicon, as did countless other people, what makes it an his- torical fact is the significance that can be attributed to the gesture in the context of the historian's analysis. A well-documented event from the past, it follows, requires fitting into an historical interpretation in order to be history. To put it more bluntly, there are no facts without interpretations. Carr in this regard concurs with Oakeshott (1983:92), who contends that 'an historical past [...] is the conclusion of an historical enquiry'. What historical analysis does, Carr argues, is strike a balancing act between facts and interpretations and hence facts and values (he explicitly rejects the fact/value distinction). The historian does this as a person who embodies progressive values that detect in history 'a sense of direction' (1961:132) that reflects the present's projection of future goals and aspirations. Our future possibilities, it follows, reveal the historical past to us and the historical past acts as a force of illumination with regard to the future, thereby conferring objectivity on historical discourse. Conservative historian G.R. Elton represents what has often been regarded as an alternative to Carr's conception of history. For Elton, Carr's conception of history is simply dangerous. Although Elton concedes that there may be no single path defining historical analysis, it is for him a pure discourse, one that ought to be untainted by additional methodological concerns (e.g. of a psy- chological or hermeneutic nature). The historian is defined by hon- esty, the professionalism that goes with the development of a practice and the refusal to allow ideals (like Carr's future-oriented ones) stand in the way of proper analysis. History itself thereby becomes a medium through which we are able to attain an ever-greater experience and knowledge of the possibilities of human life. Above all, this knowledge counters the temptation to embrace the 'vast and universal claims' about who we are or what we ought to be. Such claims are mere mythology against which the true historian works to understand the past on its own terms and in this way learn from it (Elton 1991).

More recent concerns in the theory of history might be aptly summed up by Lyotard's comment (1988) that the historian is always doomed to become part of the thing they write about. Meta-historical historical discourse, in short, is a fantasy. Such a contention is explored by the work of Hayden White (1978, 1987). Under the influence of theories of narrative developed with the domains of **analytic** and **continental philosophy** and associated with **post-modernism** and **post–structuralism** (not least the writings of Barthes, Foucault and Derrida), White has argued that historical discourse needs to be understood as essentially figural or allegorical. In other words, history cannot be said to have a literal or factual component at any level. Indeed, on White's account, history is fictional and in this regard cannot be counted amongst the empirical disciplines whose aim is the objective representation of facts. On this view, history can never stand as a metalanguage capable of referring to an objectivity that abides independently of it. What historical narratives present, it follows, are as much the inventions of imagination as discoveries. This, in turn, undermines the notion of seamless historical narrative, replacing it with concepts of rupture, fragmentation and dislocation. In this regard, White's work shares much the same spirit as the historical analyses of Foucault. As with White, Foucault's work reflects a variety of interests and influences. The writings of Nietzsche, Georges Bataille, Maurice Blanchot, Martin Heidegger and T.W. Adorno are important to his work in various ways and at different stages of his development. Like White, Foucault begins with the contention that many established perspectives and methods of enquiry (not least those epitomised by the humanism of existentialism, Marxism and phenomenology) are wanting. In their place, Foucault turns to Nietzschean conceptions of genealogy and power to develop his own approach to history. Foucault's interests are wide ranging: the construction of concepts of mental illness, the analysis of systems of discipline and punishment, sexuality and subjectivity, and the relationship between forms of knowledge and discourses of power. All his enquiries embrace the approach of close historical analysis of the development of such notions. Such meticulous historical accounts reveal the hidden structure of interests and presuppositions underlying the forms of knowledge dealing with these topics. It is partly the breadth of interest displayed in Foucault's work that makes it difficult to categorise Foucault's work as belonging to any particular discipline of academic enquiry. In his writings a concern with knowledge rubs shoulders with political and historical questions. But his concerns might be more correctly described as all falling within the realm of politics. Foucault's intellectual development can be conveniently summarised in two stages. First, the works of the late 1960s deployed an 'archaeological' and historical mode of investigation. In them Foucault sought to uncover the origins of the emergence of the human sciences, of reason and unreason, and the modern **episteme**. Second, Foucault's later work turns toward a Nietzschean historical-genealogical mode of investigation, supplementing the earlier more overtly historical analyses by concentrating instead on the power relations present in discourses of knowledge. The increased awareness of the importance of power is what underlies Foucault's contention that an awareness of 'the fine meshes of the web of power' reveals the intrinsic localism of political struggles and also thereby suspends our faith in the possibilities of an all-embracing historical narrative. Foucault's example has generated, amongst other things, an interest in hitherto marginalised aspects of historical narrative. Thus, for instance, Edward Said's interest in **orientalism** represents a development of Foucault's contention that forms of knowledge are articulations of power interests that can be revealed by patient historical analysis.

Further reading: Carr 1987; Elton 1991; Foucault 1970, 1977b, 1980; Jenkins 1995; Oakeshott 1983; White 1978, 1987.

PS

HOLISM

A contextualist theory of truth, **meaning** and interpretation favoured by some philosophers—notably W.V.O. Quine—and also by many cultural and literary theorists working in the broadly **hermeneutic** tradition that runs from Schleiermacher to Heidegger and Gadamer. On this view it is impossible to assign meanings or to interpret beliefs except in a context wider than that of the individual statement or utterance. Opinions vary as to just how widely this interpretive 'horizon' has to be drawn, or whether—in principle—there is any limit to the range of relevant background knowledge that might be involved. For the most part philosophers in the Anglo–American ('analytic') camp tend to adopt a pragmatic outlook and not worry too much about the demarcation issue, while 'continental' thinkers follow Heidegger in espousing a depth-hermeneutic approach that concerns itself centrally with just this issue.

CN

HOLOCAUST

The mass murder by the Nazis of an estimated 5.3 to 6 million Jews during the last three years of the Second World War. Between 1942 and 1945 these people were systematically annihilated in death camps. Of these camps, the one situated at Auschwitz in Poland (established in May 1940) was the largest and most notorious and has come to stand as a symbol of these horrifying events. Other camps included those at Belsen, Treblinka and Sobibor. Auschwitz itself was not simply a centre of extermination. It conveniently combined three purposes in one institution: those of a slave-labour camp, concentration camp and death camp (the latter constructed at Auschwitz-Birkenau). The Auschwitz complex in fact consisted of more than forty camps, located throughout a large industrial locality richly endowed with natural resources. From May 1940 to the beginning of 1942, Auschwitz's population consisted of just over 36,000 prisoners, of whom around one third were Russian prisoners of war. The pool of prisoners served the German war effort, working in coal mines, foundries, factories, and the like. In 1942, however, the first of an estimated 1,100,000 of the Jewish victims of the Nazi Holocaust, figuratively designated by the authorities as due for '*Sonderbehandlung*' ('special treatment', i.e. liquidation), were transported to Auschwitz, marched straight into its specially constructed gas chambers and murdered. Auschwitz-Birkenau itself consisted of a series of related constructions, including a railway platform, specially built gas chambers and adjoining crematoria (some of which could burn 8,000 bodies per day), cremation pits, a sewage plant, and a barracks in which medical experimentation was carried out on prisoners. The planning and design of the death camps, from the organisation of transport and the commissioning of specially designed furnaces from manufacturers (the company Topf and Sons had furnaces in many camps) to the selection of victims (often by qualified doctors) occurred on an industrial scale. Scientific, technical and bureaucratic skills were brought into harmony with murderous designs. The feverish rate of killing is reflected in the fact that victims were delivered to the killing complex by train without interruption between 1942 and

1944. None of these victims was registered: 'Of those murdered upon arrival, no trace remained: no name, no record, no precise information' (Gutman and Berenbaum 1994:7). Sadly, this lack of an administrative paper trail has led Holocaust deniers to assert that no evidence exists to prove that the mass exterminations ever happened. Overwhelming evidence to the contrary exists in the form of written evidence, the remains of the camps themselves and the testimony of Holocaust survivors, Nazi perpetrators and other witnesses. Clothes, food, medicine, money, hair, and even gold teeth were taken from Holocaust victims and their use value exploited. The victims' hair (some of which Soviet troops discovered on arrival in Auschwitz in 1945: '293 sacks of human hair weighing on average 20kg (44 pounds) each, and 12 sacks weighing on average 88kg (193.6 pounds) each' (Strzelecki, in Gutman and Berenbaum 1994:260)) was used in many ways. These included the making of yarn, felt, fabrics, ropes, and even stockings. Ashes and bones were also scattered in camp fields as a fertiliser. There is no doubt that the operations at Auschwitz and elsewhere were, in this regard, run at a profit.

The Holocaust is an event of such horrifying proportions that its significance defies articulation. According to Adorno (1973b), after Auschwitz no positively articulated concept of transcendence is possible unless it is one that at the same time mocks the victims' fate and thereby compromises itself. Hitler's legacy is to have imposed upon us a 'new categorical imperative' forbidding us to allow such events to recur. With regard to this demand and with an eye on recent events (whether in what was once Yugoslavia, in Rwanda, or elsewhere) one can at least say, decisively, that modern humanity has decisively failed in this regard. For Hannah Arendt (1906–75), the death camps demonstrated both the unlimited egoism of the totalitarian mind and the 'banality of evil' (Arendt 1965). Totalitarian egoism represents a shift from the nihilism of the nineteenth century which holds 'nothing is true, all is permitted', to the belief that 'all is possible'. As the word 'banality' suggests, evil, on Arendt's view, is committed in a state of thoughtlessness: executioners, like their victims, stop being agents and merely enact the duties associated with fulfilling a specified social role. For Lyotard (1988), Auschwitz stands as a prime example of a 'differend', i.e. a wrong committed against a person who is denied the means of establishing that a wrong has indeed been done. That millions were exterminated in the Nazi genocide along with the evidence of their extermination is what at the same time allows for the continued wrong to be done to them of denying the legitimacy of their victim status. The writings of Holocaust survivors such as Primo Levi, Tadeusz Borowski and Charlotte Delbo are required reading for anyone seeking to understand something of it, not merely because they represent the testimony of witnesses to the slaughter but because of their ability to communicate things about it that amount to making the Holocaust a 'shareable experience' (Langer, in Gutman and Berenbaum 1994:604).

Further reading: Borowski 1967; Delbo 1995; Gutman and Berenbaum 1994; Levi 1988.

PS

HORTICULTURE

The art of cultivating a garden has largely passed **cultural studies** by. This is unfortunate, for an important popular cultural expression is thereby overlooked. Historians of art and architecture have explored the garden (both aristocratic and domestic) (Uglow 2004), and there has recently been a strenuous attempt to recover the history of garden design, and to re-examine the work of such early twentieth-century gardeners as Gertrude Jekyll (1937) and Vita Sackville-West (so much so that praise of Jekyll is already a bit passé). Yet the domestic garden is a rich source of meaning (and thus perhaps of the construction and articulation of personal identity). The choice of plants and the layout and planning of a garden are not a matter of chance, and nor are they wholly determined by the natural properties of plant, soil and climate. Plants and especially flowering plants carry rich historical and cultural associations, even if at times these associations may amount to a nostalgic hankering after the myth of a rural idyll of the cottage garden, or a harmonious relationship with nature through the wildlife garden. The choice and arrangement of plants may therefore be seen to be governed by conventions and codes that give them meaning. In terms of consumption, the garden centre is an interesting parallel to the shopping mall. Just as shopping malls increasingly become leisure attractions (with such facilities as restaurants and cinemas), so the garden centre ceases to be simply a place to buy plants (as the old nursery might have been) and becomes a leisure facility in its own right. The garden, allotment and window box therefore offer a rich source for reflection on contemporary culture.

Further reading: Turner 2005.

AE

HUMANISM

A word with a variety of meanings. Usually, a viewpoint which advocates the supreme value of human beings: 'man the measure of all things'. During the period of Renaissance Europe, those who studied the classics (i.e. Ancient Greek and Roman texts) were deemed humanists. They espoused an optimism about human possibilities and achievements. During the twentieth century, being a humanist commonly implies an attitude antithetical to religious beliefs and institutions.

In the post-war period debates have been waged between academics over the term humanism in a variety of contexts (e.g. politics, ethics, philosophy of language). In this context, a humanist has come to signify (amongst other things) someone who advocates a view of human nature which stresses the autonomy of individual agency with regard to such matters as moral or political choice, or one who adheres to the view that human **subjectivity** is the source of **meaning** in language use. A humanist, on this view, is someone who presupposes that there are essential properties (e.g. autonomy, freedom, intentionality, the ability to use language for the purpose of producing meaningful propositions, rationality) which define what it is to be human. Such a conception of subjectivity has been criticised by way of an invocation of theories of meaning derived from **structuralism** and **post–structuralism**. Following on from such thinkers as Nietzsche, writers within these schools have argued that the production of meaning, and therefore subjectivity, is a matter of relations of **discourses** of **power** (Foucault) or processes of semantic slippage within language (Derrida) rather than a matter of an extralinguistic subject existing 'outside' the domain of language and subsequently 'uses' language to express their intentions. Such views have been taken up by advocates of **postmodernism**, who have claimed, for example, that the politics that purportedly accompanies humanism is susceptible to being undermined by these forms of analysis. Such a view depends upon whether or not one is inclined to accept the claim that the advocacy of a particular **ontology** of the subject commits one to a particular kind of politics. Certainly, many facets of liberalism are not so easily swept away by advocating an anti-humanism. For example, the anti-humanism implicit in philosopher Jean-François Lyotard's conventionalist account of language in *The Differend: Phrases in Dispute* does not circumvent certain key principles of liberal thought as elaborated by J.S. Mill in *On Liberty*, but might rather be said to be compatible with them (see Sedgwick 1998).

Other thinkers who adopt an anti-humanist attitude include Heidegger (whose conception of *Dasein* should not be confused with 'humanist' accounts of subjectivity; indeed, Heidegger explicitly rejected the humanism of Jean-Paul Sartre's existentialism in his 'Letter on Humanism' (1947)); and Louis Althusser, whose 'structural Marxism' opposed Marx's contention that humans were the authors of their own destiny with the view that social relations are instrumental in the construction of identity, belief systems and forms of consciousness.

See also: **ideological state apparatus**.

Further reading: Callinicos 1976; Davies 1997; Heidegger 1996; Sartre 1990; Sedgwick 1998.

PS

IDEAL TYPE

Ideal type is a term originating in Max Weber's **sociology**. It is a term that is easily misunderstood. For Weber, an ideal type was an abstract model, usually of some social **institution** or process. The ideal type therefore attempts to identify and isolate the key characteristics of the social institution. It will guide empirical enquiry, drawing attention to the sorts of features which the social scientist should be looking for and documenting, and may be modified in the light of empirical research. (See **bureaucracy**, for an example of a Weberian ideal type.) The ideal type is therefore 'ideal' in the sense of being an abstraction. Not all the features of the ideal type will necessarily be manifest in every (or any) empirical manifestation of the type. Crucially, the ideal type is not 'ideal' in the sense of being an account of the perfect or desirable form of the social institution.

AE

IDENTITY

The issue of identity is central to **cultural studies**, in so far as cultural studies examines the contexts within which and through which both individuals and groups construct, negotiate and defend their identity or self-understanding. Cultural studies draws heavily on those approaches to the problem of identity that question what may be called orthodox accounts of identity. Orthodoxy assumes that the **self** is something autonomous (being stable and independent of all external influences). Cultural studies draws on those approaches that hold that identity is a response to something external and different from it (an **other**).

In orthodox European philosophy, at least from Descartes's writings in the seventeenth century, it has been assumed that the self (*ego* or **subject**) exists as an autonomous source of meaning and agency. Descartes himself found that the only thing that he could not doubt was that he existed, and that this existence took the form of a 'thinking substance' (Descartes 1968). This notion of the autonomous subject, sure of its own identity and continuing throughout the individual human being's life, was dominant not just in philosophy, but also in political thought (not least as a grounding assumption of **liberalism**) and psychology. The idea was questioned however, not least by the Scottish philosopher David Hume, in the eighteenth century (Hume 1978:251–63). Hume observed that the contents of his consciousness included images (or sense impressions) of everything of which he was thinking (either directly perceiving, or recalling in memory). There was, though, no image of the self that was supposedly doing this perceiving and remembering. Hume therefore proffered what was commonly known as the 'bundle theory' of the self, such that the self is nothing more than a bundle of sense impressions, that continually changed as the individual had new experiences or recalled old ones.

In the late nineteenth century, Emile Durkheim posed a fundamental challenge to liberal individualism (Durkheim 1984). The liberal presupposed the primacy of the individual, and thus that society was composed out of individuals (brought together, for example, in a **social contract**). In contrast, Durkheim argued that the individual was a product of society (not that society was a product of individuals). His point was that a modern understanding of individuality (and thus, the self-understanding of humans in modern society) was a product of that particular culture. In pre-industrial societies, with little or no economic specialisation (or **division of labour**), all members of the society would be similar in attitudes, **values** and **norms**. Such societies were held together purely because of this homogeneity (see **mechanical solidarity**). In contrast, in industrial society, with its high degree of specialisation, individualism occurs because people live distinctive lives with distinctive experiences. Their values and attitudes can then diverge. Durkheim therefore argues that individual identity is not primary, but is a product of economic organisation.

George Herbert Mead's analysis of the self poses an alternative set of problems for the idea of an autonomous ego. For Mead, the self is constructed through its relations with others. Mead distinguishes the 'I' from the 'me', arguing that: 'The "I" is the response of the organism to the attitudes of others; the "me" is the organised set of attitudes of others which one himself assumes' (Mead 1934:175). The ego thus collapses into little more than an animal response. The self, and thus self-consciousness, rests rather upon the internalisation of the viewpoint of others. The 'I' becomes self-conscious only in so far as it can imagine how it is seen by others, and responds accordingly. The development of the self therefore depends upon the others it encounters. This line of thought is fundamental to the **symbolic interactionist** approach in sociology. In the work of Erving Goffman (1959) it is taken further. Goffman suggests that the self is a product of particular **interactions**, in so far as the individual's capacities, attitudes and ways of behaving (and possibly, of conceiving of him or herself) changes as the people around him or her change. Alone, a person is either not self-conscious, and as such does not have, at that moment, a self, or is self-conscious, in so far as he or she is aware of how he or she would appear to some more or less specific other. The self therefore has no stability, being almost as fluid as the self proposed by Hume.

Psychoanalysis opens up a further series of questions against the orthodox view of identity. For Freud, identity rests on the child's assimilation of external persons. The self is structured through the relationship of the ego, id and superego. While the id is the instinctive substrate of the self, and the superego, crucially, is the constraining moral consciousness that is internalised in the process of psychological development, the ego may be understood either as the combination of the id and superego, or as an agency separate from these two. The latter interpretation is, in the current context, possibly the more interesting, for it suggests that the ego is never self-identical. Erik Erikson's psychodynamic theory develops upon this. Identity for Erikson is a process between the identity of the individual and the identity of the communal culture. It was Erikson who coined the phrase 'identity crisis' in the 1940s. At first, the term referred to a person who had lost a sense of 'personal sameness and historical continuity' (Erikson 1968:22). As such, the individual is separated from the culture that can give coherence to his or her sense of self. Later, it came to characterise youth, as a stage in the psychological development of any individual.

In Lacan's reinterpretation of Freud, the problematic identity of the self or subject is explored further. For Lacan, self-consciousness emerges only at the mirror stage (at approximately six to eighteen months). Here the infant recognises its reflection as a reflection of itself. It therefore comes to know itself, not directly, but through the mirror image. The self emerges as the promise of control in the face of the fragmentation that occurs as the child is separated from the mother. However, as for Freud, the male child's identity depends upon that of the mother (allowing, in English at least, a pun on (m)other). The child enters language through the imposition of the law by the father, with the 'no' that prohibits incest with the mother. The child desires the mother in order to regain a primal unity. This is a desire to disobey the father's prohibition, and yet it must be repressed. Thus, Lacan can argue, the unconscious is structured like language. In effect, this is to argue that the self (or more properly the subject) is positioned by language, which is to say that it is positioned as always repressing its own lack of unity. Althusser's **structuralist** version of **Marxism** offers a parallel account of the subject, albeit now as a product of **ideology**. Social institutions such as the church, education, police, family and **mass media** 'interpellate' or hail the subject, again positioning him or her within society.

The work of Foucault may also be interpreted through the centrality of the question of identity. Thus, in his early work on madness (1971), he analyses how madness is conceived differently in different ages (comparing, for example, the Renaissance view of madness as its own form of reason, with the rationalist seventeenth century's exclusion of the insane from society). Madness is thus socially constructed and specific, and historically variable social practices exist to constrain it. Yet, crucially for the seventeenth and eighteenth centuries, madness is also the other, in comparison to which the sane and rational define themselves. The identity of the dominant group in society therefore depends upon its construction of its own other. In Foucault's later writings, he turns to the problem of the construction of the 'self (especially in relation to sexuality) through its positioning within **discourses**' (1981). From this, the self may be theorised in terms of the conceptual and other intellectual resources that it calls upon in order to write or talk about itself, and in the way in which it is written about, or written to. The way in which a **text** is composed will anticipate, and thus situate, a certain self as reader.

Structuralist and post-structuralist questioning of the nature of self-identity, as found in the work of Lacan, Althusser and Foucault, may also be linked to an identity politics. The recognition that identity is not merely constructed, but depends upon some other, opens up the theoretical space for marginal or oppressed groups to challenge and renegotiate the identities that have been forced upon them in the process of domination. Ethnic identities, gay and lesbian identities and female identities are thus brought into a process of political change.

See also: **self**.

AE

IDEOLOGICAL STATE APPARATUS

A conception developed by French **structuralist** Marxist Louis Althusser. Althusser developed the notion of ideological state apparatuses (or ISAs) in an attempt to both expand and clarify the meaning of the term '**ideology**' as it is presented in the thoughts of Karl Marx and Friedrich Engels, in line with his revision of traditional Marxist theory. Althusser argued that the traditional Marxist conception of ideology, although in essence correct, is too restrictive and insufficiently subtle as a means of elucidating the structures which underpin Marxist analysis of society. On the traditional model, the term 'ideology' is usually taken to refer to abstracted and illusory forms of thought which serve to naturalise, and thereby legitimise, the dominant social order of capitalism. The system of ideas which function as norms within capitalist society are therefore an articulation of the interests of the ruling class, and hence the base-structure of material **relations of production** is directly reflected in the ideological super-structure of ideas which serve to legitimise capitalist power. Althusser argued that such an account lacks an important aspect: although the theory of ideology provides an account of the structure of ideas which serve to naturalise the rule of the dominant class, it fails to address the way in which capitalism must at the same time seek to reproduce the conditions of production necessary to its continued survival. This is done, Althusser argued, through ideological state apparatuses.

Thus, the state, which is seen in **Marxism** as consisting of apparatuses of repression (such as a police force, armed forces, prisons, etc.) has, in addition, ideological apparatuses which carry out the function of reproducing the conditions of production. Such apparatuses include religious institutions, the education system, the system of law, political parties, the media and the family. Through these apparatuses ideology functions to construct the **subjectivity** of individuals, and in so doing it allocates them particular roles within the capitalist system of production. For example, the education system, Althusser argues, functions to satisfy the capitalist demand that a variety of roles be filled by individuals within society. The majority of school children leave school at a fairly early age, equipped with the basic skills required for a future as shop-floor labourers; a smaller number remain within the education system for a longer period, and are equipped with additional skills which suit them to fill the functions necessary to the successful management of labourers; still fewer are released from the system of education late on to take their place as senior functionaries within the state (and some, i.e. teachers and academics, are never destined to leave the system, but take on the role of educating the next generation). Likewise, the family structure is an ISA which provides the raw material of humanity required before the education system can perform its task upon them.

Further reading: Althusser 1971.

PS

IDEOLOGY

It can plausibly be suggested that a theory of ideology is fundamental to any critical social or cultural science. However, the exact meaning of the term is often elusive or confused. Its most common use may be simply to refer to a more or less coherent set of beliefs (such as a political ideology, meaning the beliefs, values and basic principles of a political party or faction). 'Ideology' is used in this sense in some branches of political science. In **Marxism** and the **sociology of knowledge**, however, it has taken on much more subtle meanings, in order to analyse the way in which knowledge and beliefs are determined by the societies in which they emerge and are held.

The term was coined at the end of the eighteenth century, by the French philosopher Destutt de Tracy, to refer to a science (*logos*) of ideas. Such a science would be based in analysis of human perception, conceived itself as a subdiscipline of biology, and the *idéologues* sought to reform educational practices on the basis of it. (This origin is more important than it may initially seem, for it presents the argument that ideas depend on some, non-ideational, substrate. For de Tracy, this is biology; for social science it will be the material, economic and political practices and structures of society.) Napoleon's ridiculing of the *idéologues* led to 'ideology' becoming a pejorative term.

It is with Marx that ideology becomes an important critical concept. Marx's approach to ideology may be introduced through the famous observation that, for any society, the ideas of the ruling **class** are the ruling ideas. This is to suggest that our understanding and knowledge of the world (and especially, if not exclusively, of the social world) is determined by political interests. There are certain beliefs, and certain ways of seeing the world, that will be in the interests of the dominant class (but not in the interests of subordinate classes). For example, it was in the interests of the dominant class in **feudalism** to believe in the divine right of kings. The authority of the king and the aristocracy is given by God, and is thus beyond question. It is in the interests of the **bourgeoisie** (the owners and controllers of industry) in **capitalism** to see the social world as highly individualistic and competitive. What for Marx is the genuinely social and collective nature of human life (not least in class membership) is thereby concealed, and the possibilities of effective **proletarian** resistance to capitalism are minimised. The dominant class is able to propagate its ideas throughout society due to its control of various forms of communication and education (such as the **mass media**, the church and schools).

While ideology in the Marxist sense is a distorted way of viewing the world, it is not strictly false (and so ideology is not simply a synonym for **false consciousness**). Marx's observation that religion is the opium of the masses (1975:244) expresses this more complex idea. On one level, religion does distort the subordinate classes' understanding of the social world, not least in its promise of a reward in heaven for the injustices suffered in this world. Yet, the metaphorical reference to opium is important, not just because opium dulls our experience of pain, but also because opium induces dreams. Heaven is therefore an idea to be taken seriously (although not literally), for it does contain an image of justice—but one that should be realised in this world, not the hereafter. In this sense, ideology is an illusory solution to a real problem (Larrain 1979). The task of the critic of ideology is therefore to recognise this—to recognise the way in which ideology inverts our understanding of real problems—and to thereby identify and tackle the real problem.

The Marxist theory of ideology presupposes that ideology is a distortion. It may therefore be set against true knowledge. In the sociology of knowledge, not least in its development by the German sociologist

Karl Mannheim (1960), ideology loses its links to class and to domination, and so challenges this notion of truth. Mannheim retains the link that Marx establishes between ideas and the material base of society, but in order to argue that people from different sections of society will understand the world in different ways. The difference between the bourgeois understanding of the world and the proletariat is not then the difference between the views of a dominant and reactionary class and a subordinated, progressive class, but simply the difference between two, equally valid, **worldviews**. For Mannheim, there is then no single truth against which all ideologies can be judged. Each ideology will have its own standards of truth and accuracy, dependent upon the social circumstances within which it is produced.

The Marxist account of ideology can be seen to have undergone two important revisions in the twentieth century. First, the development of the theory of **hegemony**, by the Italian theorist Gramsci, tackled the problem that the theory of ideology appeared to suggest that ideas could be passively imposed upon the subordinate classes. The theory of hegemony suggests, rather, that ideologies are actually negotiated in the face of contradictory evidence and life experiences. The second revision stems from the work of the French **structuralist**, Althusser. Althusser overturned the emphasis on ideas in the theory of ideology. Ideology need not be about what people think, but rather about how they act—'lived relations'. Ideological practices, which are taken for granted, constitute the human **subject** and his or her **identity** within capitalism, thus allowing him or her to function.

Further reading: Abercrombie *et al.* 1980; Althusser 1971; Barrett 1991; Eagleton 1991; Hall 1982.

AE

INDEXICALITY

A property of social actions and utterances: that their **meaning** depends upon the particular **context** within which they occur. This property is of central importance to **ethnomethodologists'** approach to the analysis of social **interaction**. For example, '2 × 2 = 4' is not a self-evidently meaningful utterance. In an elementary maths class, it has meaning. As a reply to the question: 'What's the weather like out there?' it is thoroughly perplexing. Competent members of society have the ability to recognise relevant properties in a context that give meaning to the utterance or action (and thus are said to be 'repairing indexicality'). Thus, generally we can recognise when we are in a maths class and when not. However, it would be an endless task to explain how we recognise this particular situation as a maths class. To give a simple example, Garfinkel (the founder of **ethnomethodology**) asked students to explain a sentence. Having been given what seemed an adequate paraphrase (or 'gloss'), Garfinkel pointed out that the student had not explained the words used in his or her explanation. The brighter students no doubt rapidly realised that the repairing of indexicality (i.e. the giving of a totally exhaustive account of the meaning of a particular social event) is an endless task. The remarkable thing then is that competent members of society get by perfectly well, most of the time, without being able to articulate fully what they are doing or what it means. However, confusion and 'misunderstandings' can occur when the background assumptions of one person clash markedly with those of another, and thus repair indexicality differently. (You mishear my request about the weather as an invitation to start reciting your multiplication tables.)

Further reading: Weider 1974.

AE

INDIVIDUAL/ISM

An individual is a person or **self**. Taken in the sense of something which cannot be subject to any further division, an individual is often contrasted with a group. The view that individual selves are: (i) irreducible; (ii) endowed with the ability to use their rationality according to their own dispositions and desires; and (iii) ought to be free civic agents, is associated with individualism. This conceives of the individual as a free agent in the market place and advocates a view of political and social liberties on these terms. It is a view often linked to the influence of the writings of Adam Smith (for example, in the United Kingdom in the 1980s to the impact of his ideas on Margaret Thatcher, who advocated a free-market individualism).

Further reading: Avineri and De-Shalit 1992; Lukes 1973b; MacPherson 1962; Morris 1991.

PS

INSTITUTION

As a technical term in social science, an institution is a regular and continuously repeated social practice. As such, the term has a wider coverage than in everyday usage, including not merely prisons, asylums, schools, hospitals and government offices, but also **language**, and moral and **cultural** practices.

AE

INTERACTION

In interaction, the actions of human beings are made in response to, and anticipation of, the actions of others. Interaction is of importance, for it can be argued that it is only through interaction that social events and situations are given **meaning**, that social reality is itself constructed (Berger and Luckmann 1961) and that personal identity is formed (Mead 1934).

See also: **symbolic interactionism**.

AE

INTERSUBJECTIVITY

A property is **subjective** if it is recognised only by a particular human being (so that one's experience or susceptibility to pain is subjective, as is the enjoyment one derives from chocolate). A property is **objective** if it actually belongs to the object, exists independently of any observer, and can therefore be recognised by anyone who has the appropriate senses. (Not everyone will enjoy chocolate, but everyone, independently, will perceive such properties as its colour and its weight.) The concept of 'intersubjectivity' opens up an important middle ground between these two oppositions. A property is intersubjective if human beings agree upon its existence, and thereby come to perceive it as if it existed in the external, objective world. Thus, **cultural** significance may be understood as intersubjective. A particular sound does not inherently have the meaning it does in a particular language, so it is not objective. Yet, it is not subjective, for (*contra* Humpty Dumpty) words cannot mean anything that I choose them to mean. Rather, the sound's meaning depends upon the hearer belonging to a particular linguistic community, or at

175

least understanding the appropriate language. It may then be argued that the meaningfulness and significance of all social events is inter-subjective.

AE

INTERTEXTUALITY

The term 'intertextuality' was coined by Julia Kristeva to indicate that a **text** (such as a novel, poem or historical document) is not a self-contained or autonomous entity, but is produced from other texts. The interpretation that a particular reader generates from a text will then depend on the recognition of the relationship of the given text to other texts. Thus, for example, a photograph of a politician in a newspaper may yield more meaning, or further levels of meaning, if it is interpreted, not simply as a representation of its subject, but rather through a frame constituted by other photographs of the same person (possibly in widely different situations), speeches made by him or her, newspaper reports and comments on him or her, and even cartoons lampooning the politician. Similarly, our understanding of David Lean's film *Great Expectations* is influenced by our reading of Dickens's novel, or conversely our understanding of the novel is now framed by having seen the film. Intertextuality may be understood as the thesis that no text exists outside its continuing interpretation and reinterpretation. There can then never be a definitive reading of a text, for each reading generates a new text that itself becomes part of the frame within which the original text is interpreted.

Further reading: Barthes 1974; Kristeva 1986a.

AE

IRONY

The term 'irony' is derived from the Greek *eironeia*, meaning 'simulated ignorance'. Its precise definition is, however, elusive. At its simplest, it is a figure of speech in which what a person says is the opposite to what he or she means (so referring to the tall as short, the cowardly as courageous, and so on). This inversion captures little of the subtlety of irony. A liar or confidence trickster may say the opposite of what he or she means, but the liar is not using irony, for those who understand an utterance as ironic will recognise the inversion of meaning. The point of the inversion is therefore important—why say the opposite of what you mean, unless you are trying to deceive your audience? Two reasons can be offered. First, irony is a form of mockery or critical comment. Ironically to dub the cowardly courageous is to mock their lack of courage. Irony usefully saves the speaker from committing him or herself to a positive position, and to a degree may keep the speaker detached from the issues upon which he or she comments. (A classic example of literary irony is Swift's *Modest Proposal* (1729), in which he advocated eating Irish babies as a solution to the population problem. He thereby ridicules existing solutions to the 'Irish problem', without offering a serious solution of his own.) Second, recognition of irony as irony may serve to distinguish the sophisticated members of an in-group, from the more simple creatures without.

Two special meanings of irony may be noted. 'Socratic irony' refers to the manner of argument employed by Socrates, at least as he is represented in the early dialogues of Plato. Socrates pretends both ignorance and a sympathy with the position of a supposed expert on some topic. This affectation allows Socrates to question his victims, harrying them until their arguments and contradictions collapse into contradiction and incoherence. 'Romantic irony' is especially associated with early nineteenth-century German philosopher-poets, including Hölderlin and Friedrich Schlegel. Such irony, drawing on Socratic irony, is explicitly associated with the ambiguity, uncertainty and fragmentation of meaning. For Schlegel, in irony 'everything should be playful and serious, guilelessly open and deeply hidden'. Or again: 'Irony is the form of paradox. Paradox is everything which is simultaneously good and great' (Simpson 1988:183). Irony therefore disrupts the taken-for-granted meaningfulness of utterance and writing, exposing its artificiality. It is this emphasis on the problematic and ultimately indeterminate nature of the interpretation of any utterance or **text** that carries irony into contemporary literary theory. Thus, for Barthes, irony is the 'essence of writing', in that it exposes the inability of the writer to control the interpretation of the text.

Further reading: Kierkegaard 1966.

AE

JAZZ

The word 'jazz' has obscure origins; the most common etymology is that it developed from 'jass', a turn-of-the-century USA term for semen. 'Jass music' was hence sexually charged, dissolute music played in brothels or other dubious establishments and in which musical competence was less important than infectious rhythm and performance gimmicks. Others have claimed, however, that 'jazz' is a word whose origins are North African or even Arabic (a language spoken very widely in North and West Africa) and hence that it pre-dates slavery and the music which is known by that name today. In that case, the link with 'jass' would appear to be rather pernicious.

The music has a long and complex history, and many elements of its early development are still in dispute. What is beyond question is that most of its primary musical innovators have been, and to a lesser extent continue to be, black Americans, including the earliest influential individuals, 'Buddy' Bolden, 'King' Oliver and Louis Armstrong. They played in the New Orleans style (although all three eventually left that city for Chicago), which is characterised by small groups, a regular pulse and group improvisation on simple melodies such as marching tunes. As groups grew larger and audiences became more respectable, the music evolved into 'swing', a dance-hall craze which lasted for over two decades and helped create an audience of more affluent middle-class whites. Duke Ellington is now recognised as the master of swing composition, but the Count Basie orchestra was no less successful, and white Paul Whiteman's enormous band was even more so.

Gradually, musicians in swing groups began to experiment. Players such as Coleman Hawkins, Lester Young and Charlie Christian (one of the few guitarists to have an unshakeable place in jazz history) developed a more complex solo style, and sought smaller groupings which would give them the space to develop ideas over a longer period—it is easily forgotten that for the first forty years or so of what is now called 'jazz', individual instrumental statements were not a particularly important feature of the music. In contrast, bebop groups tend to be small—between three and six players is typical—and to focus on solo statements. Charlie Parker, Dizzy Gillespie and Thelonious Monk are among the most famous innovators in the field, developing the music into a ferociously complex, competitive arena in which technical virtuosity and near-instantaneous reflexes were pitted against intricate harmonic structures and breakneck tempi.

Since the assimilation of bebop into the jazz mainstream, the music has fragmented into a large number of different schools. Perhaps most significantly, the rigours of bebop harmony were abandoned by practitioners of 'free jazz', particularly Ornette Coleman and (in his later work) John Coltrane. This music developed, through contact with the European **avant-garde**, into what is today known as 'free improvisation'. Also of very great significance was the move by many musicians into electrified instrumentation in the 1970s, an economically dry time for jazz. In effecting this change, players such as Miles Davis and Herbie Hancock revolutionised the vocabulary of the music, opening the door for genres like fusion, acid jazz and electronic music generally. Jazz from these traditions has had, and continues to have, a strong formative influence on Western popular music as a whole, and it would be fair to say that very popular forms of music such as hip hop and electronic dance music are deeply indebted to them.

All of the above is conventional wisdom, but it is also controversial; there are no neutral histories of jazz. Its racially fraught history in particular has led to massive critical distortions both negative (as when early critics denounced it as 'voodoo music') and positive (the primitivist criticism still occasionally produced today, which opposes the supposed instinctive physicality and emotionality of the black musician with the rational approach of white classical players). A useful collection of such distortions is Meltzer (1993). The most influential of studies which thematised its racial origins was LeRoi Jones's *Blues People: Negro Music in White America* (1965) (Jones is now known as Amiri Baraka; his books may be found under both names).

Another tendency in jazz criticism is to compare the music with that of the classical tradition. By far the most important study of this kind was Gunther Schuller's *Early Jazz* (1968), which argued that, if classical analytic standards are applied to jazz, the music may be better understood and appreciated. Famously, Adorno begged to differ, claiming that the comparison showed jazz to be an impoverished form of popular entertainment; on this, see particularly his 'On the Fetish Character of Music and the Regression of Listening' (1978b).

Further reading: Berlin 1980; Berliner 1994; Collier 1977; Gabbard 1995; Jost 1981; Shepherd 1991; Stearns 1956; Wilmer 1992.

RC

LABELLING

Labelling theory is an important explanatory tool within the study of **deviance**. First proposed by Lemert (1951), but most closely associated with the work of Howard Becker (1963), it is grounded in **symbolic interactionism**. The theory argues that an individual does not become a deviant simply by breaking some behavioural norm (such as a law). Rather, 'deviant' is seen as a label that is imposed upon the individual. An initial violation of a commonly accepted behavioural rule becomes significant only if others react to it. Human beings are understood, within the theory, as forming their personal **identity** or self-understanding only through interaction with others. Therefore, if others perceive one's actions negatively, and crucially talk about you and describe your actions in this negative language, then you will begin to think of yourself in those terms. Your personal identity will then be constructed through those terms. Thus, labels, such as junkie or drug addict, lunatic or mentally ill, mugger and child molester, are not neutral. They are inherently critical of the sort of person they describe. In incorporating these labels into one's own self-identity, one learns to live and behave differently (Goffman (1961), for example, has analysed the processes by which new inmates of asylums for the mentally ill learn to behave as mentally ill.) The deviant may be isolated from 'normal' society, turning to the company of other deviants. The **others** whom the individual encounters on a routine basis, and who are thus responsible for forming the individual's self-identity, change. A relatively minor violation of norms (such as the smoking of cannabis) can then be 'amplified' into more serious forms of deviance (such as the taking of hard drugs) as the deviant shifts from the norms of behaviour and language typical of 'normal' society, to those typical of 'deviant' **subcultures**. It may be added that the process by which the self-identity of the individual is reconstructed is not automatic. The imposition of a label may be resisted. Those with great economic or intellectual and educational resources will have more power to resist the application of a label (for example, by having the resources to provide a more adequate defence of themselves in court).

Further reading: Fine 1977; Gove 1980.

AE

LABOUR

In economics, labour is one of the four factors of production, alongside **capital**, land (or natural resources) and enterprise, which is to say, it is one of the four general types of input or resource required for economic production. In orthodox economics, labour includes the number of people actually employed in, or who are available for, production, or a little more abstractly, the capacity to produce (understood in terms of intellectual and manual skills, and the exertion).

In Marxist economics, labour is the source of all economic **value** (hence the **labour theory of value**). In addition, the **proletariat** (the subordinate class within **capitalism**) are characterised by having to exchange their capacity to labour (or labour power) for the **commodities** that they require in order to live.

AE

LABOUR THEORY OF VALUE

The **labour** theory of **value** is an attempt to explain the value of goods and services in terms of the costs of their production, as opposed to their usefulness (or **use value**). Elements of the labour theory can be traced back, at least to the seventeenth-century political philosopher John Locke, who analysed the appropriation of private property in terms of a person's ability to 'mix' their labour with natural resources (1980). The British economist David Ricardo (1772–1823) gave the first coherent account of the theory (Ricardo 1951), in part in response to the 'paradox of value'. It was argued that the usefulness of a commodity could not determine its value, as very useful entities, such as air and water, are generally free or very inexpensive. In contrast, apparently useless luxury goods (gold and diamonds, say) can be very expensive. The labour theory explains this in terms of the amount of labour (or labour time) that went into their production, either directly, or indirectly through having being stored up by having been expended in the production of machinery and other capital goods. Water is easily found and conveyed to consumers, in contrast to the great amount of time needed to find and extract diamonds. In practice, the actual amount of labour expended in production is of less relevance than a social average labour time (for otherwise the theory would imply that the products of the lazy would be worth more than those of the efficient). While the theory is fundamental to **Marxist** economics, in orthodox economics, since the late nineteenth century, it has been replaced by more sophisticated explanations of value grounded in usefulness (beginning with Marshall's account of marginal utility).

See also: **surplus value**.

Further reading: Meek 1973.

AE

LANGUAGE

There are many approaches to language. From a common-sense standpoint, language might be taken as a vehicle for the **communication** of thoughts. Hence, **meaning** and its 'transmission' is essential to a definition of what language is. This view would conceive of a **subject** having thoughts, and in turn expressing them *through* language in the form of speech. Taken in this way, particular languages might be produced by particular cultures, but it would not necessarily be the case that thoughts are culturally specific (the issue of meaning, in other words, might turn on questions of human nature, on psychology, physiology, etc.). In turn, meaning, on this conception, would be primarily a matter of the intentions of speakers. This view is open to question from a number of perspectives, for example, approaches associated with **postmodernism, structuralism** and **post-structuralism**. On such accounts as these, language produces meaning not through the assertion by a language-independent speaker of a proposition which expresses an intention independently of the language used, but it is only in virtue of the existence of language (understood as a system of **signs**, or as a semantic process which is ontologically independent of the constitution of subjectivity) that there are such things as 'speakers' and 'intentions'. In turn, speakers are regarded as being constituted within language, and hence are not taken as ontologically prior to it. The tradition of **analytic philosophy** has offered a number of accounts of language and meaning which simply do not rely upon a self-conscious model of subjectivity as constituting their foundation, but point towards the logical and structural preconditions of languages as being of importance in our understanding of such issues; while Lacan's model of **psychoanalysis** envisages a structural link between the constitution of the **unconscious** and language (i.e. he claims the unconscious is structured like a language).

Equally important to any account of language are the notions of **representation** and **reference**. Thus, we can ask such questions as, 'Does language represent the world to us, or construct it for us?' or 'Does language succeed in referring to entities which are "non-linguistic"?' Such questions involve the consideration of issues related to the areas of **metaphysics, ontology** and **epistemology**. For example, Derrida's account of the metaphysical tradition of the West conceives of it as embodying a set of presuppositions about the nature of meaning and intention. Such presuppositions include the attitude that meaning is a matter of the 'presence' of speakers and that 'writing', in turn, is secondary to living speech in the hierarchy of meaning:

speakers produce meaning, but need writing to preserve the living presence of meaning in their absence. Likewise, the view that subjectivity is the source of meaning presupposes a particular ontology of the **subject** (namely, that the subject is capable, in virtue of what it is, of agency with regard to the generation of meaning); while questions about the nature of knowledge (i.e. epistemological questions) are also questions concerned with language with regard to (i) its capability to refer to 'non-linguistic' experience or alternatively (ii) the linguistic **norms** or conventions which stipulate what counts as knowledge within any given community of speakers. If questions of normativity and community come to the fore, then any account of language must pay attention to the cultural factors involved in the construction of meaning.

Whether it is possible to talk about 'Language' (with a capital 'L') at all in a general sense is perhaps open to question. It has certainly been the case that many theories (e.g. structuralism) have at least an implicit investment in the belief that there are characteristics that can be described which are universally applicable to *all* languages. Only on the basis of such a view was structuralism able to lay claim to its status as a 'scientific' description of language. However, 'Language' in this sense is perhaps a conception which is bound up with problems of **metaphysics**, for what is referred to when one uses the word 'Language' in this way cannot be demonstrated or shown in the way in which the particular referents contained within a proposition can be. Another instance of such a conception would be the phrase 'universe': the referent here is a totality which cannot be shown, not least because the very act of attempting to show it would itself have to be part of what is shown. Likewise, talking of 'Language' at the very least presupposes that one can allude to a totality, of which the proposition which refers to this totality must itself be a part since it is linguistic (a problem related to Russell's aporia—cf. **grand narrative**).

PS

LANGUE

In Saussure's linguistics, '*langue*' refers to the underlying structure and components of a language. It is thus made up of a repertoire of possibilities available to the speaker of the language, along with the rules that determine the meaningful selection and combination of available units of meaning.

Further reading: Barthes 1967b; Holdcraft 1991.

AE

LEGITIMATION

A term in sociologist Max Weber's sociology of politics which means the acknowledgement on the part of a society's **subjects** of the right of their rulers to rule them. In the post-war period the issue of legitimation has become a central issue in social, political and cultural discussions. For Jean-François Lyotard, for example, the question of legitimation is one that is continually suspended within a theoretical double bind. Questions of legitimation, on this view, are really genre questions concerning appropriate means to particular ends (see **discourse**), and cannot be divorced from consideration of their social and cultural dimensions. Lyotard argues that there are no universal criteria for legitimation and that, in consequence, the political level is a realm of cultural antagonism between contending purposes rather than goal oriented. He does, however, reserve a critical space for the study of language: the open-ended philosophical analysis of **rules**. Politics, on a Lyotardean model, would be about competing claims being fought out within the space of cultural life, not in terms of some overall, most desirable state of affairs towards which society should be aiming. Jürgen Habermas, in contrast, has tried to argue against this view (which endorses a politics of conflict or 'dissensus') with a consensual reading of the social language of 'communicative action'.

Further reading: Habermas 1976b, 1984, 1987; Lyotard 1988; Weber 1958.

PS

LEISURE

The time left over after the completion of work, and the activities pursued during that time. Leisure has been traditionally defined and understood in opposition to work or **labour**. If time spent in work is considered as a period of necessary activity in order to secure one's livelihood, and thus as a period in which income is earned, then leisure is the time of freedom, in part made possible by work, and in which any surplus income is spent. A more or less explicit promise of **modernisation** is that leisure time will be increased. Indeed, in the United Kingdom in the 1920s, certain trade unions identified the need for greater leisure time as a priority over higher wages, an emphasis that led to an increase in public holidays and the shortening of the working day.

Attitudes towards leisure have, nonetheless, been complex and ambiguous. While leisure may be generally considered a good thing, the emphasis upon human beings as essentially labourers (found, for example, in **Marxism**) tends to generate a suspicion about, or at least a highly prescriptive attitude towards, the activities pursued during leisure time. The promise of increased leisure is thus not construed as a promise of mere idleness, but rather of time for personal and communal development and cultivation. As, during the nineteenth century, significant amounts of leisure time ceased to be a prerogative of the ruling classes, the leisure time of the working classes came to be seen as a potential threat to the social order. Unruly leisure activities might at once disrupt the normal running of society, and leave the worker in a state unfit for the return to work. In nineteenth-century Britain, and indeed elsewhere in the industrialised world, the ruling classes may be seen to take a more paternalistic approach to the leisure of the working classes, provide resources, such as those supporting brass bands in the North of England, **sporting** and other events, that would channel leisure in improving and non-threatening directions. Resistance to these ideals might be seen in the continuation of such activities as dog fighting amongst the working class. The Victorian 'rational recreation' movement sponsored public libraries, museums and working men's institutes. A concern with the threat posed by leisure continued well into the twentieth century, not least in relation to the enforced leisure of unemployment and its impact upon the young. While some commentators identified extended leisure as a potential threat, others, such as Alfred Lloyd, an American sociologist, identified it as a precondition of the development of a democratic culture. Significantly, in 1924, Lorine Pruette's (in *Women and Leisure: A Study in Social Waste*) focused upon the increase in women's leisure time facilitated by the development of domestic labour-saving devices, but also the danger that such leisure would be wasted due to continuing sexual discrimination inhibiting women's pursuit of more worthwhile activity.

Theorists of leisure have reflected the complexity of attitudes towards leisure. The first major sociological study of leisure was Thorstein Veblen's *The Theory of the Leisure Class* (1953). Veblen may be seen to provide an ironic comment on the self-evidence of the Marxist assumption that human dignity lies in the ability to labour. The affluent in American society have become, Veblen suggests, an idle and parasitic class, who as absentee landlords or owners of **capital** have become divorced from the 'instinct of workmanship'.

For such people, working is indicative of low status, and the pursuit of **status** matters to this group more than the pursuit of money. Status is earned through expenditure, in a competitive display amongst social **elites**, so that the rich become a 'leisure class' indulging in conspicuous consumption (although Veblen himself used the term 'conspicuous leisure'). Such consumption has to be highly visible, but also wasteful (for example, casino gambling) if it is to earn status.

Marxist approaches to leisure in the mid-twentieth century received perhaps their most sophisticated articulation at the hands of Theodor Adorno and other members of the **Frankfurt School**. In the account of the '**culture industry**', Adorno argues that leisure time within late capitalist societies is not a free time of potential creativity and self-cultivation, but rather a time subtly controlled within the economic system. In leisure, the worker becomes a consumer, but their consumption is largely constrained by the culture industry, precisely in so far as advertising and images of good living propagated by the **mass media** shape the consumer's assessment of the worth of the commodities available to them. Thus, while in the high capitalism of the nineteenth century, consumers made a free choice as to the commodities' they consumed, grounded in their own evaluation of the commodities worth (or **use value**), now that choice is mediated or shaped by the producer. Use value as well as **exchange–value** is controlled within the late capitalist production process.

More subtle and sympathetic approaches to leisure emerged with the rise of **feminism** and **cultural studies**. Feminists exposed the relatively neglected and stereotypical view of women's leisure that had dominated previous arguments. By opposing leisure to paid employment, women's domestic labour tended to be treated as leisure. If women's leisure was recognised as something distinct from housework, it still tended to be seen in the context of the home, rather than in any broader public space. Within cultural studies, the **consumption** of **commodities** came to be seen as a genuinely creative act, in contrast to the deterministic approaches characteristic of Marxism, and to have an autonomy and validity independently of work. From a broadly **postmodernist** perspective the consumer may be understood to construct and negotiate an often fleeting and fragmentary **identity** and lifestyle through leisure time consumption. In the work of, amongst others, the **Birmingham Centre for Contemporary Cultural Studies**, leisure also came to be seen as a site of resistance to the dominant **ideology** (see **subculture**) (Hall *et al.* 1976), or the site of the negotiation of political identity and a source of social cohesion independent of the work place (Elias and Dunning 1986).

The richness and complexity of contemporary leisure, not least within a global society where travel and tourism are major leisure time activities (Urry 2002), is now more readily recognised and creatively researched than ever before.

Further reading: Adorno 1991c; Hunnicutt 1988; Rojek 1985, 1993, 1995; Wimbush and Talbot 1988.

AE

LIBERALISM

A key term within political philosophy, the word 'liberalism' is associated with a large number of thinkers (including Locke, Adam Smith, Malthus, Condorcet, J.S. Mill, Rawls and, more recently, Richard Rorty). The origins of liberalism can be traced back at least as far as the writings of John Locke (1632–1704). Indeed, Locke's work exhibits many of the key features that have subsequently been used to define liberalism. For instance, in the *Two Treatises of Government* (1690) Locke is concerned to show that the analysis of political power involves the consideration of certain key attributes all human beings possess (in Locke's case this means analysing human beings in their 'natural state', or the '**state of nature**'—a notion derived from the work of Thomas Hobbes (1588–1679)). By taking this approach, Locke in effect asserts that there are a number of principles of political right that operate outside the realm of **civil society**, and indeed function to ground it. These principles are (i) freedom of action and (ii) equality of right. Thus, in the state of nature no individual has the right to transgress another individual's basic freedom. Locke justifies this claim by way of reference to a conception of natural law derived from the claims of reason, 'the common rule and measure God hath given to mankind' (*Second Treatise*, section 11). From a rational point of view, it is claimed, every individual has the right both to self-protection and to claim compensation for suffering a wrong at the hands of another. From this it is clear that a particular conception of the human individual (conceived in a manner which divorces human subjectivity from the constraints of modes of social organisation) forms the basis for Locke's political discourse.

Each individual is, in Locke's view, self-interested. From this it follows that some form of regulative body is required for the impartial administration of these rights. This forms part of the basis of Locke's justification for the existence of government, which constitutes a means of arbitrating between the disputes which necessarily will arise between individuals situated in a state of nature (section 13). Government, in turn, rests on the constitution of civil society, which is voluntarily arrived at through a contract (section 14). Thus, in Locke's view the legitimacy of governmental power should be derived from the consent of those who fall under it. In principle, one is only subject to the power of government if one has agreed to enter into civil society, and thereby become a civil agent.

For Locke, civil society is ultimately derived from one basic principle of natural law which operates within the state of nature: the right to the possession of one's own body and the products thereof. Locke's argument can be summarised thus (sections 25–30): (i) all humans situated in the state of nature have the right to self-preservation; (ii) the earth is the common possession of all human beings equally; (iii) its natural products thus belong in principle to everybody; (iv) however, since these products are available for use it follows that there must be some means whereby they may be appropriated and thereby subsequently owned; (v) there is one piece of property all humans possess, namely their own bodies; (vi) if you own your body, then the products of your labour are also yours; and (vii) hence, if you appropriate anything from the state of nature this must, by definition, be the result of your labour and consequently become yours. Once the latter point has been reached, Locke says, it follows that other persons do not have the right to take possession of what is now yours, namely the products of your labour, for goods appropriated in this manner from the state of nature become through this process a matter of 'private right'. This right is God given, since God would not have put the world of nature at humanity's disposal if it were not to be taken advantage of. There is, it follows, a 'law of reason', 'an original law of nature', which grounds the ownership of private property and thereby grounds civil society (section 30). In turn, on a Lockean account, the proper function of government is to protect the rights of individuals and of their property (both in the form of the individual's own body and the products of his or her labour). A limitation to appropriation in the state of nature is set by use: one may only own what can be used without waste (e.g. if one appropriates more apples than one can eat, they will go off and be wasted; and the same point goes for land). However, with the invention of money (which is a non-perishable good) this limitation is overcome. For instance, one may indeed own a large quantity of land, the products of which can be exchanged for cash and hence do not go to waste. In turn, it is possible thereby to justify unequal property ownership: 'since gold and silver, being little useful to the life of man, in proportion to food, raiment, and carriage, has its value only from the consent of men ... it is plain that the consent of men have agreed to the disproportionate and unequal possession of the earth' (section 50). Liberty, it follows, does not guarantee equality. Indeed, the progression from the state of nature to civil society is, for Locke, one which brings with it a necessary inequality with regard to the possession of goods.

Locke's thought exhibits a number of features common to many liberal thinkers. First, a central concern is with the basis of the individual's right to the ownership of goods, including above all his or her own body. Second, this right is paramount and it is the function of good government to protect it. Third, liberty, in turn, is understood as the freedom to be left alone to pursue one's own goals with the minimum of interference from others. Fourth, the function of the state is articulated and established within this basic assumption concerning liberty: a state should be based on consent (from which it derives its legitimacy and authority), and has as its proper function the protection of the rights of civil agents. Fifth, the state therefore has a limited role in the lives of individuals: it is not there to prescribe particular modes of behaviour which individuals ought to adhere to, but rather ought only to oversee the behaviour of individuals to the extent of ensuring that one person's actions do not infringe the rights of another. It follows that for thinkers within the liberal tradition the individual takes precedence over all other political concerns (i.e. individual liberty has priority over other values, such as equality).

These features are also evident in J.S. Mill's classic text *On Liberty* (1859). Mill's avowed aim in this text is to explore 'the nature and limits of the power which can be legitimately exercised by society over the individual' in the context of the social 'struggle between liberty and authority' (1859:59). There is, for Mill, an inherent political tension which exists between the spheres of liberty and authority, between individual freedom of thought and 'collective opinion' (manifested at its worst in the 'tyranny of the majority'). The individual is for Mill an independent entity with an accompanying right to this independence: 'his independence is, of right, absolute' (1859:69). An individual exhibits abilities (such as those of reflection and choice) as well as passions, desires and purposes. Taken together, these features allow for the identification of the individual as that which possesses interests. Given a situation in which a diversity of individuals are present in a society, it follows that such a society will also contain a diversity of interests. It is just such a form of society, one which both contains and is an expression of the diversity of human possibility, manifested in the form of the individual, that Mill favours as being the most progressive. Hence, Mill's account of individuality and political authority simultaneously implies an affirmation of a particular conception of cultural life. A more 'progressive culture' is taken to be synonymous with a liberal political culture, i.e. one in which individuality is fostered as the key basic value: 'It is not by wearing down into uniformity all that is individual ... but by cultivating it and calling it forth, within the limits imposed by the rights of others, that human beings become a beautiful and noble object of contemplation' (1859:127). As with Locke, then, for Mill the individual has rights which are established by way of reference to a regulative model of negative freedom. Freedom is, in other words, conceived as the freedom to act according to one's individual desires, providing that one does not infringe the liberties of others in the process ('freedom from ...', as opposed to 'freedom to ...'). As such, the liberal conception of individuality sets up a normative restriction which tells us what the boundaries of an agent's actions ought to be, even as it asserts the absolute right of individuals to be free from either state or consensual pressures which might impede their basic right to liberty.

More recently, John Rawls (in *A Theory of Justice* (1972)) has rearticulated many of the central tenets which underlie the thinking of both Locke and Mill. As with these two thinkers, Rawls is concerned to demonstrate that political right must be derived from the protection of individual interests, which are anchored within a rational framework capable of providing a normative model for individual agency. In Rawls's case, this framework is articulated through the postulation of the 'original position'. In the 'original position', Rawls says, a group of individuals would be placed behind a 'veil of ignorance' and asked to choose the basic rules which would underpin the society in which they will subsequently live. In such a position, these individuals have no knowledge of such things as what social status they will have, how much money they will possess, etc. Thus, the 'original position' functions as a heuristic device intended to show what choices rational agents divested of individual interest would make about the most favourable form of social order. Rawls's conception of the 'original position' shares common features with Locke's 'state of nature' theory. For example, it envisages that it is possible to describe rational human subjects removed from the constraints of social hierarchy, and in turn to adduce that they would favour a social order which maximises personal liberty. In addition, however, Rawls also argues that such individuals would elect for a society in which the possible injustices they would suffer were they to draw the short straw and find themselves at the bottom of the social pile are minimised (what is termed the 'maximin' principle). Once again, though, it is evident that Rawlsean liberalism envisages the key political issue as being concerned with individual liberty and how best to both maximise and protect it. As with Locke and Mill, individuals have liberty granted to them with the proviso that it ought not to transgress the interests of others.

It is apparent from the work of these three thinkers, however, that liberalism is not a term which may be used to define a particular procedural attitude concerning how to arrive at the best model of social order. Thus, where Locke and Rawls both resort to a model of justification which, in effect, removes the individual from their social context in order to derive the principles of right and liberty which then apply to them, for Mill this move is not necessary. In other words, Mill does not envisage a 'state of nature' theory (or something akin to it) as being necessary to the project of arguing for the primacy of the liberty of individual political agents. Indeed, Mill's conception of the individual is more socially embedded to the extent that individuality gains its meaning, for him, from the social context in which agents engage in their personal pursuits. Nevertheless, Mill is equally committed to the view that the individual's rights are paramount, and that the pursuit of the conditions which maximise individual liberty will lead to the most desirable forms of social organisation and cultural life. With regard to the state, likewise, liberals are not in common agreement. As already noted, a Rawlsean would argue that the maximisation of liberty must nevertheless be compatible with the minimisation of the risks to individual well-being that are present in society. A certain level of wealth redistribution being carried out by government is therefore justifiable in Rawls's view; whereas for a thinker like Locke, the unequal distribution of goods is a necessary consequence of human activity in civil society and one must simply accept this fact.

Along with their emphasis on the importance of individual liberty, liberals also show a commitment to a fairly rigid distinction between the public and private spheres of life. In other words, for a liberal like Mill, what an individual chooses to do with their own goods and even life is not a matter for public concern, so long as any choices that are made do not adversely affect the private rights of others. This line of thinking reflects the liberal emphasis on the individual as the basic unit of political discourse. Putting the matter another way, one might say that liberals are in general committed to an ontology of the individual—a metaphysical conception of the individual as an irreducible entity endowed with an existence that can be taken to transcend the limitations of any particular culture or society.

It may be tempting, in the light of the above, to oppose the thought of liberalism to more recent developments within **postmodernism**. For example, the postmodern critique of the **subject**, if convincing, might be regarded as sounding the death knell of the liberal conception of subjectivity and its accompanying commitment to its particular conception of liberty. However, this may not be the case. The American pragmatist thinker Richard Rorty, for example, does not shy away from describing himself as both a postmodernist *and* a liberal. Nor, it might be added, is it necessarily the case that certain liberal principles are excised by postmodernist criticism. Amongst the postmodernists, the work of Jean-François Lyotard may be cited as an example of a thinker who, in spite of his commitment to a critique of liberal conceptions of the political, nevertheless retains many features which can with justification be termed 'liberal'. Thus, in his book *The Differend: Phrases in Dispute* (and indeed elsewhere), Lyotard's advocacy of the pursuit of a plurality of 'genres of discourse' is not incompatible with the liberal's advocacy of a plurality of individual modes of existence. Indeed, it may be more germane to oppose liberal thought to that of the tradition of **Marxism** which, unlike that of the postmoderns, does not tend to regard the pursuit of multiplicity for its own sake in an uncritical light.

Further reading: Barry 1986; Grant 1987; Gray 1990; Kukathas 1989; Kymlicka 1989; Locke 1988; Lyotard 1988; Mill 1984; Moore 1993; Mulhall and Swift 1996; Rawls 1972; Rorty 1991; Sandel 1982, 1984.

PS

LIBERTARIANISM

As a political doctrine, libertarianism may be situated as an extreme form of **liberalism** and, like liberalism, it is historically rooted in the work of the seventeenth-century political philosopher John Locke. Libertarianism places a central emphasis upon the moral and political necessity of respecting human freedom, autonomy and responsibility. This freedom is principally expressed through the exercise of the right to own and enjoy property. Humans must be free to acquire property (but not by stealing the property of others) and to transfer property (by giving it away or by selling and exchanging it). The libertarian will therefore argue that state interference in the life of its citizens must be restricted. The state will have a duty to protect the basic freedoms of its citizens (and so will provide a police force and the legal apparatus necessary to support it). The state cannot, however, appropriate its citizens' property (in the form of taxation) for any other purpose. For example, to provide state education or health care would, first, require illegitimately appropriating citizens' property (to pay for these services), and second would fail to respect the autonomy and responsibility of citizens to organise their own education and health care. In libertarian thinking, the market plays a key role in the organisation of a free society.

Further reading: Nozick 1974.

AE

LIFE-CHANCES

A term used in **sociology** (especially where influenced by Max Weber) to refer to the opportunities that members of social groups have for acquiring positively valued goods and rewards, and avoiding negatively valued goods. Thus, life-chances encompass not just overtly economic goods (such as wealth, income and material possessions), but also cultural goods (including the opportunities for education and consumption of or participation in the arts), health and criminality. Typically, life-chances will be correlated with a person's economic **class**, so that the higher up the class hierarchy one is, the greater one's chances to enjoy a high income, a long and good quality education, and to avoid illness and premature mortality, and to avoid criminal prosecution.

Further reading: Dahrendorf 1979.

AE

LIFE-WORLD

The concept of 'life-world' was introduced by the German phenomenologist Edmund Husserl, to refer to the expectations and practical skills that human beings have, prior to any conscious or theoretical engagement with the world. While these beliefs and abilities may once have been consciously acquired, and thus they are the product of theoretical reflection upon the social and physical worlds, they are now taken for granted and largely unnoticed. They have become 'sedimented' in the life-world, which we acquire as we learn to become competent social agents. The life-world is thus composed of 'stocks of knowledge' (according to Alfred Schutz), or skills and expectations that allow us to give meaning to (and indeed to construct) the social world within which we live. The concept has been taken up recently in the social theory of Jürgen Habermas, where the life-world, as the everyday experience of the world as something meaningful and as within our control, is set against the systematic or seemingly objective, meaningless and constraining aspects of social life.

Further reading: Habermas 1984, 1987; Husserl 1954; Schutz 1962.

AE

LITERARY CRITICISM

Literary criticism encompasses the analysis, interpretation and evaluation of literary texts. It attempts to identify the text's meaning and addresses questions concerning the larger social relevance of a particular work. In its historical development, the original focus was on the author and has gradually moved over to the text, while incorporating some discussion of the role of the reader and the historical period when the text was written.

The emergence of literary criticism went along with the desire to become conscious of the meaning of **culture** and **society**. In many ways it is part of an emancipatory project (an inheritance of the **Enlightenment**) which attempts to understand the **self** in relation to its historical context. A self-conscious attitude towards the capacities of the mind is one of the hallmarks of criticism, and detailed investigations of the imagination produce theories of literature which not only leave far behind any simplistic equations between the poet and the liar, but deal interestingly with the complex of questions around **realism**.

The most important debate in literary criticism has always concerned the relation between **text** and historical reality. Literature unquestionably refers to external reality, but it is extremely difficult to gauge what kind of reference this is. By means of representing the experience of social relationships, the text effects a social positioning: however distanced or defamiliarised the fictional narrative may be, the text is always written from a certain perspective and deploys its **rhetoric** to implicate the reader in its own ideological stance. Because literature which is assumed to have a right to this title critically engages with its own premises, it dramatises a tension between descriptive and prescriptive standards. It is, then, criticism's task to tease out the ways and means by which literature permits certain conventions and stereotypical assumptions to be contested. An important starting point for such a task is to analyse the text's mode of address and to ask what kind of subjectivity it projects onto its readers. The analysis of **irony**, here, is as significant as the task of seeking to identify contradictions and logical inconsistencies in the text's argument. While New Critical readings claimed that it is illegitimate either to assume that poetry consists of arguments or to produce a paraphrase of its meaning, recent critical theories have insistently pointed out that a meaningful critical methodology concentrates on plural meanings and discusses the ways in which different interpretations conflict with each other.

In its original deployment as a technique of scriptural exegesis, such criticism treated sacred writings as a self-present entity because the text was taken as a direct revelation of the divine spirit. But twentieth-century hermeneutic theories point out that understanding individual textual passages is only possible on the basis of previous knowledge about the fictional rendition of experience. What is referred to by the concept of the 'hermeneutic circle' describes the difficulties with reaching through to a sense of first-hand experience which exactly reproduces the perceptions implied by the literary text. It is the idea of there being an immediate access to an ideational realm that is most sharply contested, especially by deconstructionist critiques of language and ideology.

In its New Critical guise, literary criticism expressed an authoritative view of the text's meaning. But in spite of the idea that an exclusive focus on the objectively present 'words on the page' would reduce the arbitrariness of interpretation, both **New Criticism** and **structuralism** were soon forced to abandon their appeals to objectivity. In the post-structuralist and deconstructionist view of interpretation, the problem of misinterpretation was circumvented through establishing an aesthetics of literature which hailed the plural text. This is to say that the text itself was no longer viewed as an entity that could be reduced to one singular meaning. The drawback of this view, however, is that a text could be understood as saying almost anything and the task of criticism became that of selecting relevant interpretations from a vast range of plausible or conceivable options.

Other questions belonging to the discipline of literary criticism concern the relation between literature and criticism. Because criticism is itself a textual genre, it has been claimed that no generic difference can be assumed to exist between text and interpretation. Discussions of literary value, which are now topical in relation to discussions of the status of popular fiction, are an old concern which has particular salience at a moment when **cinema** and other **mass media** have a more immediate impact on the imagination of the late twentieth century than other, more sophisticated forms of art. These issues in literary criticism make it clear that the attempt to explicate the meaning of literature is a major site of ideological struggle.

Further reading: Eagleton 1983; Lodge 1972; Rice and Waugh 1989; Wellek 1986.

CK

MARXISM

Marxism refers to those schools of social, economic, political and philosophical enquiry that derive their approach from the work of Karl Marx and Friedrich Engels. The interpretations and developments of Marx's work are extremely diverse. They share an approach to the analysis of society that gives primacy to economic activity, although key debates within Marxism centre on the degree to which the economic **base** determines the nature and structure of the rest of society. Societies are understood as being structured according to the exploitation of subordinate **classes** by a dominant class. Historical change is therefore typically analysed in terms of developments within the economic base, that are manifest as class conflict and revolution. As a political philosophy, Marxism remains committed to the realisation of a non-exploitative society (communism), typically through the liberation of the **proletariat**, the subordinate class within **capitalism**. Again, a central debate, especially in the earlier periods of Marxism, concerned the degree to which the proletariat revolution was an inevitable event, brought about by the forces of historical change, or whether Marxist political parties were obliged to actively bring about revolution. As Marx wrote little directly on **culture**, there is great scope for diverse applications of his work to cultural studies. What is perhaps common to most Marxist approaches to culture is a recognition that culture is entwined with class struggle through **ideology**. That is to suggest that culture is produced within a class-divided society, and will participate either in the maintenance and **legitimation** of existing power relations, or in resisting that power. Three broad approaches to Marxism, and thus to the Marxist theorisation of culture, can be identified.

Classical Marxism is derived, by Kautsk and Plekhanov, and later by Lenin and Trotsky, from the work carried out by Engels in the 1870s and 1880s (Engels 1947). It presents Marxism as a scientific account of social change. As such, in a dogmatic form, it became the official Marxist doctrine of the Soviet Union. The theory of culture most closely associated with this Marxism is Plekhanov's reflection theory. In *Art and Society* (1912), he develops a **sociology** of art, in explicit opposition to the doctrine of art for art's sake, that would isolate art from political and economic reality. Culture therefore comes to be seen as 'the mirror of social life'. Under the Stalinist Zhdanov, this becomes the stultifying dogmatism of socialist **realism**. In comparison to Plekhanov's account of art simply reflecting on society, for Zhdanov the artist is an engineer of the human soul, educating the working classes and portraying reality in its revolutionary development. The finest exponent of socialist realism as a literary theory was Georg Lukács. For Lukács, the nineteenth-century realist novel offered the most politically progressive form of the novel. Balzac, for example, is praised (despite his overt political conservatism), in so far as his novels articulate the underlying social forces, rather than merely documenting the surface appearance of society.

Paradoxically, earlier work by Lukács, and in particular his *History and Class Consciousness* (1923), is the key influence on the development of Western Marxism. Lukács interprets Marx as the inheritor of the German philosophical tradition, and thus sees Marx's social theory as a materialist reworking of Hegelian idealism. Marxism becomes a humanist philosophy, rather than a science. It challenges positivist approaches to social science that would attempt to explain society through the methods of the natural sciences. In contrast, Western Marxism focuses on the problem of bringing an objectified society back under the control of its human members. Hence, the theory, and indeed **metaphor**, of **alienation** (and in the work of Lukács and the **Frankfurt School**, **reification**) is of prime importance. Humanity is not at home in the world that should be its home. Culture can therefore be attributed a complex position within society, and its aesthetic worth intertwined with its political value. Regressive culture, on the one hand, is understood as ideology. It reproduces the categories of thought and reasoning that make the existing social order appear to be natural and legitimate. Walter Benjamin, for example, laments the use that fascism can make of the core categories of traditional aesthetics, such as 'originality' and 'genius' (1970b). Progressive culture, on the other hand, is interpreted as an expression of alienation and an act of political resistance. The work of the German philosopher Ernst Bloch, for example, explores the utopian aspirations, the yearnings for a better and more just society, that are embedded in the most diverse forms of culture. **Frankfurt School** theorists, including T.W. Adorno and Max Horkheimer, see high culture, especially, as being one of the few spaces in which one can think differently and challenge the ideological illusions of dominant, economically motivated (and positivistic) thought. Similarly, Bertolt Brecht's theatre, and specifically the notion of alienation effect, disrupts the illusions of politically conservative theatre. The theory of **hegemony**, developed by the Italian Marxist Antonio Gramsci, advances the theory of ideology precisely by recognising that the ruling class cannot simply impose its own interpretation of the world upon the subordinate classes. Any such interpretation will be negotiated, so that culture becomes a site of class struggle.

In the 1960s, the anti-humanist, or **structuralist** Marxism, of Louis Althusser represented a new stage in the development of Marxism. The Hegelianism of Western Marxism is rejected, in favour of a scientific approach. Further, the economic determinism of Soviet Marxism is also thrown into question, so that the economic is seen to be determinant only in the 'last instance', thereby giving the other spheres of society **relative autonomy**. Althusser opened a conception of ideology as lived practice (rather than purely intellectual reflection), which in turn offered new approaches to the analysis of everyday culture that were particularly significant for the newly emerging cultural studies. The implications of these arguments for art and literature were explored most significantly by Pierre Macherey (1978, 1995). Macherey rejects ideas of creativity and the notion of the author, and indeed of criticism as evaluation or interpretation. The **production** of the literary **text** is treated rather as a determinate material practice, working in and on the raw material of ideology. Literature generates an 'implicit critique' of ideology, exposing the relationship between ideology and the material conditions of its existence.

It may be suggested that **cultural studies** have increasingly moved into a post-Marxist phase. A number of influential thinkers, including Baudrillard and Lyotard, may be seen to have developed away from initial Marxist influences, ultimately to question not merely the understanding of culture found in Marxism, but more specifically the accounts of politics and **history** that underpin that understanding.

Further reading: Bottomore 1983; Kolakowski 1978; Lunn 1982.

AE

MASS MEDIA

The mass media of communication are those **institutions** that produce and distribute information and visual and audio images on a large scale. Historically, the mass media may be dated from the invention of the printing press, and thus, in the West, from Johann Gutenberg's commercial exploitation of printing around 1450. The early products of printing presses were religious or literary works, along with medical and legal texts. In the sixteenth and seventeenth centuries, periodicals and newspapers began to appear regularly. Industrialisation led to a further expansion in the book and newspaper industries in the nineteenth century. The twentieth century has seen the introduction and rapid expansion of electronic media (**cinema**, radio and **television**), to the point at which they have become a dominant element in the experience and organisation of everyday life.

The first significant attempts to theorise the mass media in the twentieth century began within the framework of mass society theory. Developed most significantly in the second quarter of the century, not least as a response to the rise of Nazism and **Fascism**, mass society theory typically presented industrial society as degenerating into an undifferentiated, irrational and emotive mass of people, cut off from tradition and from any fine sensitivity to aesthetic or moral values. The mass entertainment media are thereby presented as key instruments in the creation of this mass, precisely in so far as they are seen to appeal to the more base elements of popular taste (thus reducing all content to some lowest common denominator) in the search for large audiences. The media thereby serve to undermine traditional and local cultural difference, and, in the emotional nature of their content, to inhibit rational responses to the messages they present. Entertainment is complemented by the use of radio, especially, as an instrument of political propaganda, or more precisely in **Marxism**, as one of the core contemporary instruments of **ideology**. Mass society theory may therefore be seen to attribute enormous power to the media, and, as a complementary presupposition, to present the audience as the more or less passive victim of the messages foisted upon it. The **empirical** research that such theory fostered, 'effects' research, tends to look for the harmful effects that the media had, both politically (in inhibiting democracy) and morally (for example in encouraging violence). This assumption of media power was, paradoxically, in the media's own interests, in that it implied that they were a powerful and effective tool of advertising.

A more subtle approach to media research emerged in the post-war period, within the framework of sociological **functionalism**. 'Uses and gratifications' research attributes greater activity and diversity to members of the audience, in so far as they are assumed to have subjectively felt needs, created by the social and physical environments, that the media can fulfil. The central functions performed by the media include escapism (in so far as media consumption allows a legitimate withdrawal from the pressures of normal life), the establishing of personal relationships (including the use of media programmes as the focus of discussion and other social interaction) and the formation of personal identity (whereby the values expressed by programmes are seen to reinforce one's personal values).

In the 1950s, a Canadian school of media theory emerged, principally in the work of Harold Innis and Marshall McLuhan. The central argument here was that there was a causal link between the dominant form of communication and the organisation of a society. Thus, Innis (1950, 1951) distinguished 'time biased media' from 'space biased media'. The former, such as clay and stone, could not easily be transported, but were durable, thus leading to stable social phenomena, grounded in the reproduction of tradition over long periods of time. The latter (such as paper) are less durable, but are easily transported. They could therefore support the expansion of administrative and political authority over large territories. McLuhan (1994) argued that the development of new media technologies has a fundamental impact on human cognition. The introduction of printing leads to greater compartmentalisation and specialisation of the human senses, as communication comes to be dominated by the printed page (as opposed to oral communication previously). Vision thus becomes dominant, but deals with information that is presented in a linear, uniform and infinitely repeatable manner. Thought thus becomes standardised and analytical. Print also leads to individualism, as reading becomes silent and private. Print culture, which for McLuhan as for Innis is space biased, is challenged by electronic media. Electronic media, in their proliferation and continual presence, annihilate space and time. Confronting us continually, modern media do not have to be sought out. Similarly, the act of reading or consuming various media is no longer confined to particular periods of the day. Information from diverse locations and even periods in history are juxtaposed in a single newspaper or evening's television. The modern experience is thus one of an unceasing relocation of information in space and time, leading to what McLuhan termed 'the global village'. While McLuhan's theories fell from fashion in the 1970s, they bear a resemblance to much recent postmodernist thinking.

New strands of media theory emerged in the 1960s and 1970s, in no small part through increasing interest specifically in **television**. Two extremes may be identified. At one, concern is with the material base that determines cultural production. The political economy of the mass media thus focused on institutional structures that under-pinned media production (and thus its contents and value orientations). Murdock and Golding (1977), for example, looked at the structures of share ownership and control that linked media organisations into multinational **capitalism**. At the other, emphasis is placed upon media content as texts, in need of interpretation or decoding. The increasing influence of **semiotics** led to a fundamental re-evaluation of the role of the media audience. They cease to be mere victims of the media, and come to be seen as actively engaging with media products, interpreting them in a plurality of ways that may be at odds with the possibly ideological intentions of the producers. The work of the **Birmingham Centre for Contemporary Cultural Studies** and Stuart Hall is crucial here. From this, **cultural studies** may be seen to lead, less to theorisation of the mass media per se, than to the development of distinctive theories and accounts of specific media (such as television, **popular music** and even the Sony Walkman).

Jürgen Habermas (1989a) and Jean Baudrillard offer two distinct, yet general accounts of the place of the mass media in the experience and development of contemporary society. Habermas's theory centres on the concept of the public sphere. The **bourgeois** public sphere emerged in Europe in the seventeenth and eighteenth centuries, as critical self-reflection and reflection upon the state, conducted first in coffee houses and salons, and then through pamphlets, journals and newspapers. While in practice this public sphere was exclusive, allowing participation by the propertied, rational and male bour-geoisie, Habermas finds in it a principle of the open, and thus democratic, use of public reason. Contemporary electronic media are seen to have a complex, **dialectical** impact on this sphere. Positively, modern production techniques can make complex, critical and culturally demanding material widely available. In practice, cultural consumption has become increasingly privatised, breaking up the public sphere, and dominated by low-quality material, designed to have a mass appeal. In politics, this leads to the degradation of political debate and policy formation into an increasingly stage-managed political theatre.

Baudrillard (1990b, 1990c, 1993) understands contemporary capitalism in terms of symbolic (as opposed to strictly economic) exchange. The contemporary world is therefore dominated by **signs**, images and representations, to such a degree that the distinction between the sign and its referent, the real world, collapses (so that one can no longer speak to the real needs or interests of the people, for example). The mass media (and particularly television) are central to this production and exchange of signs, and it is to the nature of the consumption of these signs that Baudrillard looks in order to outline a pessimistic theory of the impact of the mass media on democratic society. Baudrillard's consumer is typically a channel hopper and couch potato. On the one hand, television transforms the world into easily consumable fragments, and yet does so within the gamut of media that produce more information than any one person could absorb and understand, so that it attracts only a superficial 'ludic curiosity'. On the other hand, the media swallow up private space, for although typically consumed privately, they intrude upon our most intimate moments by making them public. Nothing is taboo any longer, and the immediacy of media coverage inhibits the possibility of critical reflection. An opinion poll, for example, cannot appeal to a genuine public. It does not manipulate the public, for the public (and the distinction between public and private) has ceased to exist. The expression of political opinion is reduced to a yes/no decision, akin to the choice or rejection of a supermarket brand, or a film. Resistance, for Baudrillard, can then rest only in a refusal to participate in this system.

Further reading: Giner 1976; McQuail 1994; Stevenson 1995.

AE

MEANING

Philosophically, there seems little theoretical agreement as to a definition of this term or as to 'where' exactly meaning resides. Indeed, this lack of agreement is so marked that some philosophers would question its very existence. An understanding of this lack of agreement is perhaps best grasped by examining the historical development of the term.

One of the most influential theories of meaning, 'nomenclaturism', dates from philosophical antiquity. This is basically the idea that the meaning of a name or kind term is the object for which it stands. The grounding assumption of the theory is that there is an essential or natural relationship between a linguistic sign and the object it 'stands for' in a language. It was this doctrine that Plato discussed in his *Cratylus*.

A view very much akin to this is still influential today. Perhaps the best known of its modern supporters is Bertrand Russell (1918, 1924) and the *early* Wittgenstein (1921). This view, which became known as 'logical atomism', dates approximately from the turn of the twentieth century. The idea central to this philosophy is that the sentences in a language can only have a meaning if they are composed of smaller units of meaning which, in turn, derive their meaning from their direct relationship with states of affairs in the world. This view was the precursor of logical **positivism**, which was supported by the members of the 'Vienna Circle'. Perhaps the most concise exposition of this philosophical theory was given by A.J. Ayer (1946). At the core of logical positivism lies the 'principle of verification', which stipulates that the meaning of a sentence or proposition is the method of its verification. In other words, the meaning of a sentence is defined by the observations which would serve to show its truth or falsity. By definition of the theory, if a sentence is not verifiable by these means it is *meaningless*. Thus, for example, the propositions of traditional **metaphysics** would have no meaning because the conditions of their verifiability could not be given.

The opposing view to logical atomism is that of semantic **holism**. This view has its roots in the works of Frege (1892) and Saussure (1916). From the perspective of **analytic philosophy**, Frege opened the door to the view that language plays an active part in the construction of our notion of **reality** (see **reference**). Saussure, likewise from the perspective of **structuralism**, made a similar point. The most influential figure upon the modern philosophy of science is that of W.V.O. Quine (1953). Quine challenged the notion that there could be a viable theory of meaning couched in terms of any fragment of a language. Instead, language was to be viewed as a holistic structure, the meaning of whose parts were dependent upon the whole. A similar view to this was held by the philosopher of science Pierre Duhem (1962). This combined view subsequently became known as the 'Quine–Duhem hypothesis': that a physicist, when performing an experiment, is never testing a single hypothesis but, rather, a whole group of hypotheses.

A more full-blooded version of this approach to meaning in the philosophy of science was developed by Thomas S. Kuhn (1970). Kuhn said that the sciences comprised a number of **paradigms** which supplied the scientists who worked within them with their **worldviews**. These paradigms, in turn, comprised the theories and assumptions which scientists currently held to be true. The meaning of each of the terms in these theories was defined by its relation to the other terms within the paradigm. Consequently, the meaning of any term, sentence or phrase was, by implication, internal to the paradigm. Thus, when a paradigm changed, the meanings of the terms within it also changed; the net result being that members of different scientific paradigms shared different worldviews. The implication of Kuhn's theory leads to the problem of 'incommensurability'.

A similar view, with reference to ordinary language, was supported by the *later* Wittgenstein (1953) and was encompassed by his notion of a 'language game'. On this view, the meaning of a term is dependent on how it is used within a particular language game. The implication is that although certain words can share a 'family resemblance' in that they sound or look the same, their meanings will vary across language games. Although they have many theoretical differences, this view shares certain important similarities with the work of Saussure in that 'meaning' on this model is internal to and dependent upon a language or, for Wittgenstein, part of a language (Harris 1988). Both the views of Wittgenstein and Saussure have had a significant influence on the schools of **postmodernism** and **post–structuralism**.

The holist view of language has certain fundamentally important implications for not only the physical sciences but also the social sciences. If meanings are internal to a particular language or language game, then communication between one language or language game and another becomes problematic in that no common medium of communication exists between them. If languages or language games are concomitant with particular cultures or parts of a culture, then it seems to follow that communication between cultures or parts of a culture become similarly problematical (see **cultural relativism**). This being so, then the possibility of making cross-cultural comparisons seems ruled out as a matter of course since, by definition, the social scientist is as trapped within the confines of a particular language or language game as those he or she professes to study.

A possible route out of this problematic is at least promised by Quine's notion of 'radical translation' and is taken up again, more successfully, by Donald Davidson.

Perhaps the most damaging challenge to meaning comes from the work of Jacques Derrida (1967). One of the central assumptions of any theory of meaning is that a language can remain in a state of equilibrium long enough for meanings to become a possibility. Such an assumption is certainly true, at least at a methodological level, of Saussure's theory of language. At the centre of his theory is the notion that the meaning or value (*'valeur'*) of a linguistic **sign** in any language comes from its **difference** to all the other signs in that language. The stability of meaning for each sign is preserved provided that a rigid distinction can be maintained between 'la *langue*' and '*parole*'. What Derrida does, in effect, is challenge the validity of this distinction as used by Saussure. Derrida mounts this challenge by deconstructing (see **deconstruction**) Saussure's opposition between speech and writing. Saussure views writing as posing a fundamental threat to the stable oral tradition of a language. To avoid this threat he gives the privileged position in this opposition to speech. Derrida not only reverses the polarity of this opposition, but also employs the logic Saussure uses to construct it to create just the kind of linguistic deformations that the latter wishes to prevent. The net result is the loss of the necessary stability required to keep the meanings of individual signs intact.

Generally it is held, at least by analytic philosophers, that there is a close relationship between the notion of 'meaning' and that of reference.

SH

MEANS OF PRODUCTION

In **Marxism**, 'means of production' refers to all the material resources used in production. The major class divisions in any society are understood in terms of ownership and control, or lack of ownership and control, of the means of production. Thus, in **capitalism**, the **bourgeoisie** owns factories, raw materials and other productive resources, and is able to control what is produced, and the disposal of that product. The subordinate **proletariat** have only their ability to labour, which they sell to the bourgeois capitalist.

Further reading: Cutler *et al.* 1977.

AE

MECHANICAL SOLIDARITY AND ORGANIC SOLIDARITY

Terms in Durkheim's **sociology** that explain the cohesion of pre-industrial and industrial societies respectively. In industrial societies there is a complex **division of labour** which entails that each member of a society is a specialist, unable to provide for his or her needs without co-operation and exchange with others. Society therefore coheres because individuals do not have the resources to secede from it. In contrast, Durkheim characterises pre-industrial society by the lack of specialised roles. Each family unit could, in principle, live independently from the rest of the society. Cohesion is maintained through repressive laws that embody commonly shared values (see *conscience collective*), typically imbued with sacred qualities. Any individual transgressing these laws will be severely punished, typically by being ostracised from the society.

AE

MEDIATION

Mediation can have two distinct meanings. At its simplest, and its closest to ordinary English usage, it refers to anything that comes between two other things. In the study of **mass media**, mediation is therefore anything which (or anybody who) conveys a message to the audience. A reporter mediates between the event reported and the audience; or a fictional detective mediates between the audience and its understanding of the police and criminality. In German philosophy (for example as found in the **Frankfurt School** and other forms of **Marxism**), mediation has a more technical usage, closer to 'construction'. Thus, in Marxism, to observe that the **subject** is mediated by the object is to observe that the human subject—the individual or person—is substantially created or constituted by the objective forces—be these biological laws, or more likely, the coercive force of social pressures—that act upon him or her. Similarly, our (subjective) understanding of the social world will be shaped and constructed by ideological and cultural frameworks; these frameworks mediate our experience and perception.

AE

MERITOCRACY

A meritocracy is a society with an occupational hierarchy (see **social stratification**). Different occupations will enjoy different rewards, **power** and **status**. However, in a meritocracy, individuals move up and down this hierarchy (see **social mobility)** on the basis of merit, which is to say, on the basis of the talents and qualifications that they possess, and the appropriateness of these attributes to the tasks required in the given occupation. The most highly rewarded occupations will also be those which are most important to the society that requires rare skills, or requires skills and knowledge that take a long time to acquire, and which carry the highest levels of responsibility. (It is assumed that financial and other rewards are necessary, in order to motivate the most appropriate people to undertake the training necessary to fulfil the occupation.)

The **liberal** philosopher John Rawls has offered a highly influential defence of meritocracy as being fundamental to a just and fair society (1972). He is, however, at pains to distinguish what he calls a 'callous meritocracy' from fair equality of opportunity. In the former, a person's education will depend predominantly upon what his or her parents can afford. Thus, the children of successful parents will be more likely to acquire prestigious jobs, because they are likely to have had a better education. This would lead to wide inequalities in society. Rawls therefore defends an education system to which everyone has equal access, to ensure that the talents a person does have are recognised and cultivated, regardless of that person's parental background.

Further reading: Young 1958.

AE

METAPHOR

Broadly, a trope in which one thing is referred to by a term which literally describes something else—the term derives from the Greek *metaphora*, meaning transfer or carry over. Hence in Aristotle's *Rhetoric*, metaphor is presented as a word used in a changed and illuminating sense: 'ordinary words convey only what we know already; it is from metaphor that we can best get a hold of something fresh.'

More recently too, metaphor's status in the growth and development of language has invited special attention from philosophers and literary theorists. Various, more or less technical, accounts have been given of what metaphors actually are, how they function, and what, if anything, they contribute at a semantic or cognitive level. In Max Black's influential analysis, for example, the metaphorical utterance contains two 'subjects'—primary and secondary—and works by 'projecting upon' the primary subject (e.g. 'Uncle Ted') a set of associated implications (e.g. 'is a low dog') which act as a kind of filter through which a new angle on, and understanding of, the primary subject is achieved. Thus anatomised, metaphor is more than a mere ornament: it has a privileged, specific role in the application of words to world, and particularly in understanding by comparison.

The reverberating influence of Nietzsche's oft-cited description of truth as 'a mobile army of metaphors' suggests that metaphoricity may go deeper still. For if, as he suggested, literal truths are simply 'metaphors which are worn out and without sensuous power; coins which have lost their pictures and now matter only as metal, no longer as coins', metaphor, rather than being an isolable mode of linguistic meaning, becomes its very basis. Simultaneously, the distinction between the literal and the metaphorical becomes a temporal, rather than an abstractly semantic, matter; the former becoming roughly equivalent to familiar, or normal language use, and the latter to the unfamiliar, or abnormal.

Subsequent developments have pushed metaphor further up the theoretical agenda. Heidegger's interpretation of the Greek word for truth (*aletheia*) as 'disclosure' or 'unconcealment' rather than the strict 'representation' of reality lends much to the idea that the creativity of the metaphorical process is central to truth rather than a superficial distraction. In Jakobson's structuralist linguistics, metaphor, along with metonymy, it is one of the two basic poles of the functioning of language. For Jacques Lacan, metaphor, as the substitution of one word for another, is central to his linguistification of the Freudian concept of condensation. And much has been made of metaphor's importance to intellectual and cultural progress by those, like Mary Hesse, Hayden White and Richard Rorty, who would extend its pivotal status respectively to scientific hypotheses, historiography and all descriptive writing of any kind. Thus, for Rorty, the first time Copernicus claimed that the earth revolves around the sun he was simply trying out a new, abnormal, way of speaking—a metaphor which, for reasons more cultural and political than strictly veridical, happens to have 'stuck' as the now-normal, common-sense account.

For some, the conceptual prioritisation of metaphor reaches its apogee with Jacques Derrida's apparent refusal to allow any distinction between literal and metaphorical meaning at all, and the efforts of trigger-happy deconstructionists to expose the artifice of all claims to objectivity. Others, though, see Derrida as highlighting the necessity of precisely the sort of philosophical account of metaphor which the demonstrable metaphoricity of even the most mundane language would seem to demand.

In any case there are those, sold on the idea that reality is best viewed as a linguistic or discursive construction, who would extend the Nietzschean line to the point where all claims and propositions, and all forms of cultural discourse, can be read as metaphorical: where metaphor, in other words, goes 'all the way down'. The consequences are many and profound, not least the blurring of distinctions between truth and ideology, science and superstition, or simulacrum and (supposed) real life. This may, however, deny what is particular about metaphor's importance to descriptive practice. Certainly, questions remain about what an adequate definition of metaphor might be, whether and how it might be distinguished from literal meaning, and whether it *creates* meaning or simply *rehearses* it (see Davidson 1984a). Whatever the scope for final answers, few would now dispute its integral role in the functioning of discourse in general.

Further reading: Black 1979; Cooper 1986; Davidson 1984a; Derrida 1982; Nietzsche 1995.

GC

METAPHYSICS

Metaphysics is traditionally regarded as the study of reality as it is beyond mere appearance. The threefold purpose of this study is purportedly to find out (i) what the world is 'really' like, (ii) why the world exists and (iii) what our place is, as human beings, in this world. More recently metaphysicians have tended, in the main, to limit their investigations to (i) and (iii), thereby, in accordance with modern physics, regarding (ii) as largely unanswerable.

As a result of their attempts to answer all three of the questions of metaphysics, traditional metaphysicians have tended towards system building. They have attempted to explain the true nature of reality by constructing a model of that reality which integrates the answers to the three questions of metaphysics into a single, general and complete answer. Perhaps the grandest employment of this methodology was by Hegel, who held that the universe was just one substance ('mind' or 'Geist') which was in the process of coming to know itself. Examples of other philosophers who have employed this methodology are G.W. Leibniz and, to a slightly more limited extent, Bishop Berkeley. This style of metaphysics has tended to attract philosophers sympathetic to idealism and of a rationalist inclination. The rationalists regard the only reliable tools to discovering the 'true' nature of reality as being the power of reason and the faculties of the intellect. This approach complements the notion of system building in that the key to achieving a good system is to use this power and these faculties to construct a general and suitably coherent theory of the universe which could answer, in an integrated fashion, the three questions of metaphysics.

Perhaps the greatest challenge to traditional idealist metaphysics comes from the work of Immanuel Kant in the form of his 'transcendental idealism'. Kant held that the approach of the traditional metaphysician could never work because it tried to accomplish too much. His view was that although there was a world beyond mere appearance, we can never know what that world is like in itself because how we come to know that world will be restricted by what we, as rational creatures, bring to it. What we bring to the world is what Kant calls the 'categories', which are the conditions of our thinking about the world. Numbered among these categories are the concepts of 'time' and 'space', and 'cause' and 'effect'. Thus, in a sense, although there is a world independent of how we think about it, it is forever beyond our reach and, consequently, we must settle for investigating the world as it appears to us. Granted this point, it was the influence of Kant that first firmly bound the questions of metaphysics to those of **epistemology**.

The most recent debates in metaphysics have tended to centre around the dispute between those who support metaphysical **realism** and those who support anti-realism in its various more or less extreme versions. The supporters of metaphysical realism reflect and are historically rooted in the concerns of those who have traditionally opposed both rationalism and idealism, i.e. the supporters of **empiricism**. Metaphysical realists hold to the view that there is a mind-independent material/physical reality which we can come to know. Thus, not only does it *appear* that there are such things as trees, cats and stones, but these things *actually exist* in the mind-independent world (van Inwagen 1993).

Opponents of metaphysical realism have become known as anti-realists. However, it is important to distinguish here what exactly the anti-realists are opposed to, and whether they are *all* opposed to the same thing. Indeed, some anti-realists are simply opposed to any *straightforward* notion of reality but not necessarily reality per se, and there are those who seem opposed to the notion of reality in toto. The latter group includes analytic philosophers (see **analytic philosophy**) like Richard Rorty (1972) and Nelson Goodman (1978) and postmodernists (see **postmodernism**) such as Jean Baudrillard

(1988). In the former group we have philosophers such as Hilary Putnam (1981) and Thomas S. Kuhn (1970) who, claiming to work in the shadow of Kant, seem to want to note the problematics connected with reaching reality rather than rejecting it as a notion out of hand.

Some philosophers have opposed the project of metaphysics altogether. Within analytic philosophy we have the logical positivists who claim that the metaphysicians could say nothing meaningful (Ayer 1946). This is because they could not state the conditions which allow us to judge a metaphysical statement true or false (see **meaning**). More recently, there has been opposition to what Jacques Derrida calls the 'metaphysics of presence'. Derrida has been variously interpreted as either denying anything as being exterior to the **text** or, less radically, simply showing the hopelessness of speaking of **reality** outside of any particular interpretative framework (see Norris 1987: chapter 6).

Further reading: Kim and Sosa 1994; Walsh 1963.

SH

METONYMY

A form of communication in which a part or element is used to stand for the whole. At its simplest, we talk of a herd of cattle, or speak of the crown, when we refer to the monarch. However, we also understand many complex **texts** through metonymy. For example, in a news photograph, a single poor peasant farmer may stand for all peasants, or all members of a certain community, nation or continent. As such, metonymy can play a role in **mythology**, as defined by Barthes. In making the interpretative move from the element that is presented to the whole, we draw, unwittingly, upon certain politically and factually questionable, but none the less taken-for-granted (and thus apparently natural), assumptions. Thus, the single peasant farmer may reinforce the unspoken belief that all Africans, say, are the impoverished victims of an adverse climate.

AE

MINORITY

Usually a social group which is in a numerically inferior position to others within a **society**, and consequently is susceptible to suffering at the hands of majority opinion. The term 'minority', therefore, can often signify an inferior social position or marginalised interests in virtue of a lack of power when it comes to having one's views or interests voiced. Likewise, being in a minority (especially, for example, in the context of being an ethnic minority) can lead to states of inequality and misrepresentation (see **stereotype**). However, it is worth noting that an **oligarchy**, for example, is a minority in the numerical sense, although it wields power over other social groups.

The philosopher J.S. Mill (one of the most famous proponents of **liberalism**) diagnosed modern, popular democratic societies as having the greatest potential for infringing on the rights of minorities in the name of popular, majority opinion (Mill's term for this was the 'tyranny of the majority'). According to Mill, minority interests (and principally the right of minority opinion represented by the autonomy of thought which, he argued, was the preserve of the **individual**) needs to be both respected and preserved if a society is to attain its greatest potential. In Mill's terms, the greatest cultural good is synonymous with the maximisation of a plurality of views and lifestyles within a society, and hence with the preservation of the rights of expression of minority opinion.

Gilles Deleuze and Félix Guattari have argued that a distinction needs to be drawn between 'majoritarian' and 'minoritarian' systems of representation and the social effects of these systems. To be minoritarian, in their view, means to have marginalised interests within a social order; thus, being minoritarian is not synonymous with being in a minority. Women, for example, may be a majority in terms of sheer number, but are minoritarian if their interests are marginalised by the dominant power structures and signifying systems which operate in a society or **culture** in such a way as to place them in a position of social inferiority.

Further reading: Deleuze and Guattari 1987; Mill 1984.

PS

MODE OF PRODUCTION

In **Marxism**, history is understood as the determinate succession of distinct epochs or modes of production (Marx and Engels 1970). Marx identifies six historical epochs: primitive communism, ancient slave society, **feudalism**, **capitalism**, **socialism** and communism. Each has a distinctive economic character, analysed in terms of its

forces and **relations of production**, which is to say, the level of technology within the society and the relationship between producers and the owners or controllers of the resources required for production (the **means of production**). The mode of production is therefore the distinctive interrelationship of forces and relations of production, and their associated structures of economic exploitation. While strictly no historically specific **social structure** can be fully analysed in terms of a single mode of production, and there has been fruitful debate over distinctions with the capitalist modes of production (for example, as to a break between high capitalism and late capitalism), the basic Marxist account offers a powerful, if abstract model of social change.

This may be illustrated through reference to the transition from feudalism to capitalism. Feudal technology depends on sources of natural power (including animal power, wind power and human strength), while capitalism has machinery powered by the burning of fossil fuels. The relatively low production of feudal technology can be fully exploited through small-scale and predominantly agrarian production methods. The greater power of capitalist technology entails that a single source can provide the power for a large number of workers. The factory therefore emerges as the most appropriate way to exploit this power. However, the factory, and its organisation, are themselves strictly part of the forces of production. To make the factory possible, the feudal relations of production must be broken. These relations are those existing between the feudal lord and the serf, where the serf is bound to a particular piece of land, and to service for a particular lord. The lord can exploit the serf by appropriating a portion of the production of this land, and by requiring the serf to work for a period on the lord's own land. Capitalism, and thus the **bourgeois** or capitalist class that seeks to take full advantage of the new technology, requires a labour force that is free to move between employers (according to the demands and motivations of a free **labour** market). Capitalist relations of production therefore centre upon the market. The labourer is formally free to work for anyone willing and able to employ him or her, for a wage determined by the market. The capitalist will own, not just the means of production, but also the product of the labour that is exerted within his or her factories. The capitalist is free to dispose of this product as he or she wishes (again, at a price largely determined by the market in consumer goods). Exploitation of the subordinate class is now concealed within the exchanges made on the labour and commodity market, all of which are superficially fair. The value paid to the labourer as a fair and mutually agreed wage for a given amount of labour is less than the **exchange-value** received by the capitalist in selling the product. (Exploitation therefore occurs through the appropriation of **surplus value**.)

The transition between modes of production is violent (brought about through revolutions that are the overt manifestation of class conflict). This violence is necessitated by the inherently conservative or static nature of the relations of production, in contrast to the dynamic nature of the forces of production. Revolution occurs when a contradiction occurs between the forces of production and the relationships of production. This is to say that the existing relations of production are no longer adequate to exploit the productive potential of the forces of production. The dominant feudal class, and thus feudal relations of production, are seen as being incapable of making full use of industrial technology. The rising capitalist class is only able to develop the potential of industrial technology if it can first over-throw the feudal relations of production, in order to remove the feudal inhibitions on the expansion of a mobile and free labour force. Capitalist relations of production are thus seen to be somehow implicit in early industrial technology, and this implicit capitalism is in contradiction to the reality of the old feudal order.

Through appeal to the **base and superstructure** metaphor (and in various forms of twentieth-century Marxism, analyses of **commodity fetishism** and **reification**), Marxists may suggest that the economic elements of the mode of production (the economic base) has a determining influence over the legal and **cultural** aspects of society. If so, then different modes of production are not merely characterised in terms of different economic characteristics, but also in terms of different cultural characteristics (and most importantly, by the **ideological** mechanisms that are used to give legitimacy to the rule of the dominant class).

Further reading: Balibar 1970; Cutler *et al*. 1977; Marx and Engels 1970; Sweezy *et al*. 1978.

AE

MODERNISM

The precise meaning of the concepts of 'modernity' and 'modernism' depend, very much, upon the context in which they originate and are used. Thus, the concept of 'modernity' typically implies an opposition to something, and particularly to an historical epoch that has passed and has been superseded. Thus, as derived from the Latin *'modernus'* (and *'modo'*, meaning recently), modernity comes to characterise the Christian epoch (from the fifth century, in the writings of St Augustine), in contrast to a pagan past. This distinction is revised at a number of points throughout the European Middle Ages and into the Renaissance. (The Renaissance, for example, as a modern age, was initially understood in opposition to the preceding 'middle' ages, but not to the now revalued pagan epoch (or antiquity).) In the seventeenth and eighteenth centuries, modernity came to be associated with the **Enlightenment**. This entailed a revision of the historical understanding of the present. The understanding of time and **history** in the Christian Middle Ages, and even in the Renaissance, was shaped by the expectation, on the part of Christianity, of the imminent end of the world. The more secular Enlightenment presupposes that history will unfold into an open, possibly limitless future. In addition, technological and industrial development, with associated social change, became visibly more rapid during this period. As such, modernity ceases to be merely that which is most recent or new, and now becomes that which is most progressive. Thus, the contemporary social theorist Jürgen Habermas (1983) can still defend the 'unfinished project' of modernity. Such a project suggests that modernity has not merely technological, but more importantly political and moral goals (particularly in the emancipation of humanity from the superstitions and unquestioned **authority** of the past). In this context, 'modernism', in its contemporary meaning, can be seen to emerge in the political revolutions of 1848.

In sociological thinking, modernity is typically placed in contrast to traditional, and therefore pre-industrial, societies. **Sociology**, as a discipline, emerges in the theorisation of modernism in this sense. In the work of Emile Durkheim, at the close of the nineteenth century, contemporary modern society is contrasted, in terms of its complex division of labour and greater sense of individual identity and separateness, from the **mechanical solidarity** of pre-industrial societies. The German social theorist Tönnies similarly distinguished the integrated and homogeneous 'community' of pre-industrial society, from the fragmentation, isolation and artificiality of modern 'society'. In the work of Max Weber, the development of modernism is linked to increasing **rationalisation** in all aspects of social life. This rationalisation entails that all social activities (from the economy, through law and political administration, to **architecture** and music) are subject to scrutiny in order to determine the most instrumentally efficient means of achieving their goals. In these accounts, modernity is never a purely good thing. The idea of modernity as simple, unambiguous progress, is thrown into question, as the problems and tensions of existence in modern society are thrown into relief (from Durkheim's **anomie**, through Marxist theories of **alienation**, to Weber's iron cage of **bureaucracy** that curtails individual and political freedom and spontaneity).

In the arts and other areas of **culture**, modernism may be taken to refer to the development of more self-reflective art forms towards the end of the nineteenth century Thus, in 1845, the poet Baudelaire writes of the French painter Constantin Guys in an essay significantly entitled 'The Painter in Modern Life'. However, modernism in painting is typically tied to Edouard Manet (1832–83) and, under his influence, the development of Impressionism. Crucially, in this work, the conventions of **realist** art are thrown into question. The artist's concerns therefore shift away from the overt subject matter of the painting, to the process of painting itself. (As the composer Schoenberg once remarked, painters do not paint trees, they paint paintings.) Similar shifts can be seen in music (with the break from the conventions of tonality at the beginning of the twentieth century, for example in the work of the Second Viennese School) and in literature (as the conventional **narrative** of the realist novel is questioned by such figures as Proust and Joyce). Yet it may be suggested that an increasing interest in the techniques of the artistic medium itself, or in form, is only one aspect of modernist art. This emphasis on form serves to separate the artwork from anything outside art (culminating, not merely in the practice of abstract expressionist painting, for example, but also more importantly in the way in which that work is theorised and defended by such critics as Clement Greenberg (1992) and Michael Fried (1992)). In contrast, much art that can be fairly described as modernist shows a greater commitment to political and social change, or an engagement with the project of producing an art that is appropriate to contemporary (modern) social life. Thus, futurism, for example, sought to celebrate the achievements of an industrial age, and the power and speed of modern technology. Modern **architecture**, for example in the work of Le Corbusier and the Bauhaus, sought a building design and urban planning that was appropriate to a rational age, stripped of the conventions and ornaments of the past.

Modernism in art and architecture tended to be characterised by an **elitism** and insularity that made it unpalatable to a wider public. The crisis of modernism comes as its aspirations to universalism (and thus its tendency to dictate, from a privileged position, what culture and architecture should be) are revealed as concealing a closure against the many alternative voices that had in fact been excluded from modernist developments (see **postmodernism**).

Further reading: Berman 1983; Bradbury and McFarlane 1976; Giddens 1990; Habermas 1988.

AE

MYTH

'Myth' is a term that has a number of subtly interrelated meanings. At its most fundamental, a myth is a (typically anonymous) **narrative** about supernatural beings. The importance of the myth lies in the way in which it encapsulates and expresses beliefs and values that are shared by, and definitive of, a particular **cultural** group. Thus, a myth may explain the origin of the group (or of the world in general), the place of that group in the world, and its relationship to other groups, and illustrate or exemplify the moral values that are venerated by the group. Mythology has been subject to various theoretical approaches.

In **psychoanalysis**, mythical themes are typically treated as expressive of universal psychic conflicts (with the Oedipus complex being the most famous example). Through an extensive study, not just of mythologies, but also dreams, religion and art, Jung developed his account of archetypes as the basic and universal formative processes that structure mythologies. In functionalist approaches to **cultural anthropology**, myths are explained in terms of the needs they meet in the reproduction and stabilisation of society. Thus, by encoding group **norms**, a mythology serves to strengthen the cohesion and integrity of the society. In Durkheimian sociology, mythology may be seen to be expressive of the *conscience collective*, that is to say, the norms and beliefs into which individuals are socialised, and that serve as the cement that holds together both pre-industrial and industrial societies. Something akin to this understanding of myth, as that which binds and motivates a group, is found in *Reflections on Violence*, by the French Marxist theorist Georges Sorel (and first published in 1907). Sorel treats accounts of contemporary political and social events as potential myths (notably in the example of the General Strike). Such myths are necessary to evoke sentiments that would serve to motivate mass political action. This echoes, in a revolutionary manner, Plato's conservative account of golden lies. In his **utopian** republic, individuals will be motivated to keep to their place in society, thanks to a mythology of metals in the soul. The dominant guardians have gold in their souls, while the warrior class has silver and the artisans iron. The social and political relationships between groups is thereby expressed in a fictional account of natural differences.

In Lévi-Strauss's **structuralist** anthropology, inspired by Saussure's **semiology**, myths are treated as **sign** systems. While myth is still important as the medium through which the cultures reflect upon the tensions of social existence, for Lévi-Strauss, the appropriate way to analyse them is as a surface expression of an underlying deep structure (akin to Saussure's *langue*). On one level, his four-volume *Mythologies* recounts in faithful detail a vast array of myths from anthropological literature. On another level, the study attempts to identify the rules that govern the transformation from one myth to another. The semiological approach to myth is taken up by Roland Barthes (1973), particularly as a tool to analyse a wide range of images and activities in contemporary culture.

Barthes's analysis works as follows. A sign is understood to have both denotative and connotative orders. It denotes by pointing or referring to something in the world. Thus, a photograph of a family denotes two adults (a mother and a father) and, let us say, two young children. As connotation, the sign expresses or alludes to certain, culturally specific, values. The precise values involved will depend both upon the culture within which the sign is produced and interpreted, and the way in which the sign is presented. Thus, our family photograph could be brilliantly lit, emphasising bright colours and a sunny day. The photograph would then connote the contentment and security associated with family life. Conversely, a bleak, black-and-white photograph might express the pressures of family life and the tensions between generations. Mythology builds upon this structure of denotation and connotation. As myth, the sign gives concrete and particular expression to abstract concepts, through which we make sense of a particular social experience. Thus, when we look at a photograph, it does not merely evoke values of which we are consciously aware, but also values or ideas that are so taken for granted that we remain unaware of our own attention to them. Our photographs of the family then evoke myths of family life. These may be myths of the harmonious heterosexual family, and the benefits of marriage to the social and moral order (for our colour photograph), and the myth of the decline of family life in the other. The photographs work as mythology precisely in so far as they immediately give support for the taken-for-granted and oversimplified beliefs. The belief leads to a certain understanding of the photograph, and the photograph reinforces the veracity of that belief. The mythical beliefs transform complex cultural processes into apparently natural, unchangeable and self-evident ones. (The association with Plato's noble lies, where the cultural becomes natural, is worth noting.)

AE

NARRATIVE

The organisation of language into a structure which thereby conveys an account of events in a connected and ordered manner. Thus, narratives invoke the notion of sequence: 'This happened ... then this ... ', etc. There are a variety of theories which explain narrative, for example, Gérard Genette's, which explicates narrative according to the **structuralist** paradigm and hence provides a scientific explanation of narrative form (the discipline of 'narratology'). On this conception, a narrative is composed of the structured relationships between such things as the events narrated, the historical sequence in which they happened, the temporal sequence presented within the narrative, the narrator's perspective and tone, the relationship between the narrator and their audience, and the activity of narration itself. Amongst thinkers associated with **postmodernism** and **post-structuralism**, Roland Barthes sought to initiate a break with the scientific model espoused by structuralism and turned instead to an emphasis upon the role of the reader in the generation of **meaning**; while Jean-François Lyotard's discussion of the postmodern in *The Postmodern Condition* (1979) is characterised by the view that narrative forms have a plurality and heterogeneity which cannot be overcome by way of resorting to a meta-narrative (or 'grand narrative'). Thus, what constitutes one narrative form is incommensurable with another. The postmodern, in turn, is conceived of by Lyotard as the state which embodies the demise of meta-narratives and their replacement with a multiplicity of finite narratives which spurn the pretention to universality. Equally, writers such as Homi Bhabha have alluded to the relationship between narrative and issues of **identity**, principally in connection with the areas of nationalism and **post-colonialism**.

Further reading: Barthes 1974; Genette 1980; Lyotard 1989; Ricoeur 1984–8.

PS

NATION STATE

In its modern sense, a political **community** that is differentiated from other such communities in virtue of its autonomy with regard to legal codes and governmental structures, head of state, boundaries, systems of military defence, etc. A nation state likewise has a number of symbolic features which serve to present its **identity** in unified terms: a flag, national anthem, a popular self-image, etc. It is worth noting that the nation state is not synonymous with the possession of nationhood. In the nineteenth century, nationalistic struggles to achieve the political autonomy of a nation state were mounted by nations which did not possess political autonomy (e.g. the Italian states, or the unification of the German states under the leadership of Prussia in 1872). Likewise, today there are nations which do not necessarily have an accompanying status of statehood (e.g. Wales and Scotland in the United Kingdom). From this it follows that what a nation state is cannot be determined with reference to such notions as nationality, nor **ethnicity**, **culture** or **language**. It is, rather, the political, social and economic modes of organisation which appear fundamental with regard to this matter: nation states have political autonomy, different **norms** and codes with regard to their systems of social relations, and a relatively independent economic identity.

Further reading: Tivey 1981.

PS

NATIONALISM

Nationalism presents itself not simply as a political phenomenon, but also as a matter of cultural **identity**. As such, any conception of the nation to which it refers must take account of ethnic, historic and linguistic criteria, as well as political notions such as legitimacy, bureaucracy and presence of definable borders. Nationalists make a number of specific claims for the nation, which vary in relative significance according to the particular historical situation. A primary argument is that the nation has a right to autonomy, and that the people of the nation must be free to conduct their own affairs. As a corollary to this autonomy, nationalists presuppose (or demand) that the members of the nation share a common identity, which may be defined according to political or cultural (ethnic, linguistic) criteria. This notion of identity may be extended to create a sense of unity of purpose, whereby the projects of individuals are subsumed within the projects of the nation.

Nationalism thus defined is a modern phenomenon, becoming prevalent towards the end of the eighteenth century. Despite the existence of similar ideas in ancient times, the development of nationalism is concomitant with the development of the modern state, primarily in Europe and North America. The dates of the American Declaration of Independence (1776) and the French Revolution (1789) are frequently cited as marking the beginning of nationalism. Its roots as an intellectual movement are nonetheless vague; although steeped in the **Enlightenment** tradition of Rousseau and Herder, nationalism's appeal to an authentic existence based on a return to a shared cultural heritage has much in common with the themes prevalent within **romanticism** and the writings of Fichte and Hegel. Analytical study of nationalism as a political force had to wait, however, until the latter half of the nineteenth century, and it was not until the **post-colonial** era that scholarly interest became widespread.

Given the disputed nature of the nation in political and cultural theory, it is hardly surprising that a universally accepted theory of nationalism remains elusive. In particular, theorists remain divided over the relative importance of nationalism's political and cultural dimensions. Ernest Gellner's definition of nationalism as 'a political principle, which holds that the political and the national unit should be congruent' is an example of a position stressing the former aspect, whereas so-called 'primordialists', exemplified by the anthropologist Clifford Geertz, argue that nationalism stems from patterns of social ordering deeply embedded in all ethnic psyches. By contrast, Eric Hobsbawm and Elie Kedourie have proposed that nationalism is an invention on the part of social elites which fails to address the arbitrary and contingent formation of nations, instead positing invented traditions which thence constitute a superficial cultural heritage. In addition, scholars are divided as to whether a distinction can be made between 'good' and 'bad' nationalism (patriotism and chauvinism). Despite disagreement concerning its nature, however, nationalism remains a potent **ideology** in contemporary society, and its popularity appears to have diminished little in the face of potential threats such as **globalisation**, mass communication and multinational institutions.

Further reading: Gellner 1983.

CW

NATURE

'Nature' has a number of meanings. The oldest meaning is as the essential character or quality of something (see Williams 1976:219ff.). If each individual thing has its own nature, then nature is the essential quality of everything. Nature is the vital or motivating force behind the universe. More modestly, nature may be equated simply with the universe and all its contents (rather than the force behind it). More restricted still, it is the living world (of plants and animals). The most recent use of the concept 'nature' is to refer to that which is opposed to, prior to, or simply outside human **society** and **culture**. Human culture and society is artificial, having been produced, manufactured or transformed through human invention and industry. Nature may be the material that is subject to this process of transformation, but it is not properly part of human society, until it has been so transformed.

It is this last sense of nature that is most relevant to cultural studies. If nature is opposed to human society, then it can either be because nature is seen to be superior to society, or because it is inferior. In the mid-seventeenth century the English political philosopher Thomas Hobbes described the condition into which society could collapse, not least through civil war, as a state of nature (1994). Hobbes's state of nature is brutal and violent, and so the task of political philosophy is to describe the forms of government that will most effectively prevent the disintegration of society into nature. An alternative vision becomes clear, at the very end of the eighteenth century and beginning of the nineteenth, in the writings of the German philosophers Kant (1983) and Hegel (1948). Both of them offer accounts of human **history**, based on interpretations of the Book of Genesis, that begin with primitive humans (Adam and Eve, Noah and Abraham) having to be expelled from the security of nature, in order to be forced to develop their potential as human beings. Nature, be it the idyll of the Garden of Eden, or the nomadic Abraham merely following the wanderings of his flock of sheep, poses no challenge to humans, and therefore no stimulus to the development of human self-understanding and reason.

The dominant view of nature in science and political philosophy in the seventeenth-century European **Enlightenment** is of nature as superior to society. It is a source of order and reason (which was displayed, not least, by Newtonian physics). Politically, the appeal to nature and natural order served as a challenge and criticism of contemporary society. Nature promised an alternative to the seemingly arbitrary and even corrupt conventions that governed absolutist and **feudal** society. Thus, for example, the English philosopher John Locke appealed to the idea of a state of nature, but as a relatively benign condition existing prior to the formation of society (1980). In this state of nature, human beings enjoyed extensive freedoms (or natural rights). Such freedoms could easily be undermined or removed by the violent and selfish actions of others, so society (in the form of government or the state) emerged as people banded together to protect each other. It was therefore the task of any rational and acceptable form of government to protect the natural freedoms of its **citizens**. Feudal government notably failed to do this.

In the **romanticism** of the late eighteenth and nineteenth centuries, this sense of a superior nature is modified. Society is now to learn from nature, and to renew itself through that study (rather than to be overthrown by an appeal to nature). The emphasis that the **Enlightenment** places on reason, and the rational order that it found in nature, is displaced by a concern with the diversity and fecundity of the organic. Nature becomes a source of spiritual values and emotion. It stands for that which is good and innocent. It is the world of the noble savage. This use is important, because it continues today, not least in the language used in advertising. It is the claim that the wheat from which your breakfast cereal is made is 'natural'. Strictly the wheat is a product of human culture (or more precisely, **agriculture**). It is the product of hundreds of years of selective breeding. (Natural wheat would be a fairly unpalatable Ethiopian grass.) Closely associated nuances of meaning are found today in the use of 'organic'.

This final twist of meaning in 'nature' is perhaps the use that is most central to cultural studies, for it reveals much about the working of **ideology**. Ideology may be understood as sets of ideas and concepts that shape our understanding of the world, and crucially distort that understanding so that we do not challenge or question existing **power** relations. Nature plays a crucial role in ideology, for if social and cultural relations and events are perceived to be natural, then they will not be challenged. They will not appear to be the product of human agency and the exercise of political power, and to challenge them will appear no more rational or sensible than challenging the law of gravity or the fact that it is raining. The Hungarian philosopher Georg Lukács used the phrase 'second nature' to encapsulate this experience of society (1978). That which is the product of human action and invention (our society and culture) and thus that which should be full of meaning and the indications of human intention, actually confronts us as something that is as alien and as meaningless as first nature—real nature. The German Marxist philosopher T.W. Adorno summarised the challenge that this ideological inversion of nature and culture posed for a politically informed study of culture: 'What cannot be changed in nature may be left to look after itself. When it can be changed, it is up to us to change it' (Wiggershaus 1994:90). That is to say that the task of cultural theory may be to see through second nature, and so change what appears to be unchangeable.

See also: **ecology**.

AE

NEOCONSERVATISM

Neoconservatives are a branch of the political right which have occupied a place of increasing power in the United States since the occupation of the American presidency in 2001 by Republican G.W. Bush. A central influence on neoconservative thinking has been the academic Leo Strauss. According to leading neoconservative Irving Kristol, 'It is not a "movement", as [...] conspiratorial critics would have it', but is rather 'a "persuasion"'. Thus, neoconservative attitudes express a state of mind. Kristol emphasises the *echt* American nature of this state of mind; hence its legitimacy is asserted by way of its link with the cultural and political roots of American society. 'Neocons', as they are often called, favour an economy with a minimum tax burden and hence the predominance of an unfettered free market. Consequently they also demonstrate scorn for the large state systems of **health** care and social welfare in many of the nations of the European Union. Paradoxically, this attitude does not seem to sit uncomfortably with neoconservative faith in a strong and well-equipped state. This, in conjunction with an impassioned nationalism (or 'patriotism'), a respect for the ideals of religious (Christian) conservatism and opposition to international courts of arbitration may explain why neoconservatives also favour the kind of American military intervention that took place with the invasion of Iraq in 2003.

Further reading: Kristol 1999, 2003; Norton 2004.

PS

NEW CRITICISM

The most significant influences on New Criticism were the scrupu-
lous text-oriented literary interpretations of I.A. Richards. But the
movement called New Criticism consisted chiefly of the expatriate
poet T.S. Eliot and three writers from the American south: John
Crowe Ransom, Allen Tate and Robert Penn Warren. It is largely a
North American phenomenon even though it has significant parallels
with the work of the British critics F.R. Leavis and William Empson.
Through its emphasis on questions of literary form, New Criticism
expressed a poet's interest in the possibilities of language. This
entailed an aesthetic theory that moved the interest of criticism away
from the author's life towards a detailed engagement with the language of literature and thus marked a decisive shift away from phi-
lology, source hunting and literary biography to textual analysis.
Although its emphasis on close reading was admirably suited to the
classroom and still remains the starting point of most theoretically
inspired interpretations, the intellectual premises of New Criticism
were so firmly ingrained in a narrow conservative, agrarian ideology
that it became the target of fierce attacks.

New Criticism's insistent focus on the text was the result of
understanding the work of art as a timeless and self-contained artefact. Although its interest in the materiality of the text also touched
upon questions concerning text production, the institutionalised
practice of applying New Critical methodology disconnected literature from its social context, so that, by and large, it became equated
with an exclusive interest in the words on the page. This emphasis
was testified by the publications of its chief representatives: most
notably Cleanth Brooks's and Robert Penn Warren's series of text-
books, among them Brooks's *Understanding Poetry* (1938) and *The
Well Wrought Urn* (1949). Other representatives are Monroe Beardsley
and R.P. Blackmur. Although the emphasis on form had started out
as a means of introducing questions concerning the economic
requirements for the production of art, it was appropriated as a
bourgeois aesthetic in which the high valuation of rhetorical complexity displaced the need for political commitment. In the theory
propounded by W.K. Wimsatt, the text was defined as being 'iconic':
literary language figured as an end in itself and literature was taken to
describe a world which differed from all historically perceived reality
because it was thought to express a universally true perception of
what it meant to be human (*The Verbal Icon* (1958)). This was as
much as to say that literature represents profound human problems

which are independent of both author and historical context, and it is in the appeal to this fundamental sense of humanity that the critic can understand and explicate the full meaning of a work of art.

The emphasis on close reading is the result of a critical theory which focused on the workings of language rather than on the psychology of the author. At its best, however, it combined an investigation of linguistic structures with a more open-minded interest in the psychology and sociology of language production. Although his work stands apart from New Criticism, William Empson had considerable influence on the movement. Two of his books, *Seven Types of Ambiguity* (1953), written at a time when New Criticism was about to take off as a critical practice, and the later *The Structure of Complex Words* (1951), combine close attention to textual-semantic details with a discussion of culturally salient ideas. But it has to be noted that Empson always incorporated contextual considerations into his interpretations, and his work on ambiguity was careful not to posit an ultimate reconciliation through notions of 'paradox, irony', etc.

Recent approaches to art, especially those taking a **deconstructionist** line, also engage in minute textual analysis and concentrate on contradictory moments of the text. The chief difference is that New Criticism treated literature as an object that would reveal the complexities of life through its self-referential emphasis on rhetorical complexities (such as paradox, oxymoron, ambiguity, tension, irony). Poetry, especially, was taken as the highest cultural achievement because its rhetorical patterns were believed to express the possibility of reconciling contradictions, by analogy with the firmly defined system of beliefs held by Western society and Christian religion. The subsequent objections to it voiced by those who struggled for the recognition of gender and racial rights showed that even though New Critical readings may have been immensely sensitive to the contradictory semantic potential of the texts, their ultimate conclusions were politically unacceptable. This is because the method adopted by the New Critics typically reduced the meaning of a text to a singular and all-inclusive statement about the individual's existence as a member of Western (patriarchal and bourgeois) society. In contrast to this, a deconstructive critical practice, especially if it engages in politically motivated Marxist, feminist or post-colonial criticism, highlights plural interpretations of a text as instances where the meaning of central concepts, such as subjectivity or identity, are contested. Objections to New Criticism were not only raised on political grounds but also concerned its reductive understanding of language. For all its interest in rhetorical devices expressing contradiction, New

Criticism adhered to the belief that it was possible to exert control over linguistic meaning and that paradoxical statements made in literature had the special virtue of awaiting a sufficiently sophisticated mind to explain and resolve them.

Further reading: Hosek and Parker 1985; Lentricchia 1980; Litz *et al.* 2000.

CK

9/11

The shorthand phrase for the wave of coordinated terrorist assaults that struck the USA on 11 September 2001. The attacks began at 8.46 a.m. when a hijacked aeroplane (American Airlines Flight 11) was crashed into the north tower of the World Trade Center, New York. At 9.03 a.m. a second plane (United Airlines Flight 175) was flown into the south tower. Around half an hour later a third hijacked plane crashed into the Pentagon. A fourth aircraft (Flight 93 – destined for the Capitol, the centre of USA government) crashed in Pennsylvania following an on-board battle between its passengers and the hijackers. It is estimated that 2,973 people were murdered in the attacks. The attacks were revealed to have been the work of a militant Sunni Islamist group al-Qaeda, founded by Osama Bin Laden in the 1980s. Al-Qaeda was founded in opposition to growing post-war American influence over the Islamic world (it, for example, urges the destruction of Israel and the withdrawal of American forces from the East). What has contributed to making the phrase '9/11' so richly symbolic (especially in the minds of many in the West) is the detailed media coverage of the events of that day as they unfolded in New York. Live television broadcasts of the assault on the south tower and the subsequent catastrophic collapse of both towers, magnified by constant repetition in the form of global news broadcasts and subsequently in documentaries and other programmes, helped create an indelible symbolism. The power of this symbolism, along with subsequent events that arose in the aftermath of 11 September, probably stands as the fulfilment of the attackers' highest hopes. An icon of the industrial, financial and cultural might of capitalist America was transformed into rubble in a matter of hours and thereby subsumed and rendered open to reinterpretation within an iconography framed by the upsurgent power of religious fundamentalist will. It was not merely the suicidal ruthlessness of the attackers that was especially chilling, but also the ease with which the attacks were perpetrated using aircraft bound on internal flights in the USA. The symbolic power of the images of collision with the south tower is connected in no small way with this fact. The towers, icons of Western global power, were destroyed by the use of machines that themselves stand as representatives of the same global economic and industrial interests. The aeroplane, which like the telecommunications industry has served to shrink geographical space, and with it cultural and political space, has brought with it not merely convenience of travel between distant (and for the vast majority in the West hitherto almost unreachable) destinations but also an increased sense of vulnerability and, in turn, instability.

The historical and hence cultural significance of 11 September 2001 is at present difficult to fathom, although this has not prevented many from trying to do so – as indeed one must. One thing does, however, seem certain: the attacks have raised anew questions about the nature of cultural relations between the West and the Middle East. On the one hand, Arab grievances concerning Israel's treatment of the Palestinians and USA support of Israel have become issues in the West to an unprecedented degree. At the same time, aggressive American responses to the 9/11 attacks have, it could be argued, not merely deprived them of the deserved sympathy they received in the aftermath of the attacks but also deepened the crises that underlie them. The initial USA response of turning on the al-Qaeda stronghold of Afghanistan and ousting that country's fundamentalist Taliban rulers has, so far, led to inconclusive results. The expected extermination of the Taliban has not happened. As a result, Afghanistan remains an arena symbolic of the struggle between Islamic militancy and the West. Following this, in March 2003 the United States led a British-sponsored invasion of Iraq that has served further to polarise dichotomies and create resentments. The fact that American officials sought to justify the invasion by claiming that Saddam Hussein had been involved in the 9/11 attacks points to their instrumental political value. These claims were subsequently admitted to have been false, but their persuasive power (surely reflected in wide initial popular support for the invasion in America) provides ample evidence of the blow to American sensibilities that the September attacks undoubtedly represent.

Many sweeping claims have followed in the wake of 9/11. Neoconservative commentators have invoked the notion of unprincipled evil as a means of explaining the actions of those who perpetrated the 9/11 murders. Such a view tends to regard 'Islamic **fundamentalism**' as an irrational, unsophisticated literal perversion of 'genuine Islam' that merely serves those trenchantly opposed to the principles of free (i.e. **liberal**) society (see Elshtain 2003). On the other hand, left-of-centre thinkers like Noam Chomsky have argued that the horrifying events of 11 September 2001 must be understood as an expression of deeply felt grievances over several decades of American foreign policy (Chomsky 2002). Two specific theses that preceded the 11 September attacks have been brought to the fore in different lights. Francis Fukuyama's 'end of **history**' thesis (Fukuyama 1992) proclaiming the end of the Soviet Union in 1989 as marking the unstoppable ascendancy of a liberal free-market order and a conflict-free world has come to look even less persuasive than it did when it was first promulgated. On the other hand, Samuel Huntington's contention that the post-war era is increasingly marked by cultural rather than ideological or economic struggles has an obvious explanatory power, at least for some (Huntington 1998; Ruthven 2002). This is sometimes known as the 'clash of civilisations' thesis. The *prima facie* persuasiveness of the thesis lies in its undeniable simplicity: it allows us to explain the 9/11 attacks in terms of a range of invisible forces that are at once powerful yet (for Westerners) largely unintelligible and hence hardly in need of rational examination. The problem with this view is that it marginalises the political and social dimensions of history, while at the same time transforming the word 'culture' into something both absolute and impenetrable. The view that cultures stand in relation to one another with absolute borders, akin to the boundary lines that divide nation states but hermetically sealed from outside influence in a way that no state can be, is hardly convincing (see Sen 2005). As John Clark's important study shows (Clark 1997), the historical influence of Eastern thought on the West since at least the time of the Enlightenment has been profound and belies the notion of closed cultural barriers.

Some have argued that the 'War on Terror' announced by American president G.W. Bush in the immediate aftermath of the 9/11 attacks (Bush 2001a), a war aimed at crushing the 'enemies of freedom' (Bush 2001b), invoked key American cultural paradigms. According to Bostdorff (2003), Bush offered his audience a discourse that appeals to a 'Puritan rhetoric of covenant'. By accepting the covenant, the younger generation of Americans in effect accede to the **authority** of the faith of the older, World War II generation and revitalise it. The covenant brings with it the language of moral polarisation (self-appointed terrorist leaders versus democratically elected politicians, unprincipled evil versus 'the values of America') conjoined with economic pragmatism (the need for 'continued participation and confidence in the American economy' (Bush 2001b)). The potentially divisive rhetoric of good versus evil, however, is as amenable to the terrorist as the Western politician and hence does little to enlighten, as Bin Laden's talk of the 'crimes and sins committed by the Americans' against the Muslim world illustrates (Bin Laden 1998). Such rhetoric serves to give credence to the 'clash of civilisations' perspective, unintentionally acceding to Bin Laden's demand for a polarised 'holy war' against the 'evil' West and thus making things worse (Barber 2002). An analogous point has also been made by Derrida (2003). For him, the West's response to terrorist atrocity is marked by a tendency to limit the legal procedures that are their lifeblood (witness the American 'Patriot Act' that was rushed through in the aftermath of 9/11 – cf. Dworkin 2005).

The religious rhetoric noted by Bostdorff has also been remarked upon by Habermas (Habermas 2003). As he has commented, the tendency to resort to religious rhetoric was implicit in the repetition of 'biblical images' of the collapsing twin towers of the World Trade Center. Bush's subsequent retaliatory language which, with its Old Testament resonance, indicated something peculiar to be at work within secular Western society. According to Habermas, the 11 September attacks must, like the 'exclusively modern phenomenon' of fundamentalism, be interpreted as expressions of the unsettling consequences of modernisation as it takes on global proportions. In the West, the effects of modernisation were minimised not merely by its relative slowness but by concrete compensations (better living conditions ameliorated for the loss of tradition). Nevertheless, one of the defining features of modernity, its secular component, most vividly expressed in the separation of church and state, still inspires discomfort in the West even today. This reveals that the West, too, is still in the throes of change, that 'the occidental process of secularisation' is an ongoing phenomenon. The time lag between social and cultural transformations creates tensions. Today, the demise of tradition at the hands of secularising forces in the non-occidental world is all the more traumatic not merely because of its unprecedented rapidity but because the ensuing destruction of tradition lacks compensatory features. Secularisation is experienced as cultural colonisation. It is this, coupled with the West's lack of an appreciation of the extent to which it, too, has yet to bring secularisation to a conclusion that allows the threat of a clash of civilisations to present itself. The only solution to this, for Habermas, is to be found in a concrete attempt on the part of the West to undertake a critical incorporation of the religious contents of its traditions by a profane, yet emphatically '*nondefeatist* reason'. Such a form of rationality must respect the religious origins of culture and rationality itself and in doing so attempts to broach the divide between the religious and the secular, East and West, by cultivating a language of mutual understanding in the form of a 'democratic common sense'.

Further reading: Barber 2002; Borradori 2003; Bostdorff 2003; Chomsky 2002; Elshtain 2003' Habermas 2003; Huntington 1998; Margolis *et al.* 2005; Ruthven 2002.

PS

NORM

A norm is a **rule** that governs a pattern of social behaviour. Examples of norms include laws, moral principles and guidelines, customs and the rules of etiquette, but also may express desirable values and goals. 'Norm' has two meanings, which in practice it is important to distinguish. On the one hand, a norm may encapsulate the usual behaviour within a society (and is thus a norm in the sense of being statistically normal behaviour). On the other hand, the norm is a pattern of behaviour that is desired or prescribed, whether or not actual behaviour complies with this ideal. Norms, especially in this latter sense, will be accompanied by positive and negative sanctions— that is to say, respectively, rewards for conforming and punishments for breaking norms. The nature of the sanction will vary from mild approval and a hard stare to, for example, large financial rewards and lengthy prison sentences, depending upon the sort of norm involved.

The idea that individual human beings learn the norms of their society through early upbringing (or **socialisation**) helps to explain how individuals become competent social agents, who, by and large, conform with the expectations of their culture. The early sociology of Durkheim emphasised the costs of a loss of norms (which he termed **anomie**). Without the guidance of norms, a person's life loses direction and becomes meaningless. However, a danger with this approach (which is seen particularly in **functionalist sociology**) is that it tends to assume that norms exist independently of any particular social event (and that there is no ambiguity as to which norms apply here and now) and that there is a general consensus in society about its norms. **Symbolic interactionism**, precisely because it focuses upon the construction of society through **interaction** between competent social agents, argues that norms may be better understood as the subject of negotiation. Agreement upon the relevant norms will be entwined with the activity needed to make sense of the sort of social event to which one is party. Marxist sociologists, conversely, have questioned whether norms can be understood as the site of a self-evident consensus. It is suggested, rather, that the imposition and acceptance of a norm must be analysed in terms of the power structures within society (and thus as part of **ideology**).

AE

OBJECTIVITY

True knowledge that is, or should be, value-neutral. Thus, objective knowledge is knowledge of how things really are, as opposed to how they appear to be. In the natural sciences (e.g. physics) objectivity is an indispensable notion (with regard to the application of theories and, above all, their verification by experiment). Objectivity presupposes that there is a real, external world which is independent of our knowledge of it, and that it is possible to describe this world accurately. On this view of science, scientific methodology aspires to provide the rules whereby reality can be known (a variant of this can be found in **positivism**). Philosophers like Nietzsche have criticised this notion. For Nietzsche, there is no knowledge which is not interested knowledge, i.e. which does not have an interest in, and therefore does not presuppose some value with regard to, its subject matter. Likewise, Foucault has taken a similar line. The implication of this attitude is that the aspiration to value objectivity above all else in knowledge is itself generated historically and culturally.

See also: **self**, **epistemology**.

PS

OEDIPUS COMPLEX

A key term in **psychoanalysis** used to theorise the transition of the child (at approximately three to five years) from a dyadic relationship with the mother to a triadic relationship that includes the father as a figure of **authority**. The failure to move through this transition correctly is an important source of psychopathology in the adult. The term is derived, by Freud, from the Greek myth in which Oedipus kills his father and marries his mother. Freud, in part on a supposed recollection of his own childhood experience, argues that initially the child is in love with his mother and jealous of his father. (In the early theorisation of the complex, the child was presumed to be male.) The account of the Oedipus complex is complemented by Freud's account of the childhood theory of sexuality. The child assumes that all babies are born with penises. The absence of the penis in the woman is interpreted as punishment inflicted by the jealous father. The male child therefore breaks from his relationship with his mother, under the perceived threat of castration. The female child, conversely, displaces her wish for a penis by the desire for a baby.

Further reading: Freud 1910, 1924, 1979.

AE

OLIGARCHY

Government by the few. The term can be traced back to Aristotle, who classified government into three types: monarchy, or rule by the one; aristocracy, or rule by the few; democracy, or rule by the many. Thinkers associated with the Aristotelian tradition (e.g. Niccolò Machiavelli (1469–1527) and James Harrington (1611–77)) have advocated a mixed form of government, i.e. one in which each of these models was combined in a system of checks and balances in order to prevent the degeneration of these into tyranny, oligarchy or anarchy. Oligarchy thus signifies a degenerate form of government, in which the few who administer power have succumbed to corruption and no longer serve the overall good of society but rather their own personal interests.

PS

ONTOLOGY

1 Part of **metaphysics** which engages in the study of the nature of existence in general, *not* with the existence of particular entities. Thus, an ontological enquiry, such as that engaged in by Martin Heidegger in *Being and Time*, is concerned with 'the question of Being', by which he means the conditions of possibility for the existence of any particular entity.

2 Any set of assumptions about the fundamental nature of existence which are presupposed within a theory. For example, the thought of

classical **liberalism**, it has been argued, contains a conception of individual subjectivity which conceives of it as comprising a particular set of properties which make it what it is (this is sometimes termed an 'ontology of the **subject**').

Further reading: Grossmann 1992; McCulloch 1995; Sadler 1996; Sprigge 1984.

PS

ORIENTALISM

This is a term that has gained special prominence with the writings by the late Edward Said (see Said 1978a). Understood thus, 'orientalism' is the intellectual study of the East undertaken by Western **colonial** scholars. Turning for theoretical support to the writings of Michel Foucault and Jacques Derrida (see **deconstruction**, **poststructuralism**, **postmodernism**), Said sought to show how this study was in fact an extension of the logic of imperialism. The orientalist, Said argues, although professing to offer an objective descriptive analysis of Asiatic culture, in reality identified the East in terms of specific, usually negative, traits (e.g. irrationality, tyrannical government, unconstrained sexuality) that emanated from the need to furnish a definition of European identity. What was designated as the oriental 'other', in short, was in reality a projection of Western anxieties. Thus, Western scholarly representations of the East are in fact no more than ideological constructions rooted in a combination of colonial dominion and cultural revulsion. The construction of a discourse of oriental subjectivity, following Foucault's analysis of **discourse**s of knowledge and power (see **episteme**), is in this way rendered a form of control that seeks mastery over its subject matter by defining it. Amongst other things, this contention has the positive effect of raising awareness of the sense of cultural and racial superiority present in the writings of prominent Western thinkers as diverse as Hobbes, John Locke, J.S. Mill and G.W.F. Hegel. Said's analysis powerfully argues for the need to consider issues of colonial subjugation whenever we are faced with the apparent opposition between occidental and non-occidental cultures. At the same time, the persuasiveness of considering orientalism to signify nothing more than a homogeneous discursive unity guided by the aims of imperialist control can be to some extent questioned (see Rocher, in Breckenridge and van de Veer 1993). Although Said may have justification for questioning the homogeneous image of the oriental that Westerners have at times imposed, he may also, it follows, stand open to the same charge. Likewise, it has been persuasively argued that many aspects of Asian thought have exerted a decisive influence on the West that cannot be adequately understood in the passive terms that Said's ideological reading imposes. As Clark states, it can be contended that orientalism 'in the Western context [...] represents a counter-movement, a subversive entelechy, albeit not a unified or consciously organised one, which in various ways has often tended to subvert rather than to confirm the discursive structures of imperial power' (Clark 1997:9).

Further reading: Breckenridge and van der Veer 1993; Clark 1997; Said 1978a.

PS

OTHER

A concept that can be traced back to the work of Hegel, and to be found in a variety of approaches to **epistemology**, questions of cultural **identity** and **psychoanalysis**. Amongst others, a treatment of this notion is in the writings of Lacan, in Sartrean **existentialism**, Derridean **deconstruction** and Edward Said's analysis of the colonial European study of oriental cultures, *Orientalism* (inspired in part by the thought of Michel Foucault). The term, not surprisingly, is highly ambiguous. In the context of theories of culture, perhaps the most prominent contemporary use of this notion has been made by Said. In these terms, the Other may be designated as a form of cultural projection of concepts. This projection constructs the identities of cultural **subjects** through a relationship of power in which the Other is the subjugated element. In claiming knowledge about 'orientals' what orientalism did was construct them as its own (European) Other. Through describing purportedly 'oriental' characteristics (irrational, uncivilised, etc.) **orientalism** provided a definition not of the real 'oriental' identity, but of European identity in terms of the oppositions which structured its account. Hence, 'irrational' Other presupposes (and is also presupposed by) 'rational' **self**. The construction of the Other in orientalist **discourse**, then, is a matter of asserting self-identity, and the issue of the European account of the oriental Other is thereby rendered a question of **power**.

Further reading: Said 1978a.

PS

PARADIGM

1 In semiotics, a paradigm is the range of meaningful units from which a message may be composed. The letters of an alphabet, for example, are the paradigm from which words can be composed. (Thus, A, a, B and b are part of the paradigm of the Roman alphabet, while Ë and $ are not.) Within a paradigm, units become meaningful in so far as they are distinguishable from each other and are potentially interchangeable.

See also: **syntagm**.

2 Term in the philosophy of science. As explained by Thomas Kuhn in *The Structure of Scientific Revolutions* (1962), paradigms are working theories or 'world views' which, within the domains of various scientific fields, facilitate the activity of study and research. For Kuhn, a paradigm may be considered as a conceptual 'achievement' (as exemplified by key works in the **history** of science, such as Newton's *Principia* or Lyell's *Principles of Geology*) which lays down the guiding principles within a particular scientific discipline for the future interrogation and investigation of phenomena. It is thus a working model which allows scientists to engage in the activity of actual scientific practice. The achievement which marks the birth of a paradigm has two central features: (i) it 'attract[s] an enduring group of adherents away from competing modes of scientific activity'; and (ii) the model is itself not complete but 'sufficiently open-ended to leave all sorts of problems for the redefined group of practitioners to solve' (Kuhn 1962:10).

A paradigm is thus a general theory which has succeeded in its struggle against other competing theories, but which has nevertheless not exhausted all the possible facts with which it has to deal. Once a paradigm is established, both the field it covers and its practitioners are more firmly defined, and future problems in need of investigation clearly stipulated. In such cases 'normal science' is in progress. A paradigm reaches a crisis point when the phenomena encountered within the discipline it defines become difficult to reconcile with it and also sufficiently important or numerous that they cannot be ignored: 'Failure of existing rules is a prelude to a search for now ones' (Kuhn 1962:68). This crisis leads to a breakdown of the theory, which nevertheless continues to operate until a new, more adequate one arrives to explain anomalous phenomena (1962:77). The replacement of one paradigm by another in the wake of such crises constitutes a shift 'in the scientific community's conception of legit-imate problems and standards' (1962:108).

Most significantly, according to Kuhn, such paradigm shifts are not to be understood in terms of a cumulative process in which the same problems are thereby further refined and developed as objects of study (a view put forward by philosopher of science Karl Popper). A change of paradigm involves a substantive alteration with regard to the issues which are held to be of importance within a discipline. A new paradigm gains acceptance because it is more able to account for anomalous phenomena and, importantly, because it gains a sig-nificant number of adherents. Hence, such changes (or revolutions) are not to be understood as marking out a moment of **progress** in the history of a particular discipline which is to be understood in purely objective terms. Rather, these changes are to be taken as manifestations of a sociological nature. In this sense, science itself is rendered a cultural practice whose subject matter and guiding pro-blems are determined by forces which exist within the community of scientific interpreters themselves, rather than according to any objective standard of reference to an external world set apart from problems of interpretation.

Further reading: Kuhn 1970.

PS

PAROLE

In Saussure's linguistics, '*parole*' refers to actual language or to the potentially infinite instances of language use (such as written and spoken sentences, poems and reports). *Parole* is contrasted to the underlying structure of the language, or *langue*.

AE

PARTICIPANT OBSERVATION

Participant observation is an **empirical** research methodology in the social sciences that involves the researcher studying a community or cultural activity of which he or she is a part (typically if only for the length of the study). Such an approach has the advantage over more controlled and experimental approaches in terms of the richness of qualitative detail that it can yield. A number of problems are well documented. First, the presence of an observer may distort normal social action within the group (so that the group ends up doing what it thinks the researcher wants it to do). Second, the **role** that the researcher occupies in the group is important. An inappropriate role can isolate the researcher from important actors or decision-makers within the group, so giving a distorted view of how the group works. Participant observation is, in any case, frequently criticised for lacking **objectivity** and for being too vulnerable to the **value** assumptions that the observer imposes, unwittingly, on his or her observations. Conversely, a well-chosen role can facilitate the task of observation. In a study of a Welsh rural community, Ronald Frankenburg (1957) was able to take on the role of 'stranger'. This at once allowed him access to communal activities (so much so that he became secretary of the football club), without compromising his independence. Importantly, Frankenburg argues that this role existed prior to his entering the community and so did not disrupt its structure.

See also: **ethnography**.

Further reading: Spradley 1980.

AE

PATRIARCHY

The term 'patriarchy' literally means the 'rule of the father'. It has been adopted by the majority of **feminist** theorists to refer to the way in which societies are structured through male domination over, and oppression of, women. Patriarchy therefore refers to the ways in which material and symbolic resources (including income, wealth and power) are unequally distributed between men and women through such social **institutions** as the family, sexuality, the state, the economy, culture and language. While there is no single analysis of the workings of patriarchy, debate over its nature and historical development has been important in the development and differentiation of schools of feminist thought. A number of key issues can be identified in the theorising of patriarchy. The relationship of male domination to biology was an early source of contention. While patriarchal structures may be found in all known human societies, the reduction of patriarchy to biological invariants, such as the roles of women and men in childbirth and nurturing, suggests that patriarchy is an essential and unchangeable **natural** relationship. Feminism tends, rather, to argue that patriarchy is, at least, the cultural interpretation of those natural relationships, if not itself wholly cultural. Psychological, and especially **psychoanalytic**, theories may associate patriarchy in the early socialisation of the child (and especially the break of the child from the mother at the **Oedipal** stage). Feminist responses to Lacanian psychoanalysis, from for example Kristeva and Cixous, are significant in seeing dominant culture, language and reason (Lacan's 'symbolic') as inherently patriarchal. They therefore seek to recover a pre-patriarchal stage, expressed in an *écriture féminine*, through which women can articulate themselves to themselves outside the distortions of male language. The relationship of patriarchy to other forms of oppression, such as **class** and **race**, receives diverse theorisation. Questions include that of the primacy or otherwise of patriarchy over other forms of domination, and the way in which different forms of domination may interact and reinforce each other. Thus, socialist feminists have typically sought to link patriarchy to class exploitation (Barrett 1980). The importance of race and **ethnicity** has indicated that a potential flaw in an all-encompassing theory of patriarchy is that it remains indifferent to divisions between women. The exploitation and domination of all women is not alike, and women cannot therefore be theorised as a single, homogeneous group.

Further reading: Mies 1986; Spivak 1987; Walby 1990.

AE

PHENOMENOLOGY

Phenomenology refers to a cluster of approaches to philosophical and sociological enquiry and to the study of art, deriving from the work of the German philosopher Edmund Husserl (1859–1938). The diversity of approaches that have been described as phenomenology, not least in Husserl's own work (which continually changed and developed over his career), means that a precise and all-encompassing definition of phenomenology is not easily given. However, something of the flavour of Husserl's enterprise can be suggested, along with some indication of the reaction of his followers, who include Martin Heidegger, Maurice Merleau-Ponty, Jean-Paul Sartre and Alfred Schutz.

Phenomenology, as its name suggests, is concerned to describe basic human experience (and hence, a concern with phenomena, a word that is derived from the Greek for 'appearance'). The point of this is to explore that which is presupposed by the natural sciences and all other claims to knowledge, and which therefore makes those knowledge claims possible. Phenomenology attempts to describe how the world must appear to the naïve observer, stripped of all presuppositions and culturally imposed expectations. This is captured in the slogan that phenomenology returns to the 'things themselves' (*Zu den Sachen* (Husserl 1962:74ff.)). Phenomenological enquiry therefore proceeds through the method of 'bracketing'. Bracketing involves a suspension of belief. The scientist, for example, in observing a colour, observes it in terms of the assumption that it is light waves at a given frequency. Yet this assumption is not available to the untutored observer. It can therefore play no part in the phenomenologist's description. More radically, Husserl suspends what he calls the 'natural attitude'. In everyday experience, we take for granted certain assumptions about our experience, not least that there is a real object out there that is being experienced, and that we are unified egos that have that experience. These assumptions are again not given in experience. Crucially, Husserl is not arguing that the real world does not exist. Rather, bracketing draws our attention to the assumptions we (must) make in order to experience the real world at all.

This is clarified by recognising the centrality of another of Husserl's claims. He argues that all consciousness is intentional. This means that we are always conscious of something (and never just conscious). Thus, I see an oasis, I touch a desk and I long for a pay rise. Note that the objects of which we are conscious need not exist. (So the pay rise may never be granted, and the oasis might be a mirage.) Husserl's point is that the account of experience cannot be made in terms of its causation by the material object. Rather, the object exists as it does (e.g. as a real oasis or a mirage) because of the meaningful relationship that the observer has to the object. The object, for Husserl, fulfils the expectations of the observer, and in encountering an object we will have a host of expectations that structure our relationship towards it. In Roman Ingarden's **aesthetics**, which draws on Husserl, the literary work is treated as a purely intentional object (1973). Concerned with describing genuinely aesthetic attitudes to the work of art, he rejects any identification of the work of art with its material substrate. The work is ascribed an enduring identity, independently of its multiple interpretations. The proper object of appreciation is therefore the content of the artwork, in which the reader 'concretises' the work in imaginatively reconstructing what the author has left indeterminate.

Husserl's followers typically challenge his idealism. His phenomenology concentrates on the experience of a largely disembodied observer. In contrast, Heidegger (and following him, Sartre) begin from the experience of an embodied agent who is practically engaged with the problems of the real, material and contingent world. Thus, for example, Husserl strives to discover the 'meaning' of experience as necessary and universal essences. In contrast, for Heidegger, such meaning develops historically as we pursue practical problems in the world. The meaning of a 'hammer', to use a favourite Heideggerean example, depends upon the use that human beings make of hammers. The meanings of experience are not then universals to be discovered through phenomenological descriptions, but rather are ascribed to the world by human beings in the pursuit of diverse goals. As Heidegger rather elegantly puts this: 'The wood is a forest of timber, the mountain a quarry of rock; the river is water-power, the wind is "wind in the sails"' (1962:40–1). Similarly, Merleau-Ponty sees meaning as being ascribed through the body so that belief in the body cannot be bracketed (1962:147).

In the social sciences, a phenomenological **sociology** has been developed from the work of Alfred Schutz (1899–1959). Again, Schutz (1962) rejects the idealism of Husserl's own programme, in order to describe human experience as it occurs within an inter-subjectively constituted social world (or **life-world**). The 'natural attitude' becomes for Schutz the taken-for-granted assumptions that competent social actors make about the social world and the people they encounter within it. Such actors take for granted the existence of other human beings, and assume a 'reciprocity of perspectives'. The social actor therefore has a 'stock-of-knowledge-at-hand' (in the form of sets of skills, assumptions and 'typifications'—being the labels and concepts through which he or she orientates his or her actions to each other) that allow them, not merely to recognise and respond to social reality, but actively, if unwittingly, to construct it.

Further reading: Bell 1990; Schutz and Luckmann 1974.

AE

PHOTOGRAPHY

The belief that the camera never lies is, perhaps, one of the most flagrant examples of the working of **ideology** that can be imagined. The belief assumes that if the image recorded by the camera is dependent upon natural, optical processes, then what the photograph represents will be what is really out there in the world. The photograph is important to cultural studies, precisely because cultural studies attempts to expose such confusions of the natural and the artificial. In many respects, the work of Roland Barthes on photography is at the core of this approach (1973, 1981). Barthes identifies what he calls 'the photographic paradox' as the coexistence of two messages within a single photograph. One message concerns what the photograph denotes. This is the neutral referent of the photograph, the object or person of which it is a photograph. The second message is the **myth** that is invested in this image. It is the way in which the object is represented, and invokes in the spectator, often unwittingly, a series of taken-for-granted assumptions about the social and political worlds. Precisely because this invocation is unremarked, the photograph serves only to reinforce prejudices. Barthes's famous illustration of this is of a cover of *Paris-Match*. 'On the cover, a young Negro in a French uniform is saluting, with eyes uplifted, probably fixed on the fold of the tricolour.' As myth, it signifies to the viewer, 'that France is a great empire, that all her sons, without colour discrimination, faithfully serve under her flag, and that there is no better answer to the detractors of an alleged colonialism than the zeal shown by this Negro in serving his so-called oppressors' (Barthes 1973:125–6).

A more positive view of the photograph was suggested by Walter Benjamin in the 1930s, in his analysis of the work of art in the age of mechanical reproduction (1970b). Mechanically reproduced art, including photography and cinema, is seen to challenge concepts from orthodox **aesthetics** that could be of use to **fascism** (such as originality, genius and authenticity). The photography carries with it no 'aura' of being the original and authentic work of art. The audience is thus brought closer to the work, and is engaged politically, rather than being kept at a distance by the **rituals** that surround the viewing of hand-produced originals. Yet mechanical reproduction also changes the nature of the artwork, and Benjamin makes a series of richly insightful and stimulating comments on the work of specific photographers. Thus, the photographs of the early twentieth-century French photographer Eugène Atget are 'like scenes of crime. . . . It is photographed for the purpose of establishing evidence' (Benjamin 1970b:228). The photograph thus draws our attention to the otherwise taken-for-granted details of everyday life, just as Freud's analysis of parapraxis ('Freudian slips') drew our attention to the accidents, and suddenly imbued them with great significance. Thus, Benjamin compares the painter to a magician or shaman, healing through the ritual of the laying on of hands. The photographer or cameraman is a surgeon, cutting into the patient (1970b:235).

Further reading: Bolton 1989; Newhall 1982; Sontag 1973.

AE

PLURALISM

As the promotion of heterogeneity over homogeneity, difference over sameness, or the dispersal of power over its centralisation, pluralism has informed social theory in appropriately multiple ways. It can take the form of an empirical or metaphysical claim (that reality, culture, truth, values, or practices simply are irrevocably plural in nature) or a normative agenda (positing diversification, devolution and openness as values), but mostly the two will be interlinked.

A concern for the tolerance of difference (in beliefs and social practices) has motivated liberal thinking from Milton and Locke, through Kant and Mill, and down to Berlin and Rawls—whether based on scepticism about the superiority of any single conception of the good life (and thus about the state's right to enforce one), or on a conception of the autonomous individual capable of choosing his or her own ends and taking responsibility for his or her actions. Various aporias and dilemmas have emerged: is it possible, desirable, or responsible for a state to remain neutral between competing ideals? Does one grant freedom of speech to those who would deny it for others? Does liberal (representative) democracy really allow for the articulation and pursuit of the full diversity of citizens' inclinations? How does liberalism account, or cater, for the possibility that ideas of the good stem from (rather than exist prior to) particular historical forms of social organisation? And so on. Significantly, contemporary pluralist thinking emerges strongly in the work of those **communitarian** thinkers (such as Charles Taylor and Michael Walzer) and in the discourse ethics of Jürgen Habermas, which reject the atomistic individualism of traditional liberalism in favour of some account of the intrinsically *social* nature of subjectivity.

A spin-off in political science is the form of pluralism (prominent since the 1950s) associated with a largely American tradition of 'polyarchic' democracy theory, represented notably by Talcott Parsons and Robert Dahl, linking Western democratic practice to a wide dispersal of power and **authority** through a range of relatively autonomous forums and institutions. This is one way to counteract the potential tyranny of the state: ensure that rival interest groups and other factions have a definite checking and balancing role in the political process. As with classical liberalism before it, this position has been rejected, by Marxists among others, as a straightforward apologia for the systematic inequalities of liberal capitalist societies: a smokescreen to obscure the typical concentration of power in the hands of an ultimately unaccountable elite.

Wittgenstein's recasting of philosophy in terms of an exploration of the forms of life revealed and enacted in our everyday language practice preceded a much wider insistence on the incommensurability of different language games, ways of thinking and discourses, culminating in post-structuralism's scepticism towards all foundationalisms, claimed transcendences of socio-historical context and 'meta-narrative' accounts of **history**, rationality and truth. Lyotard's work, in particular, has refused any attempt to reduce the multiplicity of 'phrase-regimens' and discursive '**genres**' to any single, self-authenticating account (be this in historiography, science, or theories of political justice)—and finds the instrumentalist, cognitive genre typified in **Enlightenment**-generation discourse to wield an unfounded, exclusionary, 'terroristic' social influence. His pluralism finds its ethical articulation in a call to 'bear witness' to those discursive practices to which modernity has denied a voice.

Similarly, a pluralistic impetus underlies the 'post-Marxist' reorientation of socialist theory by those, like Laclau and Mouffe, who wish to drop its allegedly **essentialist**, foundationalist and positivistic aspects in favour of a scrupulously anti-reductive 'radical democracy' rooted in the contingent, fluid, but constitutive nature of political identities. The 'politics of difference' that arise from talk around the postmodernist holy trinity of race, class and gender typifies the present affirmation of cultural pluralism. Does this mean cultural relativism, and a transition from a hesitancy to endorse a single worldview to a more problematic (and arguably self-refuting) 'anything goes' approach that would treat all such views as being strictly on a par? One aspect of pluralism since classical liberalism has been a tendency to slide from a liberating scepticism or fallibilism to an outright refusal to judge between different views and practices.

Further reading: Dahl 1956; Laclau and Mouffe 1985; Lyotard 1988; Walzer 1985; Young 1990.

GC

POLITICAL ECONOMY

The economic analysis of government. A good example of this form of study is Adam Smith's *Wealth of Nations*, a work generally hailed as the first of its kind. Smith offered an account of society in terms of socio-economic forces, and analysed economic relationships between **individuals** in terms of their implications for the role of government. In turn, Smith's analysis presents itself as a study of the general tendencies of social development which have marked out **history**. Thus, he examines the origins of modern **civil society** in terms of its **evolution** through succeeding stages, and accounts for that development in terms of its economic, psychological and power-related features. For example, Smith contended that the actions of a particular individual inspired by greed (namely, the pursuit of personal wealth through activity in the marketplace) will have other actual social effects, namely, the production of a greater level of overall wealth in society. This, Smith says, is the operation of the 'invisible hand', which operates at psychological and economic levels to promote the conditions of wealth. Smith provided an account of the mechanisms of competition and the conditions which determine the value of commodities. He advocated a view of government which had a limited range of social duties (the provision for, and administration of, law and order; provision for defence; and the responsibility to build essential public utilities), since its main aim was to facilitate the mechanisms of the free-market.

From Smith's work it is plain that political economy can be seen to aim at a descriptive analysis of social forces. Political economy (not only Smith's, but also the work of others, such as Ricardo) was adopted by Karl Marx, who used it in the development of his theories. In the 1960s and 1970s many of the basic premises of political economy (e.g. the notion of **subjectivity** presupposed within it, its status as empirical science) were subject to criticism by thinkers such as Louis Althusser.

Further reading: McLellan 1975; Smith 1986.

PS

POPULAR CULTURE

A simple definition of the term 'popular culture' as the **culture** that appeals to, or that is most comprehensible by, the general public may conceal a number of complexities and nuances of its use within **cultural studies**. The term is frequently used either to identify a form of culture that is opposed to another form, or as a synonym or complement to that other form. The precise meaning of 'popular culture' will therefore vary, for example, as it is related to folk culture, mass culture or high culture. In addition, popular culture may refer either to individual artefacts (often treated as **texts**) such as a popular song or a television programme, or to a group's lifestyle (and thus to the pattern of artefacts, practices and understandings that serve to establish the group's distinctive identity).

Theories of mass culture (that were dominant in American and European **sociology** in the 1930s and 1940s) tended to situate popular culture in relation to industrial production, and in opposition to folk culture. While folk culture was seen as a spontaneous production of the people, mass society theories focused on those forms of popular culture that were subject to industrial means of production and distribution (such as **cinema**, radio and **popular music**) and theorised them as being imposed on the people. The approach therefore tended to assume that the audience were passive consumers of the goods foist upon them. The message and purpose of these goods were interpreted within the context of a more or less sophisticated theory of **ideology**, so that the mass of the people were seen to be manipulated through the new **mass media**. Perhaps the most sophisticated version of this approach is found in the **Frankfurt School**'s concept of the **culture industry**.

With the development of the sociology of the mass media and of cultural studies from the 1950s onwards, not least with the work of Hoggart and the **Birmingham Centre for Contemporary Cultural Studies**, the consumers of popular culture came to be seen as increasingly active, and thus the process by which the message of popular culture is communicated to be increasingly complex. The activity of the people can be identified at two levels. On the first, the people are identified as the producers of popular culture (so that popular culture becomes the folk culture of an industrial society). On the second, more sophisticated level, the people are the interpreters of this culture. Thus, using for example a theory of **hegemony**, the propagation of mass culture cannot be seen as simply inflicting a message on the audience, despite the use of industrial production and distribution techniques. Rather, the audience will interpret, negotiate and appropriate the cultural artefacts or texts to its own uses, and make sense of them within its own environment and life experience. Precisely in so far as more sophisticated (and especially semiological and structuralist) approaches to communication emphasised the fact that the interpretation of a message can never be self-evident, the audience came to be credited with greater interpretative skills, and thus with the ability to resist an interpretation of the culture that is simply in the interests of the dominant class. The analysis of women's magazines, for example, may at once recognise the systems of **codes** and other mechanisms that integrate the reader into a particular ideological construction of femininity (and thus into particular patterns of commodity consumption), but also into the space that the magazine opens up in which the reader can enjoy and indulge in this construction and yet see through it as a fiction. Thus, popular culture may be understood in terms of ideological struggles and as a central element in any cultural politics.

Popular cultural artefacts serve to articulate the differentiation of society in terms of gender, age or race, and to constitute the self-understanding of those groups. Popular music for example has a key role in articulating the gender, class and ethnic identities of teenagers (and indeed in constituting the 'teenager' as a distinctive age group). However, precisely because much popular culture continues to depend upon the resources of industrial **capitalism** for its production and distribution, a tension remains in the selection of popular cultural products between the interests of capitalism (even if these are the purely commercial interests of profit maximisation) and the cultural and political interests of the consumers. Fiske, for example, distinguishes between the financial and the cultural economies within which cultural artefacts circulate. While the former is concerned with the generation of **exchange-value**, and thus with the accumulation of wealth and the incorporation of the consumer into the dominant economic order, the latter is concerned with the production of meanings and pleasures by, and for, the audience. Precisely because the production of meanings within the cultural economy is not as readily controlled as is the production of wealth, the audience, as producer of meanings, is credited with considerable power to resist the financial forces of incorporation. Popular culture is therefore seen by Fiske as a key site of resistance to capitalism.

Further reading: Fiske 1989; Hall *et al.* 1992; Storey 1996, 1997; Strianti 1995; Waites *et al.* 1989.

AE

POPULAR MUSIC

The study of popular music has followed a trajectory that is familiar in many areas of cultural studies, from a dismissive and elitist mass society theory to a concern with popular music as a creative expression and **articulation** of personal and group **identity**. The mass society approach, predominant from the 1930s, assumes that popular music, as the product of the music industry, is a highly standardised

commodity. The differences between popular songs are seen to be largely superficial, depending on the mere rearrangement of familiar elements within a rigid formula. The consumer of this music is largely passive (with the **consumption** of music as a **leisure** time activity being a mere corollary to the work process through which the labourer is renewed and prepared for the next day's work). Popular music (especially in its emphasis on the authoritarian power of rhythm) therefore 'adjusts' the listener to his or her existence in contemporary capitalism (see Adorno 1994). Crucially, a dichotomy is set up between popular music on the one hand, and some more authentic and aesthetically and politically valid music on the other. Popular music is seen to be manufactured and thus imposed upon an artificially constructed and maintained collective (the 'mass'). The authentic music expresses the real interests of the people, be this high art music (for Adorno), **jazz** (for Hall and Whannel (1964)), or folk (for Rosselson (1979)). The presence of such a **binary opposition** is highly persistent.

A political economy of popular music (associated with the political economy of the **mass media**) emerged in the 1960s and 1970s (see Golding and Murdock 1991). To a degree, it reproduced the assumptions of mass society theory in that it examined the economic mechanisms that determined the access that the public has to musical products. Commercial control of recording studios, record manu-facturers and even record store chains was seen to radically restrict the music that was made available on the market. The cultural studies approach to popular music can be seen as a reaction to this, not least in so far as it argues that consumption is an activity, and an activity through which the consumer can resist the industry. Thus, Hall and Whannel (1964) argue that popular music and its associated com-modities (such as magazines, concerts, posters and films) are selected in order to explore and establish a sense of **identity**. Commercial popular music therefore provides the teenager with resources ('guid-ing fictions') that are valuable in dealing with the difficulties of emotional and sexual transitions. The teenager does not therefore simply buy what the record industry provides. Indeed, only 10 per cent of all records released actually make a profit for the industry (suggesting large-scale rejection of what is offered).

This approach was developed within the study of **subcultures** (Hall and Jefferson 1976). The emphasis here rests upon the use of popular music in a subordinate or minority group's resistance to the values and attitudes of a 'parent' culture. A specific form of popular music will be chosen as one of the elements that reflects a set of central values with which the subcultural group identifies. The choice is not then made arbitrarily or casually. The music is meaningful. Willis's analysis of the culture of bikers illustrates this (1978). Classic 1950s rock music is significant, for as an historically unified corpus of music it is readily opposed to the contemporary popular music and thus the biker is separated from the consumer of pop music. Classic rock'n'roll (for example by Elvis Presley and Buddy Holly) is expressive of masculine values. Finally, the driving rhythms are expressive of a life of movement (and thus the music provides an imaginary soundtrack to bike riding itself). This approach to subcultures and music is developed to an extreme by Hebdige's (1979) explicit use of **semiotics** in the analysis of punk and its precursors.

If the cultural studies approach to popular music culminates in a semiotics of subcultures, it may still be criticised for placing undue emphasis on the exotic resistance of these subcultures, as opposed to the more mundane consumption of music that is typical of much **youth culture** (so that a heavy hint of the authentic/manufactured music distinction remains). The ethnographic approach to music making and consumption explores this background. Ruth Finnegan's study of Milton Keynes (in England) reveals a rich and diverse world of music making (1989). Knowledgeable amateur musicians, valuing individual expression and innovation, are part of a complex set of social relations that draw together and serve to define local communities. Bands are not simply groups of musicians, but rather musicians supported by followers and helpers. They rely on the support of existing social **institutions** (such as schools and colleges, pubs and families) for resources such as practice and performance space, as well as instruments and equipment. Thus, the expression of an opposition or rebel stance is mitigated by this integration into the community. However, as Frith (1992) observes, this is still a world structured by **gender** and **class**. Women are largely excluded from bands, or marginalised into traditional domestic roles in support of the bands. Further, popular music is not seen by Frith as a predominantly working-class activity. Middle-class youths are not simply involved, but because they typically have more access to the resources (of money and time) necessary to promote and develop their art, they are also more likely to turn their amateur music making into professional music making.

Further reading: Frith 1981.

AE

POSITIVISM

A theory of knowledge which contends that what should count as knowledge can be validated only through methods of observation which are derived from the example set by the physical sciences. Thus, positivists hold to the view that what counts as knowledge is solely a matter of sense-experience. The roots of positivism can be traced at least as far back as the writings of Auguste Comte (1798–1857), although the seventeenth-century philosopher Francis Bacon (who propounded an account of knowledge in his *Novum Organum* (1620) which stressed the importance of empirical observation) might also be cited in connection with this approach. In the twentieth century, a number of thinkers have espoused what has been termed 'logical positivism', an approach derived from the early work of Ludwig Wittgenstein, as well as that of Bertrand Russell and Gottlob Frege. A.J. Ayer's book *Language, Truth and Logic* is often seen as a key work in the articulation of the basic tenets of logical positivism. In this work he argued that all propositions could be characterised as either true, false or meaningless. In other words, if a proposition does not assert something which can, in principle, be either validated or disproved by way of observation according to the standards of scientific verification, then, it is held, that proposition is devoid of meaning. This attempt to clarify the meaning of propositions/sentences, in these terms, represented an attempt at a kind of 'ground clearing' within philosophy, in so far as it was contended that many sorts of questions (e.g. those concerned with issues of religion or **metaphysics**) were in fact meaningless.

There have been numerous critics of positivism, including Thomas Kuhn, W.V.O. Quine, Karl Popper and **Frankfurt School** thinker Max Horkheimer. Amongst other things, Horkheimer's attack on positivism argues that methods adapted from the sciences cannot be taken as the sole criterion for knowledge, since positivists ignore the fact that the social and cultural domains within which scientific investigation is undertaken represent a fundamental factor in the construction of knowledge. By reducing the meaning of the term 'knowledge' to being equivalent to 'method', Horkheimer says, positivists conceptualise knowledge according to the precepts of a socially determined instrumentalism (i.e. the view that knowledge is a matter of the appropriate means for a given end) which characterises the tendency in modern industrial culture towards an abandonment of critical reflection with regard to its own nature and constitution.

Further reading: Ayer 1959, 1967; Hanfling 1981; Horkheimer 1992.

PS

POST-COLONIALISM

A term generally used to indicate a range of global cultural developments which occurred in the aftermath of the Second World War. To this extent, it has both historical nuances and theoretical ones. On the one hand, 'post-colonialism' signifies something distinctive about this period as one in which the cultural, economic and social events which have constituted it mark the decline of European imperialism. On the other hand, theories of 'post-coloniality' concern themselves with a wide range of **metaphysical**, ethical, methodological and political concerns. Issues which are addressed from this perspective include the nature of cultural **identity** and **gender**, investigations into concepts of **nationality**, **race** and **ethnicity**, the constitution of **subjectivity** under conditions of imperialism and questions of **language** and **power**. One of the earliest writers who brought attention to such issues was Frantz Fanon (1925–61), who sought to articulate the oppressed consciousness of the colonised subject. He argued that imperialism initiated a process of 'internalisation' in which those subjected to it experienced economic, political and social inferiority not merely in 'external' terms, but in a manner that affected their sense of their own identity. Hence, material inferiority creates a sense of racial and cultural inferiority. In turn, Fanon attempted to show the role of language within this process. Colonisation, he argues, also took place through language: under French domination the Creole language is rendered 'inferior' to French, and the colonised subject is compelled to speak the tongue of his or her imperial rulers, thereby experiencing their subjugation in terms of their own linguistic abilities and identity (an experience, it might be added, not uncommon within the context of Europe itself, e.g. the colonial experiences of Irish and Welsh cultures under the dominion of English expansion since the sixteenth century).

In the wake of the work of such figures as Fanon, writers have raised questions about the applicability of definitions of culture and humanity (for instance, the question of nationhood) which have been offered within the context of Western cultural domination (see, for example, Bhabha 1990), or have elucidated the cultural bias inherent in particular forms of European discourse (see Edward Said's writings on **orientalism**). Likewise, notions, such as those of 'hybridity' and diaspora, have been developed in order to emphasise the notion of an implicit cultural diversity underlying the identities of so-called 'Third World' or post-colonial cultures (see, for example, the writings of Stuart Hall or Homi Bhabha). Within this context, theories of **discourse** and **narrative** have often been deployed as a means of articulating the distinctions between Western and non-Western culture, and in turn questioning its hierarchical superiority. Some of these theories have been derived from **Marxism** or the thinking of **postmodernism** and **post-structuralism**— although the anti-**realism** implicit in the work of thinkers associated with these last two movements has led to some criticism, for instance by Said, of its applicability to the experience of 'post-colonial' subjects (and, perhaps, one ought to mention the possible criticism that much of the thought inherent in postmodernism and post-structuralism has itself been produced within the Western academy).

It is also worth noting that the use of 'post-colonialism' to define such theories, or indeed even an historical period, is controversial. This is not least because it is possible to argue that the word preserves within it the presupposition that Western culture retains the predominance it attained during the past two or three hundred years as a consequence of colonial expansion. To be identified as 'post-colonial', in other words, involves a retention of the belief that colonialism continues to exert its influence through providing a definition of the identity of 'post-colonial' subjects and their cultures. Equally, whether the post-war period can be seen as really signifying a move away from colonial forms is questionable. The rise of colonial imperialism rooted in the political form of the European nation state occurred in conjunction with capitalism in the modern era, and the predominance of this form has perhaps subsided. But the cultural and economic power of the West, it is arguable, retains its dominance in the form of those processes of **globalisation** which have been delineated by some critics as characteristic of developments within late capitalism (see the discussion of David Harvey's work in the **postmodernism** entry).

Further reading: Bhabha 1990, 1994; Fanon 1989; Said 1978a, 1993.

PS

POST-HUMANISM

The typically enthusiastic exploration of the impact that **technology** will have on embodied human existence, manifest in philosophy, cultural theory and science fiction. Post-humanism focuses primarily on the enhancement of the human **body** and mind through such technologies as cybernetic implants, **genetic** modification and, more recently, nanotechnology.

The term post-humanism may be understood as articulating a position that lies beyond the **humanist** philosophies that have characterised much Western thought since the Renaissance. Thus, a humanist presupposes that there is a given human **nature** that cannot be changed, and that is shared by all humans through **history** and across cultures. (The French philosopher René Descartes (1596–1650) is frequently taken to be exemplary of such a humanist approach.) While such a position does not necessarily entail that humanity cannot improve or progress, the humanist typically assumes that any such progress is towards a predetermined goal – the essence of perfect humanity. These more historical dimensions of humanism were being explored extensively in the nineteenth century, not least by philosophers such as Hegel and **Marx**, who recognised that human nature was in a process of historical flux and development. Marx in particular recognised that human nature was bound up with humanity's use of technology (see **forces of production**), and changed as the technology itself became more sophisticated, and thus begins to suggest that there is no such thing as an essential human nature. This challenge to an ahistorical humanism was complemented by Darwin's theory of **evolution**, that presented humans as just one more species, and not as God-given or in any way separate from the forces of natural selection that shaped the evolution of other species. Thus, in 1923 a British biochemist, J.B.S. Haldane (1924), could already begin to explore the positive consequences to humanity of genetic and other forms of technological enhancement.

For the post-humanist, humanism does not merely represent a philosophical position concerning the nature of human existence, but also the presupposition that 'humanness' is a grounding normative value. Such 'humanness' presupposes the positive valuation of human autonomy (articulated, most profoundly, in the moral philosophy of the eighteenth-century philosopher Immanuel Kant, but also encoded in such political and moral documents as the United Nations Declaration of Human Rights). Within a humanist perspective, autonomy is the unique source of human dignity. This notion had already been challenged, for example by **structuralist** thinkers such as Louis Althusser (1918–90). For Althusser, the focus on individual autonomy is an **ideology**, concealing the actual dependence of human action on social and cultural structures. The individual human being is at best a bearer of any such structures, their actions more or less determined (or over-determined) by those structures.

The distinctiveness of the post-human perspective may be seen in the emphasis that it places upon technology, and upon the openness and unpredictability of the nature of the human (or post-human) in the future. Baudrillard, in a gesture that anticipates something crucial to post-humanist thinking, suggests that (post)modern humans are so dependent upon the technology that surrounds them, that they are in a position akin to 'the boy in a bubble' (Baudrillard 2000b:34). The 'boy in a bubble' is a child whose immune system is so weak that he cannot survive outside an artificial and precisely controlled, sterile environment, and thus outside of the NASA-designed 'tent' in which he lives. Perhaps the key move in post-humanist thinking is to shift attention from the technological control of an environment (that may be seen to develop Marx's thinking), to the possibility of that technology intruding into the human body itself, so that any possible human essence is overridden from within.

The twentieth century saw a sustained, if at times rather marginalised, debate over the future of the human, and thus the post- or transhuman. The term transhuman can be taken to be more or less synonymous with post-human, although it has the nice double association of referring to both a transcendence or humanity, and a transitional humanity (the latter being the sense given to it by F. W. Esfaniary (aka FM 2030 (1989), founder of the Upwingers). The contributions from scientists (such as Robert Ettinger (1972) and others involved in cryonics), utopian thinkers (such as Max More (2003), the founder of the Extropy Institute, where 'extropy' is the opposite of 'entropy), novelists and film-makers have all contributed to developing both the theory and popular awareness of the post-human. A World Transhumanist Association was founded in 1998 by Nick Bostrom and David Pearce.

Within cultural theory, Donna Haraway's 'Cyborg Manifesto' (1991) is a key text. Working from a **feminist** perspective, Haraway challenges three core **binary oppositions** that she identifies in humanist thinking: human as against animal; organism as against machine; and physical as against non-physical. In the post-human, these distinctions will be blurred, and the patriarchal privilege given to the first element in each pair will be undermined. The task of a post-human feminism is therefore to find **codes** that will allow the interface of previously separated components, leading to a machine–organism symbiosis: the cyborg as 'a kind of dissembled and reassembled, postmodern collective and personal self' (Haraway 1991:163). In Katherine Hayles's account, in 'the post-human, there are no essential differences or absolute demarcations between bodily existence and computer simulation, cybernetic mechanisms and biological organisms, robot technology and human goals' (1999:3).

The moral debate over post-humanism has intensified in the face of the growing potential of genetic technology. This debate may be seen to take up the humanist theme of dignity, and centrally to ask whether genetic and other modifications of the human being leave the resultant being with an acceptable degree of dignity and, indeed, in what this dignity might consist. Some thinkers resist the idea of genetic (and other) modification of the individual human being or the human species, typically on the grounds that this would violate human dignity (and thus, again, the grounding values of 'humanness'). Thus, Jürgen Habermas has argued that a human being who was genetically modified to enhance certain capacity or potentials would be denied rational choice over its life goals. Such enhancement is contrasted with normal **education**, where the very process of educating someone gives them the ability to reflect upon and if necessary to reject the goals and purposes for which they are being educated. The genetically modified person is denied such a choice (Habermas 2003). Perhaps the best-known and most widely read opponent of the post-human is Francis Fukuyama (2002). For him, genetic modification will undermine the unknowable 'factor X' that is common to all humanity, and which thereby grounds the common dignity and rights of all humans within the community. This undermining will lead to new forms of discrimination and oppression, as certain groups or individuals are determined to be genetically inferior or superior.

This conservatism has been challenged by, amongst others, Bostrom and Hughes. Bostrom (2005b) has sought to explore a wider notion of dignity, that will articulate a space within which all possible modes of being can be accepted and respected. Hughes (2004) envisions a society in which safe post-human technologies are made available to all, with the right according to all individuals to shape their bodies as they wish. The state is thus accorded the role of guaranteeing the safety and efficacy of new technologies, and ensuring that such technologies are not the preserve of a wealthy or powerful elite.

Further reading: Badmington 2000; Bostrom 2005a.

AE

POST-INDUSTRIAL SOCIETY

The idea of a 'post-industrial state', grounded on an economy of small-scale, workshop-based craft production was first proposed in the late nineteenth century by followers of the utopian socialist William

Morris. However, in current usage, 'post-industrial society' was articulated, almost simultaneously in the early 1960s, by Daniel Bell (1973) and Alain Touraine (1968). The concept of 'post-industrial society' is intended to encapsulate the changes that have occurred within **capitalism** in the post-war period. The post-industrial society was presented as a new social form, as different from industrial capitalism as capitalism had been from **feudalism**. The central idea is that theoretical knowledge has now become the source of social change and policy formation. The society is highly educated, with significant levels of resources invested into the production of theoretical knowledge (in higher education and commercial research and development). The economy therefore shifts from the production of goods and raw materials, to the production of services. The dominant industries become those which are dependent upon theoretical knowledge (such as computing and aerospace). This is accompanied by a decline in the old working **class**, and the rise of 'white collar' (or non-manual) classes. New professional and technical classes (or a 'knowledge class') become dominant. The difference between Bell's and Touraine's accounts rests largely upon the enthusiasm with which they embrace post-industrial society. For Bell it is a positive development, leading to greater social integration, and the reduction of political conflict. For Touraine, post-industrial society threatens to become a society dominated by a technocratic **elite**, who are insensitive to the humanist values of traditional university education.

Further reading: Kumar 1978.

AE

POSTMODERNISM

'Postmodern, if it means anything,' Anthony Giddens argues, 'is best kept to refer to styles or movements within literature, painting, the plastic arts, and **architecture**. It concerns aspects of *aesthetic reflection* upon the nature of modernity' (1990:45). Giddens in fact also links it to Nietzsche and Heidegger, and an abandonment of the **Enlightenment** project of rational criticism. Postmoderns, though, Giddens continues, have nothing better to offer in the place of the ideals of the Enlightenment. Amongst other critical works which have dealt with postmodernism, David Harvey's *The Condition of Postmodernity* has sought to analyse it in socio–economic terms. Harvey argues that the postmodern can be taken to signify a decentralised, diversified stage in the development of the market place, in which the Fordist rationale of production concentrated in a single site (the factory) has been replaced by a form of manufacture which co-ordinates a diversity of sources (e.g. parts of one final product are made in more than one place and then shipped elsewhere for purposes of assembly) in search of greater flexibility of production. In turn, this has had the effect of producing workforces which are mobile and disposable in a way in which the earlier labour markets of Fordist period were not. Thus, for Harvey postmodernism is in fact an extension of those social processes which Marx diagnosed as being characteristic of the logic of capitalist society. In effect, on this view, postmodernism (at least in its philosophical guise) may well be regarded as a form of apology for **capitalism**.

One thing, therefore, is certain about postmodernism: the uses of the word display such a diversity of meanings that it defies simple definition. In architecture, for example, postmodernism has been taken to mean the overcoming of earlier, rigid conventions underlying modernist tastes (as exemplified by Le Corbusier's functionalism) in favour of a more eclectic, playful and non-functional aesthetic. The 'postmodern' novel, in contrast, could be described as embodying an experimentalism with narrative form through which a rejuvenation of the established conventions of the form itself is sought (by way of a simultaneous retention and redeployment of those conventions in the name of an avant-gardism which harks back to modernism). Writers often associated with postmodernism include Jean Baudrillard, Jacques Derrida, Michel Foucault, and Luce Irigaray.

Perhaps the most coherent account of what constitutes postmodernism has been offered by the philosopher Jean-François Lyotard in *The Postmodern Condition: A Report on Knowledge* and most succinctly in the essay included at the end of that volume, 'Answering the Question: What is Postmodernism?'. In *The Postmodern Condition*, Lyotard provides an account of postmodernity which stresses the collapse of 'grand narratives' (e.g. that of **Marxism**), and their replacement with 'little narratives' in the wake of **technologies** which have transformed our notion of what constitutes knowledge. To that extent, the view offered in this text concentrates on the **epistemology** of postmodernity, i.e. the postmodern conceived of in terms of a crisis in our ability to provide an adequate, 'objective' account of reality.

In the essay 'Answering the Question: What is Postmodernism?', Lyotard offers an analysis of Kant's notion of the **sublime** (as presented in the *Critique of Judgement*) as a means of elucidating the postmodern. The sublime, Kant argues, is a feeling aroused in the spectator by the presentation to the intellect of something which defies conceptualisation. Likewise, Lyotard holds, the postmodern can be characterised as a mode of expression which seeks to put forward new ways of expressing the sublime feeling. In other words, postmodernism is an **avant-garde** aesthetic discourse, which seeks to overcome the limitations of traditional conventions by searching for new strategies for the project of describing and interpreting experience. Significantly, Lyotard argues that the postmodern ought not to be understood in terms of an historical progression which signals a present departure from a past modernism. Rather, modernism is in fact characterised as a response to a set of concerns which are themselves already postmodern. According to Lyotard, modernism embodies a nostalgic yearning for a lost sense of unity, and constructs an **aesthetics** of fragmentation in the wake of this. Postmodernism, in contrast, begins with this lack of unity but, instead of lamenting it, celebrates it—a claim made most evident by Lyotard's comparison of the modernist 'fragment' (i.e. the artwork conceived of as a part of a greater, albeit unattainable, whole) with the postmodern 'essay' (taken in the sense of an essaying-forth, in the spirit of an experimentalism which disdains either to construct or lament totality—the characterisation of the latter bearing a strong resemblance to T.W. Adorno's analysis in his 'The Essay as Form').

More recently, Lyotard has moved away from his earlier exposition of postmodernism. On the one hand, he has sought to redefine it in terms of a 'rewriting' of the project of modernity (see the essays collected in *The Inhuman*). On the other hand, a work like *The Differend: Phrases in Dispute* at least hints that postmodernism may be considered in a rather less positive (and certainly more modest) light than that afforded it in *The Postmodern Condition*: 'an old man who scrounges in the garbage-heap of finality looking for leftovers ... a goal for a certain humanity' (*The Differend*, section 182).

Italian philosopher Gianni Vattimo has also offered an account of the postmodern in his essay 'Nihilism and the Postmodern in Philosophy' in *The End of Modernity*. Contrary to Giddens's view, Vattimo specifically relates postmodernism to philosophy, rather than the arts. As with Giddens, two thinkers mark the opening of postmodernity: Nietzsche and Heidegger. Vattimo turns to Heidegger's notion of *Verwindung* as a means of explicating his position. The word *Verwindung* represents neither an *Überwindung* (i.e. a critical overcoming of **contradiction** through the use of reason) nor a Kantian *Verbindung*, which seeks to establish a priori modes of combination as a means of grounding transcendental critique in primary rules of understanding and principles of reason. A *Verwindung*, rather, is a 'twisting' of meaning which makes room for a form of relativistic criticism which disdains all pretensions to objectivity. This, then, allows for Vattimo to account for the 'post-' in postmodernism, for it does not presuppose the possibility of transcendental critique. Interestingly, it is Nietzsche, and not Heidegger, whom Vattimo regards as the first philosopher to talk in the terminology of *Verwindung*. Indeed, for Vattimo, postmodernity is born with Nietzsche's writing (*The End of Modernity*, p. 164). Turning to Nietzsche's book *Human, All-Too-Human*, Vattimo argues that this work defines modernity as a process of constant replacement, wherein the old (expressed through notions such as 'tradition') is abandoned in favour of the new, which in its turn decays and is replaced by ever-newer forms. Within such a context, the modern can never be overcome, since each overcoming is merely another repetition of the fetish of the new. Having offered this diagnosis, Nietzsche's text refuses to envisage a way out of modernity by way of recourse to, for example, a Kantian transcendentalism. Rather, a Nietzschean account seeks to radicalise the modern through a dissolution of 'its own innate tendencies' (p. 166). This is achieved through the following chain of reasoning: (i) a criticism of mores (dominant forms of ethical behaviour) is undertaken by Nietzsche through a strategy of 'chemical reduction' (see *Human, All-Too-Human*, sections 1ff., where Nietzsche writes of constructing a 'chemistry of the moral and religious sensations'); which leads to (ii) the realisation that the ontological ground and methodological basis for this reduction (i.e. truth) is destined likewise to dissolve under such scrutiny; and (iii) that truth, in consequence, is rendered the product of historical contingency. As such, it is realised that truth (and consequently the language of truth) is both (a) subject to and (b) moulded by forces such as the need for survival, and rests on such notions as the untenable belief that reality can be known; this, in turn, leads to the conclusion that (iv) truth is rooted in the metaphorical function of language (language as a tool for coping with the world, not as a means of describing reality). Within this context, truth is dissolved and (most famously) God dies, slain by his own metaphysics (the Christian metaphysical demand for truth having turned on Christianity itself, finds it unable to live up to its own ideal). For Vattimo, this nihilistic conclusion offers a way out of modernity, and marks the birth of postmodernity, i.e. an interest in grounding knowledge in concepts of truth and Being is replaced by one which stresses the historical analysis of 'appearance' and the predominance of contingency in our forms of knowledge. It is worth noting that such an account leaves out many aspects of Nietzsche's thought which would not conform with Vattimo's view (e.g. his later diagnosis of modernity as a decadent form which must be 'overcome', and likewise his criticisms of modern 'nihilism' as a symptom of 'decadence' or cultural decline).

Further readings: Giddens 1990; Harvey 1989; Hassan 1987; Jenks 1991; Lyotard 1988, 1989, 1991; Vattimo 1988.

PS

POST-STRUCTURALISM

Movement of thought in various fields—literary criticism, cultural studies, political theory, sociology, ethnography, historiography, psychoanalysis—which grew out of (and to some extent reacted against) the earlier structuralist paradigm adopted by mainly French theorists in the 1950s and 1960s. **Structuralism** took its methodological bearings from the programme of theoretical linguistics devised some four decades earlier by Ferdinand de Saussure. This work was rediscovered—with considerable excitement—by structuralist thinkers who proceeded to apply his ideas to a range of social and cultural phenomena supposedly exhibiting a language-like (systemic) character, and hence amenable to description and analysis in terms deriving from Saussure's structural-synchronic approach. Thus, in each of the above-mentioned disciplines, the aim was to break with an existing (merely 'empirical' or case-by-case) treatment of the innumerable narratives, myths, rituals, social practices, ideologies, case histories, cultural patterns of belief, etc., and to focus rather on the underlying structure—the depth-logic of signification—which promised to fulfil Saussure's great dream of a unified general **semiology**. Such would be the structuralist key to all mythologies, one that explained how such a massive (empirically unmanageable) range of cultural phenomena could be brought within the compass of a theory requiring only a handful of terms, concepts, distinctions and logical operators. Among them—most importantly—were Saussure's cardinal distinctions between **signifier** and **signified**, *langue* and *parole*, and the twofold (diachronic and synchronic) axes of linguistic-semiotic research. Beyond that, the main task was to press this analysis to a point where it left no room for such supposedly naïve ideas as that of the subject—the 'autonomous' subject of humanist discourse—as somehow existing outside or beyond the various structures (or 'subject-positions') that marked the very limits of language and thought at some specific cultural juncture.

Thus structuralist thinking most often went along with a strain of theoretical anti-humanism which defined itself squarely against such earlier 'subject-centred' movements of thought as **phenomenology** and existentialism. In this respect, and others, there is a clear continuity between structuralism and post-structuralism. Indeed, there has been much debate among theorists as to how we should construe the 'post-' prefix, whether in the strong sense ('superseding and displacing the structuralist paradigm') or simply as a matter of chronological sequence ('developing and extending the structuralist approach in certain new directions'). Post-structuralism also finds its chief theoretical inspiration in the programme of Saussurean linguistics, though it tends to play down—or reject outright—any notion that this might give a 'scientific' basis for the analysis of texts, semiotic systems, cultural codes, ideological structures, social practices, etc. That claim is now viewed as just a species of 'metalinguistic' delusion, an example of the old (typically structuralist but also Marxist) fallacy which holds that theory can somehow attain to a critical standpoint outside and above whatever it seeks to interpret or explain. On the contrary post-structuralists argue: there is no way of drawing a firm methodological line between text and commentary, language and metalanguage, ideological belief systems and those other (theoretical) modes of discourse that claim to unmask ideology as a product of false consciousness or—in the language of a structural Marxist like Louis Althusser—a form of 'imaginary' misrecognition. Such ideas took hold through the false belief that theory could achieve a decisive 'epistemological break' with the various kinds of naturalised 'common-sense' knowledge which passed themselves off as straightforwardly true but which in fact encoded the cultural values of a given (e.g. bourgeois-humanist) socio-political order. However, this position becomes untenable once it is realised that *all* subject-positions—that of the analyst included—are caught up in an endless process of displacement engendered by the instability of language, the 'arbitrary' relation between signifier and signified, and the impossibility that meaning can ever be captured in a moment of pure, self-present utterer's intent.

Thus the 'post-' in 'post-structuralism' is perhaps best understood—by analogy with other such formations, among them 'post-modernism', 'post-**Marxism**' and, more lately 'post-feminism'—as marking a widespread movement of retreat from earlier positions more directly aligned with the project of political emancipation and critique. However, post-structuralism does lay claim to its own kind of radical politics, one that envisages a 'subject-in-process' whose various shifting positions within language or discourse cannot be captured by any theory (structuralist, Marxist, feminist or whatever) premised on old-style 'Enlightenment' ideas of knowledge and truth. Most influential here, at least among literary theorists, was the sequence of changing allegiances to be seen in the work of Roland Barthes, from his early high-structuralist phase (in texts such as *Mythologies* (1957) and 'The Structural Analysis of Narratives' (1977b)) to his late style of writing (e.g. *S/Z* (1970) and *The Pleasure of the Text* (1973)) where he renounces all claims to theoretical rigour, and instead draws freely and idiosyncratically on whatever sources come to hand—literature, linguistics, structuralism, psychoanalysis, Marxism and a vast range of intertextual allusions—while treating them all with a consummate deftness and irony which disclaims any kind of orthodox methodological commitment. In *Mythologies* Barthes had provided by far the most convincing application of a highly systematic (Saussure-derived) structuralist method to the analysis of various items of late-bougeois 'mythology', from advertising images to French culinary fashion, from 'The Romans on Film' to the myth of the jet pilot, and from 'the brain of Einstein' (a fetish object created by the modern ideology of scientific genius) to the spectacle of boxing as a prime example of cultural artifice passing itself off as a natural sporting event. A decade later he reflected ruefully that this method could now be applied by anyone who had picked up the necessary analytic tools and learned to demythologise just about everything that came their way. So one had to move on, renounce that false idea of 'metalinguistic' analysis, and instead produce readings that would 'change the object itself'—the title of a later essay—by actually *rewriting* the myths concerned through a process of creative textual transformation. Otherwise there would always come a stage—repugnant to Barthes—when radical ideas began to settle down into a new orthodoxy, or when theories that had once seemed challenging and subversive (like those of 'classical' structuralism) were at length recycled in a safely packaged academic form.

In Barthes's later writing one can see this diagnosis applied to certain aspects of post-structuralism even though that movement had not yet acquired anything like its subsequent widespread following. Thus, for instance, it became a high point of post-structuralist principle (deriving from the psychoanalytic theories of Jacques Lacan) that the unconscious was 'structured like a language', that its workings were by very definition inaccessible to conscious thought, and that the human subject was irreparably split between a specular realm of false ('imaginary') ego-identification and a symbolic realm where its 'identity' consisted of nothing more than a series of shifting, discursively produced subject-positions. Then again, post-structuralists have been much influenced by Michel Foucault's sceptical genealogies of knowledge, his argument that 'truth' is always and everywhere a product of vested power interests, so that different regimes of 'power-knowledge' give rise to various disciplinary techniques or modes of subjectively internalised surveillance and control. These ideas are presented as marking a break—a radical break—with the concepts and values of a humanist discourse which concealed its own 'will to power' by fostering the illusion of autonomous freedom and choice.

So the claim is that post-structuralism affords a potentially liberating space, a space of 'plural', 'decentred', multiple or constantly destabilised subject-positions where identities can no longer be defined according to such old 'essentialist' notions as gender or class affiliation. For some theorists, Ernesto Laclau and Chantal Mouffe among them, it points the way towards a politics—an avowedly 'post-Marxist' politics—that acknowledges the sheer range and variety of present-day social interests. On this view it is merely a form of 'meta-narrative' delusion to suppose that any one privileged theory (like that of classical Marxism) could somehow speak the truth of **history** or rank those interests on a scale of priority with socio-economic or class factors as the single most important issue. Rather we should think—in post-structuralist terms—of subjects as 'dispersed' over a range of multiple positions, discourses, sites of struggle, etc., with nothing (least of all some grand 'totalising' theory) that would justify their claim to speak on behalf of this or that oppressed class or interest group. Still there is a problem when it comes to explaining how anyone could make a reasoned or principled choice in such matters if every such 'choice' were indeed just a product of the subject's particular mode of insertion into a range of pre-existing discourses.

Nor is this problem in any way resolved by the idea that subjects are non-self-identical, that subjectivity is always an ongoing process, or again—following Lacan—that there never comes a point where the ego escapes from the endless 'detours' of the signifier and at last achieves a wished-for state of 'imaginary' plenitude and presence. For this still works out as a determinist doctrine, a theory of the subject as constructed in (or by) language, whatever the desire of some post-structuralists to give it a vaguely utopian spin by extolling the 'freeplay' of the signifier or the possibility of subjects adopting as many positions—or 'performative' roles—as exist from one situation to the next. In Barthes's later work it is the very act of writing, exemplified in certain **avant–garde** literary texts, that is thought of as somehow accomplishing the break with oppressive (naturalised or realist) norms, and thus heralding a new dispensation where identity and gender are no longer fixed by the grim paternal law of bourgeois 'classical realism'. Such ideas have a certain heady appeal when compared with the bleak message conveyed by theorists such as Foucault and Lacan. Nevertheless, they are open to the same objection: that the subject remains (in Lacan's phrase) a mere 'plaything' of language or discourse, and that reality likewise becomes just an optional construct out of various signifying codes and conventions.

One result—as seen in post-structuralist approaches to historiography and the social sciences—is a blurring of the crucially important line between fictive discourse (novels, stories, imaginary scenarios of various kinds) and those other kinds of narrative that aim to give a truthful account of past or present events. That confusion of realms is carried yet further in the writing of postmodernist thinkers like Jean Baudrillard who argue—largely on the same premise—that we now inhabit a world of ubiquitous mass-media simulation where the very idea of a reality 'behind appearances' (along with the notions of truth, critique, ideology, false consciousness and so forth) must be seen as belonging to a bygone age of nai?ve Enlightenment beliefs. This is all—as post-structuralists would happily concede—a very long way from Saussure's original programme for a structural linguistics based on strictly scientific principles. Whether or not their more radical claims stand up to careful scrutiny is still a topic of intense dispute among theorists of various persuasions.

Further reading: Attridge *et al.* 1987; Barthes 1975; Belsey 1980; Harari 1980; Harland 1987; Sturrock 1979; Young 1981.

CN

POWER

A term which has a variety of meanings. Most usually, power is taken to mean the exercise of force or control over individuals or particular social groups by other individuals or groups. Power, in this view, is something extrinsic to the constitution of both individuals and society. For example, the theory of the role of the state in the writings of **liberalism** normally conceives of legislative power in terms of limitations on the state's ability to use justifiable force with regard to the behaviour of individuals who fall under its jurisdiction. On such a view, it does not follow that the exercise of power is a priori coercive in nature, since power exercised within the limits of legality is taken to be justly exercised. On the other hand, liberals would regard any exercise of power which compels individuals to behave in ways that they would not freely choose as coercive.

Power and **authority** are not necessarily synonymous. Thus, for example, the seventeenth-century political philosopher James Harrington (an exponent of **civic humanism**) drew a distinction between *de facto* power (the possession of power as a matter of fact) and *de jure* authority (authority by right, i.e. by means of justification). Harrington notes that one may have the one without the other. Power without authority expresses for him the essential feature of the modern or 'Gothic' form of government, which corresponds with the *de facto* possession of power by a monarch, who is not answerable to those citizens who fall under his or her jurisdiction and thereby rules without the authority of their consent.

The writings of French philosopher Michel Foucault have often been taken as influential (principally amongst exponents of one form or other of **post-structuralism** or **postmodernism**, both of which Foucault has been identified with at one time or another) in their attempt to redefine what the term 'power' means. Foucault, following Nietzsche, seeks to redefine power in a way that is notably different from how it is conceived within more traditional theory. Thus, power, in Nietzsche's view (see especially *The Will to Power*, 1968b: section 1067), does not so much express differences in the relationships that exist between individuals or groups as permeate the entirety of reality and thereby become its essence. Likewise, Foucault conceives of power as existing *not* as something that is exercised over individuals or groups, but as being constitutive of both the relations which exist between groups and hence equally of individual and group identities themselves. Important in Foucault's analysis is the claim that power is not only constitutive of social reality and of such social forms as **subjectivity**. He also claims that discourses of knowledge are in fact an expression of power relations and themselves embodiments of power (a view that goes back to English philosopher Thomas Hobbes, who saw knowledge as an expression of power, and indeed well beyond him—for example, the Ancient Greek figure Georgias, discussed in Plato's dialogue of the same name). On this view, power becomes so universal and immanent to social relations that it is difficult not to regard it as a metaphysical conception.

Further reading: Foucault 1980; Harrington 1992; Mill 1984; Nietzsche 1968b.

PS

PRAGMATISM

A philosophical movement that exerted a profound influence upon American thought during the first part of the twentieth century. Principal thinkers associated with pragmatism include C.S. Peirce (1839–1914), William James (1842–1910), John Dewey (1859–1952), George Herbert Mead (1862–1931) and Clarence Irving Lewis (1883–1964). However, these thinkers do not share one basic doctrine on the basis of which they may all straightforwardly be classified as pragmatists. It is, rather, in virtue of a shared approach to philosophical problems that the term 'pragmatism' is best applied to each of them. Although an exclusively American movement, unsurprisingly (given the fact that its thinkers were schooled in European philosophy and literature) pragmatism owes much to British and continental European philosophy. Thus, pragmatists like Peirce devoted their attention to elucidating problems in the sphere of the theory of knowledge that they had encountered in the work of Descartes or Kant. It is perhaps best to turn to Peirce's own account of pragmatism, given in the essay 'What Is Pragmatism', for a concise exposition of his notion of pragmatism:

> a *conception*, that is, the rational purport of a word or other expression, lies exclusively in its conceivable bearing upon the conduct of life [...] if one can define accurately all the conceivable experimental phenomena which the affirmation or denial of a concept could imply, one will have therein a complete definition of the concept, and *there is absolutely nothing more in it*.
> (Peirce 1998:332)

In other words, in Peirce's view, pragmatism involves placing emphasis upon the concrete outcomes of our concepts as a means of determining their value as expressions of knowledge. Thus, according to Peirce in 'Definition and Description of Pragmatism', there is 'an inseparable connection between rational cognition and rational purpose'. Hence, Peirce outlined pragmatism as 'the doctrine that the whole "meaning" of a conception expresses itself in practical consequences, consequences either in the shape of conduct to be recommended, or in that of experiences to be expected, if the conception be true'. In turn, he argued for viewing enquiry as a process which proceeds from a state of doubt and is resolved in belief. According to Peirce, the best way of establishing belief is according to the dictates of scientific method.

William James is probably the most famous thinker associated with pragmatism. James was a friend of Peirce and therefore formulated his ideas in conjunction with the development of Peirce's thought, so it is not easy to separate the intellectual development of the two men. However, James's conception of pragmatism differs from that offered by Peirce in so far as whereas Peirce (who, as a realist, formulated pragmatism primarily as a theory of meaning) sought to ground meaning in the sphere of practical and concrete human action, James looked elsewhere. For James, in contrast, what is highlighted is his account of the role of concepts and ideas in human experience. Our beliefs, he claims, affect our actions in the world, and his pragmatism therefore concentrates upon the ways in which ideas and beliefs relate to our experiences. In turn, James is not committed to the realism that Peirce endorses, but instead embraces a kind of nominalism. More significantly, for James, pragmatism involves constructing a more general account of human thought and action (including psychology) of which a pragmatic theory of **meaning** is merely one part.

John Dewey's work represents another variant of the pragmatist theme. As with James, Dewey started out by developing a psychological approach. However, he later turned to a more behaviouristic and socially nuanced account of human action. In time, Dewey came to term his own brand of pragmatism 'instrumentalism'. Principal amongst his philosophical concerns was **education**, which Dewey came to regard as having supreme importance as the primary means for the transmission of knowledge and ideas within **society**. Society, for the mature Dewey, comes to be regarded as a kind of educational institution, which, as the sphere in which human life is actually lived, is taken as the educative means to the end of living. In turn, Dewey developed a view which emphasised the links between human action and the social realm: action does not occur 'in' a social space, since the social is itself an essential aspect of human behaviour. Dewey's criticism of the Cartesian conception of **subjectivity** (i.e. mind–body dualism) clarifies his view of the social realm: the philosophical division between mind and body allows us to ignore the fact that the thinking individual is itself a part of the social structure in which thinking occurs. Dewey envisaged this relationship in terms of a 'circuit' (see his 'The Unit of Behaviour: The Reflex Arc Concept in Psychology' of 1896). Equally, he was also interested in developing an account of the relationship between knowledge and value, arguing that self-reflexive scientific enquiry, understood as an active selecting and therefore valuing of what it investigates, is a prime example of ethical action.

From the consideration of Peirce's and James's 'pragmatism' and Dewey's 'instrumentalism', it is evident that the primary question pragmatists ask with regard to knowledge is 'does it work?'. Dewey's term is thus apposite: pragmatists are essentially instrumentalists when it comes to the issue of what counts as reliable knowledge.

Amongst recent thinkers, Richard Rorty (1931–2007) has adopted a form of pragmatism which endorses an anti-**essentialism** with regard to questions of rationality, cultural identity and politics. This is coupled with an extolling of bourgeois **liberalism**. Rorty's approach is perhaps more Jamesean than Peircean. For example, he consistently criticised realism, which is a central component of Peirce's pragmatism. For instance, in one of Rorty's arguments, since we cannot escape from language our thinking must relate only to language, i.e. there is no 'reality' independent of language to which we refer when we speak (in philosophical parlance, there are no 'matters of fact'). Those who believe that there is an 'outside' to language Rorty deemed 'representationalists'; and it is against this position that he espoused his own 'anti-representationalism':

> By dropping a representationalist account of knowledge, we pragmatists drop the appearance–reality distinction in favour of a distinction between beliefs that serve some purposes and beliefs that serve other purposes [...] We drop the notion of beliefs being made true by reality.
>
> (Rorty 1998:206)

Hence, on Rorty's view, since our language cannot be identified in terms of some mind-independent realm, it must be culturally situated, and our knowledge of the world depends upon the cultural **norms** at our disposal and our aims. In short, Rorty viewed himself as a 'pragmatist' in so far as he, too, advocated an instrumentalism. Rorty likewise advocated a **cultural relativism**. Aspects of his views have been criticised by, amongst others, another thinker with a pragmatist heritage, Hilary Putnam (1926–), who has claimed that Rorty's argument in support of his account of language is 'terrible'. As

Putnam remarks, what if it were instrumentally useful for us to believe in things like 'matters of fact'? If so, then Rorty's argument hardly goes very far towards mounting a serious objection to such notions. Although not following Rorty's line of thought, Putnam too, has sought to develop some of the ideas first outlined by his pragmatist predecessors (addressing, for instance, the importance of education to democratic forms of life in the wake of Dewey's writings).

Further reading: Gallie 1975; Mounce 1997; Putnam 1995; Rorty 1982, 1991, 1998; Thayer 1982.

PS

PRAXIS

Strictly, 'praxis' is German for 'practice' (and is derived from the Greek). Thus, its use in English, which is common, can verge on pretension. When used with theoretical precision, it refers to the precise meanings that the young Marx ascribes to 'practice'. Two key senses can be usefully identified. At its simplest, and most dramatic, praxis suggests revolutionary practice. As such, it is a fusion of theory and practice, and thus the point at which philosophers have ceased to interpret the world (Marx 1975:423) and have developed a (materialist) account of the world that will allow the **proletariat** to understand their place in it and thus transform it. In the second, more complex sense, praxis refers to the early Marx's account of human nature and human **history**. The core of human nature is presented as the ability to transform the environment consciously. Humans therefore live in a world that they have built, and that they continue to rebuild and change. It is through this practical engagement with the world (this praxis) that humanity can come to understand itself. However, in class society, humanity is alienated from what it produces and thus does not understand its essential nature. Labour is a burden, rather than fulfilment.

AE

PREJUDICE

1 An aggressive and negative attitude towards, for example, a particular social group. Thus, **racism** can be described as a form of prejudice, in so far as the racist is predisposed to judge a designated racial

group as being inferior (cf. **stereotype**). Other attitudes may be regarded as embodying prejudice. For instance, attitudes towards women. The issue of how prejudice functions can be raised in relationship to such matters as its relationship both to systems of **representation** (whereby stereotypical images are disseminated through the **mass media**) and questions of **power.**

2 A term employed within the **hermeneutics** of H.-G. Gadamer. According to Gadamer, 'prejudice' is a precondition of an act of interpretation and consists of the presuppositions which any interpreter brings to bear as a necessary precondition of achieving an understanding of a text.

Further reading: Banton 1977; Fanon 1989; Hartmann and Husband 1974; Miles 1989; Said 1978a.

PS

PRODUCTION

Production has its most basic use and meaning in the field of economics, where it refers to the transformation of natural resources or already manufactured items through their being combined with **labour** and **capital**. Production is therefore always the transformation of something that already exists. The concept has usefully been applied to culture, not least by Marxists, in order to indicate the link between the production of cultural artefacts or events and economic production: either in so far as cultural production is grounded in, and determined by, economic production; or in that cultural production imitates certain aspects of economic production. Such an approach poses an effective challenge to orthodox **aesthetics** that tends to isolate the work of art from the social and economic circumstances in which it is created. Benjamin's essay on Brecht, 'The Author as Producer' (1937), neatly illustrates this challenge.

Further reading: Macherey 1978; Wolff 1981.

AE

PROGRESS

As contested a concept as its question-begging dictionary definition ('forward movement' or 'improvement over time') would suggest.

The idea of progress has been in circulation for upwards of 2,500 years (see Nisbet 1980), but gained its most sustained momentum during the **Enlightenment**. Whether as the rationalisation of the capacity of things in general to get better, or with a tighter focus, say on the expansion of scientific knowledge, progress became bound up with the steady emancipation of humankind from blinkered sub-servience, blind faith, and the pull of myth and mysticism. Thus Condorcet and Kant among others proclaimed progress as a tra-jectory of increasing reflexive self-awareness, on a cultural as well as individual level. Even so, Kant's writing on the topic makes see-mingly incongruous reference to a 'hidden plan of nature' to bring about 'the sole state in which all of humanity's natural capacities can be developed'.

The tension has proved stubborn. Treated on the one hand as a matter of uninterruptible historical **evolution**, the idea of progress took strongest hold as the interventionary power of human agency began finally to displace the fatalistic acceptance of providence in the tenor of social thinking. How, then, to *quantify* progress? Its intimate relations with notions as ideologically charged as development, civilisation and technological advancement have made it eminently deconstructible—not least in its most emphatic, Hegelian version in which (since the real is rational and the rational is real) philosophy sets itself the task of revealing the gradual triumph of human reason in all departments of cultured and social life. Marx, in subverting Hegel's abstract, sanguine diagnosis of the seamless unfolding of universal reason, invoked a materialist conception of progress as emancipation through the rea-lisation of hitherto-suppressed human potentialities and control of our natural environment. 'The philosophers have only interpreted the world, in various ways', as he famously stated in the *Theses on Feuerbach*; 'the point is to change it'. But for all Marx's emphasis on active participation in **history**, and the integral role of classed-based schism and revolution, crucial to both schema is an objective linearity to the historical process. This is progress as teleology: as a more or less vital journey towards a given, universally redemptive, end.

As such, it is a prime example of what postmodern theorists deem a 'meta-narrative', their incredulity towards which accompanies the jettisoning of all ideas of Progress with a capital 'P'. This is usually on the basis of an appeal to recent history as flatly contradicting the very idea that general social improvement has, in any real sense, been afoot. Lyotard and Bauman, to name but two, have linked the atro-cities and excesses of the twentieth century (for example, Auschwitz, the Gulag Archipelago, the nuclear build-up) to the overweening hubris of the Enlightenment's prediction of an emancipatory triumph of reason and virtue. Like Adorno and Horkheimer before them (though without their residual Marxist affinities), they trace the fruition of 'instrumental' reason exemplified in recent barbarities back to modernity's fetishising of universal reason and the concurrent banishment of the irrational, illusory or retrograde. Thus, scientific or technological advance does not by itself a good society make; and indeed the valorisation of science as the supreme source of knowledge makes more likely the regimentation, normalisation and silencing of those not party to the expert culture—hardly 'progress' in the modern definition.

Whether this disposes of, or rather asks anew, the question of the nature of progress is another matter. Does the *nai?veté* or danger of conceiving progress as structurally guaranteed bury too those alternative accounts which would put it down to collective human agency? Can we really look at the history of science or medicine and deny that substantive advances have taken place? Is the end of slavery just a culturally determined and administered value? 'We have stopped believing in progress', remarked Borges; 'What progress that is!' It is a pregnant contradiction. Hedgy and unfashionable as progress-talk has become, it is hard to see how normative social theory—whether at the *fin* of a given *siècle* or not—can get along without it. Nor has its theoretical beleaguering served fully to extinguish its obviously cultural and rhetorical import.

Further reading: Bauman 1989; Horkheimer and Adorno 1972; Kant 1983, 1971; Lyotard 1989; Nisbet 1980.

GC

PROLETARIAT

The term 'proletariat' has been popularised through its use in Marxist theory, where it refers to the subordinate class within **capitalism**. The proletariat is composed of that proportion of the urban population who own only their own ability to **labour**. They are therefore compelled to sell this labour power in order to be able to purchase all other goods that are required for their continued existence. Less formally, the term is frequently used as a synonym for working **class**. Strictly, the working class, composed of those who are occupied in any form of manual labour, are only a portion of the proletariat, for few if any of the (non-manual) middle class owns enough productive property or **capital** to generate enough income to do away with the necessity of working for a living.

Further reading: McCarthy 1978; Perkins 1993.

AE

PROPERTY

1 The possession of private goods. Land, wealth, even ideas can be property (e.g. patents, copyrights). Property is an area of central interest in the writings of many political philosophers. Both John Locke and Jean-Jacques Rousseau equated the private ownership of property with the development of **civil society**—albeit with very different conclusions (for a discussion of Locke's account of the basis of property ownership see **liberalism**; see also **state of nature**)—while **Marxism** advocates the dissolution of the private ownership of goods and their redistribution on the basis of need. What is clear from the work of these thinkers is that both the possession of property and the issue of what rights (i) ground and (ii) accompany property ownership, have important implications for the way in which the social and political domains may be understood.

If there is an important political idea which has been linked with property ownership it is that of *interest*. Locke draws our attention to this matter when, in the second of his *Treatises of Government*, he holds that the primary possession of each and every individual is his or her own body. If each of us is the legitimate possessor of their own body then, in turn, each individual has an interest which is related to their physical well-being, and rights also devolve from this. Equally, for Locke, since the investment of labour involves an extension of the characteristic of self-possession associated with the body, labour thereby gives what is associated with it that same characteristic: a person can pick an apple or plough a piece of untended ground and, so long as nobody else already owns them, these become his or hers by virtue of the investment of labour involved. Equally, legislative **authority** is in turn devolved by Locke from the right to own property, for the protection of property is regarded by Locke as the principal function of legitimate government.

It is possible to read Locke's argument as an implicit and *post facto* justification for the development of mercantile capitalism. Hence, if private property is held to be a legitimate form of ownership and, in turn, the role of government is primarily to protect individuals from being deprived of their property as Locke argues, then it is private rather than public interest which is foregrounded in rank of social importance. Political freedom can be defined in the wake of such a commitment: on such a view, freedom always means 'freedom from . . . ' In other words, 'freedom' is taken to mean the freedom to pursue one's self interest with minimal hindrance from the activities of others, including the state. By contrast, a Rousseauean or Marxian reading of property would hold that its possession is the product of interests, but not, contrary to Locke, a priori legitimate interests. Thus, Rousseau, in his *Discourse on Inequality*, held that the invention of private property is a central component in the corruption of humanity, in so far as with property comes the unequal distribution of goods and, in turn, the domination of personal greed over virtue. For Marx, the private and unequal distribution of goods in society is one of the defining characteristics of the capitalist mode of production, and this form of production functions through the exploitation of a majority of the population at the hands of a property-owning minority. Indeed, from this perspective, one might say that the advocacy of the possession of private property is *the* defining feature of **capitalism**, for unless this right is granted legitimacy the capitalist **mode of production** is impossible. In contrast to the view advocated by liberal thinkers, a Marxian approach would tend to regard the private possession of goods as something which inhibits the freedom of others (understood as 'freedom to . . .').

In modern technological societies, the issue of property ownership has come to take on a more complex aspect with the advent of technologies of reproduction. For example, in the recorded music industry the increased public availability of convenient carriers for the transfer of music between formats (recording from the company-manufactured compact disc to the privately owned recordable compact disc or to mp3 format, for instance) has highlighted a problem with regard to the ownership of copyright on recordings. Legally, of course, the question of who owns a copyright (i.e. the legal owner of a recorded product) is not usually a problematic one. One might be tempted, however, to turn to the fact that copyright is being constantly infringed and claim that this will, in the long run, problematise what we mean when we talk about the ownership of such goods. Whether such a claim is justifiable is, though, another matter. Even if **technology** affects the practicalities of enforcing copyright on recordings, ideas or even designs, it is an open question as to whether the notion of property implicit within copyright is likely to be challenged seriously by such practices. Likewise, even if this does prove to be the case, it does not follow that 'property' in its more general sense will thereby be subject to some form of redefinition. It is, perhaps, more germane to recall that the issues surrounding property ownership identified by thinkers such as Locke, Rousseau and Marx (e.g. questions of the right to ownership as it relates to the concept of the 'individual', or of the social relationship between the distribution of goods and issues of political freedom and power) still remain central to our conception of it and its cultural ramifications. For example, when Locke's argument concerning the justifiable acquisition of untended land through the investment of labour is applied to geographical areas outside Europe, such as 'the wild woods and uncultivated waste of America left to nature' (second *Treatise*, section 37), it is worth noting that such a theory amounts to a justification for the appropriation of land occupied by other cultures.

2 Feature or characteristic (cf. **essentialism**).

Further reading: Locke 1988; Marx 1976; Rousseau 1984.

PS

PSYCHOANALYSIS

Psychoanalysis is both a method of scientific investigation and a discipline that is concerned with the role of the unconscious in the mental life of the subject. It is primarily based on the interpretation of the analysand's free associations within the context of the transference in the analytic situation. Freud introduced the term 'psychoanalysis' as an analogy to the process of chemical analysis in a laboratory. Like a chemist, the analyst is engaged in the act of deconstructing the patient's symptom into its component parts.

> The patient's symptoms ... are of a highly composite kind ... we trace the symptoms back to the instinctual impulses which motivate them ... which are present in his symptoms and of which he has hitherto been unaware—just as a chemist isolates the fundamental substance, the chemical 'element', out of the salt in which it had been combined with other elements and in which it was unrecognisable.
>
> (Freud 2001:159)

Psychoanalysis takes under its purview all the productions of the unconscious like dreams, parapraxes, etc. According to Freud, all the formations of the unconscious are characterised by a similar set of mechanisms (condensation, displacement, dramatisation and secondary revision). Hence, its results are not restricted to the so-called 'neurotic' subject but comprise the 'normative' as well. Since these mechanisms can be simplified along the lines of the primary linguistic topes, namely metaphor and metonymy, Jacques Lacan, following the lead of the linguist Roman Jakobson, understands the unconscious to be structured like a language.

It is difficult to date the exact origins of psychoanalysis as Sigmund Freud, its founder, was fond of finding an endless number of precursors starting with his nineteenth-century contemporaries, Arthur Schopenhauer and Friedrich Nietzsche, to the ancients like Plato. However, most histories of psychoanalysis begin with Freud's early work in collaboration with the Viennese physician Josef Breuer. Freud's association with Breuer was prompted by the case of Bertha Pappenheim (better known under the pseudonym 'Anna O'). The results of the psychoanalytic investigations in this and other cases were published as *Studies in Hysteria* in 1895. Hysteria was defined as the product of a psychic trauma that had been repressed by the patient. The treatment was an attempt to get the patient to remember the trauma in order to abstract the cathexis which was attached to the causative event. The association between Freud and Breuer did not last long as they disagreed on the role of sexuality in the aetiology of hysteria.

Freud, unlike Breuer, believed that the trauma had a strong propensity to be of a sexual nature. Though there have been several attempts to revise the definition of hysteria in the subsequent history of psychoanalysis, it continues, at least in the Lacanian interpretation of psychoanalysis, to be the central problematic of the Freudian field. The term hysteria however is used less often in psychiatric and psychoanalytic circles in the United States, where it has been subdivided into a host of mental disorders characteristic of women. Though it was Freud's insistence on the sexual aetiology of the neuroses that lead to charges of 'pansexualism', the dialectical opposition between Eros and Thanatos must not be overlooked. It may well be true that the real scandal of psychoanalysis is not sexuality but death, and that the former has functioned as a Trojan horse in popular perception. For Lacan, the end of analysis must mark 'death's death'. The subject must come to terms with the structural inevitability of symbolic castration: the fact that symbolic systems tear the subject away from the historical possibility of plenitude is a price which the subject must pay in order to distance itself from the trap of psychosis.

There has also been considerable debate within the psychoanalytic movement on whether psychotics can be 'reached' by the analytic method, given their resistance to the transference. Subsequently, psychoanalysis has concerned itself mainly with the neuroses and not psychosis, though there have been sporadic attempts to develop a theory of the latter. The most ambitious of these efforts has emerged from the work of French theorists influenced by psychoanalysists like Gilles Deleuze and Félix Guattari. Disagreements in psychoanalytic models generally emerge around the role of the Oedipus complex and infantile sexuality in the constitution of the subject. Psychoanalysts tend to overemphasise the Oedipal moment while schizoanalysts de-emphasise it radically. It should be possible to write the entire history of psychoanalysis around the changing fortunes of the term 'Oedipus'.

Further reading: Deleuze and Guattari 1977, 1988; Ellenberger 1970; Freud 1966; Goux 1993; Grunbaum 1984; Henri 1993; Laplanche and Pantalis 1988; Lebovici and Widlocher 1990; Mehlman 1972; Meltzer 1987.

SKS

QUEER THEORY

Since the early 1970s, there has been a steady and significant development in the study of gay, lesbian and bisexual experiences. While the term 'queer theory' may usefully be taken to embrace that body of research, it cannot be characterised by any simple methodological or disciplinary unities. Queer theory refers to a range of work occurring, for example, in **history** (David 1997), literary criticism (Sedgwick 1994, 1997), sociology, philosophy (Butler 1990), art history, musicology (Brett, Thomas and Wood 1994) and cultural studies (Doty 1993; Morton 1997) that seeks to place the question of sexuality as the centre of concern and as the key category through which other social, political and cultural phenomena are to be understood. Queer theory may therefore be seen to explore the processes through which sexual identity is, and has been, constituted in contemporary and past societies. Sexuality is thus to be presented as a meaningful activity or achievement that is continually undergoing negotiation and dissemination, rather than as a mere natural (let alone medical) fact (see LeVay 1996). Such meaningful constitution of identity will entail study of both the active embracing and articulation of alternative experiences and lifestyles, and their repression, marginalisation and suppression. Crucial to any queer history will be the recovery of the otherwise concealed and denied presence of gay and lesbian protagonists and activities. While queer theory is inevitably to be linked to the propagation and defence of the politics of gay and lesbian groups in the face of repression and homophobia, the ramifications of its research spill out into fundamental questions about the political nature and even coherence of the supposedly normal and dominant categories of heterosexuality (Richardson 1996).

Further reading: Abelove, Barale and Halperin 1993; Weeks 1989.

AE

RACE/RACISM

A mode of classification of human beings which distinguishes between them on the basis of physical properties (e.g. skin colour, facial features) which purportedly derive from genetic inheritance. The key problem with this mode of classification is that the processes of selection regarding what ought to count as 'racial' and therefore 'natural' (i.e. non-cultural) differences are themselves inextricably linked to the existence of cultural **norms** concerning what defines a 'difference' as peculiarly 'racial'. The criteria of differentiation between what are designated as 'races' may, it follows, be established as a result of other factors that have a predominantly social dimension and are related to, for instance, socially determined questions of **power** and **representation**. This particular point has been made by writers such as Edward Said. In his book *Orientalism* (1978a) Said argues that the concept of the 'oriental' (taken in the sense of both a **subject** and a culture) as outlined in the European discipline of **'orientalism'** in fact represents a projection of European concepts and values on to the 'oriental' subject. Thus, purportedly 'objective' descriptions of the oriental can be read as expressions of the European imperialist desire to conceptualise and thereby control the identity of the colonised subject. Equally, when the oriental is discussed in negative terms (for example, by attributing the characteristic of 'irrationality'), this too can be interpreted as a projection of Western fears rather than as an accurate description of the oriental subject's 'racial' and 'cultural' attributes.

The belief that physical differences in turn validate the attribution of additional characteristics which are not simply physical but denote the existence of, for example, a determinate set of abilities, propensities or forms of behaviour, is associated with the attitude of racism. The reader will scarcely need reminding that the twentieth century has seen some of the most powerful and disturbing expressions of racist sentiment, and indeed of the catastrophic outcome of this sentiment in the form of German National Socialism. Although it may not always be too difficult to describe racist attitudes, how one accounts for racist phenomena such as anti-Semitism is a difficult question. Doubtless, it is possible to point to a wide number of intellectual domains (including even the physical sciences) and claim that racism has at various times found expression within them (the German philosopher Hegel springs to mind in such a context, with his ill-informed comments on the African continent, which is portrayed as an 'undeveloped' stage in the dialectic of Absolute Spirit). To this extent, too, the discipline of 'orientalism' criticised by Said can with validity be regarded as a manifestation of racism. Yet Nazi ideology seems to have been far too ad hoc an affair to have required comprehensive grounding in intellectual respectability, although its anti-Semitism may have gained support from certain practitioners of genetics. As Eric Hobsbawm has observed:

> Hitler's racism was [. . .] a late nineteenth-century post-Darwinian farrago claiming (and alas, in Germany often receiving) the support of the new science of genetics, or more precisely of that branch of applied genetics ('eugenics') which dreamed of creating a human superrace by selective breeding and the elimination of the unfit.
>
> (Hobsbawm 1995:118)

So, although Hitler's racism was itself supported by some **eugenics** theory (and thereby laid some ill-founded claim to 'scientific' respectability), the origins and intellectual justification for this racism were an altogether thinner affair. More basic to this manifestation of racism was, Hobsbawm argues, the mass xenophobia which the late nineteenth century bequeathed to the twentieth (to which one might add the influence of a romantic and nostalgic conservatism). Thus, the culture of Nazi racism was, like the movement itself, a mass phenomenon and pays ample testimony to the dangers which may be inherent in manipulative mass cultural forms.

Whatever the causes of racism, it is clear that racists subordinate purportedly 'significant' physical or normative (i.e. behavioural) differences to the presupposition that the possession of one particular set of characteristics does not merely signify a physical difference but also an inherent difference of **identity**, nature and 'intrinsic value' (cf. **stereotype**). Racism thereby draws a hierarchical distinction between races, opening a gulf between them and setting one racially designated group over and above another on a scale of moral worth, intelligence or importance. A racist **ideology**, therefore, is constructed on the basis of hierarchical distinctions drawn between different groups. From the point of view of such ideologies, race is taken to be a more fundamental basis for the social differentiation between individuals and groups than, for example, that of **class**. Racism thus embodies the attitude of a rigid and naturalised conception concerning the nature of individuals and groups (see Miles 1989). Whether or not racism should therefore be defined solely in terms of ideologically constructed attitudes, or additionally in terms of the norms and practices of a given society, is a matter of some debate. In this connection, a number of commentators on racism have pointed to the role of representation in contemporary society, e.g. the construction of racial identity through the presentation, for instance in the media, of stereotypical images of different cultural groups (a factor which, once more, raises the question of the links between racism and mass culture in the modern world).

The significance of racism is not necessarily limited to active discrimination against people, whether through the institutions, ideologies, or norms and practices of a given society. The sense of **self** that those subjected to racism may have, may likewise be affected. In the context of European colonialism, for instance, the construction of racial **identity** and its consequences have been studied not only by Said, but also by Frantz Fanon whose book *Black Skin, White Masks* (1952) considered the damaging influence of colonialism on the self-image of colonial subjects.

Further reading: Banton 1977; Fanon 1989; Hartmann and Husband 1974; Hobsbawm 1995; Miles 1989; Said 1978a.

PS

RATIONALISATION

Rationalisation is a term most readily associated with the German sociologist Max Weber. While rationalisation has numerous meanings in Weber's writings, it is centrally used to account for the rise to global dominance of **capitalism**. Capitalist society is seen to be uniquely rational, not merely in its economic and technical organisation, but also in science, law, religion, art and government. Rationalisation, in each case, consists of the refinement of instrumental rationality. That is to say, that each social **institution** is rational because it is structured according to rules that determine the most efficient means for achieving any given end, independently of any inhibition from traditional or conventional practices, or the personalities or **values** of any of the social agents involved. Weber's analysis of **bureaucracy**, as the most rational form for the exercise of power, manifests the darker side of rationality, as bureaucracy is seen to become an 'iron cage' that stifles individual liberty and democratic accountability. Weber's account of rationality, in so far as it comes to confront human agents as an external and constraining force, has much in common with Marx's analysis of **alienation**. The work of the Hungarian Marxist Lukács, as well as that of the **Frankfurt School**, explore the interrelationships of Marxist and Weberian sociology precisely at this point.

Further reading: Brubaker 1984.

AE

REALISM

1 In literature and **aesthetics**, the term realism refers to those styles of artistic representation that are supposed to work through some resemblance or verisimilitude between the artwork and what it represents. Thus, a painting by Vermeer or a novel by Walter Scott seem to offer a depiction or a description of events that resembles how those events would have been experienced in real life. In contrast, an expressionist painting by Munch offers at best a distorted image of reality. In Marxist literary criticism and aesthetics, realism has been placed in opposition to **modernism**, with a significant debate occurring as to which is the most politically progressive. On the one hand, Georg Lukács has defended realism (for example in the work of Balzac) as serving to express the social totality, which is to say the social, economic and political forces that work beneath the surface of seemingly contingent social events. On the other hand, theorists within the **Frankfurt School** criticised realism for its failure to reflect upon the conventions that governed the production of the artistic image (so that rather than expressing society as it reality was,

realism merely reproduced a naturalised and **ideological** account of society) (see Bloch *et al.* 1977).

Certain non-Marxist philosophers, and most notably Nelson Goodman (1976), have questioned the distinction between realist and non-realist works. By picking up on a number of problems in explaining exactly in what the resemblance between the artwork and reality consists (for example, by pointing out that one painting resembles another painting far more closely than either resemble their subject matter, yet one painting is rarely a representation of another painting), Goodman suggests that realism is in fact governed by conventions for interpretation, and thus is highly artificial. We are confused into thinking that the relationship between a realist painting and its subject matter is immediate or natural, simply because we have learnt these interpretative conventions so well and so early in our development.

2 In philosophy in general, realism is the doctrine that certain things exist independently of any human observer or of any description of them that may be offered. As Danto has pointed out, philosophy emerges only in those rare **cultures** where the question, 'Is it real?', can sensibly be asked of objects (such as tables) that self-evidently do exist. In effect, philosophy (and it may be noted, for Danto, art as well) presupposes a culture in which the 'real' world can be set against something that is not real (such as an image, appearance, illusion, representation, sensory impression or concept) (Danto 1981:78–80). Thus, I might for example doubt the reality of the table if I were to argue that I had no direct evidence for its existence, only the sensory data I have of seeing, smelling and touching it. Thus, if I was of a mind, I might argue that only these sensory data are real, and not tables.

In the philosophy of science, more precisely, realism has come to refer to an account of science that, again, presupposes that the objects of scientific enquiry exist independently of the process of enquiry itself, and then argues that science progresses by building theoretical models of those objects of enquiry. While the object of enquiry may itself be unobservable (as, for example, in the case of atoms or molecules), the model will allow predictions of observable events to be made. The model can be revised so that it becomes an ever more accurate representation of reality in the light of experimental evidence.

See also **reason**.

Further reading: Bhaskar 1975; Chalmers 1982; Harré 1970.

AE

REASON

The question of the nature of reason is at least as old as philosophy. Plato (*c.* 428–348 BC), for example, held that rationality is an intrinsic feature of reality. According to Plato (1998), there are two distinct realms, the intelligible and the sensible. The realm of the senses corresponds to what would now be more usually called empirical experience. It is a realm in which things come to be, decay and pass away, and is dominated by appearances and opinions. The intelligible, in contrast, is a realm of ideas. As opposed to the mere opinion which experience affords, the realm of the intelligible yields true knowledge. In other words, the realm of thought points towards a reality that exists apart from the world of the senses. In turn, Plato argues that the world of experience gains what reality it has from the realm of the intelligible. This contention relates to Plato's 'Theory of Ideas', which states that all experiential particulars that share the same identity do so because they are particular instances of a universal idea that precedes them logically. Thus, if we take three different individual cats, each one having specific differences separating it from the other two cats, what they have in common is that they are in each case an instance of the universal idea 'cat'. What conjoins each one with the other is the common property of 'cat-ness'. The same goes, Plato argues, for more abstract notions, such as beauty, goodness and justice. Every instance of these things presupposes a universal. All universals exist in themselves: the 'good in-itself', 'justice in-itself', etc. It follows for Plato that the kind of knowledge that we can have of the world of experience merely amounts to obtaining opinions about it that are correct (i.e. it *appears* that such-and-such is the case). In contrast, true knowledge (such-and-such *is* the case) concerns the highest reality, i.e. the forms and, in turn, these gain their reality from the Idea of the Good. The Idea of the Good is what bestows upon life the standard of measurement whereby actions, beliefs and the like can be judged good, true, etc. In other words, there is a reality independent of an individual's inclinations or psychology that endows what he or she does and is capable of doing with meaning. Since the Idea of the Good occupies and constitutes the basis of intelligibility, it does not change (as the realm of experience does relentlessly) but remains eternally consistent. The knowledge of this is the highest form of knowledge ('dialectic') and finds its highest expression in human reason. Goodness, rationality and happiness are, for Plato, all necessarily linked to one another. Thus, he holds reality to be determined by objective rational conditions. In short, for Plato, reality is intrinsically rational.

There has been much philosophical debate about the nature of reason since Plato's time. Aristotle (384–322 BC) challenged his teacher Plato's notion of universal ideas, disagreeing with the view that the individual disciplines of enquiry can be unified in the universal principles of dialectic. Aristotle nevertheless agrees with the notion that absolute knowledge rests upon definition and believes that truth concerns what is eternal. The rationalist René Descartes (1596–1650) concurs with the Platonic contention that reality is to be judged according to the yardstick set by our rational abilities (Descartes 1968). Descartes's philosophy is rooted in the view that it is possible to construct an account of knowledge on the basis of rational introspection (see **Cartesianism**). Reason, he claims, is a God-given 'universal instrument' that presents us with the surest means of assessing what knowledge is and thereby facilitates its foundation. An essential feature of Descartes's account of rationality is his contention that our rational abilities form the core of subjectivity and consciousness. This view forms the basis of his mind–body dualism. We are essentially beings who think and are rational and defined in terms of mental substance. Animals, in contrast, are no more than machines, devoid of the ability to think and reason and constituted out of no more than material substance. An irresolvable problem for Descartes is negotiating the link between mind and matter, in so far as we are for him both material beings but ultimately defined in terms of our mental capacities.

In contrast to rationalists like Descartes, who considered all knowledge to be derivable from rational principles, empiricist thinkers such as John Locke (1632–1704) and David Hume (1711–76) argued that the origin of knowledge was experience. Locke nevertheless concurred with the Cartesian view that reason has a divine origin. For Locke, it may be the case that our knowledge derives from the senses rather than innate rational principles, but the notion that reason and thought could come from the interaction of brute matter is repugnant to him. Reason in fact involves a universality that points to the existence of God. Hume, in contrast, hit upon the notion that our rational abilities are derived from psychological propensities rather than universal conditions. For Hume, the self is a bundle of habits, an amalgam of customs and practices that have no life independently of their embodiment. The self, the central bearer of our innate rational abilities in Descartes's philosophy, becomes fragmented and loses its core in Hume's thought. With this the significance of our rational abilities is transformed. Hume's famous analysis of the concept of causality sought to show that it cannot be derived from innate principles or from objective conditions. We may think in causal terms all the time, and indeed must do so in order to live, but we should not be deceived into believing that the notion of causality can be derived from principles of knowledge or scientific reasoning. All reasoning about cause and effect, for Hume, has its origin in sense impressions and the ideas that they generate in the mind. In turn, rather than serving to secure the foundations of universal knowledge, our reason becomes for Hume at best a means of limiting the possibility of wandering too far from the bounds of common sense. Our reason has the causal power of being able to give rise to truth, that is its 'natural effect'. But we are creatures of habit and hence governed by our passions and drives. Consequently, Hume argues, our rationality is prone to being subverted by our other propensities and with this all knowledge becomes a matter of probability rather than certainty.

Hume's contention that psychological conditions underlie our rational abilities is derived from his adherence to the spirit of scientific enquiry (associated with the sixteenth- and seventeenth-century researches of figures like Galileo and Newton). In this regard he typifies the tradition of **Enlightenment**. The thinkers associated with the Enlightenment were committed to the view that just as the workings of nature were amenable to rational, empirical scientific investigation, so the workings of the human mind and society could be analysed on the same basis. Hence, Hume's contention at the beginning of his *Treatise of Human Nature* (1739) that it is possible to elucidate nothing less than a 'science of MAN' that will have the same standing as the sciences that deal with mathematics and physics. Other Enlightenment thinkers, in their various ways, followed the same basic path. They considered it possible to construct a rational account of human society that, if acted upon, would put an end to the irrationality of injustice, cruelty, prejudice and myth. In short, the Enlightenment proposed a radical political agenda of social transformation through technology and science. The philosophy of Immanuel Kant (1724–1804) both reveals the continuity of thematic concerns between thinkers of the Enlightenment and the differences internal to it. Kant disagreed with Hume and the empiricists that it is possible to construct an account of thought and reason that relies solely upon the notion of experience. In the *Critique of Pure Reason* (1781/1787) Kant argues that experience is essential to knowledge, but cannot be its only source. To contend, as the empiricists do, that experience is the source of all our ideas ignores the fact that in order to have any experience we must, in some manner, be equipped with the ability to notice it in the first place.

All particular experiences, in other words, presuppose a priori conditions, i.e. conditions that precede them. These conditions, Kant argues, are transcendental. They do not transcend experience, but are constantly present as a condition of all human thought about experience. This amounts to the contention that there are objective conditions of knowledge, but that such conditions reside not in the external world but in the manner in which human subjectivity is constructed. This construction Kant calls the 'transcendental ego'. The transcendental 'I' is not a person but an impersonal structure to whose demands every human being must conform in order to be who he or she is. Thus, human understanding is, for Kant, governed by rules. These rules constitute the basis of human reason, in so far as they are both necessary for thought and are universal (i.e. shared by every human subject). Reason is thereby understood as being linked to our ability to recognise and follow rules. It has legitimacy in the same way in which law has legitimacy.

G.W.F. Hegel (1770–1831) extended Kant's criticisms of empiricism. For Hegel, however, Kant's analysis of the conditions underlying rationality did not go far enough, in so far as the concepts of universality and necessity are for Kant disclosed by the subject through experience rather than by way of an immanent analysis of them that considers them in themselves. For Kant, our knowledge of objects is determined by the rational conditions that we impose upon them. Hegel, in contrast, contends that thought and reality share a common logical structure that is disclosed through the unfolding of historical experience. This is exemplified in the most famous (and often least understood) Hegelian dialectic. Dialectic, for Hegel, represents the logical unfolding of conscious thought as it engages with the material world through the senses. This unfolding, however, is reflected in the material world itself: physical reality conforms to the logical dictates of the dialectic. In short, reality conforms to the rules of logic no less than thought. Hegel thereby advances the view that rationality is objective, rather than subjective.

The distinction between objective and subjective reason is one of the most important for understanding the era of post-Kantian thought. As Horkheimer and Adorno argue (Horkheimer and Adorno 1972; Horkheimer 1992), the tradition of Enlightenment, in conforming to the demands of the scientific conception of rationality, effectively sanctions the transformation of reason into little more than an *instrument* of pre-existing subjective desires. The latter is epitomised by 'rational choice theory', which takes reason to be no more than the maximum satisfaction of individual preferences (Green and

Shapiro 1994; Taylor 1990). Such a notion of reason has had a profound effect on recent public policy in the West, sanctioning as it does the view that cultivating the inherent ability of free-market economies to provide for individual preferences amounts to the most concrete realisation of individual freedom. The simplistic and atomistic conception of the **self** that underlies this notion, however, renders it questionable. Rationality, as mere instrument, serves the demands of such desires well enough, but this in its turn creates a moral lacuna. Where for Plato or Hegel our reason provides an objective standard for judgement, thereby grounding the possibility of ethical discussion, instrumentalism brings with it the demise of ethical objectivity. Especially worrying is the potential of instrumental reason to serve dominant social interests. Thus, the sciences develop their respective fields of specialist knowledge in response to dominant relations of power. Reason, in this way, abandons its critical potential and accedes to the subservient status of being hooked to the 'social process'. In *Dialectic of Enlightenment*, written when Horkheimer and Adorno were in American exile during the Second World War, they seek to expose this sinister underbelly of Enlightenment. Thinkers such as Friedrich Nietzsche (1844–1900) and the Marquis de Sade stand as the 'dark' bourgeois thinkers of Enlightenment, denouncing the limitations of the Enlightenment conception of reason by pushing its logic to extremes.

Nietzsche, no less than Horkheimer and Adorno, stands as one of the central figures in recent debates about the concept of reason. Nietzsche's thoughts on reason are hard to summarise without descending into parody. On the one hand, he is often tempted to consider reason as merely an instrument of the greater totality of relations that constitutes the self. With this, consciousness, too, slips off its pedestal of philosophical **authority** and is replaced by 'will to power'. This aspect of Nietzsche's thought has been characterised by Jürgen Habermas (1929–) as representing the proclamation of the demise of critical reason and the initiation of **postmodernism** and **post-structuralism**. Against this, Habermas (himself a pupil of Adorno and Horkheimer) has sought to revitalise a linguistic version of Kantian transcendentalism (see **Frankfurt School**). On the other hand, it is possible to detect in Nietzsche's work a rigorous account of the development of the normative structures that underlie human rationality in the form of his notion of the 'morality of custom' (see Nietzsche 1982) that does not so easily conform to this view. More recently, Habermas has proposed a rethinking of our concept of rationality and secular thought in the light of a critical acknowledgement of their intimate relationship with religious traditions (Habermas 2003, 2007). This idea may have profound implications for further developments with regard to understanding the nature and limits of reason.

Further reading: Descartes 1986; Hegel 1977; Horkheimer 1992; Horkheimer and Adorno 1972; Hume 1978; Kant 1964; Sedgwick 2001.

PS

REFERENCE

The term 'reference' is generally used to indicate the relationship which linguistic terms have with an extralinguistic reality. In its most traditional and most straightforward sense it indicates the relationship between a name and its object or referent. Thus, on this model, a name is taken as 'standing for' the object it refers to in a language (see the discussion of 'nomenclaturism' in **meaning**). 'Reference' is a primary concern of those working within the tradition of **analytic philosophy**.

This view, in its most modern guise, is reflected in the 'causal theory of reference', the seminal theorist of which is Saul Kripke (1980). On this view, once a proper name or kind name comes to stand for an object in a language it retains its referential power regardless of how it is used or misused by individual speakers. It is via this supposed referential stability that supporters of this theory hope to avoid the more radical implications for the physical and social sciences of semantic **holism** (see also **meaning**). However, it is far from certain that such stability can be guaranteed by the theory, granted that the referential use of kind names and proper names seems to depend unavoidably upon the intentional capacities of individual language users (Evans 1973).

The alternative view of reference is the 'description theory of reference'. This theory has its roots in the work of Frege (1892) and his seminal 'sense determines reference' thesis. On this view a proper name or kind name is a shorthand term for one of a number of definite descriptions which come to be associated with it. Accordingly, we can only refer to an object if we can, first, describe it in some way. If we accept this view, we appear to be defining the properties of one part of language, i.e. proper names and kind names, in terms of another part of language, i.e. definite descriptions. Thus, in effect, we have introduced a linguistic wedge between language and the world. Bertrand Russell (1905) held to a qualified acceptance of this theory, although ultimately he thought it needed to be backed up by a form of 'logical atomism'. Peter Strawson (1966) supports a somewhat stronger version of the theory.

Accepting the implication of the description theory, i.e. that we can only refer to an object via some definite description or other, effectively accepts that we can only reach the world *through* language. Again, if we admit that we need descriptions to speak about or think about the world, then it seems that how we think about or speak about the world and the 'objects' of which it is comprised depends on the meanings available to us within a particular language. The fear of the theory's critics is that from here it is but a short step to an acceptance of full-blown semantic holism (see Devitt and Sterelny 1987).

SH

REFLEXIVITY

Reflexivity is the property of referring to oneself. Thus, a reflexive cultural theory will take into account its own position and construction as a cultural artefact.

Further reading: Elders 1974.

AE

REIFICATION

Reification is literally the transformation of something **subjective** or human into an inanimate object. In social and cultural theory it therefore refers, most generally, to the process by which human society (that is ultimately the product of largely conscious and intentional human actions) comes to confront its members as an external, seemingly **natural** and constraining force. In a more precise or technical sense, the theory of reification (or *Verdinglichung* in the original German) was developed by Georg Lukács (1923) from Marx's theory of **commodity fetishism**. Marx analysed the process in **capitalism** by which relationships between human beings (i.e. the meeting of humans in commercial exchange in the market) take on the appearance of relationships between things (such that the relationships between humans come to be governed by properties—**exchange-values**—that appear to be inherent to the **commodities** exchanged). For Lukács, this inversion is manifest in all social relations (and not merely in the economy). This is because an increasingly **rationalised** and **bureaucratic** society, that which is qualitative, unique and subjective in human relationships is lost. Human beings are governed according to the purely quantitative concerns of the bureaucrat and the manager.

See also: **Frankfurt School**.

Further reading: Rose 1978; Thomason 1982.

AE

RELATIONS OF PRODUCTION

In **Marxism**, the relations of production are the social relations that exist between the **class** of producers and the class of owners within an economy. In Marxist theory, all societies are characterised in terms of conflict between two major classes. The subordinate class is the class that actually produces goods and services, through the exercise of its **labour** power. The dominant class owns and controls the resources that are used in the production process (the **means of production**), and as such are able to control the production process and the fate of the product. Different modes of production, or historical epochs, are characterised by distinct relations of production and levels of technology (or **forces of production**). The relations of production are inherently static, and social revolution occurs when the productive potential inherent in developing forces of production can no longer be contained or fully exploited within the existing relations of production.

See also **mode of production**.

AE

RELATIVE AUTONOMY

The notion that the social forms or structures which operate within a **culture** are *neither* wholly determined by *nor* wholly independent of the cultural whole (a notion which is well illustrated by Louis Althusser's conception of **ideological state apparatuses**).

PS

RELIGION

Many attempts have been made to define religion from the points of view of a number of different disciplines: psychologists have characterised it as a projection of human desires (or even as a kind of neurosis), while political thinkers have understood it to be a means of social control which preys upon instinctive human fears. Anthropological definitions, by contrast, attempt to describe religion on its own terms—to understand it from within.

Emile Durkheim argued that the cardinal distinction between the sacred and the profane lies at the heart of all religious experience. It is, he claimed, 'the most profound distinction ever made by the human mind'. On this basis, he defined religion as 'a unified system of beliefs and practices relative to sacred things, that is to say, things set apart and forbidden'.

In more recent times, Durkheim's notion of the sacred has come to be viewed as inadequate on the grounds that it cannot be defined by scientific criteria. Alternative definitions have tended to be more descriptive, avoiding the use of privileged terms like 'sacred' and 'profane'. Clifford Geertz, for example, has proposed the following definition: 'a religion is: (i) a system of symbols which acts to (ii) establish powerful, pervasive, and long-lasting moods and motivations in men by (iii) formulating conceptions of a general order of existence and (iv) clothing these conceptions with such an aura of factuality that (v) the moods and motivations seem uniquely realistic.'

The problem of definition attested to by the bewildering array of claims and counterclaims aimed at uncovering the essence of religion, is a reflection of the sheer scope and diversity of its formulations, both temporal and geographical. As Ninian Smart has said: '[W]e are not confronted in fact by some monolithic object, namely religion. We are confronted by *religions*. And each religion has its own style, its own inner dynamic, its own special meanings, its uniqueness'. In order to reflect this diversity, and to attempt to do justice to the multifaceted nature of each and every example, Smart proposes a kind of anatomy of religion rather than a definition: 'a religion is ... a six-dimensional organism, typically containing doctrines, myths, ethical teachings, rituals, and social institutions, and animated by religious experiences of various kinds' (Smart 1971: 31).

Another problem associated with the issue of definition is that it is difficult to be clear about the nature of a phenomenon whose origins are obscure. There is evidence to suggest that Neanderthals practised ritual burial of their dead, which may indicate that they believed in an invisible realm or some kind of an afterlife. But it is open to question whether such beliefs can be termed 'religious'. Smart points out that where life is bound up in cultural practices associated with an all-embracing belief system, people are not free to opt in or out of 'religion'. There is, in such circumstances, no secular life by contrast with which religious life can be defined.

The development of religion is also contested. Those who have propagated evolutionary theories (Rudolf Otto, for example) have construed the history of religion as a process by which primeval polytheisms have been refined. Sometimes such refinements result in monotheism, sometimes in more highly developed versions of polytheism. E.B. Tylor, influenced by Darwinian theory, contended that all religion has its roots in animism. According to his developmental narrative, belief in the existence of the human soul led to the inference that natural objects also have souls. Gradually, natural phenomena came to be perceived as working together, and a controlling influence was inferred: a single deity emerged from the primeval dispersion. Wilhelm Schmidt, on the other hand, claims that the most primitive form of religion was monotheistic, and that, subsequently, it was overlaid with animistic and spiritistic elements.

Some approaches to the subject characterise religious phenomena as purely human constructs. On this account, religious beliefs grow out of the need to explain human existence, to answer its problems and to account for its sufferings. Raymond Firth writes: 'Everywhere belief in religion arises from attempts to save man or console him from the consequences of his own and other people's impulses, desires, fears and actions.'

This **humanistic** view is the result of the decline of Christianity in Western cultures after more than a thousand years of dominance. That is to say: in order for religion to be defined 'from the outside', its grip had first to be loosened sufficiently to make such a perspective possible. It was, above all, the rise of science in the West in the seventeenth century that opened a way beyond religious thought. Human life and natural phenomena came to be explained in radically different ways. The mysterious cosmos, controlled by capricious, and in some cases malign, entities, was supplanted by a rational universe which operates according to fixed laws, and which can be grasped by human reason. Once this leap was made, religious explanations began to appear obsolete.

A post-mythological paradigm is evident in the philosophies of seventeenth-century rationalism as well as in scientific study. In the eighteenth century, Immanuel Kant attempted to redefine the role of religion in the new age of enlightened thought. It should be confined, he contended, 'within the limits of reason alone'. In Kant's view, morality does not require religion, but the former inevitably produces the latter. Human capacities are inadequate to ensure that moral goodness leads to happiness, so it is necessary to postulate the existence of an omnipotent, moral Being who can act as the cosmic guarantor of the benefit of behaving according to the dictates of reason.

Nineteenth-century thinkers like Auguste Comte and Ludwig Feuerbach sought to take the Kantian critique of religion even further by removing God altogether. They argued for a 'religion of humanity'. 'The divine being', Feuerbach asserted, 'is nothing else than the human being.' Karl Marx, acknowledging the humanist argument, pressed for the abandonment of the idea of a 'religion' of humanity, in favour of a policy of action aimed at overthrowing the social order which religion had produced. He described religion as: 'man's self-consciousness and self-awareness ... the sigh of the oppressed creature ... the opium of the people.'

Alongside the rise of Reason and the concomitant decline of religion in Western thought, a stream of sceptical (and in some cases irrationalist) thought has persisted. Kant's contemporary, J.G. Hamann, pointed out the strains and contradictions inherent in the **Enlightenment** valuation of Reason. He had a marked influence on the work of the Danish philosopher S½ren Kierkegaard, and on the strain of German romanticism which produced Friedrich Nietzsche's anti-Kantianism. Today, the so-called '**postmodern**' thought, which draws on the work of writers like Michel Foucault, Jean-François Lyotard and Jean Baudrillard, owes much to this intellectual lineage. The suspicion aimed by such thinkers at the categories and concepts of the Kantian tradition has given rise to a rethinking of religious possibilities. It has produced an anti-humanism, which, while it has not reasserted pre-humanist, religious values, has, according to Philippa Berry, 'dissolved the clear-cut distinction between secular and religious thinking which Kant and the Kantian tradition had carefully secured.'

Further reading: Durkheim 1975, 1976; Geertz 1976; Schmidt 1935; Smart 1960, 1972, 1973.

KM/GH

REPRESENTATION

1 On some theories, a function of **language** (i.e. representation conceived of as (i) the representation of thoughts in language, (ii) the linguistic representation of the world of empirical experience).

2 In social terms, representation has (i) a political meaning (in the sense of meaning the representation through institutional bodies or pressure groups of the interests of political **subjects**—a notion inextricably linked with modern, **liberal** conceptions of the democratic process), and (ii) a more nuanced meaning, which has linked the practices and **norms** of representing and which may, for example, be used in the **mass media**, in order to present images of particular social groups. In sense 2(ii), representation does not necessarily signify the representing of the interests of the group or individual represented. A group can be represented in a manner which might be conceived of as **stereotyping** them. Thus, in this context, 'representation' may be characterised as misrepresentation: as the 'presentation' or construction of **identity**. Such constructions of identity may be closely allied to questions of **ideology** and **power**, and to the forms of **discourse** implicated in the procedures whereby such images are created. Thus, the construction of concepts relating to issues of **gender**, **race** or **sexuality** are questions of representation. Sense 2(ii) is, in many ways, a matter related to senses 2(i) and 1(ii). In terms of the representation of political subjects (2(i)), the constitution of modes of representation may have an important role to play within the political process, in so far as such issues as those concerned with the construction of discourses surrounding matters of race or **ethnicity** can also be conceptualised as being political issues. Likewise, the view that language may have a role in constructing 'reality', rather than simply reflecting it (1(ii)), is an important one in this connection; for, if we were to be convinced that language does not merely 'mirror' the world of experience but constructs it, the same must go for its role in the world of social experience. The question of the role of representation can also be raised in the context of discourses of knowledge (cf. **orientalism)**.

Further reading. Haldane and Wright 1993.

PS

REPRODUCTION

See **cultural reproduction**

RHETORIC

The art of persuasion. Rhetoric is the putting to work of language in order to influence other people, either in terms of their future actions or their beliefs. 'Rhetoric' also signified the formal study of persuasion. In the medieval period this was a branch of academic learning akin in status to the study of grammar, mathematics or logic. In the Renaissance, rhetoric was regarded as a practical field of study for those interested in politics and law (and handbooks of rhetoric were included in Erasmus's *De copia* (1521)). A new interest in rhetoric has been developed in the post-war period by figures associated with **post-structuralism**, such as Paul de Man (1919–83). De Man, who developed a form of **deconstruction**, analysed linguistic tropes and their functions, paying paticular attention to rhetorical language in critical and philosophical texts.

Further reading: de Man 1979, 1989.

PS

RISK

A situation in which the outcome is not known with any certainty. In economics, risk is sharply distinguished from uncertainty. In a condition of uncertainty, the actor has no knowledge of what might happen. In conditions of risk, the actor is aware of possible outcomes, and may be able to calculate the probabilities associated with each possible outcome, but cannot determine which will happen (as, for example, in the case of throwing a die) (Knight 1921). Approaches to risk in economics and psychology have typically explored the ways in which actors calculate risks, with particular reference to the discrepancy between the calculations of an ideal rational agent and a real agent. Risk aversion is typically assumed to govern individual choices and actions. It is well recognised that people are poor at estimating risks, so that for example an unlikely but newsworthy event (such as mugging) is judged to be a greater threat than a routine action (such as car driving). This insight already suggests that risk is to some degree socially constructed.

In **sociology** and cultural theory, the work of the **cultural anthropologist** Mary Douglas on the categories of 'purity' and 'danger' has highlighted the social construction of risk (Douglas 1969). The 'other' is construed as an object of fear and fascination, and thus of danger and pollution, in the sense of a threatened disruption to accepted cultural boundaries. The perception of risk as danger of pollution is thus shaped by a culturally imbued sense of normality, morally and ritually appropriate boundaries. In pre-modern societies, pollution will be blamed upon someone who is already unpopular, which is to say that even natural events will be given a social and politically significant interpretation. In modern societies, a secular view allows for risks to be traced to causal factors, but also to be blamed upon those victims who are 'at risk' (see Douglas 1985, 1992; Douglas and Wildavsky 1982).

Ulrich Beck's theory of 'risk society' has been highly influential in sociology. Beck (1992) distinguishes between pre-modern and modern societies. In pre-modern society, risk is not a relevant category. Fate, associated with natural disasters such as plagues and famines, is more relevant, precisely because the events are beyond human control. Risk implies the possibility of a human response, and the possibility of calculation and risk assessment. Thus, modern societies have the technological means necessary to assess, and where possible, avoid or mitigate risk. This leads, for example, to the rise of the welfare state as a means of protecting individuals from social risks (of unemployment, illness and infirmity). However, a 'risk society' only emerges in the post-war period, in a stage of **'reflexive** modernism' (Beck *et al.* 1994). In reflexive modernism, the central concern of society shifts from the question of the development and deployment of new technology, to the managing of the risks associated with existing technology. Beck's point is that industrial society does not merely produce 'goods', but also 'bads', or the risks and burdens associated with technology (such as pollution, nuclear waste, global warming, and the side effects of medical treatment). These 'bads' are the unintended consequences of industrial activity. Beck argues that, ironically, their very management can itself have unintended consequences. Further, such risks do not typically fall only on specific groups within society, but upon all. Smog, Beck reminds us, is democratic (Beck 1992:36). This entails that 'bads' fall upon individuals rather than upon traditionally defined classes.

Risk society can then be characterised, first, by the breakdown of trust in scientific experts, and in the power of technological reasoning. For Giddens, the project of the New Labour government, that came to power in the United Kingdom in 1997, was precisely to respond to this new culture (Giddens 1998). Second, beyond this breakdown of trust, Beck suggests that risk society also undermines traditional **class** structures. Increasingly aware of their place in society, individuals calculate the risks associated with different lifestyle choices, and take responsibility for those chosen lifestyles. Political struggle thus shifts from issues to class to those of **identity** (centring on ethnicity, gender, sexuality or culture, for example).

Beck's work has been criticised for underplaying the degree to which risk is a social construction. His initial assumption appears to be that the risks generated by contemporary society are real, and that perception of them is largely accurate. This approach is challenged through Foucault's concept of 'governmentality' (Foucault 1991). Here the argument is that risk is socially constructed through the actions of governments in managing their populations. Foucault's own work focuses on the role that demographic studies have played in European government since the seventeenth century (Foucault 1977a). Governments have inculcated in citizens an awareness of certain risks, alongside the individual's responsibility to respond to those risks. This approach has influenced significant studies of health care (Rose 2002; Flynn 2002), policing (Ericson and Haggerty 2002) and social policy formation (Rose 1996), but may also be considered to be of great relevance during a period in which Western governments mobilise their citizenry in a 'war on terror' (see also : **Terrorism**).

Further reading: Beck 1999a, 1999b; Lupton 1999; Taylor-Gooby and Zinn 2006.

AE

RITES DE PASSAGE

The term '*rites de passage*' comes from **cultural anthropology**, and refers to those public ceremonies or **rituals** that mark the transition from one stage of life to another. The *rites de passage* tend to presuppose the complete submission of the individual to the collective, and thus the exact execution of the requirements of the ritual. A typical example would be the ceremonies associated with the transition from childhood to adulthood. While such ceremonies are readily associated with pre-industrial societies, they continue to play a significant part in contemporary society, for example, in the forms of baptisms, the high school prom, graduation ceremonies and funerals.

AE

RITUAL

A ritual is a formal action, following set and repeatable patterns, that is expressive of communal **values**, meanings and beliefs. The original use of ritual would suggest that the ritual entailed some link with sacred, supernatural or magical worlds. Indeed, Durkheim argued that the distinction between the 'sacred' and the 'profane' is fundamental to ritual, which entails crossing the usual boundary between the two. For Durkheim, the sacred is expressive of the community within which individuals live. Ritual therefore serves the function of integrating the individual more closely into the social whole. Taking this theme further, ritual may also be seen as a response to threats to the community. Ritual activity intensifies in the face of social change or during other periods of social instability. Within cultural studies, these notions of ritual have been used more or less precisely or **metaphorically** to explore the ways in which secular groups (and especially **subcultures** or **ethnic** groups) define and articulate their identity, and resist external pressures in contemporary **capitalism** (hence, for example, the title of Hall and Jefferson's collection, *Resistance through Rituals* (1976)).

AE

ROLE

At its simplest, 'role' is a useful **metaphor** for the social activities that members of **society** undertake in their day-to-day life. Thus, being a 'daughter', 'student', 'fan' and 'party-goer' are all roles (and indeed roles that one person could take on, either sequentially or in combination).

Behind this metaphor lie at least two diverse theoretical approaches. In functionalist **sociology**, a role is seen as a more or less precisely prescribed set of behavioural expectations, that effectively define the role. The role is thus circumscribed by a set of **norms**, rules and **values** that determine how the individual in that role is to behave. Failure to behave appropriately will be punished through some form of negative sanction. Thus, the role of 'teacher' would be understood in terms of the rules that govern the technical skills and stocks of technical knowledge that the teacher must possess, along with the moral rules that govern his or her relationship to pupils and to colleagues, and the aspiration to certain values (such as a belief in the value of teaching as a profession). **Socialisation** (the process of learning to be a social and cultural being) is thus understood as the preparation of individuals to take on certain roles.

In contrast, roles within **symbolic interactionist** approaches are seen as more fluid, and in need of achievement and negotiation. This approach is grounded in the work of George Herbert Mead (1934), who argued that we come to understand and fulfil our own roles only by imaginatively taking the roles of others. A role, and thus in part our own **self**-understanding or self-identity, is composed in response to, or in anticipation of, the actions of others. The teacher's role does not then exist in isolation. It is constructed (or 'made' in Mead's terminology) only in relation to the expected behaviour of pupils, and in responding to their actual reactions, and each teacher may work this role out in his or her own way. Roles are continually modified through **interaction**. Mead thus defines a role as a sequence of gestures that highlight and refer to an individual's actions and dispositions. The concept of role thus indicates how we read, and give **meaning** to, each other's actions or gestures (and indeed think about the meaning of our own actions), in order to anticipate and respond to the future actions of others.

Two important associated concepts are 'role conflict' and 'role distance'. Role conflict occurs either when an individual finds that two of the roles that he or she performs make incompatible demands, or when two groups have different, and again incompatible, expectations of one's role. Thus, an off-duty friendship may clash with the need to impose discipline while on duty; or a trade union shop steward may find that managers and workers have radically different expectations as to what he or she can do. Role distance was coined by Goffman (1959) to refer to the degree to which performers of a role are detached from it and, in being aware that they are performing a role for a specific audience, can manipulate it to achieve some end.

See also: **dramaturgical model**.

Further reading: Biddle 1979.

AE

ROMANTICISM

The Romantic period in European culture runs from approximately 1780 to 1850. While Romantic works of art are generally readily identifiable as such (for example in the painting of Turner and Delacroix, the poetry of Wordsworth and Byron, and the music of Wagner), the precise formulation of what Romantic artists and thinkers have in common is elusive. Romanticism is perhaps best seen as a cluster of attitudes and themes, rather than as a single coherent doctrine. At its core is a reaction to **Enlightenment** emphasis on reason and order, and thus as a reaction to classicism in the arts.

Originally 'Romantic' referred merely to the romance languages, and hence to writing in the vernacular French, rather than Latin. In 1755, Dr Johnson defined 'Romantick' as 'resembling the tales or romances; wild . . . improbable; false . . .; fanciful; full of wild scenery'. This definition already begins to capture something of the cluster of Romantic concerns. The Romantic breaks free of classicism through a renewed appeal to emotion, and crucially to the darker emotions of fear and suffering. Thus, while the Enlightenment was interested in **nature** as a source of reason and order (exemplified by Newtonian mechanics), the Romantic found in it organic growth and diversity. For the Romantic, the natural and the supernatural are entwined, giving nature an emotional and spiritual force that is alien to Enlightenment thinking. In addition, romanticism marked a renewed interest in medieval and even pagan culture. The Romantic therefore turned to the Gothic (culminating in the revival of Gothic **architecture**), and where classicism had looked to Greek and Roman mythology, romanticism looked to European mythology and folk culture (for example in the German *Nibelungenlied*, or the Finnish *Kalevala*). Above all, romanticism celebrates the exceptional individual.

Writing towards the end of the eighteenth century and beginning of the nineteenth, Friedrich and August Wilhelm von Schlegel are key figures in the development of romanticism. Both emphasise the fluid and fragmentary nature of the Romantic work of art. For Friedrich, Romantic poetry is always in a state of becoming, and thus never achieves the perfection or harmonious coherence to which classical art aspires. For August, the Romantic is encapsulated in the problem of interpretation, and the ultimate incomprehensibility of the work of art. His doctrine of Romantic **irony** stresses the paradoxical nature of the poem, so that no objective or definitive meaning can ever be derived from it. In drama, Shakespeare is celebrated for his ironic detachment from his characters. He is thus able to portray contradictory positions, through the opposition of characters, without resolving the drama in favour of one viewpoint.

In philosophy, the emergence of romanticism may be associated with the work of Jean-Jacques Rousseau, both in his criticism of the corrupting effect of contemporary civilisation on humanity, in the emotional and sentimental tone of his novel, *Julie, ou la Nouvelle Héloi?se,* and in the self-exploration of the *Confessions.* As Rousseau turns to the image of a state of nature, prior to civilisation, in order to recover an image of a noble and uncorrupted humanity, so the German philosopher Johann Gottfried Herder (1744–1803) turns to folk cultures and to non-European cultures, understanding them not as primitive precursors of European civilisation, but as having their own validity, and their own criteria of meaning and excellence. While Herder writes in reaction to the rationalism of Kant, Kant himself stands in a complex relationship to romanticism. His ethics are dominated by reason, but his theory of knowledge and **aesthetics** explores the limits of knowledge and reason (constraining scientific enquiry in order to make 'room for faith'). However, it is Arthur Schopenhauer (1788–1860), himself reinterpreting Kant, who is the purest example of a Romantic philosopher. His pessimistic account of the world in terms of the continual strivings of the will, from which art provides one of the few sources of relief, was influential on the archetypal Romantic artist, Richard Wagner.

Further reading: Cranston 1994; Honour 1979; Le Huray and Day 1987; Lovejoy 1948; Praz 1970; Rosen and Zerner 1984; Simpson 1988; Wu 1994.

AE

RULE

A term which has gained an increasing importance in the sphere of the analysis of language, where it has sometimes come to be used in a manner which is akin in meaning to 'convention'. Rule-based views of language assert that it is by way of rules or conventions that meaning is constituted, not through, for example, the manner in which words refer to non-linguistic states of affairs. The work of the later Wittgenstein provided much of the impetus towards the analysis of rules in language in the post-war period (principally through the notion of 'language games'). One good example of a rule-based account of language is Jean-François Lyotard's *The Differend: Phrases in Dispute* (1983). On this conception, the rules which constitute any particular way of speaking make up a **genre** of discourse. A genre has a purpose, and the rules tell you what to do in order to achieve that purpose. One might draw the analogy between this notion and cooking: if one wishes to make a cake, then the genre of cooking contains within it the rules one needs to observe in order to attain this goal. It follows that rules are not of themselves obligatory—there is no rule which tells you that you ought to follow a particular rule—since they are dependent upon the existence of particular goals; nor do they tell you how to 'play well': one can follow the rules of chess and still play badly (although, if a man allows himself to be beaten at chess by his boss, one might be tempted to argue that he is playing another game with a different set of stakes). Conventions differ from rules at the level of social interaction when this term is taken as signifying a way of behaving in a particular context which is adopted by the members of a community as a norm (e.g. shaking hands when meeting; knocking on a door before going in a room; wearing a particular style of clothes in a particular context, e.g. a wedding). Taken in this sense, conventions also underlie the identities of particular genres (e.g. in literature the novel form stipulates a set of conventions which, at least in theory, all novels share in some manner or other, although the 'goal' of any individual novel is not stipulated by way of its conforming to the conventions which characterise the genre).

PS

SELF

A term which is linked to issues of **subjectivity** and **identity**, and which also has ramifications in a variety of discursive contexts (e.g. politics, **liberalism**, **individualism**, **epistemology**, ethics).

The notion of the self is invoked as soon as one asks a question like 'Who am I?' At first glance, this might not seem very difficult to answer, and you might respond by just giving your name. But giving your name does not adequately answer the 'Who am I?' question if you also take it to mean 'What am I?' In general, philosophers have held that asking who you are necessarily also involves considering *what* you are. Here is one possible answer to this question: 'I am a mind and a body. I think and I also move about in the world as a material being'. But answering in this way does not solve the problem, unless you are also able to say how such things as minds and bodies are related to one another. In turn, then, a consideration of the nature of the self usually entails a number of related questions;

e.g. *how* is the mind connected to the body? (put another way: What is the relationship between mind and body?). Also, if one holds the view that each of us is a mind plus a body, another issue arises, namely, which came first?

A number of approaches to this issue are possible. Plato, in the *Phaedo* (*c.* 380 BC, cf. 63e ff.), argued that the soul (mind) and the body are distinct. Moreover, he held that the soul must have existed prior to the body. The essence of what each of us is resides in this contrast. The essential part of each of us (the mind/soul) never changes, because what is essential (and hence true) must by definition never change. In contrast, the realm of the material world changes. Here is Plato's argument, presented by Socrates in the *Phaedo*: (i) There are two sorts of existence: the seen (the physical world) and the unseen. (ii) The world of experience (the seen) is a realm of change, whereas the unseen is unchanging. (iii) We are made of two parts—body and soul. (iv) The body is akin to the seen, and therefore changing; and the soul is akin to the unseen, and therefore unchanging. (v) Of these two, the soul is akin to the divine (which is unchanging)—in short, we have an immortal soul. (vi) Therefore, the soul is indissoluble. From this, it follows that the self is the immortal part of each of us, and the body the mere vessel in which this essence is instantiated. Plato, following this chain of reasoning, held that what is essential about each of us endures after death (i.e. that the soul/mind is immortal).

Such a view can be contrasted with eighteenth-century philosopher David Hume's treatment of the matter in the *Treatise of Human Nature* (1739: cf. Book 1, part iv, section 6). According to Hume, whenever I speak of *myself* I always do so in the context of some particular thought or feeling. There is no self over and above thoughts and feelings which can be held to be independent of them. What 'I' am is a bundle of sensations; the self, therefore, is a product of a body's ability to have sensations, experiences, etc. Hence, on Hume's account, nothing about the self can be said to exist independently of such sensations: the self is mortal. Moreover, the self is therefore something *added* to experiences; it is a fiction or an illusion. Put another way, the self is not an entity independent of the sensations a body is capable of feeling, but is produced by them. Thus, for Hume the self is a kind of *interpretation* of these sensations.

These two accounts, whatever their respective shortcomings, offer contrasting ontological views about the nature of the self. In making some claim about the nature of the self (i.e. what the self is), we are committed to some kind of ontology. This is the case even if, like

Hume, we are tempted to deny that the self exists in any ontological sense: we are still making an ontological claim about the self on the basis of what we hold reality to be.

Important elements of Plato's view are by no means restricted to him. Many philosophical, religious and ethical attitudes and ideas contain within them the (albeit perhaps tacitly held) belief that mind and body are distinct from one another in kind. Likewise, with regard to knowledge, considered from both a philosophical point of view and from the vantage point of science, the question of the self is a significant one. This is because in talking of knowledge the question necessarily arises concerning who or what it is that has, or is the subject of, knowledge. For example, within the sciences some notion of what an enquirer is must be pre-supposed.

The seventeenth-century philosopher René Descartes, in reply to the writings of contemporary sceptics who questioned whether we can have any certain knowledge, attempted to show that there is at least one certain piece of knowledge we are in possession of. Descartes starts by claiming that he has been struck by the large number of false beliefs he has accepted since being a child. He resolves to 'demolish' all his beliefs as a prologue to constructing the foundations of knowledge (this approach is often known as the 'sceptical method', since it preceeds from doubt). In order to do this, it is sufficient to bring into question all one's opinions, i.e. to show that they are *not certain*, rather than that they are false. However much one may doubt the veracity of one's beliefs, Descartes claims, one thing remains true: whatever happens I am still thinking: 'I must conclude that this proposition, *I am, I exist,* is necessarily true whenever it is put forward or conceived by me in my mind'. This is most famously expressed in the phrase 'I think, therefore I am' (*cogito, ergo sum*).

What is this 'I' that thinks? Descartes draws a distinction between (i) the mechanical structure of the human body and (ii) the activities which humans pursue: they walk about, eat, have perceptions through their senses, etc. These activities are, he claims, the actions of a soul or mind. The properties of a body are physical: it can be seen, touched, occupies a particular space, can be moved, etc. The 'power of self-movement', however, is not a property we can attribute to a body. In line with the precepts of the sceptical method, the body can be doubted. But the self that thinks, Descartes argued, cannot be doubted. Thus, Descartes holds that he is a mind, 'not that structure of limbs which is called a human body' (a view termed 'mind–body dualism'). In other words, this standpoint contends that what is essential about humans is that they are thinking things, and that the property denoted by the term 'mind' is essentially different from that denoted by the term 'body'. This forms the basis for his view of knowledge: certain (i.e. true) knowledge derives from the 'I think', the self conceived as a mental essence. Amongst those who have criticised this approach was Nietzsche, who, in *Beyond Good and Evil* (section 16), pointed out that there was no necessary causal connection between thinking and the self; that is, we cannot show with complete certainty that it is the self which is the agency behind the activity of thinking. For Nietzsche, in contrast, the self is always to be comprehended as being situated within particular contexts and, indeed, as the product of human **culture**, rather than an ontological category which grounds the basis of experience and therefore knowledge.

With the 'linguistic turn' in philosophy during the twentieth century and also in the light of intellectual developments such as **psychoanalysis**, accounts have been offered of the self which address, for example, the question of its construction within the domain of language and **discourse**. For Jean-François Lyotard, for example, the notion of a self apart from language derives from an anthropocentric view of the nature of meaning which can be challenged. Selves, on this account, are not situated in a language-independent realm, nor are their attitudes, dispositions and intentions alone sufficient to secure an epistemological foundation for knowledge. Rather, such things as intentions, dispositions and interests are realised in and through language. Thus, Lyotard criticises Wittgenstein's conception of 'language games' as being too limited. For instance, in drawing an analogy between language games and the game of chess, Wittgenstein, says Lyotard, remains trapped within a view of meaning which privileges a self which is independent of language: he presupposes that a 'player' moves a piece in a chess game, yet remains apart from the game. Equally, Jacques Derrida has argued that the meaning of such things as propositions is not simply a matter of the intentions of a speaker. For Derrida, although 'meaning has its place', what is instrumental in the production of meaning are language and context. Also, the work of Michel Foucault has, following Nietzsche, concentrated on reconceptualising the notion of the self in terms of the relations between discourses of power.

Further reading: Derrida 1988b; Descartes 1986; Hernadi 1995; Lyotard 1988; Nietzsche 1968a; Plato 1975.

PS

SEMIOTICS/SEMIOLOGY

The terms 'semiotics' and 'semiology' alike refer to the theory of **signs**, and thus to the way in which a study of signs and systems of signs can explicate problems of **meaning** and communication. (While 'semiotics' was coined in the seventeenth century by the English philosopher John Locke and 'semiology' by the twentieth-century linguist Ferdinand de Saussure, the former term is perhaps used more frequently.) The study of signs can be broadly traced back to ancient Greece, for example in the medical study of symptoms as signs of disease. Similarly, modern semiotics may embrace everything that can act as a sign, and which can therefore generate and communicate meaning. Zoosemiotics, for example, is concerned with the natural processes that exist in animal communication. However, the importance of semiotics for cultural studies lies in the insight that it can provide into communication within human cultures, and thus with the artificial (as opposed to natural) processes that make possible human communication. It may not be an exaggeration to suggest that semiotics is the single most important set of theoretical tools that is available to cultural studies, precisely because of its power to recognise and analyse meaningful relationships in a vast range of human activities and products. Within cultural studies, semiotics may be applied, equally productively, to such diverse artefacts as literary texts, popular songs, photographs, advertisements, road signs, food and clothing. Crucially, semiotics therefore allows cultural studies to break from the evaluative approach of traditional literary criticism and **aesthetics**, for it does not seek to assess the worth of **texts**, but rather to understand the processes through which they become meaningful and how they are variously interpreted.

Language is the dominant model of a sign system for semiotics, and the linguistics of Saussure has had a major influence on the development of modern semiotics. At the core of Saussure's approach to language is the claim that language (and thus the words or signs within a language) do not merely correspond to a pre-existing (extralinguistic) reality. Rather, language is seen as constituting the reality we experience. Thus, the word 'herb' does not point to some pre-existing segment of reality, for the distinction between, say, herbs, flowers and vegetables depends upon our possessing a language that allows us to recognise differences between these three types of plant. (We might readily imagine a language that did not make this distinction, and perhaps then imagine the difficulty we would have in explaining the difference to someone who did not speak English, even if we were fluent in this other language.) Saussure therefore argues that language, as a sign system, works, not through the simple relationship of its component signs to external objects, but rather through the relations of similarity and difference that exist between signs (and thus wholly within language). Part of the meaning of 'herb' is that it is not 'vegetable'. Similarly, to use a common example, the word 'man' in English means 'not animal', 'not woman' and 'not boy'. This may be extended to suggest that it has further associations, such as 'not vulnerable' or 'not emotional'. The meaning of the word 'man' therefore depends upon the particular understanding of masculinity that is current in the language-user's culture. One more example will serve to develop this point, and particularly to emphasise the arbitrariness of semiotic structures. In Western cultures, 'white' is typically associated with positive emotions and events (hence a white wedding dress). White is therefore not black, for black is associated with negative emotions and events. In Eastern cultures, while the opposition of white and black may be retained, the associations may be reversed. The white is therefore the colour associated with funerals.

The above examples may begin to indicate how semiotics moves from language, as the model of a sign system, to other forms of sign system. A person's choice of clothing, for example, is meaningful. A black dress is appropriate in certain social contexts, inappropriate in others, precisely because it communicates a message about the wearer (she is in mourning; is being formal; is being sexy). Just as there are conventions governing the meaning of a written or spoken word in a sentence, so there are conventional rules governing the meaning of a chosen item of clothing. Crucially these rules govern the choice of one item from a range of possibilities (a black dress, not a white or yellow or blue dress) (see **paradigm**) and the combination of the chosen items (see **syntagm**). Thus, one may differentiate between funeral wear, a suit for the office and a party dress, although all may be black, by recognising the combination of colour (as one sign) with style, hemline, material, and so on (as other signs), just as a sentence or any other spoken or written **text** makes sense through the combination of words.

The examples of 'man' and 'black' used above indicate that signs typically have a range of meanings, some of which are fairly literal (man is not woman), while others are more allusive (man is not emotional). Thus, a distinction is made between the denotations of a sign, being its most literal and stable meanings, and the connotations, being the associations or more emotional, expressive and evaluative nuances of meaning that the sign evokes. In practice, no sign (with the possible exception of those used in mathematics and formal logic) is purely denotative. To choose to talk, say, of 'steeds' rather than 'horses' places a small but important twist upon what is said. Using the distinction between connotation and denotation, Roland Barthes builds upon Saussure's original conception of semiotics in order to argue that connotation should be understood as calling forth the value system of the culture within which the sign is used and interpreted. Crucially, these culturally specific evaluations are linked to the distribution of power within the society (so that, for example, the association of masculinity—in the sign 'man'—with rationality, action and strength is indicative of a patriarchal society). The fact that we take connotations for granted, confusing them with denotations and thereby accepting them as if they were natural or unchangeable, leads to what Barthes calls **myth**. The evaluative, and ultimately political, implications of signs are concealed, so that the reader may unwittingly absorb the dominant value system as he or she responds to the text. Thus, in looking at an advertisement, the nai?ve reader will absorb evaluations of masculinity and femininity, simply through the way in which men and women are portrayed and related to each other and to other signs in the advertisement. (Fiske and Hartley have therefore argued that an understanding of semiotics and mythology, in Barthes's sense of the term, leads to a theory of **ideology**.)

For all the analytical power that semiotics offers to cultural studies, not least in the model of Barthes's work, the Saussurean approach to signs may be seen to have certain weaknesses. An early alternative to Saussurean semiotics was posed by the Russian theorist V.N. Voloshinov. Voloshinov sees Saussure's emphasis on the linguistic or sign system as giving a false objectivity to language. Voloshinov is concerned not with the ahistorical structure of language, but rather with the realisation of language and meaning in particular social situations. A sign may thereby be understood as a potential area of class struggle, for although all members of a society may share a common language, different classes will appropriate that language to different political uses. Signs thus have a 'social multiaccentuality', although this will be most explicit only in times of crisis and revolution.

A further criticism may be made through reflection on the great emphasis that Saussurean semiotics places on the role of language in structuring, and indeed creating, the world which we experience. This gives rise to the danger that semiotics collapses into a form of anti-realism, which is to say that it says too little about the restraints that the world external to languages and sign systems places upon us, and the way in which signs refer to that external, non-linguistic world. A number of approaches have been developed to deal with this problem, not least through elaborating some notion of **reference**. However, the work of the American philosopher Charles S. Peirce has received attention, precisely because his semiotics is, from the first, more sensitive to the problem of the relationship of the sign to an extralinguistic object.

Peirce's theory of signs involves a three-part scheme. What Peirce terms the 'sign' is related to an 'interpretant', via an 'object'. A simple example (borrowed from Hookway) best illustrates this. If I see bark stripped from a tree, then this may be a sign that a deer is around. The stripped bark is the sign, the real deer that did the stripping is the object, and my idea of a deer is the interpretant. The interpretant is thus the mental response of the reader to the original sign. Crucially, Peirce goes on to argue that signs generate chains of interpretants, which is to suggest that a sign is not self-evidently or transparently meaningful. Each reader will generate his or her own interpretation of the sign. The reader is therefore always separated from the real object by the sign and its interpretation. However, as the chain of interpretants progresses, Peirce argues (at least for certain types of sign, such as those used in communication within the community of scientists) that interpretants (and thus the reader's understanding) gradually become more adequate to the object. In effect, the object, outside language, may then be seen to exert pressure on signs and sign systems. Thus, while different cultures may classify the realm of plants differently, a practical engagement and study of plants will, for Peirce, eventually lead the botanist and the cook to distinguish herb from vegetable, and rosemary from carrot.

Peirce's semiotics offers one further, useful set of concepts, in so far as he distinguishes three types of sign. Symbols are signs that are only conventionally related to the objects to which they refer. Thus, the word 'dog' has nothing physically or otherwise in common with real dogs. A flag may signify a nation, but need be nothing more than an abstract design. Indices, conversely, have some causal or existential link to the object. Thus, the stripped bark is an index, because it is caused by the deer. Smoke is an index of fire. Finally, icons share certain properties with their object. A map is thus iconic, as are representational paintings and photographs.

Further reading: Barthes 1967b, 1973; Eco 1976; Fiske and Hartley 1978; Hookway 1985; Innis 1986; Peirce 1986; Saussure 1983; Voloshinov 1973.

AE

SEXUALITY

'Sexuality' is probably the most misunderstood concept in Freudian **psychoanalysis**. It is commonly conflated with the term 'genital'. For Freud, sexuality functions as a superordinate term: the genital is merely one of the aspects of sexuality. The pansexualist criticism of psychoanalysis is based on the idea that Freud reduces everything to sexuality (i.e. the genital). In his *Three Essays on the Theory of Sexuality* (1905), Freud widens the ambit of sexuality to include infantile sexuality, polymorphous perversity, the function of symptoms (all of which represent the sexual life of the subject), and the sheer diversity and deviations that pertain to object choice. Sexuality cannot be reduced to instinctual behaviour since the relationship between the drive and the object is arbitrary Sexuality does not merely frame the phenomenology of the neurotic symptom but helps the psychoanalyst to understand its aetiology as well. It was Freud's insistence on the sexual aetiology of the neuroses that led to a parting of ways between him and his early followers, Alfred Adler and Carl Gustav Jung.

Sexuality in psychoanalysis is described through a developmental model where the infant progresses through different stages: the oral, the anal, the genital and the phallic. Contingent disturbances in any of these levels will determine the distributions of libido that structure the subject's life. Neuroses were initially understood as regressions to one of these levels of libidinal fixation. The regression is made necessary by the subject's inability to respond to the demands of 'reality'. Sexuality is understood to manifest itself from the time of early infancy. The premature demands of the sexual drive are repressed in the so-called Oedipal phase and the child switches from an *imaginary* identification with the mother to a *symbolic* identification with the father. This is followed by a period of latency. At puberty, sexuality once again makes its exorbitant demands on the subject, thereby leading to the revival of modes of behaviour that constitute the libidinal matrix of childhood.

In subjects who fail to make a proper Oedipal crossover from the mother to the father, sexual impressions of early childhood take on a traumatic aspect during puberty resulting in the return of the repressed. This leads to the production of neurotic symptoms, which constitute the sexual life of the subject. The typology of neuroses can also be classified along a model of stages. For example: in terms of fixation, hysteria is to orality what obsessionality is to anality. Lacan, however, called this model of biological stages into question without doing away with it completely. In the Lacanian model, though the infant must travel through these stages, there is nothing specifically biological about it. It is the fear of castration that mediates the subject's relation to any of these 'stages'. Castration has a specifically symbolic dimension in Lacan. Symbolic castration is the radical disjunction between the subject and its object of desire, such that no object can exhaust the restlessness of the drive. The Oedipal drama is the symbolic realm where the subject is first alienated in its desire. Subsequently, the sexual drive can only seek an object in a complex imitation or distortion of the lost object. Sexuality therefore cannot be reduced to instinctual behaviour, instead it takes on a dialectical relationship with the absent, the forbidden and, finally, the impossible.

Further reading: Freud 1977, 1979; Laplanche and Pontalis 1973.

SKS

SIGN

A sign may be understood as anything that stands for, refers to, or represents something else. A sign is analysed into two elements. A **signifier** is the material form the sign takes, such as a written word ('rose'), an object (the stem and flower of a rose), a trade mark, photographic images, scents, colours, and so on. A **signified** is the abstract concept to which the signifier points (so that a rose or the image of a rose may signify the idea of love more adequately than the word 'love', giving you, as a sign, what Barthes has called a '"passionified" rose'). Signs may be understood as the most important units that carry and produce **meaning** in any act of communication. Signs are meaningful due to their position within a conventional and culturally specific set of rules (or **codes**) that govern their use and appropriateness.

See also: **semiotics**.

Further reading: Silverman 1983.

AE

SIGNIFIER/SIGNIFIED

In **semiotics**, a **sign** is analysed in terms of two constitutive components: the signifier and the signified. The signifier is the physical form taken by the sign, such as a spoken or written word ('remembrance'), an object (a herb, the drawing of a herb), and so on. The signifier is distinct from any particular utterance, use or presentation of it. Thus, a dozen people with diverse accents and intonations of voice may all say 'remembrance' in their own way, and yet we will recognise the signifier that is common to each of these utterances. The signified is the concept to which the sign refers (and thus, in these examples, the idea of remembrance). Crucially, the signified is not to be understood as a particular object or event in the real world. So the word 'remembrance' no more signifies a particular act of remembrance than the word 'herb' refers to any particular herb. Similarly, a photograph of the herb rosemary, for example in a botany book, signifies what might be called 'rosemary-ness', and not the particular plant that the photographer used for a model.

It must also be noted that a signifier may have many signifieds, and a signified may have many signifiers. Thus, the word 'remembrance', the herb rosemary, or an artificial poppy, as signifiers, may all have the abstract concept of remembrance as their signified. Similarly the word 'rosemary' might well signify different concepts if used within a poem than if used in a cookery or botany book. The relationship between signifier and signified is thus recognised as largely arbitrary, and dependent on the cultural conventions that govern a particular sign system.

Further reading: Barthes 1967b.

AE

SIMULACRUM

Conventionally, a simulacrum is a copy of a copy in Plato's **ontology**. A copy is inferior to the ideal form of which it is a copy, while the simulacrum is further still from the form, and is therefore inferior to the straight copy. In particular, a drawing of an object, since it is a copy of the thing, which itself is simply a copy of the form, is undesirable because it contains less inherent truth about the form than the object itself.

In the wake of Nietzsche, some philosophers associated with the more extreme kinds of **postmodernism** have tended to stress the importance of the simulacrum. This is probably connected with their general aesthetic disposition. Jean Baudrillard has given particular importance to the simulacrum, while Gilles Deleuze and Jean-François Lyotard also took this approach, especially in their earlier works.

The general consensus is that the simulacrum is not simply a copy of the copy: it somehow avoids contact with the ideal form. Given that the order of forms represents, for Plato, the rational ordering of the universe, the simulacrum comes to stand for that which is incommensurable with conceptual reason.

Further reading: Deleuze 1990b.

RC

SOCIAL CONTRACT

A social contract theory envisages the drawing up of a contract between free individuals with a view to establishing the basic political, civil or moral principles of a community. A contract theory therefore aims to legitimise these principles by invoking the notion of consent. Through consent the contract lays claim to a form of **authority** which is derived from the agreement of those who undertake to be bound by it. A variety of philosophers have dealt with this notion: Hobbes, Locke and Rousseau all propounded social contract theories, while thinkers such as Hume, Hegel and Marx have provided criticisms of this approach.

See also: **liberalism**.

Further reading: Boucher and Kelly 1994.

PS

SOCIAL DARWINISM

An appropriation of the evolutionary principles outlined in Charles Darwin's *Origin of Species* (1859), social Darwinism was first propounded by Herbert Spencer (1820–1903). Spencer's theories in fact pre-date the publication of Darwin's own text; he first drew on contemporary science as a means of justifying his hypotheses, and later used Darwin's work in order to validate the **authority** of his own. Spencer's project aimed to integrate different disciplines (e.g. the then developing discipline of **sociology**, and the methods and theories of the physical sciences) within an evolutionary account of human **society**. Thus, whereas Darwin's model of **evolution** is concerned with physical fact (the realm of nature), Spencer's conception of evolution may be characterised by way of its claim to be a science of society.

Spencer holds that the evolutionary process is one in which there is a spontaneous 'change from incoherent homogeneity (i.e. unity) to a coherent heterogeneity (i.e. diversity), accompanying the dissipation of motion and integration of matter' (*Structure, Function and Evolution* (1971:92)). From this premise he constructs a depoliticised model of society which is both naturalised and ahistorical: left alone, society will regulate itself according to the principle of the 'survival of the fittest', which is driven by this movement towards increasing coherence and diversity. His view is highly conservative in its implications: hierarchical stability is considered by Spencer to be essential to the 'coherence' (i.e. stability) of **social structure**. Hence, any outbreak of social disorder which threatens hierarchy is conceived of as a negative force, akin to illness in the human body. Both are disorganising regressions and obstruct the evolutionary process by causing heterogeneity *without* coherence. Defining the production of disease in the human body, Spencer comments on how, in successive stages, 'lines of organisation, once so precise disappear' and parallels this description with social disorder, which is a 'loosing of those ties by which citizens are bound up into distinct classes and subclasses' (1971:94). The 'survival of the fittest' is thereby taken as being fought out in the form of an economic and social struggle for existence, and the only justifiable attitude to matters of social organisation is one which lets the forces of progressive evolution take their course. Spencer held his view to be the most 'scientific' of philosophical theses because it could, he thought, be tested empirically. The theory attracted a number of adherents associated with **fascism**, most notably Nazi leader Hitler.

Leaving the question of the **history** of authoritarianism to one side, there are, of course, a number of objections to Spencer's evolutionary theory. For instance, although the 'survival of the fittest' principle may apply to nature, it is not clear that it is applicable in the same way, if at all, to the sphere of human **culture**. Also, recent empirical work in palaeontology has suggested that natural forms do not necessarily develop from states of relative 'simplicity' and homogeneity to states of 'complexity' and heterogeneous diversity. (See Stephen J. Gould's account of the enormous diversity of forms of life found in the Burgess Shale—a deposit of sedimentary rock around 530 million years old. Gould argues that, on this evidence, evolutionary history cannot be thought of as a straightforward progression towards increasing diversity and heterogeneity, since the forms of animal design existing today represent a reduction of the number of designs found in the *older* Burgess Shale. Interestingly, Gould holds that seeking to explain why certain forms survived and others became extinct only in terms of which had 'better' body-designs will not work, since it is not always possible to see what perceptible advantages one Burgess form may have had over another. He argues that chance may play a key role in the process of evolution: run the clock of history again from the same starting point and it might turn out differently—i.e. there might have been no humans.)

Further reading: Appleman 1970; Gould 1991; Lacquer 1988; Spencer 1971.

PS

SOCIAL FACT

In Durkheim's **sociology**, especially, a social fact is a social phenomenon that has a coercive effect upon the individual. Thus, although social facts may originally be the product of human action, they have developed an autonomy from their human authors, and now confront humans as something external to them, They have an objectivity akin to that of natural objects and physical laws. For Durkheim (1982), the goal of sociology is to study these facts.

AE

SOCIALISATION

Socialisation is the process by which the individual learns to be a member of a particular society and **culture**, and thus to be a genuinely social and cultural being. The individual internalises his or her culture. While this process is of fundamental importance to understanding how cultures work, and particularly how they **reproduce** themselves over generations, the precise nature of socialisation has been theorised in widely different ways, and continues to be at the heart of a number of key debates over the nature of human being and human society.

In the **functionalist** tradition in **sociology** and **cultural anthropology**, socialisation adapts the individual to perform the social **roles** that will be expected of him or her. The newborn human was largely presupposed to be a blank slate (or *tabula rasa*) onto which society could inscribe almost any characteristics. These characteristics would include: fundamental beliefs about the natural, social and, indeed, supernatural worlds, along with an associated cosmology; **values** and preferences, be these aesthetic, culinary or moral (what else could explain Icelanders' ability to eat rotten shark?); the moral **norms** of which he or she would approve and by which he or she would abide and judge others; and his or her patterns of behaviour (including, most significantly, those patterns associated with **gender**). Thus, an individual's personality or **self** could be seen as a product of the particular society into which he or she was born.

Functionalism focused heavily upon the 'primary' socialisation that occurs in the family. As such, socialisation tended to be theorised as a process that was largely completed in the early years of childhood, and could be completed more or less well. If socialisation failed, the consequence would be that the individual would be ill-adapted to his or her society. This would lead to criminality or some other form of **deviance**, in that the individual would be unable to abide by the norms and goals valued within his or her society. This view was challenged, famously, by Denis Wrong (1980), as the 'oversocialised' view of human being. The view of socialisation thus changes, most notably in the **symbolic interactionist** tradition, to recognise that the individual is not simply a passive recipient of the process, and further that the process is not necessarily ever concluded. This tradition draws on the work of George Herbert Mead and Alfred Schutz. Mead (1934), for example, distinguishes between the 'I', as the unselfconscious subject that responds to the actions and attitudes of others, and the 'me', as our self-understanding of ourselves as an object. Socialisation works, most significantly, through the 'me', in so far as the individual actively assumes an organised set of attitudes from others, and thus comes to recognise him or herself in terms of socially constructed concepts. This approach to socialisation recognises the space that individuals have to negotiate and challenges the values and beliefs with which they are confronted in a struggle to make sense of the situations within which they find themselves, and thus in a struggle to understand and interpret their own self-identity.

Socialisation need not then be understood as a finite process. This is because the process of negotiation and the struggle to find **meaning** in new and unpredictable situations that are inherent to socialisation will continue throughout the individual's life. Socialisation in the family is followed, reinforced and challenged by the formal education of school; contact with equals and contemporaries; the **mass media**; participation in **subcultures**; and work. If socialisation is a continuing process, then it cannot easily be seen as successful or unsuccessful. The symbolic interactionist approach to socialisation may suggest that the apparent failure of socialisation may be the failure of the external culture to meet the needs of the individual, rather than that of the individual to meet the needs or expectations of society. Paradoxically, Willis (1977) has shown how the active resistance of underprivileged schoolboys to socialisation from school, leads to their socialisation into unskilled labour.

Ultimately the analysis of socialisation is complex, dealing with possibly irresolvable questions concerning the relationship between **nature** and culture. It inquires into exactly how much an individual absorbs from his or her society (and thus the degree of malleability that there is in human nature), and how much is innate or biologically determined.

Further reading: Berger 1963.

AE

SOCIALISM

A political creed whose origins are normally traced back to the mid-nineteenth century. There have been many types of socialist (e.g. utopian socialists, Fabian socialists, Guild socialists) but they share in common an adherence to particular principles with regard to how human **society** should be organised. In contrast to **liberalism**, which advocates the primacy of the individual's liberty and rights, socialists have traditionally placed emphasis upon the importance of equality as a political principle. This is, in turn, expressed in terms of the importance of economic relationships within society. Socialists are particularly opposed to the **individualism** of liberal capitalist society, holding that a desirable form of social order (which would be based upon mutuality, co-operation and shared public ownership of the means of production) is not possible as long as human relationships are dominated by the self-interested and antagonistic principles which underlie **civil society**. In contrast to liberals, therefore, socialists see justice as a matter of how society is ordered with regard to the distribution of goods within it, not in terms of the guardianship of freedoms which enable individuals to pursue their own purposes. Socialism thus has much in common with communism with regard to its holding that the most desirable form of social organisation embodies principles of egalitarianism. However, whereas advocates of communism traditionally adhere to a theoretical perspective derived from Marx's claim that his analysis of the development of capitalist societies pertains to a scientific status, which in turn holds that proletarian revolution is the inevitable outcome of class antagonisms, socialism has tended to be more pragmatic and less confrontational in its approach. Socialists have, for example, emphasised the importance of democratic procedures within the political process.

Socialism like communism can be defined as an internationalism. This tendency can be traced back to the organisation (by Marx) of the First Socialist International in London in 1864, although the spirit of unity embodied by this event gave way to fragmentation into opposed groups (socialists, communists, anarchists) by the time of the Second International nearly a quarter of a century later. The international aspect of socialism can be seen in its adherence to values associated with **humanism**, for instance, the notion of a universal conception of value with regard to such things as the establishment of supranational mutuality, shared norms of justice and human rights between different nations.

Further reading: Berki 1975; Crozier 1987; Forman 1973.

PS

SOCIAL MOBILITY

Social mobility refers to the movement of individuals between hierarchical social groups, most typically between **classes**. Study of social mobility is an important complement to studies of **social stratification**, because a hierarchical society may not be considered undesirable if there is free movement between the different levels of the hierarchy. Such free movement would suggest that the ruling class or **elite** may not be a closed and self-serving group and, similarly, that a person born in the lower strata of society is not condemned to a life of relative powerlessness and low income. However, Marxist approaches to social mobility have long suggested that the ruling class will recruit the most able members of the lower classes into its ranks in order to prevent them becoming effective agents of revolution.

Further reading: Heath 1981.

AE

SOCIAL STRATIFICATION

The differentiation of society into separate groupings becomes social stratification when these groupings can be seen as forming a hierarchy.

Traditionally, in **sociology**, three major types of strata have been recognised. In a caste system, different strata are characterised in terms of ethnic purity, with no movement between castes (so that a person lives his or her entire life within the caste into which he or she is born). In an estate system, typical of **feudal** societies, again there is little or no mobility between strata. The estates are defined through land ownership (on the part of the dominant stratum) and bondage. In industrial societies, stratification is in terms of **class**, with classes understood as economically defined. Class hierarchies formally allow for **social mobility** (although the actual amount of mobility, and thus the real opportunities to leave the class of one's birth, may be restricted through unequal access to economic and cultural resources such as **education**). Disputes continue, first over the relevant criteria for defining class. In the Marxist tradition, two major classes are identified and distinguished in terms of ownership and control of the **means of production**. (In **Marxism**, estates and castes are subsumed within the concept and theory of class, being understood as different forms that class and exploitation take in different historical epochs.) In other sociological traditions, defining class in terms of occupation allows for a more subtle and comprehensive account of social stratification. However, it is not clear that other hierarchies, such as power, material reward and **status**, necessarily map onto class hierarchies in any simple manner. (Thus, as Max Weber noted, the *nouveaux riches* may have the income and wealth typical of the highest class, yet they will not have the status or respect that traditionally attends old money.) Further, a predominantly economic analysis of social stratification can fail to recognise the significance of other hierarchical social groupings, such as **gender** and **ethnicity**.

Further reading: Scott 1996.

AE

SOCIAL STRUCTURE

While social structure is one of the most widely used of concepts in sociology and social theory, and indicates some regular and stable patterning of social action and social **institutions**, its precise meaning is not easily determined. While 'structure' itself may be defined as the organising relationships between parts in a whole, and in social structure the whole is **society** (albeit that 'society' is by no means an unproblematic term), the parts or elements of the whole may be variously understood. In the organic analogy, whereby society is compared to an organism, the elements are institutions which perform functions necessary to the survival and stability of the whole. Thus, in **functionalism**, social structure may be understood as a set of relationships between institutions. Conversely, the elements may be understood as **roles** or as variously defined (or self-defining) groups within the society. The validity of the concept may however be challenged. While critical theorists, such as the first generation members of the **Frankfurt School**, tend to adopt the concept very much in the sense in which it is used in functionalism, they do not treat it as a value-neutral description of society. That society is structured, and that these structures can confront the individual as natural forces constraining and determining their action, is taken to be indicative of a **reified** and thus false society. Conversely, the existence of social structures is denied altogether by certain micro-social theories, such as **ethnomethodology**. This is to reject the idea of any social entity existing independently, or prior to, individuals' mundane competences to produce that entity (through common acknowledgement of each other's skills and practices) in social **interaction**. Thus, while particular interactions may be structured, in the sense of being ordered and meaningful events, this order is produced spontaneously and co-operatively by the agents involved, and is not determined by some independent mechanism.

Further reading: Crothers 1996; Merton 1968.

AE

SOCIETY

In its modern sense, an arrangement of **institutions**, modes of relationship, forms of organisation, **norms**, etc., constituting an interrelated whole within which a group of humans live. That said, there is no simple definition which will fit all theories with equal ease. How one understands the term usually depends upon how one conceives of the distinction between the **individual** and society. Traditional **liberalism** (e.g. Locke, Mill, Rawls) conceives of society as a collection of free agents whose properties and characteristics are constituted independently of the modes of relationship which operate within any particular context. Thus, society is not coterminous with the individual, and the institutions which go to ground social relations are independent of the individual's **identity**. **Communitarian** critics have argued against the liberal view, asserting that there is a necessary link between being a social entity and any conception of the **self** we might have. Marxists traditionally view society in terms of the **history** of economic and institutional relationships (the economic base-structure and ideological superstructure) which have exerted a determinant effect on **class** interests and differences, and would likewise oppose the liberal conception.

Writers associated with **fascism** also attacked the view that individuals could be contrasted with society. On the fascist model, the assertion of a fundamental division between individual and society embodies a 'mechanistic' attitude, which is opposed to the unity of collectivity and tradition that underlies the organic whole that makes up human relationships. Equally, **conservatives** (e.g. Edmund Burke) have often discussed society in terms of the organic unity of its traditions and, in contrast to the liberal conception of it as an aggregate of individuals, have used this to argue that the life of society must be preserved by way of safeguarding these traditions.

Within **sociology** (the science which studies society) a similar contrast is detectable. Thus, functionalism shares in common with the conservative viewpoint an adherence to the organic model, while the Weberian and **interactionist** approaches tend to view society in terms of the abilities of individuals to make sense of their social environment and react to it in an independent way.

Further reading: Frisby and Sayer 1985; Welford *et al.* 1967.

PS

SOCIOBIOLOGY

While the term sociobiology was in use in the 1940s, it came to popular attention as the title of Edward O. Wilson's synthesis of current work in population biology, ecology and the study of invertebrate and vertebrate animal behaviour, *Sociobiology: The New Synthesis* (1975). The book (and its proposed discipline) caused a public sensation because Wilson extended methods for studying animal behaviour that had been developed in the biological sciences to the study of human beings. Sociobiology is controversial, precisely because it offers an approach to the study of **culture** that is radically at odds with a number of basic assumptions made in such social sciences as **sociology** and **cultural anthropology**.

Sociobiology had its real origins in a paper by W.D. Hamilton (1964) that offered an evolutionary explanation of self-sacrificial behaviour in animals. The problem for evolutionary biology was this. An individual member of a species should be striving to pass its particular genes on to the next generation. To do this, it must reproduce. Yet there are plentiful cases of individual animals sacrificing themselves, prior to reproduction, in order to allow other members of the species to survive and reproduce. This self-sacrifice, if a genetically determined trait, should die out (precisely because it is not being passed on). Hamilton accounted for the survival and spread of genes that determine such altruistic behaviour by recognising the importance of kinship. The animal that sacrifices itself will be close kin with the animal it saves. If they are close kin, they will share many genes, including the genes for altruism. The altruistic animal is then, after all, protecting its own genes, or at least the sorts of gene that have made it the animal it is. (This insight has led most famously to Richard Dawkins's (1976) account of the 'selfish gene', and thus the proposal that individual animals are merely the bearers and instruments of their genes. As an aside, this is an interesting bit of anti-**humanism**—or is if applied to human beings—and as such is not so different, at least in form, to the anti-humanism of Lacan's **structuralist psychoanalysis**—where human subjects are determined by the structures of language—or Althusser's structuralist **Marxism**—where subjects are bearers of ideological and economic structures.)

This new approach to evolutionary explanation was widely applied in biology, for example to problems of how animals choose mates, optimise their chances of reproductive success, or develop successful strategies in foraging for food. The problem as far as human beings go is that it appears to reduce some of the most noble and valued characteristics of human life, morality and altruism to a matter of genetics and evolutionary survival at the expense of free human choice. Nature appears to be completely dominant over nurture (or **socialisation**). The possibility that human nature could be transformed, over **history**, through the development and change of culture is seemingly denied or sidelined. In practice, few if any sociobiologists would actually deny the influence of **culture** over human life (even if particular analyses frequently seem to be insensitive to the cultural and historical construction of **gender** and **sexuality**, for example). What sociobiology does is to pose important, and at times uncomfortable, questions about the biological heritage of human beings, or the relationship between the biological (or genetic) and the cultural and artificial in human life.

What is perhaps most disturbing about sociobiology, or at least sociobiology at its least sensitive and most territorial, is its assumption that sociology (cultural anthropology and presumably cultural studies) can be reduced to (or replaced by) biology. Sociobiology appears to be informed by a crude philosophy of science that assumes that the only way to account for any phenomenon (be it natural or social) is through explanatory models that are associated with the natural sciences. The alternative methodologies of the social and cultural sciences, not least in so far as they focus on problems of **meaning**, interpretation and **ideology**, are ignored, misunderstood or ridiculed. If this crude understanding of the nature of science and scientific inquiry is dealt with, cultural studies might find that questions of importance for human society can be stimulated by the study of ants.

Further reading: Wilson 1994.

AE

SOCIOLOGY

Sociology is the study of **society**. (The word is derived from the Latin for companion (*socius*) and the Greek *logos,* for study or reason, and was coined by the French **positivist** philosopher Auguste Comte around 1830.) In practice, this simple definition is rather uninformative, first because there are clearly other disciplines that study part of the whole of society (for example, economics, **history**, geography, political science) so that the precise meaning of 'society' is left unclear, and second because it says nothing about the manner of this study. The history of sociology may, in consequence, be seen as an extended debate over precisely these issues: What is society? and, How is it to be studied?

It is usual to cite Karl Marx (1818–83), Emile Durkheim (1858–1917) and Max Weber (1864–1920) as the three founders of sociology (with Georg Simmel (1858–1918) sometimes being included, depending upon current fashion). Indeed, it is fair to say that most of the approaches and problems in contemporary sociology can be traced back to some problem raised by these founders. From Durkheim, there arises a tradition of sociology that grounds itself as a science (closely modelled on the natural sciences of either physics or biology), and understands society as a form of objective reality. Society is seen as having a reality over and above that of the individuals from whom it is composed. A sociological explanation cannot then be broken down into an explanation grounded in the psychology of individual human beings. Rather, a genuinely sociological explanation will appeal to regularities and laws that exist uniquely at the level of society, and of which ordinary members of society need not even be aware. (Durkheim's own spectacular illustration of this phenomenon concerns suicide. While suicide is a uniquely personal and isolated act, the annual number of suicides occurring within a given society are more or less constant. This suggests that the individual decision is actually influenced by overarching social forces.) Durkheim's approach to sociology led to **functionalism**, the approach that was dominant in America until the 1960s. Functionalism drew on the analogy of society to an organism, to argue that the key feature of any society was its ability to maintain its stability and form over many generations (akin to the homeostasis of organisms). The various parts or **institutions** within a society were therefore explained in terms of the contribution that they made to that continued stability. All social institutions therefore have specific functions.

In contrast to Durkheim, who very much saw himself as a sociologist, Weber's intellectual affiliations are broader (encompassing law, history and economics). His approach to sociology can, however, be characterised by a central concern with the development (and technical superiority) of western European civilisation particularly in terms of its rationality. He is less concerned with universal laws of social organisation than with the specific conditions that led to the rise of **capitalism** in western Europe, and not elsewhere. His work is thus a good deal more historically sensitive than Durkheim's. Further, Weber's approach to sociology as a discipline owes less to the natural sciences, and more to the methods of historical interpretation (or **hermeneutics**). Weber is concerned to empathise with social actors, and grounds explanations in the motivations and meanings that they ascribe to particular situations, and the way in which they then respond. In effect, while functionalist approaches to sociology tend to reduce the individual actor to a mere tool of the **social structure**, and thus a creature that needs little skill or awareness, for it meekly acts as society tells it to, Weber presents individuals as having social competence. This approach is taken up in the work of **interactionists**, such as Alfred Schutz (who is also influenced by Husserl's **phenomenology**) and the **symbolic interactionists**. These schools of sociology placed great emphasis on the ability of individuals, acting with and in response to other individuals, to construct and make sense of the social world about them. Society is not then seen as some special form of objective reality that simply constrains individuals (as it is by Durkheim and the functionalists), but rather is presented as a product of **intersubjective** action. (This approach is pursued to its theoretical extreme in **ethnomethodology**.) While phenomenological and interactionist schools of sociology had flourished at least since the 1930s (for example, in the Chicago School), they came to the fore of sociological work only in the 1960s, displacing functionalism.

Marxism has, in certain respects, a marginal role in the history of sociology. It was initially influential as the form of sociological explanation to which Weber reacted. Thus, Weber's own approach to the explanation of the origin of capitalism (that placed a central emphasis on the role of cultural and especially religious factors as stimulants to social change) challenged Marx's materialist account. Similarly, Weber developed a many-layered account of **social stratification**, in contrast to Marx's exclusive emphasis on **class**. Despite, or perhaps because of, this tension, the core developments of Marxism in western Europe in the first half of this century came about through a fusion of Marx and Weber, for example in the work of Georg Lukács and in the **Frankfurt School**. A Marxist sociology entered the mainstream of sociological debate, at least in the English-speaking world, in the 1960s and 1970s, not least through the assimilation of the French structuralist Althusser and the recovery of the work of the Italian Marxist Gramsci.

Sociology in the 1970s, and at least in the British case, sociology as the intellectual context from which a significant part of cultural studies developed, was a rich source of conceptual and theoretical tools for the analysis of social and also cultural life. The rise of forms of interactionism and phenomenology had shifted sociology away from large-scale social structures, to allow an emphasis on the competence of ordinary human beings, and thus the importance of everyday life. The re-emergence of Marxism (along with the rise of **feminism**) complemented this focus, by providing new tools to analyse power relations (the lack of which had always been a weakness of interactionism) and **culture**. The theorisation of **ideology** and **hegemony** by Althusser and Gramsci opened up a new awareness of the way in which culture is the outcome and site of negotiation between conflicting social groupings.

The difficulty of generating a single, coherent approach to sociology that can encompass the insights of macro-sociologists (such as the functionalists and Marxists) along with those of the micro-sociologists (the phenomenologists and interactionists) continues to be a central concern of sociological theory. The work of Jürgen Habermas on the relationship of society as an objectified system to the everyday experience of the **life-world** and the work Anthony Giddens developed on **structuration** represent important attempts to respond to this problem.

See also: **agency and structure**.

Further reading: Bilton *et al.* 1996; Bocock *et al.* 1980; Elias 1970; Giddens 1997.

AE

SOCIOLOGY OF KNOWLEDGE AND CULTURE

Sociological approaches to knowledge, science and art have posed fundamental challenges to orthodox understandings of the nature and **value** of these activities and their products. Scientific knowledge, for example, would aspire to be valid independently of the particular society or culture in which it was produced. While such knowledge may be refutable (which is to say that it may well be revised or improved upon in the future), the assumption would be that such improvement would come about through better observation or accumulation of information from the external world. The value of scientific knowledge would therefore depend upon the degree to which it corresponds to how an external and independent world really is. Similarly, orthodox **aesthetics**, at least since Kant's *Critique of Judgement* was published at the end of the eighteenth century, tends to presuppose that the value of a work of art lies in the degree to which it expresses or possesses some ahistorical aesthetic value. Equally, the artwork is understood as the product of genius, and genius transcends the restrictions of its age. The value, and indeed **production**, of works of art is therefore indifferent to the social conditions of the audience or artist. **Sociology** challenges these assumptions by suggesting that knowledge and cultural artefacts are fundamentally conditioned by the societies within which they are produced.

While the concept of the 'sociology of knowledge' was coined by the German philosopher Max Scheler in the 1920s (1980), elements of a sociology of knowledge were already present in the work of Karl Marx and Emile Durkheim. Marx's analysis of society according to the **metaphor** of the **base and superstructure** (where the base is the economic activity in society and the superstructure is composed of legal and cultural forms) suggested that different economic formations could lead to different cultures, not least in so far as these cultures were involved in the **class** struggle as forms of **ideology**. Durkheim (1976) (along with the **cultural anthropologist** Marcel Mauss (1966)), through the study of the social organisation and classificatory systems of small-scale pre-industrial societies, argued, perhaps even more radically, that the very way in which we perceive reality (down to our experience of time and space) was conditioned by our social experience. Thus, where Kant, in his theory of knowledge, had argued that our experience of time and space depend on the way in which the universal human mind structures experience, Durkheim argues that the human mind is itself socially structured, and thus people from different cultures will experience the world differently (or more radically, that they will live in different worlds). For the Marxist Lukács, the experience of time and space that Kant takes to be fundamental and universal is in fact a product of life in **capitalism**, with its **division of labour** and the spatial and temporal disciplines of the factory.

Karl Mannheim (1960) developed Marx's account of ideology into a sociology of knowledge. He extended Marx's concern with a purely economic base, in order to suggest that different groups in society will experience the world differently, and will therefore accept different claims as knowledge. Mannheim's approach appears to open the way to a cultural **relativism**, such that there is no knowledge that can be deemed true, independently of the social standpoint in which it is produced and used. The relativistic implications of the sociology of knowledge were boosted by the influence of Thomas Kuhn's philosophy of science on sociology (1970). Kuhn argued that scientific inquiry depended not simply, or even primarily, on independent observation of an external world, but rather upon a **paradigm** or set of assumptions (about the nature of that world, and about the nature of science and scientific knowledge) that would structure any experience of the world. It is a small step from the theory of paradigms, to the argument that paradigms themselves depend upon wider social and cultural conditions. Thus, it may be observed that Newton's conception of absolute time and space depended, not upon observation, but upon prior theological and cosmological beliefs. (More concretely, Newton apparently observed only five colours in the spectrum. Being influenced by alchemy and the magical significance of numbers, he added two extra colours to get to the magical seven.) At its extreme, the sociology of science may therefore advocate that science constructs the physical world, rather than responds to an independent world.

If science falls to the sociological assault with such apparent ease, art is an even softer target. The production and consumption of art can readily be placed within a political and economic context. Thus, prior to the rise of a market for the arts, most noticeably in seventeenth- and eighteenth-century Europe, much that is now regarded as art had a clear and unproblematic social function. (Music, for example, could serve to structure the ritual movements of a religious service, or maintain co-ordination within a group of workers. The visual arts, more indirectly, might serve as ostentatious displays of the wealth and power of their patrons.) With the rise of a middle-class market in art, art comes to appear as something that is useless. It does not have the instrumental utility of other **commodities**. The contemporary development of **aesthetics** has therefore been interpreted as a response to this problem. The attribution of aesthetic value serves, on the one hand, to justify the consumption of something that is otherwise useless, and on the other hand, promotes the economic value of the artwork (see Bourdieu 1984). More subtly, and in line with the sociology of knowledge, the work of art may be seen to articulate the values and worldview of particular social groups. (Thus, the **Frankfurt School** theorist Lowenthal approaches literature as an expression of class ideologies and strives to account for 'the extent to which particular social structures find expression in individual literary works and what function these works perform in society' (1989:44). His analysis of Knut Hamsun's novels, for example, places them in relation to an authoritarian cult of nature (1978).)

While the extreme positions in the sociology of knowledge and culture may reduce the value of both knowledge and art to mere functions or effects of some social or political base, the more complex approaches attempt to incorporate sociological insight into the more traditional concerns of interpretation and criticism. Thus, art historians such as Tim Clark (1973) and Baxandall (1980) (following on a tradition of interpretation that runs back, at least, to the work of the Warburg Institute in the 1930s) or musicologists such as Treitler (1989) and Tomlinson (1984) have drawn significantly on sociological approaches to enrich the reading of art. Perhaps pre-eminently, within the Frankfurt School, T.W. Adorno's aesthetic theory (1984) and theory of knowledge (1967) revolve about the recognition of the **dialectical** tension between the autonomy of art and science on one hand, and their status as '**social facts**' (and thus the legitimate subject matter of sociological analysis) on the other.

Further reading: Meja and Stehr 1990; Wolff 1981.

AE

SPEECH ACT

A speech act is an action which is performed *when* a word is uttered. Speech act theory is derived from the work of British philosopher J.L. Austin (1911–60), and has been taken up subsequently by philosophers, linguists, literary theorists and even psychologists. Austin distinguishes between different classes of word which perform different functions. Thus, he holds that the activity of uttering words is a complex matter which can in turn be analysed in terms of the individual functions of various types of word. Austin's analysis concentrates on everyday language, which is used in as direct and literal a manner as possible.

In outlining his theory, Austin was resisting the view of **language** (put forward by, for example, exponents of **positivism**) which held that all meaningful sentences or propositions which declare something are descriptions of states of affairs ('constatives') and hence either true or false. Austin's point is that some parts of language express meanings which may be neither true nor false. These Austin terms 'performative utterances'. Performatives are those utterances with which people do things like make promises, warn others, make declarations, etc. (e.g. 'I promise I will give you the money', 'Look out!', 'I name this ship ...'). Performatives do not pertain to truth conditions, but are conventional (i.e. they are either appropriate or inappropriate). However, Austin does not rest content with the constative/performative distinction. Instead he complicates the distinction by attempting to show that there is a sense in which constatives can pertain to a performative status, and vice versa. On this model, *all* utterances are susceptible to being described as speech acts in so far as any fact-stating utterance can be rephrased in the form 'I hereby assert that ... ' (i.e. all language use can be viewed as speech acts).

John Searle has developed Austin's theories by attempting to stipulate the particular rules specific to different forms of speech act. On this view, a promise can be characterised as necessarily involving some form or other of future action; additionally, it must be about something that the person promising would not do in any case, and must involve consideration of the intentions of the promiser, who is undertaking to be bound by that promise. Prominent amongst those who have been influenced by speech act theory is German philosopher and critical theorist Jürgen Habermas, who has turned to the notion of performativity as a means of elucidating his theory of 'communicative action'. The notion of speech acts is significant not least because it offers an approach to issues concerning **meaning** which can be contrasted with those theories that draw upon the heritage of **structuralism** (i.e. **post–structuralism**). This may explain its appeal to Habermas who, against thinkers such as Lyotard, has used the notion of perfomativity to argue that a normative model of communal consensus is fundamental to both the functioning, and the reproduction, of the conditions necessary for human existence.

Further reading: Austin 1975; Searle 1969.

PS

SPORT

Rule-governed physical activities that serve to test the athletic pro-wess of competitors, either against each other (in the case of com-petitive sports) or against natural and other challenges (in the case of non-competitive sports such as mountaineering). The precise defini-tion of sport is highly contested, being both a topic for dispute within the philosophy of sport (see Suits 1978; Morgan and Meier 1995), and a matter of political and economic concern for organisa-tions such as the International Olympic Committee and national sporting federations (precisely because the classification of an activity as a sport can entitle it to new sources of funding, as well as to new competitive opportunities).

The history of sports within the Western tradition may be traced back at least as far as the ancient Olympics (first held in 776 BCE), and broadly sport may be seen to be grounded in the training of essen-tially military skills. Modern sport begins to take shape from the seventeenth century onwards, notably with an attempt to revive the Olympics in 1612 in the English Cotswolds. For much of the early modern period 'sport' may be taken to refer most readily to field sports, including hunting and fishing. It is indeed from these activities that modern notions of a sporting ethics emerge. The moral con-notations of being 'sporting' or giving a 'sporting chance' relate to giving some fair chance to the hunter's quarry (for example, not shooting a bird while it is on the ground). The nineteenth century saw the development of sport within the English public-school system, and thus something like the competitive sports that dominate contemporary sporting activity (as well as patterns of supporting teams, in part modelled on a pupil's loyalty to their house and thus to the house's sports teams). The link between sport and **education** thereby becomes significant and lasting. Sport, particularly in the ethos of Thomas Arnold of Rugby School, was seen to inculcate in boys a sense of team spirit and loyalty, as well as expending excess energy. Sport is also linked in this period to **religion**. The notion of 'muscular Christianity' for example is celebrated in the novel centring on Rugby School, *Tom Brown's School Days*.

The end of the nineteenth century also saw Pierre de Coubertin's successful revival of the Olympic movement. Again, Coubertin was motivated by a complex moral agenda, expressed not least in his commitment to amateurism. The history of sport in the twentieth century is in large part the history of the erosion of that amateur spirit in the face of the possibilities offered by **mass media** coverage of sport, and its development into a key form of mass entertainment (Whannel 1992). The twentieth century also saw the increased politicisation of sport, not least in terms of its importance to national identity (see, for example, Jarvie and Burnett 2000).

Sport has a longstanding, but perhaps rather marginal place in **sociology**, and issues typical to sociological inquiry have been explored, such as sport's relationship to **class** (Gruneau 1983), to **race** (Jarvie 1991), and to **gender** and sexuality (Cahn 1994; Messner 1992), as well as the question of sport as a profession and its relationship to the economy (Cooke 1994). Earlier studies were dominated by **functionalist** theory, although already in the 1930s **social interactionists** were introducing more interpretative approaches to sport (for example, in the work of G. H. Mead). During this early period Marxists also showed some interest in sport, not least in terms of its relationship to **ideology**. Hints of a sophisticated if highly critical theory of sport can, for example, be found in the work of the **Frankfurt School** theorist T.W. Adorno (Morgan 1988). Dunning's adoption of Norbert Elias's notion of the 'civilising process' for the sociology of sport marks a further key stage in the development of a social theory of sport, and one that further breaks from the early functionalist perspectives (Elias and Dunning 1986; Dunning and Rojek 1992). Elias's 'figurational' sociology explores the processes through which social relations emerge. The problems of the functionalist neglect of the agent (see **agency and structure**) are corrected, without overemphasising the autonomy of individual. The human being is not seen as an autonomous individual, but rather as a being who is dependent upon others. Individuals act together, mutually oriented to each other and dependent upon each other, in dynamic constellations that they create and sustain, but that also constrain them. This approach has been used to explore the early development of sport and the control of violence, the development of professionalism, football hooliganism and sport's relationship to **globalisation** (see, for example, Dunning 1999; Dunning and Sheard 1979).

A **cultural studies** of sport begins to emerge in the 1980s, led by feminists who sought to explore the male domination of sport and the role of sport in the construction of gender and sexuality (see Hargreaves 1994, 2000, 2006). Hargreaves and MacDonald argue that the cultural studies approach is theoretically inspired by Gramsci's theory of **hegemony**, and thus the recognition of sport as a site of cultural and political struggle, at once intrinsically worthwhile and a source of political oppression (2002). Grant Jarvie's work on the Highland games and shinty, and thus upon the relationship of sport to local communities and local identities, may be placed within this tradition (Jarvie 2000).

Perhaps the most remarkable and thought-provoking book written on sport remains C.L.R. James's *Beyond a Boundary* (1987). The importance of cricket to James's upbringing and adult life provides the backbone to a series of reflections on personal and national identity (as James negotiates the tensions between his Caribbean origins and love of English literature and culture), politics and even **aesthetics** (with an extraordinary chapter on cricket as an art form).

Further reading: Coakley and Dunning 2002; Giulianotti 2005; Morgan 1994.

AE

STATE OF NATURE

A conception deployed by a number of political philosophers of different persuasions (e.g. Thomas Hobbes, John Locke, Jean-Jacques Rousseau). In brief, a state of nature theory envisages the human individual in a state of existence outside the constraints of civil society or civilisation. In Hobbes's *Leviathan* (1651) the state of nature is famously described in violent terms, a form of life devoid of the rule of law and entailing the 'war of all against all'. In this state, individuals have absolute freedom to pursue their own ends, but unfortunately so do others. Without the rule of law, it follows, the individual has no rights of protection beyond their own physical capabilities to defend themselves. Hobbes uses this view as a means of arguing that it is reasonable to trade-off individual freedom in return for the protection afforded by an absolute monarch (the leviathan of the book's title) through the establishment of a **social contract**. Equally, for Locke and Rousseau the state of nature is one which prefigures the bonds of civil society. On the Lockean view, individuals in the state of nature possess rights which are God-given (namely, the right to self-protection, the possession of their own bodies and the right to own the products of their labour). With the growth of **property** ownership, Locke argues, individuals seek to protect their interests through the formulation of a social contract which grants legal protection to these rights—although, contrary to Hobbes, he is clear about the fact that, on his view, individuals do not as a consequence divest themselves of all their rights. Interestingly, Locke claims that a state of nature still exists in the relationships which exist between absolute monarchs or nation states. Rousseau in constructing a state of nature narrative in his *Discourse on Inequality* (1754) was more interested in deploying an heuristic device (he writes at the beginning of the work of his interest being in humans as they are now) with the aim of laying bare the social injustices of contemporary civilisation. His account envisages the emergence of humans from the state of nature into a state of tribal social organisation (that of the 'noble savage'), and the subsequent development of an unjust and corrupt **civil society** which ensues from the institution of property. A more recent exponent of the state of nature theory is Robert Nozick (see **libertarianism**); whilst a variant of it is offered by John Rawls's use of the notion of the 'original position' to ground his conception of justice (see **liberalism**).

Further reading: Hobbes 1994; Locke 1988; Rousseau 1984.

PS

STATISTICS

The branch of mathematics that is concerned with the collection, classification, and quantitative interpretation of numerical data. The purpose of statistical analysis is to demonstrate relationships between two or more variables, which is to say, to demonstrate that when one property or characteristic changes, so to does another. Hence, for example, a statistical analysis might demonstrate that people in lower-income groups have worse **health**. Perhaps the most famous use of statistical analysis in social science is that made by the French sociologist Emile Durkheim of suicide statistics. By examining the statistics that had been collected by different European governments on suicide, Durkheim was able to argue that suicide rates (which is to say the number of suicides per head of the population) varied, quite predictably, in response to changes in other social factors (and not least, to the degree of solidarity felt within the society) (Durkheim 1952). Durkheim thus used statistics to demonstrate the influence that society has over the individual. The seemingly most personal of action, the individual's decision to commit suicide, appears none-theless to obey statistical laws and to be a response to social forces.

The two branches of statistics are descriptive statistics and infer-ential statistics. The former is concerned to describe the properties of the whole of a population, or subgroups within the population. Social statistics take this form, and will consist of the compilation of the age structure of the population, occupational structures and other forms of **social stratification**, mortality rates (or life expectancy), birth rates, **health**, marriage patterns, religious belief, patterns of **consumption**, **social mobility**, and geographical mobility and migra-tion, and so on. Such statistics play an important part in the under-standing and administration of complex contemporary societies, although the government collection of statistics is as characteristic of pre-industrial civilisations as it is of modern capitalist societies. If descriptive statistics uses given data, then inferential statistics extrapolates from data about a small (but representative) sample of that population, to the characteristics of the population as a whole. Inferential statistical analyses are a core part of the methodology of the social sciences. Opinion polls are one of the most familiar forms of inferential statistics, as the responses of a small, but carefully chosen, sample of the population, for example about voting intentions or consumer preferences, are taken to be representative of the responses that would be given by the population as a whole.

The importance of statistical analysis rests upon the recognition that knowledge of social processes (and indeed of many nature pro-cesses) can be established as only being *probably* true (and so not established with certainty). Thus, for example, statistics that link smoking to lung cancer cannot demonstrate that a given person will certainly suffer from lung cancer if they smoke. Rather, they demonstrate that their likelihood of suffering from lung cancer increases (and increases to a precisely quantifiable degree) if they smoke. Perhaps because of ineffective mathematical **education** in schools, lay under-standing of the significance of statistical arguments is often poor. Thus, for example, statistical links between smoking and lung cancer are popularly refuted by appealing to one's grandfather who smoked twenty a day and never had a day sick in his life. The point is that if 80 percent of smokers suffer lung cancer, then 20 percent will not, and your grandfather was fortunate enough to be in the 20 percent. Sta-tistics, properly understood, allow more effective decisions to be made under conditions of uncertainty, and in particular for **risk** to be accurately assessed.

While statistical analysis may not be an important methodological tool of the cultural theorist, precisely because theorists are typically more concerned with qualitative analyses of data and social phenomena (and thus of questions of **meaning**), as noted above, statistics are important in other social sciences (**sociology**, economics, and psychology, for example). They are also an important social phenomenon, and thus a crucial part of the culture of all complex societies. They are thus potentially part of the subject matter that cultural theory studies (see, for example, Foucault on the **history** and significance of medical statistics (Foucault 1980:166–82)).

As a final thought, an aphorism attributed to Stalin is worth bearing in mind: One death is a tragedy; a million deaths are a statistic.

AE

STATUS

Social status refers to the prestige and honour publicly ascribed to particular positions and occupations within society. The possibility of identifying a hierarchy of status groups within society that would strictly be independent of **class** hierarchies was recognised by Max Weber (1946c, 1946d). The classic example is that of priests and other religious professionals in contemporary society, whose status is disproportionate to their income or political power (although it may be indicative of their influence on the formation of public opinion). Status groups may be expected to have distinctive lifestyles, including patterns of behaviour, belief systems, and patterns of preference and **consumption**. For Weber a caste system was representative of a hierarchy of status groups, not of classes. Crucially, social status is to be understood as the prestige that is ascribed to the social position, which need not necessarily correspond to an individual member's self-perception.

Further reading: Turner 1988; Weber 1978.

AE

STEREOTYPE

A stereotype is an oversimplified and usually value-laden view of the attitudes, behaviour and expectations of a group or individual. Such views, which may be deeply embedded in **sexist**, **racist** or otherwise **prejudiced cultures**, are typically highly resistant to change, and play a significant role in shaping the attitudes of members of the culture to others. Within cultural studies, the role of stereotypes is possibly most marked in the products of the **mass media** (including the portrayal of women and ethnic minorities in drama and **comedy**, and in the shaping and construction of news coverage), although they are also significant in **education**, work and sport (in channelling individuals into activities deemed appropriate to their stereotyped group).

Further reading: Macrae *et al.* 1996; Oakes *et al.* 1994.

AE

STIGMA

A stigma is a culturally recognised attribute that is used to differentiate and discredit a person. The stigma may be physical (a bodily deformity), behavioural (for example, a sexual preference) or social (in the sense of membership of a group). The identification of the stigma is used to reduce the person from a complex whole, to a single, tainted and discounted trait, upon which all social **interaction** with the person will be based.

See also: **stereotype**.

Further reading: Goffman 1963; Page 1984.

AE

STRUCTURALISM

A methodological approach which has been employed in a wide range of fields (e.g. the social sciences, anthropology, literary criticism). It is generally accepted that structuralism can be traced back to Ferdinand de Saussure's book *Course in General Linguistics* (1916), although the term itself was coined by Russian structuralist theorist Roman Jakobson. In his work Saussure attempted to construct a scientific account of the process of **signification** which he termed **semiotics**—the science of **signs**. On Saussure's view, all **language** (the definition of which includes forms of **communication** other than simply spoken language) can be analysed as a structural system of relations. Saussure held, that **meaning** is determined by this relation, rather than by the referential function of the signs in language. A sign is thus held to have meaning because of its relationship to the other words, not because it refers to a particular object. In turn, Saussure argued for the view that language could be described in terms of one fundamental distinction: that between *langue* and *parole*. *Langue* constitutes the fundamental structural element of language (the network of meanings which must be in place at any given time if a speaker is to be able to speak); *parole* is the actual use of these elements as they are actualised within any individual utterance.

An important notion within structuralism is that of **binary opposition**, which in effect contends that meaning is determined by the oppositional relationship which inheres between different signs (good–bad, light–dark, etc.) and exerts a fundamental determining force on the construction of meaning. This, on Jakobson's view, at least, has been taken to constitute the fundamental structure of any language. This notion has led to the development of a number of critical approaches—for instance, that of structuralist literary criticism, which has sought to use the notion of opposition as a means of scientifically decoding the organisation of meanings which are to be found in literary **texts**. Thus, there is an explicit commitment to the view that an objective, universal account of meaning can be used in order to uncover the particular meanings hidden within texts. Likewise, the structuralism of anthropologist Claude Lévi-Strauss concentrates on seeking to elucidate the universal structures which operate in human **society** and **culture**, while Louis Althusser's structural **Marxism** sought to rearticulate the ideas of Marx within a structuralist framework (most notably in his account of the nature of **ideology**).

Structuralism can therefore be described as an attempt to elucidate the objective conditions which constitute all linguistic and social relations. As such, it put forward a claim to be regarded as an objective science. The emphasis on structure has often led exponents of structuralism to take a critical stance towards **empiricism** and **humanism**. This is basically due to the structuralist presupposition that meaning is a matter of nothing more than the causal relationships which pertain within a given structure. Thus, such questions as those pertaining to matters of human agency, individual or shared interests, **community**, etc., have generally been either ignored by structuralists or explained within the confines of the structural–causal framework of analysis.

A number of criticisms of the structuralist approach are possible. Thus, in the wake of structuralism itself, an attack on the purported **objectivity** of its methods of analysis was made by such writers as philosopher Jacques Derrida (see, for example, his essay 'Force and Signification' in *Writing and Difference* (1967)) or literary theorist Roland Barthes (both of whom came to be associated with **post-structuralism**). Such criticisms began by casting doubt on the notion that there is a fixed and universal structure of linguistic or social relations. Other criticisms, however, can be made. For instance, the relationship between structure and **agency** as it is articulated within the confines of structuralist analysis could be accused of embodying a reductive approach to questions concerning how subjectivity is constituted. Likewise, structuralism has difficulty accommodating the fact of change: if meaning is determined by rigid structures, then how **history** is possible is a question which falls outside the domain of a structuralist mode of analysis. For if these structures themselves are subject to change then either (i) the process of change must be an immanent feature of any such structure— which implies that the very notion of 'structure' is itself a problematic one, or (ii) change itself is external to structure, and hence structure is not decisive with regard to the constitution of social relations or meanings but is itself subject to some other causal factors that are different in kind. Also, the 'meaning is use' thesis advocated by the later Wittgenstein (admittedly a thesis which has its own problems) might be opposed to the view that meaning is a structural matter, for what constitutes 'use' need not necessarily be defined in terms of the structural metaphor.

Further reading: Clarke 1981; Culler 1975; Derrida 1978; Harland 1987; Jameson 1972; Kurzweil 1980; Lévi-Strauss 1968a, 1977; Pettit 1975; Saussure 1983; Sturrock 1979.

PS

STRUCTURATION

Structuration is a concept and theory, developed by the British social theorist Anthony Giddens, that is offered as an explanation of the relationship between individual human agency and the stable and patterned properties of society as a whole. On the one hand, ortho-dox social theories such as **functionalism** or **structuralism** tended exclusively to emphasise the organised nature of society, so that society was presented as existing independently of the agents who composed it (and indeed, as a force that constrained and determined their actions, much as natural forces do). On the other hand, another strand of social theory (including **symbolic interactionism** and **hermeneutics**) emphasised the skills of social agents in creating and managing the social world in which they lived. Giddens recognises a partial truth in both extremes, for society is patterned so that the isolated and self-interested actions of its individual members take on the appearance of having been planned or co-ordinated. Annual social statistics, for example, show remarkable stability for the occurrence of many everyday events and activities. Furthermore, precisely because this stability and order is outside the control of individual agents, society does appear to constrain and control them. However, agents are highly competent, with a vast stock of knowledge and range of skills that allow them to make sense of complex and often unique situations, and to manage their relationships with others.

Giddens therefore talks of the 'duality of structure'. **Social structure**, which is to say the organised and enduring character of social life, is dual in that it is at once external to the society's members and internal (constituting the agent as a competent member of society). As Giddens rather cryptically puts it, 'the structural properties of social systems are both medium and outcome of the practices they recursively organise' (1984:25). The social structure exists primarily as the competence that the society's members have to organise their own social life. Social structure is thus a set of rules and resources available to the competent agent. It exists in agents' memories. The crucial point that Giddens makes, though, is that agents do not have to be consciously aware of this. A great deal of their competence is non-discursive, which is to say that agents would not be able to give a verbal account of what they know. They do, however, know how to 'go on' in a given situation. They have 'practical consciousness'. In practice, the social structure is then realised as something external to the agents. The consequences of the agents' actions in a particular situation are likely to go beyond anything that is simply intended by them. Giddens draws on geography as well as sociology to analyse the external stability of social structures as **institutional** relations that are articulated across time and space. It is important to the agent that social structure does confront him or her as something external. Giddens's concept of 'ontological security' captures this. Competent social agents are confident that the social and natural worlds (and indeed their own **self**-identity in relation to those worlds) is stable and secure. The world is made a matter of routine. Anything that disrupts this expectation of the routine is highly disturbing (a feature exploited in Goffman's analysis of embarrassment and in the 'breaching experiments' carried out by **ethnomethodologists**).

In summary, Giddens presents social life (and centrally the **repro-duction** of society) as a circle. Agents interact with others. Their taken-for-granted social competence allows them to make sense of the situation, and to carry on within it, according to routine prac-tices. Agents thereby create (and sustain) the very conditions that make their social action possible. Their knowledge of society and social competence is thereby regenerated (along with society) by the very success with which they conduct the interaction, or repair dif-ficulties encountered within it.

See also: **agency and structure**.

Further reading: Cohen 1989; Giddens 1984; Held and Thompson 1990.

AE

STYLE

'Style' has many meanings, or nuances of meaning. Consider the association of style with fashion, or with a style of dress (whether it is a stylish style or not); or style in the performance of music, so that one may perform with style or just in a style that is distinguishable from other styles. These examples suggest a value-laden use of 'style', in which it refers to some preferred **aesthetic value** and to a more neutral sense in which it suggests a meaningful combination of ele-ments (be these the components of dress, of musical performance, of literary writing, or whatever). In the neutral sense of style, the choice of elements and the rules by which they can be combined may be analysed as **semiotic codes**. As such, styles may be understood as expressive of the values and **identity** of social groups.

See also: **subculture**.

AE

SUBCULTURE

The concept of a 'subculture', at its simplest, refers to the **values**, beliefs, attitudes and lifestyle of a minority (or 'sub-') group within society. The **culture** of this group will diverge from, although be related to, that of the dominant group. Although now associated in large part with the cultures of young people (mods and rockers, skinheads, punks), it may also be applied to **ethnic**, **gender** and **sexual** groups. The concept was in fact developed largely through work in the **sociology** of **deviance** (referring, for example, to the culture of 'delinquents', criminals or drug users). An early explanation of the behaviour of working-class delinquents saw it as youths over-conforming to the working-class values of their parents (such as toughness and masculinity, cunning as against gullibility, risk taking), and that in over-conforming they come to violate the dominant norms of middle-class culture (Miller 1958).

The concept of 'subculture' is important, precisely because it allows recognition of the diversity of cultures within a society. While the older concept of **youth culture** tended to assume a single, homogeneous, culture amongst young people, the subcultural approach stresses the fragmentation of that culture, especially along class lines. As with the concept of '**counterculture**', 'subculture' tends to presuppose some form of resistance to the dominant culture. However, 'counterculture' increasingly comes to refer to groups that are able to provide an intellectual justification and account of their position. Subcultures articulate their opposition principally through exploiting the **significance** of **styles** of dress and patterns of behaviour (or **rituals**). (**Semiotic** approaches, decoding the dress and behaviour of subcultures, have therefore been highly influential. The skinhead's dress of braces, cropped hair and Doc Martens makes sense as a comment upon an imagined industrial past and as an attempt to come to terms with powerlessness in the face of a predominantly middle-class culture in which the skinhead has neither the financial nor the cultural resources to participate.) The subculture may therefore be seen to negotiate a cultural space in which the contradictory demands of the dominant parent culture can be worked through, or resisted, and in which the group can express and develop its own **identity**. The subcultural approach can therefore be characterised by its sympathy with the position of the subculture, suggesting that subcultures are an important source of cultural variation and diversity—as opposed to the implicit or explicit condemnation of subcultural activity that accompanied earlier studies of deviance.

The 1960s mods offer a neat illustration of a subculture and its analysis. Mods may be characterised by their concern with fashion and **consumption**, and a hedonist lifestyle. Typically, the mod was employed in low-grade, non-manual (clerical) work. The mod is thus very much part of his or her time, responding to the increased consumerism of the 1960s, and the shift in economy from traditional manual and manufacturing work, to non-manual, service industry. Indeed, the mod takes consumerism to its limits. Unlike so many other sub-cultures, the mod is disturbing, not because he or she shuns the 'parent' culture's demands for smart dress, but because he or she is just too smart. The problem faced by the mod is that employment (which is traditionally associated with a work ethic of self-denial and self-discipline) is at once necessary, in order to pay for a hedonistic lifestyle, and yet at odds with the lifestyle (for self-discipline is the oppo-site of hedonism). The mod therefore conforms to the paradoxical demands of consumerism and work, through the use of amphetamines.

Certain criticisms have been made against the subcultural approach as it has developed within cultural studies. It has been seen to be overly selective in the subcultures it has studied. Crucially, much of its work has focused on masculine activities, at the exclusion of either female participation in the subculture, or more importantly, the recognition of distinctive female subcultures. Similarly it may be argued that it has been excessively concerned with working-class subcultures, leading to a romanticising of the subculture as a source of resistance (and politically progressive values). Further, an over-emphasis on sub-cultures may serve to distort the picture that cultural studies has of youth as a whole. The concept of youth culture remains important. An emphasis on subcultures may serve to highlight the spectacular at the cost of ignoring the more mundane forms that are of concern to the majority of young people. This majority may be more appro-priately seen as belonging to youth culture (or cultures), not to a resisting subculture. A crude opposition between conformist youth (or even 'pop') culture and a radical subculture is itself inappropriate, as it fails to recognise the degree to which the two merge.

Further reading: Clarke 1982; Hall and Jefferson 1976; Hebdige 1979; McRobbie 1991, 1994; Mungham and Pearson 1976; Willis 1990.

AE

SUBJECT/IVITY

A term whose contemporary significance can be traced as far back as the philosophy of seventeenth-century thinker Descartes. Descartes sought to refute the arguments of contemporary sceptics, who claimed that nothing could be known for certain. Against this view, he propounded the famous dictum 'I think, therefore I am' as an instance of the one certain piece of knowledge any thinking being must have even if it is engaged in doubting everything else. The subject, therefore, is that which thinks and, in thinking, possesses certain essential properties which serve to define it. Likewise, the term 'transcendental subject' is used by Kant in his philosophy to signify the structural precondition of all thinking (cf. *Critique of Pure Reason*, 'Transcendental Deduction' B). The transcendental subject is the 'I think' which, Kant argues, must accompany all my representations when I am in the process of thinking. It is this which makes all the thoughts I have mine. The transcendental subject is not an empirical (i.e. material) entity, but a necessary metaphysical precondition of my having any thoughts at all. In this sense, the subject is the source of self-consciousness. The word is also associated with Lacan's version of **psychoanalysis** (where the subject is contrasted with the 'ego'). Additionally, it has been discussed and criticised by advocates of **structuralism** (e.g. Althusser, who holds that the subject is a product of **ideology**) and **post-structuralism** (e.g. Foucault, who argues that the subject is an effect of relations of **power**—an argument derived from Nietzsche). Both approaches share in common the view that subjectivity (i.e. the property of being a subject) is constituted by social forces and relationships; in other words, that all conceptions of subjectivity are dependent upon political, social and cultural factors. Likewise, thinkers such as Lyotard have argued that subjectivity cannot be taken as something which is independent of forms of **language**; rather, subjectivity is constituted both within and by ways of speaking. Thus, from a Lyotardean standpoint, the notion of 'language games' propounded by the later Wittgenstein, wherein he draws an analogy between language games and the game of chess, contains within it the anthropocentric presupposition that human agents are the source of meaning (i.e. that something external to the language game 'moves' the pieces in the game). Such criticisms can be contrasted with the perspective propounded by advocates of classical **liberalism**, who have in general contrasted the notion of subjectivity to that of **society** or language. Equally important therefore is the notion of a 'political subject', i.e. of an entity which has a specified political status and a particular set of characteristics which exist either independently of or in virtue of (depending on your point of view) a given socio-political mode of organisation (cf. **citizenship**).

See also: **individual**, **self**.

Further reading: Block *et al.* 1997; Bowie 1990; Dallmayr 1981; Farrell 1994.

PS

SUBLIME

The meaning and significance of the sublime has been most famously considered by Kant in his *Critique of Judgement* (sections 18ff.). Put simply, the sublime moment of cognition is one in which an object is presented to the mind which, in turn, can comprehend it only in terms of an absolute magnitude which itself defies conceptualisation (e.g. the overwhelmingly large): 'That is sublime in comparison with which everything else is small' (ibid., section 25). As such, the sublime moment is one which involves the aesthetic rather than cognitive/empirical capacities of the human mind: it embodies a feeling. Within the Kantian model there are two modes of representing an object as sublime: the dynamical and the mathematical. The mathematical relates to the notion of largeness or magnitude, in that the mathematically sublime involves the presentation of something of such sheer magnitude (such as huge objects) that our understanding is unable to provide a concept capable of containing it. The dynamical sublime, on the other hand, involves the presentation of such magnitude in terms of force or might (exemplified by the fearful might of nature, e.g. volcanoes, storms, hurricanes), which again cannot be contained within a concept. The sublime is ultimately a consequence of the demands of our rationality, in so far as reason demands that any object presented to the mind through the imagination (which structures our empirical intuitions of the world around us) be presented as a totality. The imagination itself, however, is incapable of doing this since it is tied to the empirical world of nature, and no empirical presentation of the feeling of absolute magnitude involved in the sublime is possible within this domain, i.e. it is impossible on the empirical level to present an object of absolute largeness, since the empirical world itself can only be understood in terms of relationships of relative, not absolute, magnitude. For Kant, therefore, the sublime moment, and resultant feeling which arises from it, resides not in the actual object which inspires it, but in the human mind: 'It is a magnitude that is equal only to itself. It follows that the sublime must not be sought in things of nature, but must be sought solely in our ideas' (ibid.). The sublime, therefore, involves the presentation of an idea which can have no empirical referent. Rather, the sublime object is the object of an idea (the idea of absolute magnitude).

For Kant, this chain of reasoning leads to two conclusions. First, when we consider ourselves as 'natural beings', the sublime moment allows us to 'recognise our physical impotence' (ibid., section 28), i.e. it demonstrates finitude of human existence when understood in the context of the sheer and fearful might of nature. On the other hand, however, since the sublime feeling does not reside in nature, but only in the human mind, it allows us at the same time to consider ourselves as being to some extent independent of nature, and thereby demonstrates our superiority over it: 'This keeps the humanity of our person from being degraded, even though a human being would have to succumb to that dominance [of nature]' (ibid.). The sublime feeling thus functions as a means of elevating the human imagination in such a way that the displeasure which accompanies it (namely the feeling of impotence in the face of nature) is off-set by the fact that it also causes a feeling of pleasure, in that 'this very judgement ... is [itself] in harmony with rational ideas' (ibid., section 27). Reason is thus identified by Kant with the absolute measure of what is great— the sublime. Moreover, since the attainment of rationality is the pre-requisite of the attainment of freedom, and such freedom makes us cultured and moral beings, the Kantian account of the sublime is linked to his account of the nature and purpose of culture.

More recently, Kant's analysis of the sublime has been taken up, by thinkers such as Jean-François Lyotard, as a means of explicating **postmodernism**.

Further reading: Kant 1987; Lyotard 1994.

PS

SUPERSTRUCTURE

See **base and superstructure**.

SURPLUS VALUE

'Surplus value' is a key term in Marx's economics, and particularly in his explanation of exploitation. In any historical epoch (or **mode of production**) the dominant **class** will extract surplus value from the subordinate, labourer class. In pre-capitalist societies, this is done explicitly (thus, for example, the slave works directly for his or her master, with no reward other than his or her subsistence; in **feudalism**, a portion of the serf's product is directly appropriated by the lord). The position in **capitalism** is more subtle. According to the labour theory of **value**, the price of a commodity depends upon the amount of labour time that has gone into its production. Ideally, the money that the labourer receives for the expenditure of his or her labour time should be equivalent to the value of the product he or she has produced. So, if you have worked for 5 hours and have produced, say, 10 yards of linen, and if 10 yards of linen has the same **exchange-value** (which is to say, sells at the same price) as 5 loaves of bread, your wages should be enough to purchase 5 loaves of bread. Marx argues that the capitalist system is such that the labourer's wage will typically be less than the value of his or her product. The difference is the surplus value, which the capitalist appropriates for him or herself. Thus, the worker is working part of the day for him or herself, and part of the day for the capitalist. Crucially, workers will not typically recognise this exploitation, for, as far as they are concerned, the wages they receive will be the 'fair' wages, as determined by a free labour market.

A more precise analysis of surplus value recognises that the capitalist is required to buy certain resources before production can take place. On the one hand, machines, buildings and raw materials are required (which Marx terms constant capital). On the other hand, labour power and variable capital must be bought. Marx argues that the value of the constant capital is simply transmitted into the finished product. (Thus, if the capitalist buys linen for coat manufacture, the value of that linen must be included in the value of the finished coats.) As such, the surplus value cannot be extracted from constant capital. This nice technicality leads Marx to prophesy the eventual collapse of the capitalist system, because, as technology gets more powerful, the proportion of constant capital to variable capital will increase. If the capitalist can only extract surplus value from variable capital, and that is an ever-reducing proportion of his or her total capital expenditure, the capitalist can only continue to maintain the profitability (that is to say, maintain the level of surplus value) of the capitalist enterprise by reducing payments to labour (so impoverishing the **proletariat**). Much of the most interesting work in twentieth-century **Marxism** has focused on the problem of how late capitalism has avoided this fate.

Further reading: Mandel 1972; Marx 1976.

AE

SYMBOL

A word with a variety of meanings. Symbols pervade human life, and are used in a wide range of specialised **discourses**, as well as in everyday living. Usually, the word 'symbol' is taken as referring to a **sign** or action of some kind which is used to communicate a **meaning** to somebody in virtue of a shared set of **norms** or conventions. A symbol therefore communicates a meaning because it stands for something else, although there is no necessary connection between it and what it stands for (hence its use and meaning are both matters of convention; a conception which Peirce uses in his **semiotics**). In **analytic philosophy**, 'symbolic logic' involves the substitution of symbols for terms which occur in natural language ('~' means 'not'; 'þ' means 'or', etc.) as a means of analysing the structure of arguments. In Freudian **psychoanalysis**, symbols are taken to stand in place of some object which has been repressed (in this sense, symbols usually have some (often metaphorical) relation to their referents; although Freud—a smoker—stated that there are times when a cigar is simply a cigar, from the psychoanalytic point of view the latter could be taken as a metaphor for the phallus when it occurs in a patient's dreams). In Peirce's **semiotics**, a symbol is a kind of sign which bears no relation or resemblance to what it stands for. A symbol can also have historic significance and a multitude of resonances of meaning linked to this (e.g. in European **culture**, the sign of the cross can be a potent symbol not only for Christian faith, but also for the institutions, **identity**, traditions and **values** associated with that culture).

PS

SYMBOLIC INTERACTIONISM

Within **sociology**, symbolic **interactionism** is a theoretical framework that focuses upon the relationships between human **agents** (and as such, upon 'micro' social phenomena, rather than the large scale or 'macro' concern with social structure found in **Marxism** or **functionalism**). Crucially, it is concerned with the way in which competent social agents construct and make sense of the social world which they inhabit. Such explanations are typically grounded in the detailed recording of everyday life, through **participant observation** or non-participant observation. Symbolic interactionism was developed at the University of Chicago in the early part of this century, not least under the influence of the pragmatist philosopher G.H. Mead. The term itself was coined by Herbert Blumer in 1937, although symbolic interactionism became a widely accepted approach only in the late 1960s and 1970s.

Mead (1934) argued that the **self**, or our personal identity and self-consciousness, does not exist independently of our social relationships with others. It is produced and continually modified through our actions with respect to others, their responses and our anticipation of those responses (and hence, through our social interaction). Mead compares the **communication** between humans with that between non-human animals. In communication between non-human animals, one animal responds to the patterns of behaviour (or gestures) of another, by modifying its own gestures. What, for Mead, is distinctive about human communication is that the human does not simply respond to a gesture, but to the relationship between the gesture and the object or event that stimulated or motivated that gesture. Above all, the human does so from the standpoint of the original actor. In effect, the human attempts to understand why the other is acting so. The gesture becomes symbolic, and thus meaningful, precisely in so far as one person empathises with the position, **role** and attitudes of the other. Humans can therefore imagine the effect that a gesture will have upon others through an internal conversation between the 'I' (or spontaneous side of the self) and the 'me' (crudely, the self as seen by others). The human self is therefore constituted and continually reconstituted by internalising the 'generalised other', i.e. the typical attitudes and perspectives of the group.

Blumer, simplifying Mead's philosophy, presented symbolic interactionism as a programme for sociological research, by focusing on the manner in which social agents negotiate the meaning of the particular social situations in which they are involved. Functionalists, for example, tend to assume that social roles and norms exist prior to the individual (and have objectivity as **social facts** that constrain and determine social behaviour). A competent social agent simply has the ability to apply the appropriate rules (or to adopt the appropriate role) in a given situation. In contrast, the interactionist stresses the work that social agents must do—not in recognising the already existing meaning and significance of a situation—but in creating a shared understanding of a situation, and thus a common approval of the roles and norms that are adopted. Society is not therefore objective, existing independently of the social agents, but is constructed and maintained by agents through interaction.

In the 1960s, Erving Goffman's work developed a form of symbolic interactionism with particular reference to face-to-face interaction. He explored the fragility and fluidity of such interactions. Analysis of such phenomena as embarrassment pointed to moments when social interaction breaks down (with one or more of the participants being exposed as incompetent). A significant part of social life may then be seen to revolve about the avoidance, or fending off, of charges of being incompetent (so that, echoing Mead's interior conversation, it is important for the competent social actor to mark their isolation as atypical moments of incompetence, for example through swearing at oneself). Goffman further suggests (again echoing Mead, albeit in a more extreme form) that our 'selves' are constructed, uniquely, in each distinct social interaction. Our attitudes and patterns of behaviour are shaped according to the people around us (and thus in Goffman's (1959) now classic example, the waiter's attitudes before a customer are fundamentally different from those before colleagues in the kitchen).

Despite its important insights into **socialisation** and **deviance** (and especially **labelling theory**), symbolic interactionism has been criticised for its failure to take full account of power relations.

Further reading: Becker 1963; Berger and Luckmann 1961; Blumer 1969; Denzin 1992; Goffman 1959.

AE

SYNCHRONIC/DIACHRONIC

The distinction between the synchronic and diachronic was used by Saussure in developing his linguistics, and has become fundamental to much work in **structuralism**. To take a synchronic approach to a phenomenon is to approach it at a single moment in **history**, or as something existing outside history. The diachronic is therefore concerned with the historical or temporal aspects of a phenomenon. Saussure's structural linguistics examines language as an unchanging structure, in contrast to the approach of nineteenth-century linguistics, that was concerned with the historical origin and development of language.

AE

SYNTAGM

In **semiotics**, a combination of signs, from a **paradigm**, that constitutes a meaningful whole. A set of rules or **codes** will determine the correct and thus meaningful way in which potentially meaningful units can be combined, in order to form a syntagm. For example, considered as a syntagm, a European road sign is a combination of one of a small set of coloured, geometric shapes (such as a red triangle, a blue circle), with one of a set of silhouettes or more abstract shapes (an arrow, the silhouette of a motor car).

AE

SYNTAX

The rules which stipulate the ways of ordering words into sentences and propositions within a language. The syntax patterns of a language in effect state how individual words relate to one another. The observation of syntactical rules thereby allows for the construction of 'well-formed' sentences, although from the basic rules which determine the syntactical structure of any language an effectively infinite number of combinations of words is possible. The fact that children are able to construct new sentences on the basis of encountering different combinations of words led linguist Noam Chomsky to argue that all humans possess a common grammatical capacity which transcends social and cultural differences.

Further reading: Chomsky 1957.

PS

SYSTEMS THEORY

Various forms of systems theory have been used in analyses of **society** throughout the twentieth century, with **functionalism** being perhaps the longest-lasting and most influential variant. In general, a system may be understood as a collection of interrelated parts. The system is divided from an external environment by a boundary. The environment is more complex than the system. The system is thus characterised by the degree of order it manifests, not least in so far as it excludes certain relationships between its parts and enforces others. (For example, a meaningful sentence is a relatively simple affair, its meaning being determined by the rules of its language. The sounds of traffic, other people, bird song, rain, and so on around me, when I utter that sentence, are far more complex and indeed seemingly chaotic.) A system maintains this boundary between itself and its external environment, both maintaining an internal order and also drawing the resources necessary for its survival and reproduction from the external environment. (Thus, an animal organism can be understood as a system. Its skin is a boundary between it and the external world. It must be able to draw sustenance from that world, and maintain itself as a vital organism. At its death, the boundary collapses, and the organism decays into its environment.) It may be argued that any system must satisfy a set of abstract conditions in order to remain stable and vital. These include adaptation to the external environment, internal integration and the motivation to realise the goals of the system as a whole.

Society may be treated as a system at a number of different levels. For example, the **interaction** between two people can be understood as a system. That interaction will have a purpose. The system, strictly, co-ordinates not the people, but their actions. Other people and other irrelevant events and actions will be excluded from it. It will be conducted according to various rules that give it coherence and integrity. Thus, for example, a market is a system that co-ordinates together the actions, not merely of two, but potentially of many, people. In systems theory the market is not understood as a meaningful exchange between people (so the systems theorist is not interested in the social backgrounds or motivations of those involved in the market) but only in the co-ordination of the actions of buying and selling. Society as a higher level, for example that of a nation state, or country, may similarly be understood as a system. The systems theorist therefore responds to a particular aspect of contemporary societies: the way in which those societies confront their members as having a power to constrain and control them. (The point is, not simply that a market can be viewed as a system, theoretically blanking out our subjective experience of it, but that markets are increasingly becoming pure systems. The argument would be that markets, like **bureaucracies**, increasingly only recognise the ability of agents to buy or sell. Money alone matters in co-ordinating our actions together. The market thus takes on the force of an objective law, so that we are thus obliged to obey it, whether we like it or not, and in addition, despite the fact that we may realise that the market is really just one more set of cultural conventions.) It has then been argued that **modern** societies may be characterised by this high level of systematisation: social actions are increasingly co-ordinated by sets of rules and conventions that fall outside of the understanding (or even experience) of society's members. For some, such as Niklaus Luhmann (who has done much to revive systems theory in the social sciences), this is a good thing, for it removes a burden of responsibility from the individual. For others, such as Jürgen Habermas, it can pose a threat, in removing society from the control of the people who constitute it (1984 and 1987).

Further reading: Habermas 1984, 1987; Luhmann 1982; Parsons 1951.

AE

TECHNOLOGY

The word 'technology' is derived from the Ancient Greek word *'tekhne'*, meaning either 'art' or 'craft'. In modern parlance, however, the meaning of 'technology' has tended to take on the instrumental aspect implied by the word 'craft'. The use of the word 'technology' can in turn be divided into two separate but linked domains. First, 'technology' concerns that web of human practices within which the manipulation of (raw) materials is undertaken with a view to giving them a functional and useful form. In this sense, technology is primarily a matter of technique, and its employment presupposes some notion of purpose or design with regard to the manner in which materials are subsequently used. Second, the end product of such a process of manipulation is also called 'technology'. Thus, when we refer to a 'piece of technology', such as a computer or an aircraft, we are not referring to the manipulation of materials which gave rise to them, but in each case to something which, by its very nature, is deemed different in kind to other types of object that we might encounter in the world (e.g. rocks and stones, plants, animals, etc.). 'Technology', therefore, refers both to a web of human practices and to the products of those practices.

In the late modern era, it might, with some good cause, be argued that the burgeoning of particular forms of technology has been a significant element in the social and political transformations which mark out the **history** of the industrial and post-industrial periods. Thus, with the rise of industrial forms of production in Britain dating from the late eighteenth century there were accompanying changes in the distribution and concentration of population (an increased concentration in urban centres), and the concentration and distribution of wealth (a burgeoning capitalist **class**). Equally, there were accompanying developments in the political constitutions of representative bodies (e.g. by the end of the nineteenth century, there was an increasingly widening political franchise who elected members of parliament). Without attempting to fill in the historical picture, it is clear what the possible links between technological developments and such social and political developments might be. First, the development of industrial technology increases the viability of producing more goods at cheaper prices, since such technology brings with it the possibility of mass production. In economic terms, this implies an increased turnover both at the levels of production and consumption: speaking from the vantage point of the mercantile capitalist, the more items of a product you can make efficiently (i.e. cheaply) the cheaper you can sell it, and the cheaper you can sell it the more you can sell. In turn, the efficient mass production of goods requires the concentration of **labour** forces in restricted areas, and this is achieved through offering more financial enumeration for labour than can be obtained in what can subsequently be deemed 'rural' (i.e. nonindustrialised) areas. Such movement and concentration of population, it is clear, will have important social effects, in so far as some of the social relations which predominated in rural social forms will no longer apply. Hence, there may be increased fluidity of labour and job opportunity; likewise, there is the possibility that new social antagonisms will develop (e.g. between those who own systems of production and those who work for them) and, following the account offered by **Marxism**, individuals will develop self-consciousness through the development of class divisions resulting from the **division of labour** that mass production institutes. These social ramifications can have knock-on effects, in that the development of wealth among the mercantile class is probably going to be accompanied by an increased desire to see that wealth realised in terms of concrete political **power**. Likewise, one might expect those who work for the capitalists to want to see an expression of their interests in political terms.

Alongside the approach represented by, for instance, Marx's analysis of social relations, the kind of understanding of the significance of technology implicit in the above approach is also present in the work of thinkers associated with more recent intellectual developments that are often classified under the rubric of **postmodernism**. One such example is Jean-François Lyotard's *The Postmodern Condition* (1979). In this book, Lyotard puts forward the view that technology has a determining influence on forms of knowledge. In other words, Lyotard is claiming that the social and cultural effects of technology are not limited to such matters as the socio-historical development of classes with defined interests which spring from the predominance of the economic relation to industrial technological forms. Rather, according to Lyotard, the ways in which we think about, categorise and valorise experience are also subject to change at the hands of technological forces. In short, the question concerning what knowledge is (cf. **epistemology**), on Lyotard's account, an issue which must itself be transformed by the advent of modern technology. This is because technology comes to provide the primary criterion by which what counts as knowledge is evaluated within contemporary culture. Technology, in this sense, transforms knowledge to the extent 'that anything in the constituted body of knowledge that is not translatable in this way will be abandoned [...] [T]he direction of new research will be dictated by the possibility of its eventual results being translatable into computer language' (1979:4). Thus, on Lyotard's view the postmodern era is one which bears witness to the '**hegemony** of computers', for it is this hegemony which serves to dictate what counts as knowledge by imposing the criterion of 'translatability' upon those propositions which make claims about reality. One outcome of this is that the primacy of human subjectivity is displaced by the machinic tendencies of modern technology. This displacement, in turn, renders the thinking subject a secondary phenomenon with regard to knowledge, simply because subjectivity can no longer be taken as the foundational principle which underlies what counts as knowledge. Speaking from the point of view of an inwardly oriented conception of subjectivity (as exemplified by, for example, the Cartesian *cogito*—cf. **self**), knowledge, under the conditions dictated by technology, becomes externalised. Knowledge, transformed in this way, becomes linked to market **exchange-value** and the play of exterior forces. What is noteworthy in Lyotard's account is the claim that material forces (in the shape of technology) have the capability to transform not merely social **norms** and relations, but can alter radically the ways in which we think about ourselves and our abilities. How 'radical' an insight this is may well be a point of some debate. For example, if one understands 'knowledge' to be best defined in terms of justification (i.e. as justifiable belief), then what has been transformed through the technological process Lyotard alludes to is not necessarily something delineated by the proper name 'Knowledge', but rather the criteria and practices which serve to define what justification is. In other words, even if we might accept that what counts as knowledge must now be judged in terms of its suitability for translation into technological terms, this does not necessarily entitle us to the further claim that knowledge 'itself' has been thereby transformed, since the definition of knowledge as 'justifiable belief' has not changed, only the criteria which constitute justification.

As with Lyotard, aspects of Jean Baudrillard's conception of the postmodern are articulated in the wake of technological developments. Thus, on Baudrillard's argument, technology is again regarded as something capable of transforming our conceptions of experience and knowledge. On Baudrillard's view, the power of technology to influence our understanding of the significance of events through processes of **representation** is highlighted. Most famously (or notoriously, depending on where your sympathies lie in this context) Baudrillard claimed that the Gulf War was a staged spectacle enacted through the technology of the **mass media** which, in 'reality', never happened. In other words, the issue of what constitutes an 'event' is taken by Baudrillard to be a matter which is now determined by the representational function of technology. His views, understandably, have been met with a variety of responses.

Whatever their merits as forms of possible explanation of sociohistorical events, such accounts as those mentioned above do not, however, necessarily take us any further towards a clear understanding of what technology is. Equally, if we do not understand what technology is, then it might be somewhat problematic to claim that we can construct a persuasive account of its social or cultural significance. One possible approach to this problem has been offered by the German philosopher Martin Heidegger. In his 1953 essay 'The Question Concerning Technology' (Heidegger 1996), he attempts to show that a purely instrumental understanding of technology is a reductive one: it is reductive because if we discuss technology only in instrumental terms we miss out of our account what technology presupposes, and thereby something essential concerning what technology is. Thus, Heidegger claims, if we do not account for technology in terms of what is presupposed by it, then we ignore its 'essence'. Equally, Heidegger is careful to show that 'the essence of technology is by no means anything technological' (1996:311). In other words, what is presupposed by technology (namely what is essential to it in order for it to be what it is) cannot be accounted for in technological terms. The contemporary view of technology, in contrast, is regarded by Heidegger as being both 'instrumental' and 'anthropological'. In short, this means that technology is generally taken to be a means to an end, and this implies that the desires and purposes of humans constitute an exhaustive definition of it. Such a view is, according to Heidegger, correct as far as it goes. But this view does not go far enough, for it presupposes that we can define notions like 'means' and 'ends' in an unproblematic manner. '[W]herever instrumentality reigns there reigns causality' (1996:313), and therefore if we do not provide an acceptable account of *causality*, then we cannot be said to have engaged with the question of what technology is in sufficient depth.

On Heidegger's account, causality can be best elucidated in terms of its 'fourfold' nature: (i) the matter out of which a thing is made; (ii) the form which is imposed on the material; (iii) the purpose of the thing; (iv) that which brings about this transformation (the agent). Heidegger claims that it is essential to see the relationship between each of these four elements as an immanent one. In other words, the agent (iv) does not stand 'outside' of, or independently of, (i)–(iii). Rather, each of these is a mode of 'bringing forth', i.e. a process in which what is hidden in the world is made manifest. Moreover, 'bringing forth' is itself 'grounded in revealing' (1996:318), and revealing involves uncovering and thereby showing how things are. 'Technology is [. . .] no mere means. Technology is a way of revealing. If we give heed to this, then another whole realm for the essence of technology will open itself to us. It is the realm of revealing, i.e. of truth' (1996:318). Above all, it is in its capacity as a *mode* of revealing, *not* as a mere 'manufacturing', that technology is a 'bringing forth'. The 'bringing forth' involved in modern technology is a 'challenging' which 'sets upon' nature so as to impose order upon it with the aim of achieving 'the maximum yield at the minimum expense' (1996:321). Nature, in short, is conceptualised as a mere resource by modern technology, a storehouse of energy. But even this is 'no mere human doing' (1996:324). In the same way as a mountain range is formed and folded by forces which are not to be confused with the range itself, so humans are propelled into this 'challenging' by what Heidegger calls *'Gestell'* (enframing). 'Enframing means the gathering together of the setting-upon that sets upon man' (1996:325). In modern technology, humans are themselves 'set upon' and thereby engage with the world in a manner which cannot be accounted for in purely anthropological terms. Although the process of enframing which occurs as technology takes place within the sphere of human action, enframing does not 'happen exclusively *in* man, or definitively *through* man' (1996:329). This is because humans are themselves set upon by the conditions of their existence and hence challenged into responding to these conditions through the enframing which underlies technology. Thus, the essence of technology is revealed in the process of enframing, and enframing itself is shown to be a mode of engaging with, and thus revealing, the conditions of existence. This mode of engagement 'starts man upon the way of that revealing through which the actual everywhere [...] becomes standing reserve [i.e. a resource]' (1996:329). In this sense, there is a determinacy with regard to how humans encounter the conditions of their existence, once the enframing which constitutes the essence of technology has set them upon the course of revealing which technology embodies. This process, which underlies all modes of revealing, Heidegger calls 'destining' (*Geschick*). Humans exist within the domain of destining, but are never compelled by it, since destining is itself the 'free space' within which human action is rendered possible. As such, it is 'the realm of freedom' (1996:330). Technology, in turn, is thus always already situated within the domain of freedom. Given this last point, it cannot make sense to talk of our being 'compelled' by technology, either in the sense of 'a stultified compulsion to push on blindly' with it 'or, what comes to the same, to rebel helplessly against it and curse it as the work of the devil' (1996:330).

On Heidegger's view, then, we cannot take a stand either 'for' or 'against' technology. However, the danger presented by technology lies in the fact that it may come to subvert all other possible modes of revealing in its pursuit of ordering the world (i.e. mastery over it). In turn, such mastery would reduce both humanity and all other entities to the status of a mere resource for technological goals. Nevertheless, the technological mode of enframing can never entirely subvert the very conditions which gave rise to its historical development, and for Heidegger this means that a space must remain within which articulate different modes of thinking that can engage with the world. For Heidegger this means, above all, formulating a poetic form of dialogue with which to engage with Being—a theme which pervades much of his work.

Of other accounts of technology, thinkers associated with the **Frankfurt School** have alluded to the relationship between the rise of technology and the development of modern forms of rationality. Significant amongst these is Max Horkheimer's conception of 'instrumental rationality' and his accompanying criticisms of **positivism**. According to Horkheimer, modernity can be characterised in terms of a modulation towards a conception of reason which highlights its purposive/instrumental aspect. In short, by 'reason' what is meant in modern culture is a form of thinking which gives priority to the attainment of a given purpose or end, rather than any process of critical reflection upon a broader range of issues which fall outside the purview of the 'means and ends' rationality of instrumental reason. Instrumentalism is thus a form of thinking which takes purposes as 'givens' which are then to be acted upon, rather than a reflective and critical engagement with the question as to whether particular purposes are justifiable. In philosophy, Horkheimer argues, this has led to the development of 'positivism', which seeks to emulate the methodology of science. Positivism, in seeking to emulate science, Horkheimer claims, merely becomes a passive and uncritical voice with regard to questions of knowledge, since it is content to leave the arbitration of what counts as justification to the hegemony of modern instrumental reason.

Further reading: Heidegger 1996; Horkheimer 1992; Lyotard 1989.

PS

TELEVISION

The decisive developments in the technology of modern television broadcasting, such as electronic scanning, were made in the 1920s, and the first experiments in public broadcasting occurred in the 1930s. In the post-war period, television rapidly developed its now central position as the dominant form of popular entertainment (displacing radio and **cinema** in the USA in the 1950s, and in Britain in the 1960s). The cultural, economic and sociological theorisation of television, however, did not come to maturity until the 1970s. Perhaps, more accurately, it could be suggested that the theorisation of television as a distinctive medium, separate from more general theories of the **mass media**, did not occur until the 1970s. At this time, key studies of television were published by Williams (1974), Hall (1973) and the Glasgow University Media Group (1976).

A concern with television may be seen as an extension of Raymond Williams's earlier and continuing work on cultural transformation and democratic forms of communication. The dominant approach in Marxist analyses of the mass media had been to treat them as instruments of **ideology**, not least in terms of the threat that they were seen to pose to any politically emancipatory cultural practice. While sharing these concerns, Williams develops one of the more subtle versions of Marxist cultural theory. This may be seen in the three elements of his analysis of television. First, he is concerned to relate television as a cultural phenomenon to an account of the material conditions of society. Rejecting any simple **base–superstructure** model, according to which the development of a technology determines the cultural superstructure, he identifies the social preconditions of the growth of television in what he terms 'mobile privatism'. Television technology could only be commercially exploited by being adapted for consumption within the home. This privatism was to some extent (and especially within the United Kingdom) balanced by the dominance of public service broadcasting, and thus the state control of television. Crucially, Williams recognises in the public aspect of television (not least in its possible responses to an American dominated global television culture) the potential for increasingly local and democratic forms of communication. Williams's second concern is with the structure of the experience and content of television. Programmes are ordered in a sequential flow, as opposed to a sequence of discrete units. This structure may be seen to lead the audience into passivity, as the programmes make only a superficial and transient impression, during periods of relaxation. Finally, Williams begins to question the dominant models of audience research. These are seen to entail a crude examination of the isolated effects that television was supposed to have on its audience (e.g. in causing violence), and thereby ignoring the complex institutional structures within which television is produced and consumed.

Stuart Hall, similarly, questions the assumption that there is any simple causal model that can account for the impact that television has upon its audience. Hall is concerned with the (ideological) message that television is supposed to communicate. By recognising the complexity of the processes of production (or encoding) and interpretation (or decoding) of a message, Hall argues that the makers of television programmes cannot determine the sense that the audience will make of them. The message will be encoded in the context of a set of cultural preconceptions and taken-for-granted knowledge, **relations of production** and technologies (that will influence, for example, the way material from the everyday world is selected and transformed for transmission). These frameworks may or may not correspond to those of the audience. Audiences may therefore be understood as responding within one of three broad categories. The 'dominant-**hegemonic** position' entails decoding the message (for example of a news or current affairs programme) within the same, ideological framework as it was encoded. A 'negotiated position' entails a partial (and contradictory) reinterpretation of the message in the light of the immediate experience of the viewer. Finally, an 'oppositional position' entails that the viewer sees through the dominant framework, for example, recognising an appeal to national interest as a promotion of **class** interest. Morley's (1980) analysis of the news and current affairs programme *Nationwide* provided an empirical test of the utility of this typology, as well as allowing further exploration of the relationship between positions of interpretation and other social variables, such as **class**, **education** and age.

The Glasgow University Media Group published a series of **empirical** and **semiotic** analyses of British television news. Extensive analysis of videotaped programmes indicated a systematic ideological bias. Thus, for example, the coverage of industrial action was demonstrated to distort the actual level and nature of industrial action occurring in the country The level of television coverage, for industry as a whole, or for specific industries, did not correspond to the nature or number of strikes occurring. The newsworthiness of strike action was, rather, determined by the perceived inconvenience that the strike would have on the public. Further, coverage and commentary would presuppose the interests of capitalism and the middle classes (from which the producers of these programmes are disproportionately recruited). While this research has come in for subsequent criticism as to its theoretical presuppositions and methodology, it may be seen to have influenced not just subsequent research, but also news broadcasting practices, at least in the United Kingdom.

While the work of Hall, and to a lesser extent the Glasgow Group, opened up issues of the analysis of television as **text**, they focused on news coverage. Subsequent analysts broadened the range of programmes under consideration (including soap operas and sitcoms). Further, while media sponsored research typically focused on the number and types of viewer for particular programmes (for advertising purposes), sociological and cultural studies research examines the diversity of ways in which television programmes were interpreted and used. Ang (1985) examined the consumption of the soap opera *Dallas*. The programme is understood as 'emotional realism', in that while the situations portrayed will not correspond to the life experience of the audience, the emotions expressed will. She emphasises the diverse pleasures that are gained from consuming *Dallas*, including, for example, an 'escapism' that makes the boundaries of reality and fiction fluid (so that the pleasure may lie in accepting *Dallas* as part of the drabness of everyday life, rather than a simple flight from it). Other feminist theorists have developed on this work through appeal to **psychoanalytic** theory, and thus further question the relationship between television consumption and the construction of gendered identity. Taking television as typical of **popular culture**, Fiske (1987 and 1989) again focuses on the pleasure of consumption, and identifies a necessary separation between the programme as a commercial product and its interpretation (and thus cultural production) by 'the people'. The 'people' embraces diverse sets of allegiances, so that the programme will be variously interpreted and used in ways that are not prescribed by the makers. The consumption of popular culture therefore amounts to an irreverent and pleasurable opposition to the dominant power bloc. (A counter to this conclusion may be found in Eagleton (1991). While critical of approaches that over-emphasise the ideological content of television programmes, he argues that television has an ideological effect in the political passivity that privatised television consumption engenders.)

The work of Baudrillard has been central to the development of **postmodernist** theories of television. At the core of Baudrillard's approach (the theories of hyperreality and simulations) is an attempt to undermine the opposition between reality and fiction. The current level of media technology is seen to be such that it does not repro-duce a pre-existing reality, but rather produces the real. The world that we experience is produced through the interplay of various media (television, cinema, video, **popular music**, and so on), in so far as simulations now have real consequences. Thus, Baudrillard (1991) could notoriously claim that the Gulf War did not take place. Behind this rhetorical flourish is a claim that the Gulf War was conducted not simply under the gaze of television cameras, but rather that it was conducted for those cameras. The war becomes a spectacle (manifest most clearly in guided missiles carrying cameras), albeit a spectacle that will leave death and destruction in its wake. The very nature of war is thus seen to be changed by television.

Further reading: Morley 1992; Stevenson 1995.

AE

TERRORISM

The perpetration of violent acts against civilians designed in order to create a sense of terror in a general population (or national or ethnic group) with the intention of achieving political, ideological, eco-nomic, or religious goals. Terrorism is usually differentiated from war, which sanctions violent behaviour between combatants that is conducted on the basis of shared rules of engagement. As everybody knows, at its most extreme level, terrorist violence involves killing people; however, it can also include acts directed against property or natural resources, the damage or destruction of which leads directly to harm. Terrorist acts include several essential features. Terrorism can be national or international. It can also be perpetrated by terrorist groups opposed to particular states or by states themselves. There must be an *agent* (or agents) to which the act of violence can be attributed. That agent must necessarily be understood as acting with a view to achieving a *purpose* without which the act of terror is unthinkable. In this sense, the contingent act and the intention to cause harm are, for the attacker, justified by the purpose. The purpose endows the act of terror with *intelligibility*. Strictly speaking, there can, it follows, never be any such thing as 'senseless' terrorist violence. All terrorist violence is, in principle, intelligible. This does not, however, mean that the beliefs motivating such violence cannot be deluded or illusory, which is where their genuine senselessness thus lies. The terrorist act must have intended *victims*, but never a single, isolated victim. Whereas it is in principle possible to consider an act of murder as pertaining to a solitary victim (assuming that the victim had no dependants, living relatives or friends who might care about what happened to them) acts of terror presuppose a widespread effect. In simple terms, the effect is an emotional one upon the witnesses: the inducement of a kind of fear that pertains to feelings of limitlessness (the anti-social excess of the violence) on the one hand and impotence (the ever-present threat of such violence) on the other. Hence, the effect is of such a kind as to transform the witness into a participant in the events they have seen or heard reports of. Terrorist acts thereby create their desired effect by forming a seemingly inescapable interpretative context of fear around the unwilling participants who are their central target. Thus, victims of terror are not limited to those who happen to die or suffer physical or emotional injury as a direct result of such acts, but to 'they' who need (from the point of view of the terrorist) to take notice if their purposes are to be achieved. Terrorism is, in this regard, always a form of instrumentalism: the end justifies the means. Modern, international terrorism is in many ways unthinkable without reference to systems of media and communications. The more efficient and explicitly representational (especially visually) the network of communication, the greater the potential impact of terrorist violence, since the greater the ease of dissemination the greater the number of potential victims (witnesses).

Many individual arenas of terrorist activity could be cited since the beginning of the twentieth century, each with a subtly different dynamic. In spite of politicians' attempts to resolve tensions in the 1920s, the United Kingdom's involvement in Ireland, its second (after Wales) oldest colony, sparked a chain of violence that, from the late

1960s, led to forty years of terrorist activity in the province of Northern Ireland. Likewise, terrorist struggles in the Lebanon have accompanied the destruction of the Lebanese State, while the Israeli occupation of Palestine has led to outbreaks of terrorist violence in Israel. Terrorist outbreaks have also characterised the post-war **history** of Italy, Germany, Spain and Russia. Most notoriously, the al-Qaeda attacks on the United States on 11 September 2001 (see **9/11**) epitomise the excessive violence typical of international terrorism. In many of these cases, terrorism is seen to exert a decisive impact on the political systems against which it is focused. Among its consequences, especially in liberal democratic forms of government, is the delimiting of spheres of legality, in so far as these spheres relate to the rights of the individual and concerns about security. The autonomy of the legal system is thereby compromised with the result that the freedom before the law that liberal democracies so value is threatened. Tensions between judiciary and executive often arise in consequence. In cases where terrorists portray Western powers as imperialistic colonisers (as is the case with al-Qaeda, see Bin Laden 1989), legislation that gives the executive increased power can undermine the rhetoric of freedom. Another consequence of the attacks of 11 September 2001 has been increased international co-operation between the executive arms of national governments. Most notoriously, USA president G.W. Bush responded by declaring a 'war on terror' (Bush 2001a). The consequences of this are currently too broad to summarise. However, among its principal features must be numbered the military action in Afghanistan that came as a response to the presence there of al-Qaeda, and the American imprisonment, without trial, of hundreds of Muslims in Guantanamo Bay, Cuba, justified by the contention that these people are prisoners of war. The invasion of Iraq in March 2003, and the toppling and subsequent execution of Iraqi leader Saddam Hussein, may also be directly related to the rhetoric of the 'war on terror': (false) claims that Iraq had a role in the 9/11 attacks were used to justify the invasion. On a theoretical level, if taken seriously, the notion of a 'war on terror' introduces confusions with regard to the concept of war, which has since the time of St Thomas Aquinas exclusively concerned relations between nation states. The concept of 'war' that is implied with regard to the combating of terror is different in kind from the conception that has traditionally been theorised. For example, combatants do not meet on a specified field of battle or behave as they do in war (at least as a general rule) according to pre-established codes of military conduct and dress. Codes of conduct, of course, are of necessity ethical codes. The confusion of such codes thus invites ethical confusions.

Further reading: Borradori 2003; Dror 1983; Elshtain 2003; Primoraz 2004; Sterba 2003; Walzer 2004.

PS

TEXT

The concept of a 'text', particularly within **semiotics**, is a meaningful structure, understood as being composed of **signs**. The meaning of a text is determined by rules (or **codes**) governing the choice and combination of those signs. The rules that govern this meaningful combination of signs will be conventional, so that any reader of the text will require certain skills or competences in order to interpret (or decode) the text. Readers from different social and cultural backgrounds, who have different socially acquired skills and expectations, may therefore read the same text in very different ways.

A text typically has a material existence, but is not necessarily simply a written message (such as a sentence, memo, report or novel). Thus a photograph, a song, an advertisement (combining photographic or other visual signs with written signs), a video or a costume may all be understood as texts.

AE

THEOLOGY

In Western cultures theology has been dominated by Christian approaches to the doctrine of God since Roman times. Broadly speaking, this view characterises God as an all-powerful, all-knowing Being, who created the universe, and who made himself known to humankind in the person of Jesus of Nazareth. Jesus is worshipped as God the Son, along with the other persons of the divine trinity: God the Father and God the Holy Spirit. These are not thought of as three co-equal gods, but as one Divine essence manifest in three persons.

While it serves as a basic description, the above overview is somewhat misleading. Christian theology has never been a monolithic system of dogmatic assertions to which all believers subscribe. Within the New Testament itself there is evidence that a number of different approaches divided the primitive Church. By the second century, certain long-standing theological tendencies associated with Gnosticism had developed into sects like that which grew up around Marcion. He expressed the view (shared by many thinkers ever since—including the nineteenth-century philosopher J.S. Mill) that the God of the Old Testament is not the God of whom Jesus spoke as a loving Father.

Other conflicts centred on ways of interpreting the Bible. Some, like Origen (*c.* 185–254), favoured allegorical interpretations, while others, like Tertullian (*c.* 155–222), stressed what they saw as the literal truth of biblical texts. This was still a major issue for Martin Luther and the theologians of the Reformation in the sixteenth century. Many other theological conflicts arose during the Reformation period, including that between those who asserted that the Pope and the bishops wielded a legitimate, God-given right to decide on doctrinal matters, and those who appealed to the Bible as the highest **authority**. The same era also saw the emergence of unitarianism: the denial of the divine trinity in the assertion that God is one person.

In the wake of the Renaissance and Reformation in Europe, the study of the Bible took a critical turn. Richard Simon's *Histoire critique due Vieux Testament* (1678) began the process of textual criticism of the Bible which resulted in the gradual dismantling of its authority. As this process quickened and deepened during the eighteenth century, a liberal theology grew up which jettisoned all things supernatural and judged religious matters by the criteria of an elevated Reason.

One development which pre-dates the Reformation is of particular importance in contemporary theological thought. Early in the fourteenth century, the mystical writer Johannes 'Meister' Eckhart developed a negative theology which drew on the writings of a fifth- or sixth-century Syrian monk called Dionysius the Areopagite (or Pseudo-Dionysius). Dionysius had argued that God is beyond the grasp of the human intellect, and that, consequently, human language is inadequate to express anything wholly true about the divine nature. Negative theology thus describes God only in terms of what 'he' is not: 'a not-God, a not-spirit, a not-Person, a not-image . . .' (Eckhart *Sermon XCIX*).

The suspicion with regard to language and conceptuality evident in the works of Eckhart, John Ruysbroeck, and other mystical theologians of the period, has found an echo in a strain of contemporary philosophical thought to draw its inspiration from Friedrich Nietzsche (1844–1900) and Martin Heidegger (1889–1976). In *The Trespass of the Sign,* Kevin Hart explores the relationship between negative theology and contemporary continental philosophy concluding that the former is a species of deconstructive thought which has strong affinities with the work of Jacques Derrida.

Nietzsche's work has had a profound influence on twentieth-century theology, not only because he questioned the philosophical presuppositions upon which the Christian theological tradition depended, but also because he (famously) announced God's death. This conclusion was premised upon the fact that science had offered new, non-theological explanations of many natural phenomena. God was no longer required and religious belief appeared to be in terminal decline. In response to this, theologians such as Paul van Buren and Thomas Altizer in America, and Don Cupitt in Britain, have propounded a 'theology' of the death of God—a paradoxical Christian atheism.

Chief among the God-obscuring scientific advances of the nineteenth century was Charles Darwin's theory of **evolution** by natural selection. *The Origin of Species* (1859) divided Christian opinion, provoking the rise of **fundamentalism** on the one hand, and, on the other, influencing more liberal thinkers to produce new accounts of the relationship between Creator and creation.

Profoundly influenced by Darwin, the work of the twentieth-century Catholic mystic Teilhard de Chardin (1881–1955) has had a significant impact upon the work of subsequent Christian theologians. 'Evolution,' he claimed, 'is a light illuminating all facts, a curve that all lines must follow.' For Teilhard, the world is unfinished, and is progressing towards its 'Omega point'—the moment at which God will be fully manifest in humanity and in nature. The so-called 'process theology' of Schubert Ogden, John Cobb *et al.* owes much to this kind of approach, as do recent developments in Creation spirituality.

Among proponents of the latter trend, Matthew Fox has had the highest profile. His book *Original Blessing* (1983), its title implicitly rejecting the traditional Christian notion of 'original sin', seeks to shift Christian theology away from its emphasis on a primeval 'fall' and the need for redemption, towards a celebration of Creation as the central theme of worship. Ecological consciousness, New Age thinking, Celtic Christianity, negative theology and various forms of non-Christian mysticism all combine in Fox's work. What Fox thinks of as the 'creation-centred tradition' is also broadly feminist in character. It rejects both the male image of God as Father and the patriarchal structure of Church tradition.

Feminist theology has grown up alongside political and cultural movements towards the equalisation of female/male roles in society. Since the production of Elizabeth Cady Stanton's *The Woman's Bible*, in the last few years of the nineteenth century, the masculine construction and male domination of Christianity have come under ever-intensifying scrutiny. Today there is a substantial (and increasing) body of work, covering all areas of theological concern from a variety of feminist perspectives. In her introduction to *Feminist Theology: A Reader* (1990), Ann Loades writes:

> feminist theologians are particularly concerned with the way [religious] traditions work, the symbolism they use, the characteristics of roles within them, the way the traditions reflect social assumptions and shape and reshape those assumptions, and especially the genderrelated way in which we talk about God.

Taken together, the 'death of God', ecological consciousness, feminist reinterpretations and the cross-fertilisation of different faith traditions are elements of a major shift in attitudes to the study of divinity. It is probably not an exaggeration to speak of the combined effect of these changes as the dawn of a new era in theology.

Further reading: Altizer 1968, 1977; Cobb 1977; Cupitt 1988; Fox 1983; Loades 1990; Milbank 1990; Ogden 1979, 1996; Stanton 1990.

KM/GH

UNCONSCIOUS

Though the concept of the unconscious pre-dates Freud, it was through **psychoanalysis** that it took on a radical dimension. In Freud's metapsychology, the unconscious is defined as that which comes between perception and consciousness. It is the realm of the primary process (as opposed to the secondary process of consciousness that is characterised by a greater 'binding' of affects). It is marked by a fluidity of cathexes, of displacements, condensations, symbolism and the substitution of external reality by the subjective Real. It lacks a sense of time or the substitution of external reality by the subjective Real. It also lacks logical contradictions. Opposing tendencies can coexist within it. It partakes of the infantile but is not reducible to it. In Freud's early topographical model, the unconscious is opposed to the preconscious and the conscious. The unconscious becomes less important in the later structural model where the psyche is divided into the id, the ego and the superego. Freud argues that the better part of all these agencies may well be unconscious. The concept is necessitated by the fact that there are gaps in the analysand's memory which have a traumatic significance. Moreover, Freud argues, these gaps in the mental life must be understood as belonging to someone *other* than the subject. It is this notion which Lacan takes up in his formula: 'the unconscious is the discourse of the Other'.

The term 'unconscious' must be rigorously differentiated from the notion of 'repression'. Though the repressed is the prototype of the unconscious, it is the latter which has a wider compass. All that is repressed is unconscious but not all that is unconscious is repressed. Though a final cleavage between the conscious and unconscious does not appear until puberty, the unconscious must be presupposed in the infant to explain the act of repression. Repression is not characteristic of neurotics, as the popular depiction of someone as 'repressed' would imply. The 'neurotic' is merely the subject in whom repression has failed. All subjects must undergo primary repression during the **Oedipal** phase. For Lacan, the fall of this first signifier from the chain of signification is a structural necessity. The Lacanians refer to this as a **signifier** *en plus*. Secondary repression is a derivative of primary repression: it distorts the expression of those signifiers that bear a traumatic link to the complex ideas associated with primary repression. It is always the signifier that is repressed and not the affect. Affects can only be displaced in relation to the logic of the signifier. The formations of the unconscious can therefore be understood as an interplay between those elements which offer themselves to interpretation (desire) and those which resist it (fantasy). Hence (contrary to **postmodernist** misinterpretations) the Lacanian analyst Jacques-Alain Miller has argued that the unconscious is not reducible to the **metonymy** of desire. The unconscious is structured *both* like a language and unlike a language. For Lacan, ultimately, the unconscious is not just an-*other* scene, which requires an alternate ontology. It is instead *pre*-ontological: it is, more fundamentally, the order of the unrealised.

Further reading: Freud 1991a; Klein 1992/3; Lacan 1977a, 1977b; Laplanche and Pontalis 1973; Miller 1988.

SKS

UNDERCLASS

'Underclass' is a term often used vaguely, referring to a structured group at the bottom of the class hierarchy in capitalist societies and refers to a structured group at the bottom of the **class** hierarchy in **capitalist** societies. The presence of a 'new working class' in the North American cities was proposed by S.M. Miller (1965). This class was composed of ethnic minorities (including Puerto Ricans, Mexicans and African-Americans), who were employed in low-income service occupations, without union representation, and who suffered long periods of unemployment (and could thus be compared to the more affluent and secure, and predominantly white, 'old working class'). Further theorisation of this concept would include women alongside ethnic minorities as typical members of the underclass.

AE

URBANISM

Urbanism or urbanisation is the growth in the proportion of the population of a country who are living in towns and cities, and the social and cultural effects of this predominantly urban life. Urbanisation is caused either by the migration of people from the countryside to the town, or by the fact that the birth rate of the urban population is higher than its death rate. Urbanisation is a historically recent phenomenon. For example, in the United Kingdom, in 1800 approximately 24 per cent of the population lived in urban centres. By 1900, this figure was 77 per cent. However, with the growth of suburbs, and changes in the structure of towns and cities due to the decline of manufacturing industry, the rate of urbanisation typically tends to slow and even decline.

Two broad, if inevitably overlapping, approaches to the problem of urban life can be identified. On the one hand, there is the description and characterisation of what is distinctive about urban existence. On the other hand, there are attempts to explain this way of life. The first approach is perhaps the more relevant to **cultural studies**. In the nineteenth century, the city had already become a central theme of novelists such as Dickens and Balzac and poets such as Baudelaire. Within cultural and social theory will be found, in the early years of the twentieth century, the work of Georg Simmel, Walter Benjamin, the Chicago School and a host of contemporary writers offering **modernist**, **postmodernist** and **feminist** approaches. For Simmel (1950b), life in the metropolis is characterised by a relative increase in mental stimulation. Rural existence, or life in a small community, is more emotional and stable, yet lacking in personal freedom. The overstimulation of metropolitan life, however, paradoxically threatens the individual in his or her search for **identity**. The excess of stimuli and threat of others leads to reserve, or a blasé attitude, expressed in a perpetual search of novelty and eccentricity. Benjamin's analysis of nineteenth-century Paris (1973a) offers a dazzling range of fragmentary readings of the city, the most famous of which is the image of the *flâneur* (and which is not dissimilar to Simmel's characterisation of urban humanity). The *flâneur* strolls anonymously about the city (like Edgar Allan Poe's 'The Man of the Crowd' (1982)), consuming it in a succession of transient impressions.

Louis Wirth (1938), following in the tradition of the Chicago School of urban sociology, summarises the urban experience in terms of the loss of personal relationships, and thus of a greater instrumentality in our dealings with others. He explains this way of life by appealing to features of the urban environment itself: the size, density and heterogeneity of the population. Subsequent approaches within urban sociology question the assumption that there is a single distinctive urban experience. H.J. Gans, for example, recognises the impersonality, anonymity and superficiality of urban relationships that are formed under conditions of transience and heterogeneity, but argues that such conditions apply to only a portion of the urban population, and need to be understood in terms of sociological factors, such as **class** and employment opportunities (1968). The city therefore comes to be seen more as the context within which other social and political forces are played out. Thus, Marshall Berman explores the relationships between cities, modern art and modernisation (1983). In contemporary geography, Harvey (1989) and Castells (1989), working within **Marxist** frameworks, analyse the role of **capitalism** and the state in the structure and development of the city. Advocates of postmodernism, conversely, find in the city of the late twentieth century its transformation as a centre for consumption and spectacle. Las Vegas replaces Paris as the archetypal urban experience. Wilson's (1991) feminist approach questions the masculine bias in much work on the city, analysing the city, not merely as a place of threat and danger to women, but also as a positive site.

See also: **architecture**.

Further reading: Leach 1997; Pahl 1968; Saunders 1981; Soja 1989.

AE

USE VALUE

The concept of use value is fundamental to Marxist economics. For Marx, it refers to the usefulness of a thing, and as such is grounded in the inherent and natural properties of the thing. Bread has use value because it satisfies our hunger. Use value thus indicates something that is qualitatively distinctive about the thing in terms of the particular purpose it serves. Marx contrasts the use value of **commodities** with their **exchange-value**.

Further reading: Cunningham-Wood 1988.

AE

UTILITARIANISM

An approach to questions of ethics which argues that an action can be evaluated in terms of its moral worth by calculating its effects or consequences. The view is associated with thinkers such as Jeremy Bentham (1748–1832) and J.S. Mill (1806–73). Utilitarianism is generally associated with the maxim which advocates 'the greatest happiness of the greatest number', or principle of Utility, as providing the basis for understanding the worth of an action. This states that, faced with a moral dilemma, one should act in such a way as to maximise the greatest happiness of the greatest possible number of people who would be affected by that action ('happiness' in this context signifies the presence of pleasure and absence of pain; while 'unhappiness' would mean the presence of pain and diminution of pleasure). In the twentieth century, utilitarians have come to be divided into two kinds: (i) 'act utilitarians', who argue that individual actions should be judged according to the principle of Utility; and (ii) 'rule utilitarians', who hold that different actions can be sub-divided into different types, and that each action can be brought under a rule which applies to all such instances of that type.

There are a number of criticisms of the utilitarian theory. First, how is it possible to assess exhaustively the consequences of any action? Second, although the 'greatest number' may benefit from an act, what about those in a minority who suffer as a result of it? Third, utilitarians presuppose that 'happiness' is something quantifiable; but there is no way of showing what, exactly, 'happiness' or 'pleasure' is, nor, therefore, that there is any universally applicable definition of the term. Fourth, it is not clear that the meaning of social and cultural life can be reduced to the pursuit of happiness or pleasure, as the utilitarians must, at least implicitly, hold (a point made by Nietzsche, when he noted, somewhat dryly, that only the 'English' (i.e. utilitarians) strive after happiness, not humanity).

Aspects of utilitarian theory embody a view of cultural **identity** implicit in **liberalism**. For example, it presupposes that agents are the authors of their own destinies and are basically self-interested beings (in so far as they all seek to maximise their pleasures and that such maximisation is good).

Further reading: Glover 1990b; Mill 1984; Plamenatz 1958; Scarre 1996; Sen and Williams 1982; Singer 1993.

PS

UTOPIA/NISM

The word 'utopia' means 'nowhere'. The common use of the term as meaning 'unrealistic', 'fanciful' or 'illusory' is derived from Sir Thomas More's book *Utopia* (1516), which offers a description of an ideal and imaginary state. Utopianism is the belief that it is possible to establish a **society** which is not merely 'better' than present society, but a perfect one. Utopian texts thus seek to provide a vision of future possible worlds in which the conflicts and injustices which dominate contemporary societies are overcome. The attempt to describe such a society and the principles which underlie it can be traced as far back as the Ancient Greek philosopher Plato. His *Republic* seeks to justify the view that the rule of philosopher-kings (who are envisaged as being rational beings endowed with true knowledge who, in turn therefore, possess knowledge of the good) will lead to the perfect social order. On Plato's account, the highest form of cultural life is envisaged as being realisable through the elucidation of a model of human nature which reflects the order of objective reality and reason. Other works in this **genre** include Francis Bacon's *New Atlantis* (1624) and William Morris's *News from Nowhere* (1890).

Civic humanist thinker James Harrington's *The Commonwealth of Oceana* (1656) also provides a good example of the utopian genre and the uses to which it may be put (although it is disputable as to whether the substance of Harrington's thought could be called 'utopian'). Harrington uses an 'imaginary' state, *Oceana*, as a means of outlining the basic structure which, he argues, a society should adopt with regard both to establishing legitimate political authority and the conditions necessary to a fulfilling civic life. The interest of *Oceana* lies in its combination of utopian elements, political theory and **allegory**. The city of *Oceana* is an allegorical discourse on the historical developments which led up to the English revolution and the establishment of the British Commonwealth under Oliver Cromwell, and Harrington's text presents in utopian form what he considers to be the best constitution of government that the Commonwealth might adopt.

Some forms of **Marxist** and **socialist** thought could be described as containing utopian elements (e.g. Bakunin)—although Marx himself contrasted his 'scientific' analysis of economic and social relations with the work of earlier 'utopian' socialists. In the twentieth century the utopian genre seems to have given way to **narrative** forms which envisage more disturbing possible futures, e.g. Aldous Huxley's *Brave New World* (1931) or George Orwell's *1984* (1948). Likewise, the conception of harmonious social order underlying utopian thought has been questioned by, amongst others, advocates of **postmodernism**.

Further reading: Davis 1981; Kelly 1982; Kumar 1991.

PS

UTTERANCE

For V.N. Voloshinov, the utterance is the basic unit of the 'concrete reality of **language**' (1973:93). It is to be distinguished from concepts such as 'linguistic form' which, unlike it, are derived through abstraction from the reality of language, but which certain theorists, including Saussure, nevertheless have a tendency to imply correspond to that reality (see Voloshinov 1973:71, 79, 82, 98). Although Voloshinov sometimes uses the term 'speech act' as a synonym for 'utterance', his writings make clear that his concept covers all forms of language use and thus is applicable to, say, written **texts** or thought as well as to the spoken word.

According to Voloshinov, the utterance is dialogic and social. In outlining the former characteristic he advances some of the better-known (although by no means the only) ideas on the concept of dialogism to be offered from within the Bakhtin Circle of intellectuals to which he belonged (see Morson and Emerson 1990; Hirschkop 1986; Morson 1986). These include the theory that each utterance is an element in an ongoing dialogue—or a 'moment' in a 'continuous process of verbal communication'—and that, consequently, each responds to a previous utterance or utterances and, also, is shaped by the utterer's anticipation of potential responses and objections to what she might utter (Voloshinov 1973:95, and see pp. 72–3).

Voloshinov's thought on the social nature of the utterance may be summarised by saying that, for him, it is socially situated, oriented and determined. In *Marxism and the Philosophy of Language,* the account of the social character of the utterance overlaps with that of its dialogic character. A major component of it is the theory of the addressivity of the utterance. The utterance is always oriented towards an addressee. The addressee need not be a person in the presence of the utterer. Nor, Voloshinov intimates, need it be an actual person. Rather, an addressee may be presupposed in the form of a 'representative' of a particular social group (1973:85). Voloshinov (1973:86) theorises the utterance as determined equally by, and as a 'product of the reciprocal relationship between' addresser and addressee, and thereby implies that it may be thought of as socially authored, that is to say, co-authored.

Further reflections on the utterance are contained in Voloshinov's essay 'Discourse in Life and Discourse in Poetry'. There, he puts forward the theory that, in addition to a verbalised component, an unverbalised context, assumed by utterer and 'receiver', is a part of the utterance (Clark and Holquist 1984:204). He posits (1988:11) three elements which may comprise the context of the utterance in everyday life: the common spatio-temporal situation of the interlocutors involved; their shared knowledge and understanding of the situation; and their shared evaluation of it. He indicates that the assumed context of an utterance contributes to its sense, and, in a comparison of the everyday utterance with the aesthetic verbal utterance, theorises that the latter cannot be as dependent for its sense as the former upon its unverbalised context.

He holds, additionally, that in the everyday utterance aspects of the 'social essence' of all utterances are relatively manifest. Intonation in the everyday utterance, in particular, is of significance in this respect. It discloses, through its expression of communal values, the connectedness of utterances with their surrounding social milieus. It also reveals the existence of a relation of 'social interaction' (1988:17) not only between utterer, or author, and 'listener', but also between utterer and the topic or 'hero' of the utterance. This second relation can be seen through intonation's direction of social values towards the object of the utterance and its related tendency to personify that object.

Theories of the utterance similar to those offered by Voloshinov are forwarded by Mikhail Bakhtin (1986), although, unlike Voloshinov (1973:97), Bakhtin does not understand himself as contributing to a Marxist philosophy of language. In Bakhtin's writings, moreover, there is greater emphasis on the conventional distinction between utterance and sentence, with the former being portrayed as, *inter alia*, the employment of the sentence or sentences in speech communication. A similar distinction is present in the work of Jürgen Habermas (1979), where the utterance is theorised as the object of universal pragmatics, a discipline which Habermas contrasts with linguistics which is concerned with the abstract sentence.

Further reading: Bakhtin 1986; Clark and Holquist 1984; Hirschkop 1986; Morson 1986; Morson and Emerson 1990; Voloshinov 1988.

RW

VALUE

To value something may be defined as ascribing worth to it, and thus placing it within some hierarchy. Three core areas of value are of relevance to cultural theory: the **aesthetic**; the moral; and the economic.

Aesthetic value includes the worth of cultural goods and activities. Orthodox aesthetics is, in part, concerned with the principles that ground the ascription of value to particular works of art. While aesthetics may not itself be concerned with valuing particular works of art (which is more properly the task of art criticism), the attention that it gives to art, and especially the cultural products consumed by the dominant **classes** within society (not least, European society since the eighteenth century), presupposes that they are valuable objects and activities, and that there is such a thing as aesthetic value. At the end of the eighteenth century, Kant's *Critique of Judgement* (1987) is significant for proposing and defending a distinction between the pleasure that is derived from beauty (and thus art) and the mere sensuous enjoyment of useful, non-art objects (such as food). The autonomy and distinctiveness of aesthetic value has been increasingly challenged. On the one hand, politically, links have been drawn between art and **ideology**. The aesthetically valued art of the dominant class is explained by reference to the role it plays in legitimating and propagating the political and moral values of the dominant class. On the other hand, aesthetic value may be linked to economic value. It may be argued that the prime purpose of aesthetics is not to ascribe the ultimately illusionary aesthetic value to objects, but to give that which is otherwise of minimal use an economic value. Aesthetically valued objects can be traded at high prices (Bourdieu 1984).

The development of **sociology** as a discipline may be seen to centre on the empirical study of values, not least in Emile Durkheim's conception of 'moral facts' (1982). The integration and stability of a society is seen to depend upon the internalisation of the consensual values of the society (encapsulated in Durkheim's concept of the '*conscience collective*') through the process of **socialisation**. **Functionalism**, as the dominant American approach to sociology up to the 1960s, presupposed a consensus on moral values as a precondition of a stable society. This presupposition was increasingly challenged by the sociology of **deviance**, with the recognition of a wide-range of alternative **subcultures**, with markedly divergent value systems, within a single society. Similarly, the re-emergence of **Marxism** as a significant force within sociology in the 1960s led to an increased recognition that consensual values were themselves the products of political and above all **ideological** and **hegemonic** practices, as conflicting groups sought to defend, promote and negotiate conflicting value systems. The work of Michel Foucault (1971) on punishment (1977a) and sexuality (1981) served to restore to sociology Nietzschean perspectives on the power struggles that underpin value systems, and in which values are inculcated.

The question of economic value centres upon explanations of the value and price ascribed to **commodities**. Marxism is characterised by an appeal to the **labour theory of value**, whereby the **exchange-value** of a good depends upon the amount of labour time that has gone into its production. Orthodox economics, in contrast, explains value (or price) through appeal to the interaction of supply and demand in the market.

Further reading: Hechter *et al.* 1993; Squires 1993.

AE

VALUE-FREEDOM

A view advocated by sociologist Max Weber, which states that those involved in scientific enquiry (e.g. in analyses within the discipline of **sociology**) should avoid making **value** judgements with regard to the individuals, communities or institutions that they study.

See also: **objectivity**.

PS

VISUAL STUDIES

An emerging discipline that studies the production and in particular the **consumption** of the products of contemporary visual media, such as **television**, film and advertising.

Visual studies may be understood broadly as applying the approaches and concerns of **cultural studies** to the study of the visual arts and visual **culture** in general. As such, it is closely related to, and indeed may be taken as a synonym for, the slightly older term 'visual culture'. Visual culture represents a 'pictorial turn' in cultural studies (akin to the 'linguistic turn' in philosophy), through which the theorist turns away from the (verbal or literary) **text**, and towards the visual image. Its core theorists are: Walter Benjamin (and in particular his study of the work of art in the age of mechanical reproduction (1970b), but also his work on photography (1999a: 507–30) and on the consumerism of the nineteenth-century Parisian arcades (1999b)); Michel Foucault (and in particular his work on the notion of the 'gaze' (1976)); Roland Barthes (1973); and Jacques Lacan (and the envisioning of the Other (1977b)). It may then be seen to adopt the methods borrowed from literary theory and critical theory, alongside those of the sociology of art and of art history.

The subject matter of visual studies may, most effectively, be constructed through comparison to art history. Visual studies implicitly or explicitly criticises traditional approaches to art history for being excessively concerned with high or **elite** culture, preoccupied with the past (and thus neglecting contemporary art and new media), and for continuing to embody **post–colonial** values. Following cultural studies, questions as to **identity** politics and the social construction of the viewer or consumer are placed to the fore. The material studied will include photography, film, television, video and the internet, and their manifestation in commercial and popular cultural forms (such as advertising, toys, sport and the visual ephemera of everyday life). Little interest is expressed in the **canonical** works of art history, or indeed anything created before 1950. Having said that, a core text in the development of visual studies is Michael Baxandall's *Painting and Experience in Fifteenth Century Italy* (1972). Visual studies may also be seen as the most appropriate theoretical framework within which **avant–garde** art may be studied.

Visual studies status as a discipline is still disputed. The antagonism expressed to it in a special issue of the journal *October* (see Kraus (1996)) is illustrative of the tensions that run through academia, as more conservative academics strive to defend their position, and as more progressive academics strive to introduce courses and to conduct research that appeals to their students. While debates over the future of visual studies are debates over the forms and methods of research that are appropriate to specific forms of culture, and about the need to recognise the importance of otherwise neglected cultural forms, yet they are also debates shaped by academic politics and the need to engage new generations of students.

Further reading: Elkins 2003; Holly *et al.* 1994; Mirzoeff 1999.

AE

WORLDVIEW

From the German '*Weltanschauung*'. A shorthand term signifying the common body of beliefs shared by a group of speakers about the world and their relationship to it. There is a close interrelationship between this notion and that of 'language game' (see **meaning**), **discourse** or **paradigm**. Thus, it is one's place within a language game, discourse or paradigm which supplies one with the beliefs and assumptions necessary to construct one's worldview. It therefore follows from this close interrelationship that, given a change of language game, discourse or paradigm, there will be a corresponding change of worldview.

See also: **cultural relativism**.

SH

YOUTH CULTURE

The idea of a youth culture emerges in sociology in the 1950s and 1960s, in recognition of the fact that the **culture** of young people, especially in their teens or early twenties, is distinctive to that of their parents. Youth will have different **values**, attitudes and patterns of behaviour to those current in the dominant culture. Youth cultures are seen to emerge under certain conditions. First, youth must form a sufficiently large cohort. Second, rapid social change may disrupt young people's integration into the adult world, through, for example, changes in industry removing the traditional occupations or simply causing unemployment. Finally, an increasing **pluralism** in society will provide a stimulus to new ideas and **lifestyles**. The idea of a youth culture, however, came under criticism for assuming that youth culture is largely homogeneous. It was particularly challenged by theories of youth **subcultures**, that recognise the fragmentation of youth culture according to class, gender and ethnic divisions. A swing back in favour of theories of youth culture may now be perceived, as subcultural accounts are seen to place too much emphasis upon exotic or marginal aspects of the everyday life of young people.

See also: **counterculture**.

Further reading: Clarke 1982; Frith 1984; Gillis 1974; McRobbie 1991.

AE

BIBLIOGRAPHY

Abelove, H., Barale, M.A. and Halperin, D.M. (eds) (1993) *The Lesbian and Gay Studies Reader*, New York: Routledge.

Abercrombie, N., Hill, S. and Turner, B.S. (1980) *The Dominant Ideology Thesis*, London: Allen & Unwin.

Adorno, T.W. (1967) *(1955) Prisms*, London: Spearman.

—— (1973a) *(1948) The Philosophy of Modern Music*, London: Sheed & Ward.

—— (1973b) *(1966) Negative Dialectics*, London: Routledge & Kegan Paul.

—— (1978a) *(1951) Minima Moralia: Reflections from Damaged Life*, London: New Left Books.

—— (1978b) *(1938)* 'On the Fetish Character in Music and the Regression of Listening', in A. Arato and E. Gebhardt (eds), *The Essential Frankfurt School Reader*, Oxford: Blackwell.

—— (1982) *(1956) Against Epistemology*, tr. Willis Domingo, Oxford: Blackwell.

—— (1984) *(1970) Aesthetic Theory*, London: Routledge & Kegan Paul.

—— (1991a) *The Culture Industry: Selected Essays on Mass Culture*, ed. J.M.Bernstein, London: Routledge.

—— (1991b) *(1957–1963) Notes to Literature*, volume 1, New York: Columbia University Press.

—— (1991c) 'Free Time', in his *The Culture Industry: Selected Essays on Mass Culture*, London: Routledge.

—— (1992a) *(1965–1974) Notes to Literature*, volume 2, New York: Columbia University Press.

—— (1992b) *(1963) Quasi una fantasia: Essays on Modern Music*, London: Verso.

—— (1994) *(1941)* 'On Popular Music', in J. Storey (ed.), *Cultural Theory and Popular Culture: A Reader*, London: Edward Arnold.

—— (2006) *(1949) Philosophy of New Music*, Minneapolis, MN: University of Minnesota Press.

Adorno, T.W., Frenkel-Brunswik, E., Levinson, D.J. and Sanford, R.N. (1950) *The Authoritarian Personality*, New York: Harper.

Aggleton, P. (1987) *Deviance*, London: Routledge.

Allport, G. (1980) *The Nature of Prejudice*, Reading, MA: Addison-Wesley.

Althusser, L. (1969) *(1959) For Marx*, tr. Ben Brewster, London: New Left Books.

—— (1971) *Lenin and Philosophy and Other Essays*, London: New Left Books.

Althusser, L. and Balibar, E. (1970) *Reading Capital*, London: New Left Books.

Altizer, T. (1968) *Radical Theology and the Death of God*, Harmondsworth: Penguin.

—— (1977) *The Self-Embodiment of God*, New York: Harper & Row.

Amin, A. (ed.) (1995) *Post-Fordism: A Reader*, Oxford: Blackwell.

Amin, S. (1973) *Neo-colonialism in West Africa*, tr. Francis McDonagh, Harmondsworth: Penguin.

Anderson, P. (1979) *Lineages of the Absolutist State*, London: Verso.

Ang, I. (1985) *Watching 'Dallas': Soap Opera and the Melodramatic Imagination*, London: Methuen.

Ansell-Pearson, K. (1991) *Nietzsche contra Rousseau: A Study of Nietzsche's Moral and Political Thought*, Cambridge: Cambridge University Press.

Antoun, R.T. (2001) *Understanding Fundamentalism: Christian, Islamic, and Jewish Movements*, Walnut Creek, CA: AltaMira Press.

Anyon, J. (1980) 'Social Class and the Hidden Curriculum of Work', *Journal of Education*, 162: 67–92.

Apel, K.-O. (1976) 'The Transcendental Conception of Language Communication and the Idea of a First Philosophy', in H. Parret (ed.), *The History of Linguistic Thought and Contemporary Linguistics*, Berlin and New York: De Gruyter.

—— (1981) *Charles S. Peirce: From Pragmatism to Pragmaticism*, tr. John Michael Krois, Amherst, MA: University of Massachusetts Press.

Appleman, P. (ed.) (1970) *Darwin*, London: W.W. Norton & Co.

Arato A. and Gebhardt, E. (eds) (1978) *The Essential Frankfurt School Reader*, Oxford: Blackwell.

Arendt, H. (1965) *Eichmann in Jerusalem: A Report on the Banality of Evil*, New York: Viking.

—— (1966) *(1951) The Origins of Totalitarianism*, New York: Harcourt & Brace.

Armstong, D. (1983) *Political Anatomy of the Body: Medical Knowledge in Britain in the Twentieth Century*, Cambridge: Cambridge University Press.

Arnold, M. (1993) *Culture and Anarchy and other Writings*, ed. Stefan Collini, Cambridge: Cambridge University Press.

Atkinson, J.M. and Heritage, J. (eds) (1984) *Structures of Social Action: Studies in Conversation Analysis*, Cambridge: Cambridge University Press.

Attali, J. (1985) *Noise: The Political Economy of Music*, Manchester: Manchester University Press.

Attridge, D., Bennington, G. and Young, R. (eds) (1987) *Post-Structuralism and the Question of History*, Cambridge: Cambridge University Press.

Austin, J.L. (1975) *(1955) How to Do Things With Words*, second edn, Oxford: Oxford University Press.

Avineri, S. and De-Shalit, A. (eds) (1992) *Communitarianism and Individualism*, Oxford: Oxford University Press.

Ayer, A.J. (ed.) (1959) *Logical Positivism*, London: Allen & Unwin; Glencoe, IL: Free Press.

—— (1967) *(1946) Language, Truth and Logic*, second edn, London: Victor Gollancz.

Bachelard, G. (1964) *(1938)* *The Psychoanalysis of Fire*, London: Routledge & Kegan Paul.

—— (1969) *(1957)* *The Poetics of Space*, Boston, MA: Beacon Press.

Badcock, C.R. (1975) *Lévi-Strauss: Structuralism and Sociological Theory*, London: Hutchinson.

Badmington, N. (ed.) (2000) *Posthumanism*, Basingstoke: Macmillan.

Bahro, R. (1982) *Socialism and Survival*, London: Heretic.

—— (1984) *From Red to Green*, London: Verso.

Bakhtin, M. (1981) *The Dialogic Imagination: Four Essays by M.M.Bakhtin*, ed. M. Holquist, tr. Caryl Emerson and Michael Holquist, Austin, TX, University of Texas Press.

—— (1984) *Rabelais and His World*, tr. Hélène Iswolsky, Bloomington, IN: Indiana University Press.

—— (1986) *Speech Genres and Other Late Essays*, ed. C. Emerson and M. Holquist, tr. Vern McGee, Austin, TX: University of Texas Press.

Balibar, E. (1970) 'The Basic Concepts of Historical Materialism', in L. Althusser and E.Balibar, *Reading Capital*, London: New Left Books.

Bantock, G. (1975) 'Towards a Theory of Popular Culture', in M. Golby, J. Greenwald and R. West (eds), *Curriculum Design*, London: Croom Helm; Milton Keynes, Open University Press.

Banton, M. (1977) *The Idea of Race*, London: Tavistock Publications.

Barber, Benjamin (2002) 'Democracy and Terror in the Era of Jihad versus McWorld', in *Worlds in Collision*, Basingstoke: Macmillan.

Barker, M. (1989) *Comics: Ideology, Power and the Critics*, Manchester: Manchester University Press.

Barrett, M. (1980) *Women's Oppression Today: Problems in Marxist Feminist Analysis*, London: New Left Books.

—— (1991) *The Politics of Truth: From Marx to Foucault*, Cambridge: Polity Press.

Barry, N.P. (1986) *On Classical Liberalism and Libertarianism*, Basingstoke, Macmillan.

—— (1989) *An Introduction to Modern Political Theory*, second edn, Basingstoke, Macmillan.

Barthes, R. (1967a) *(1953)* *Writing Degree Zero*, New York: Hill & Wang.

—— (1967b) *(1964)* *Elements of Semiology*, New York: Hill & Wang.

—— (1973) *(1957)* *Mythologies*, St Albans: Paladin.

—— (1974) *(1970)* *S/Z*, New York: Hill & Wang.

—— (1975) *(1973)* *The Pleasure of the Text*, New York: Hill & Wang.

—— (1977a) *Image, Music, Text*, tr. Stephen Heath, London: Fontana.

—— (1977b) 'Introduction to the Structural Analysis of Narratives', in *Image, Music, Text,* London: Fontana.

—— (1977c) 'The Death of the Author', in *Image, Music, Text*, London: Fontana.

—— (1977d) 'From Work to Text', in *Image, Music, Text*, London: Fontana.

—— (1977e) *(1975)* *Barthes, R. by Barthes, R.*, New York: Hill & Wang.

—— (1978) *(1977)* *A Lover's Discourse: Fragments*, New York: Hill & Wang.

—— (1981) *(1980)* *Camera Lucida: Reflections on Photography*, New York: Hill & Wang.

—— (1987) *(1966)* *Criticism and Truth*, Minneapolis, MN: University of Minnesota Press.

Baudrillard, J. (1983) *Simulations*, tr. Paul Foss, Paul Patton and Philip Beitchman, New York: Semiotext(e).

—— (1988) *Selected Writings*, ed. Mark Poster, Cambridge: Polity Press.

—— (1990a) *Revenge of the Crystal: Selected Writings on the Modern Object and its Destiny, 1968–1983*, London: Pluto Press.

—— (1990b) 'Mass Media Culture', in *Revenge of the Crystal: Selected Writings on the Modern Object and its Destiny, 1968–1983*, London: Pluto Press.

—— (1990c) *Fatal Strategies*, London: Pluto Press.

—— (1991) 'The Reality Gulf', *Guardian*, 11 January.

—— (1993) *Symbolic Exchange and Death*, London: Sage.

—— (2000a) *The Vital Illusion*, New York: Columbia University Press.

—— (2000b) 'Prophylaxis and Virulence', in N. Baddington (ed.), *Posthumanism*, London: Palgrave Macmillan.

Bauman, Z. (1989) *Modernity and the Holocaust*, Cambridge: Polity Press.

Baxandall, M. (1972) *Painting and Experience in Fifteenth Century Italy: A Primer in the History of Pictorial Style*, Oxford: Clarendon Press.

—— (1980) *The Limewood Sculptors of Renaissance Germany*, New Haven, CT: Yale University Press.

Bazin, A. (1967) *What is Cinema?*, Berkeley, CA: University of California Press.

Beck, U. (1992) *Risk Society: Towards a New Modernity*, London: Sage.

—— (1999a) *Globalisation*, Cambridge: Polity Press.

—— (1999b) *World Risk Society*, Cambridge: Polity Press.

Beck, U., Giddens, A. and Lash, S. (1994) *Reflexive Modernization*, Cambridge: Polity Press.

Becker, H. (1961) *Boys in White: Student Culture in Medical School*, Chicago, IL: University of Chicago Press.

—— (1963) *Outsiders: Studies in the Sociology of Deviance*, New York: Free Press.

—— (1982) *Art Worlds*, Berkeley, CA: University of California Press.

Becker, H., Geer, B. and Hughes, E.C. (1968) *Making the Grade: The Academic Side of College Life*, New York: Wiley.

Beetham, D. (1996) *Bureaucracy*, second edn, Buckingham: Open University Press.

Behr, S., Fanning, D. and Jarman, D. (eds) (1993) *Expressionism Reassessed*, Manchester: Manchester University Press.

Bell, D. (1960) *The End of Ideology*, Glencoe, IL: Free Press.

—— (1973) *The Coming of Post-Industrial Society: A Venture in Social Forecasting*, New York: Basic Books.

—— (1976) *The Cultural Contradictions of Capitalism*, London: Heinemann.

—— (1990) *Husserl*, London: Routledge.

—— (1993) *Communitarianism and its Critics*, Oxford: Clarendon Press.

Bell D. and Kennedy, B.M. (eds) (2000) *The Cybercultures Reader*, London: Routledge.

Bell, M. (1988) *F.R. Leavis*, London: Routledge.

Belsey, C. (1980) *Critical Practice*, London: Methuen.

Bendix, R. (1960) *Max Weber: An Intellectual Portrait*, Garden City, NY: Doubleday.

Benedict, R. (1935) *Patterns of Culture*, London: Routledge & Kegan Paul.

—— (1989) *Chrysanthemum and the Sword*, New York: Houghton Mifflin.

Benjamin, W. (1970a) *Illuminations*, ed. H. Arendt, London: Jonathan Cape.

—— (1970b) *(1936)* 'The Work of Art in the Age of Mechanical Reproduction', in *Illuminations*, London: Jonathan Cape.

—— (1970c) *(1940)* 'Theses on the Philosophy of History', in *Illuminations*, London: Jonathan Cape.

—— (1973a) *Charles Baudelaire: A Lyric Poet in the Era of High Capitalism*, London: New Left Books.

—— (1973b) *Understanding Brecht*, London: New Left Books.

—— (1977) *(1928) The Origin of German Tragic Drama*, tr. John Osborne, London: New Left Books.

—— (1978) *(1937)* 'Author as Producer', in A. Arato and E. Gebhardt (eds), *The Essential Frankfurt School Reader*, Oxford: Blackwell.

—— (1979) *One-Way Street and Other Writings*, London: New Left Books.

—— (1996) *Selected Writings: Volume 1, 1913–1926*, Cambridge, MA: Belknap Press.

—— (1999a) *Selected Writings: Volume 2, 1927–1934*, Cambridge, MA: Belknap Press.

—— (1999b) *The Arcades Project*, Cambridge, MA: Belknap Press.

—— (2002) *Selected Writings: Volume 3, 1935–1938*, Cambridge, MA: Belknap Press.

—— (2003) *Selected Writings: Volume 4, 1938–1940*, Cambridge, MA: Belknap Press.

Bennett, J. (1966) *Kant's Analytic*, Cambridge: Cambridge University Press.

—— (1974) *Kant's Dialectic*, London: Cambridge University Press.

Bennett, T., Martin, G., Mercer, C. and Woollacott, J. (eds) (1981) *Culture, Ideology and Social Process*, London: Batsford in association with the Open University Press.

Bennington, G. (1988) *Lyotard: Writing the Event*, New York: Columbia University Press.

Berger, J. (1972) *Ways of Seeing*, Harmondsworth: Penguin.

Berger, P.L. (1963) *Invitation to Sociology*, Harmondsworth: Penguin.

Berger, P.L. and Luckmann, T. (1961) *The Social Construction of Reality: A Treatise in the Sociology of Knowledge*, London: Allen Lane.

Berkeley, G. (1975) *Philosophical Works: Including the Works on Vision*, London: Dent.

Berki, R.N. (1975) *Socialism*, London: Dent.

Berlin, E.A. (1980) *Ragtime: A Musical and Cultural History*, London: University of California Press.

Berlin, I. (ed.) (1979) *The Age of Enlightenment*, Oxford: Oxford University Press.

Berliner, P.F. (1994) *Thinking in Jazz: The Infinite Art of Improvisation*, Chicago, IL: University of Chicago Press.

Berman, M. (1983) *All This is Solid Melts into Air: The Experience of Modernity*, London: Verso.

Bernstein, B. (1977) *Class, Codes and Control*, volume 1, *Theoretical Studies Towards a Sociology of Language*, London: Routledge & Kegan Paul.

—— (1996) *Pedagogy, Symbolic Control and Identity: Theory, Research, Critique*, London: Taylor & Francis.

Bernstein, R.J. (1983) *Beyond Objectivism and Relativism: Science, Hermeneutics, and Praxis*, Oxford: Blackwell.

Bhabha, H.K. (ed.) (1990) *Nation and Narration*, London: Routledge.

Bhaskar, R. (1975) *A Realist Theory of Science*, Hemel Hempstead: Harvester.

Biddle, B.J. (1979) *Role Theory: Expectations, Identities and Behaviours*, New York: Academic Press.

Bilton, T., Jones, P., Skinner, D., Stansworth, M. and Webster, A. (1996) *Introductory Sociology*, third edn, Basingstoke: Macmillan.

Binford, S.R. and Binford, L.R. (1968) *New Perspectives in Archaeology*, Chicago, IL: Aldine Press.

Bin Laden, O. (1998) 'Jihad Against Jews and Crusaders', World Islamic Front Statement, 23 February 1998 (www.fas.org/irp/world/para/docs/980223-fatwa.htm).

Biriotti, M. and Miller, N. (eds) (1993) *What is an Author?*, Manchester: Manchester University Press.

Black, M. (1979) 'More about Metaphor', in A. Ortony (ed.), *Metaphor and Thought*, Cambridge: Cambridge University Press.

Blair, T. (2006) 'Valedictory Address to the Labour Party Conference Kegan Paul.

Block, N., Flanagan, O. and Guzeldere, G. (eds) (1997) *The Nature of Consciousness: Philosophical Debates*, Cambridge, MA: MIT Press.

Blumer, H. (1969) *Symbolic Interactionism: Perspective and Method*, Englewood Cliffs, NJ: Prentice-Hall.

Blumer, M. (1984) *The Chicago School of Sociology: Institutionalization, Diversity, and the Rise of Sociological Research*, Chicago, IL: University of Chicago Press.

Bocock, R. (1986) *Hegemony*, London: Tavistock.

—— (1993) *Consumption*, London: Routledge.

Bocock, R., Hamilton, P., Thompson, K. and Walton, A. (eds) (1980) *An Introduction to Sociology*, London: Fontana in association with the Open University Press.

Bogue, R. (1989) *Deleuze and Guattari*, London and New York: Routledge.

Bolton, R. (ed.) (1989) *The Contest of Meaning: Critical Histories of Photography*, Cambridge, MA: MIT Press.

Bookchin, M. (1980) *Towards an Ecological Society*, Montreal: Black Rose Books.

Boorse, C. (1975) 'On the Distinction between Disease and Illness', *Philosophy and Public Affairs*, 5: 49–68.

—— (1977) 'Health as a Theoretical Concept', *Philosophy of Science*, 44: 542–73.

Borowski, T. (1967) *(1959) This Way for the Gas Ladies and Gentlemen*, tr. B. Vedder, New York: Penguin.

Borradori, G. (ed.) (2003) *Philosophy in a Time of Terror*, Chicago, IL: University of Chicago Press.

Bostdorff, D.M. (2003) 'George W. Bush's Post-September 11 Rhetoric of Covenant Renewal: Upholding the Faith of the Greatest Generation', *Quarterly Journal of Speech*, vol. 89, no. 4.

Bostrom, N. (2005a) 'A History of Transhumanist Thought', *Journal of Evolution and Technology*, 14 (http://jetpress.org/volume14/freitas.html).

—— (2005b) 'In Defence of Posthuman Dignity', *Bioethics*, 19 (3), 202–14.

Bottomore, T. (ed.) (1983) *A Dictionary of Marxist Thought*, Oxford: Blackwell.

—— (1985) *Theories of Modern Capitalism*, London: Routledge.

—— (1993) *Elites and Society*, second edn, London: Routledge.

Boucher, D. and Kelly, P. (eds) (1994) *The Social Contract from Hobbes to Rawls*, London: Routledge.

Boundas, C.V and Olkowski, D. (eds) (1994) *Gilles Deleuze and the Theater of Philosophy*, New York: Routledge.

Bourdieu, P. (1973) 'Cultural Reproduction and Social Reproduction', in R. Brown (ed.), *Knowledge, Education and Cultural Change*, London: Tavistock.

—— (1984) *(1979) Distinction: A Social Critique of the Judgement of Taste*, London: Routledge & Kegan Paul.

—— (1993) *The Field of Cultural Production*, Cambridge: Polity Press.

Bowie, A. (1990) *Aesthetics and Subjectivity: From Kant to Nietzsche*, Manchester: Manchester University Press.

Bowles, S. and Gintis, H. (1976) *Schooling in Capitalist America*, New York: Basic Books.

Boyer, R. and Durand, J.-P. (1997) *After Fordism*, tr. Sybil Hyacinth Mair, Basingstoke: Macmillan.

Bradbury, M. and McFarlane, J. (eds) (1976) *Modernism: 1890–1930*, Harmondsworth: Penguin.

Brasher, B.E. (ed.) (2001) *Encyclopedia of Fundamentalism*, London: Routledge.

Braudel, F. (1972) *(1949) The Mediterranean and the Mediterranean World in the Age of Philip II*, London: Collins.

—— (1958) 'History and the Social Sciences', in *On History*, London: Weidenfeld & Nicolson.

Braverman, H. (1974) *Labour and Monopoly Capitalism: The Degradation of Work in the Twentieth Century*, New York: Monthly Review Press.

Breckenridge, C. and Van der Veer, P. (eds) (1993) *Orientalism and the Post-colonial Predicament*, Philadelphia, PA: University of Philadelphia Press.

Brett, P., Thomas, G. and Wood, E. (eds) (1994) *Queering the Pitch: The New Gay and Lesbian Musicology*, New York: Routledge.

Breuer, J. and Freud, S. (1974) *(1895) Studies on Hysteria*, ed. A. Richards, tr. James Strachey, Harmondsworth, Pelican Books.

Bronner, S.E. and Kellner, D.M. (eds) (1989) *Critical Theory and Society: A Reader*, London: Routledge.

Brooks, C. (1938) *Understanding Poetry: An Anthology for College Students*, New York: Henry Holt.

—— (1949) *The Well Wrought Urn: Studies in the Structure of Poetry*, London: Dennis Dobson.

Brubaker, R. (1984) *The Limits of Rationality: An Essay on the Social and Moral Thought of Max Weber*, London: Allen & Unwin.

Bruce, S. (2000) *Fundamentalism*, Cambridge: Polity Press.

Brundtland, G.H. *et al.* (1987) *Our Common Future: World Commission on Environment and Development*, Oxford: Oxford University Press.

Buck-Morss, S. (1991) *The Dialectics of Seeing: Walter Benjamin and the Arcades Project*, Cambridge, MA: MIT Press.

Bukofzer, M. (1939) 'Allegory in Baroque Music', *Journal of the Warburg Institute*, 3:1–21.

Bullough, E. (1957) *Aesthetics: Lectures and Essays*, Palo Alto, CA: Stanford University Press.

Bourdieu, P. (1977) *Reproduction in Education, Society and Culture*, trans Richard Nice, London: Sage Publications.

Bürger, P. (1984) *Theory of the Avant-Garde*, Minneapolis, MN: University of Minnesota Press.

Burke, E. (1982) *(1790) Reflections on the Revolution in France*, Harmondsworth: Penguin.

Burke, J. and Moore, S. (1979) 'Reification and Commodity Fetishism Revisited', *Canadian Journal of Political and Social Theory*, 3(1): 71–86.

Burke, P. (1990) *The French Historical Revolution: The Annales School, 1929–1989*, Cambridge: Polity Press.

Burke, S. (1992) *The Death and Return of the Author: Criticism and Subjectivity in Barthes, Foucault and Derrida*, Edinburgh: Edinburgh University Press.

Burley, J and Harris, J. (2002) *A Companion to Genethics*, Oxford: Blackwell.

Burns, T. (1992) *Erving Goffman*, London: Routledge.

Bury, M. and Gabe, J. (eds) (2006) *The Sociology of Health and Illness: a Reader*, second edn, London: Routledge.

Bush, G.W. (2001a) 'Statement by the President in His Address to the Nation, 11 September 2001' (www.whitehouse.gov/news/releases/2001/09/20010911–16.html).

—— (2001b) 'Address to a Joint Session of Congress and the American People, 20 September 2001' (www.whitehouse.gov/news/releases/2001/09/20010920–8.html).

Butler, J. (1990) *Gender Trouble: Feminism and the Subversion of Identity*, London: Routledge.

Cage, J.M. (1966) *Silence*, Cambridge, MA: MIT Press.

Cahn, S. (1994) *Coming on Strong: Gender and Sexuality in Twentieth Century Women's Sport*, New York: Free Press.

Callinicos, A. (1976) *Althusser's Marxism*, London: Pluto Press.

—— (1983) *Marxism and Philosophy*, Oxford: Clarendon Press.

Camus, A. (1990) *(1942) The Myth of Sisyphus*, tr. Justin O'Brien, Harmondsworth: Penguin.

Canguilhem, G. (1978) *(1966) On the Normal and the Pathological*, Dordrecht: Reidal.

Carr, E.H. (1987) *(1961) What is History?*, Harmondsworth: Penguin.

Carson, R. (1972) *(1962) Silent Spring*, Harmondsworth: Penguin.

Carver, T. (1975) 'Marx's Commodity Fetishism', *Inquiry*, 18(1): 39–63.

—— (ed.) (1991) *The Cambridge Companion to Marx*, Cambridge: Cambridge University Press.

Castells, M. (1989) *The Informational City*, Oxford: Blackwell.

Cavell, S. (1971) *The World Viewed: Reflections on the Ontology of Film*, New York: Viking.

Chadwick, R.F. and Cazeux, C. (eds) (1992) *Immanuel Kant: Critical Assessments*, London and New York: Routledge.

Chalmers, A.F. (1982) *What is This Thing Called Science?*, second edn, Milton Keynes: Open University Press.

—— (1990) *Science and its Fabrication*, Milton Keynes: Open University Press.

Chancy, D. (1996) *Lifestyles*, London: Routledge.

Charon, R. (2004) 'Narrative and Medicine', *New England Journal of Medicine*, 350: 862–4.

Childe V.G. (1927) *The Dawn of European Civilization*, London: Kegan Paul.

—— (1956) *(1936) Man Makes Himself*, third edn, London: Watts & Co.

—— (1964) *(1941) What Happened in History?* Harmondsworth: Penguin.

Chipp, H.B. (1968) *Theories of Modern Art: A Source Book by Artists and Critics*, Berkeley, CA: University of California Press.

Chomsky, N. (1957) *Syntactic Structures*, The Hague: Mouton.

—— (1966) *Cartesian Linguistics*, New York: Harper & Row.

—— (1972) *Studies on Semantics and Generative Grammar*, The Hague: Mouton.

—— (1973) *For Reasons of State*, New York: Pantheon.

—— (1978) *Language and Politics*, Montreal: Black Rose Books.

—— (2002) *9/11*, New York: Seven Stories Press.

Christie, R. and Jahoda, M. (eds) (1954) *Studies in the Scope and Method of 'The Authoritarian Personality'*, Glencoe, IL: Free Press.

Churchland, P. (1988) *Matter and Consciousness: A Contemporary Introduction to the Philosophy of Mind*, Cambridge, MA: MIT Press.

—— (1995) *The Engine of Reason, the Seat of the Soul: A Philosophical Journey into the Brain*, Cambridge, MA: MIT Press.

Cixous, H. (1981) *(1975)* 'The Laugh of the Medusa', in E. Marks and I. de Courtivron (eds), *New French Feminisms*, Brighton: Harvester.

—— (1987) *The Newly Born Woman*, Manchester: Manchester University Press.

Clark, D.L. (1968) *Analytical Archaeology*, London: Methuen.

Clark, J.J. (1997) *Oriental Enlightenment: The Encounter Between Asian and Western Thought*, London: Routledge.

Clark, K. and Holquist, M. (1984) *Mikhail Bakhtin*, Cambridge, MA: Belknap Press of Harvard University Press.

Clark, M. (1988) *Jacques Lacan: An Annotated Bibliography*, New York: Garland Publishers.

Clark, T.J. (1973) *The Absolute Bourgeois: Artists and Politics in France 1848–1851*, London: Thames & Hudson.

Clarke, G. (1982) *Defending Ski-Jumpers: A Critique of Theories of Youth Sub-Cultures*, Stencilled Paper 71, Centre for Contemporary Cultural Studies, Birmingham University.

Clarke, K. (1956) *The Nude*, New York: Pantheon.

Clarke, S. (1981) *The Foundations of Structuralism: A Critique of Lévi-Strauss and the Structuralist Movement*, Brighton: Harvester.

Clement, C. (1983) *(1981) The Lives and Legends of Jacques Lacan*, tr. Arthur Goldhammer, New York: Columbia University Press.

Coakley, J. and Dunning, E. (eds) (2002) *Handbook of Sports Studies*, London: Sage.

Cobb, J. (1977) *Process Theology: An Introductory Exposition*, Belfast: Christian Journals.

Cohen, G.A. (1978) *Karl Marx's Theory of History*, Oxford: Clarendon Press.

Cohen, I.J. (1989) *Structuration Theory: Anthony Giddens and the Constitution of Social Life*, London: Macmillan.

Cohen, P. (1980) 'Subcultural Conflict and Working-Class Community', in S. Hall, D. Hobson, A. Lowe and P. Willis (eds), *Culture, Media, Language*, London: Hutchinson.

Cohen, S. (1980) *Folk Devils and Moral Panics*, second edn, Oxford: Martin Robertson.

Collier, G. (1977) *Jazz*, Cambridge: Cambridge University Press.

Collini, S. (1988) *Arnold*, Oxford and New York: Oxford University Press.

Collins, R. (1975) *Conflict Sociology: Toward an Explanatory Science*, New York: Academic Press.

Condit, C. (1999) *The Meanings of the Gene. Public Debates about Human Heredity*, Madison, WI: University of Wisconsin Press.

Connerton, P. (ed.) (1976) *Critical Sociology*, Harmondsworth: Penguin.

Conrad, Joseph (2000) (*1902*) *Heart of Darkness*, London: Penguin.

Cook, D. (1996) *The Culture Industry Revisited: Theodor W. Adorno on Mass Culture*, Lanham, MD: Rowman & Littlefield.

Cooke, A. (1994) *The Economies of Leisure and Sport*, London: Routledge.

Cooke, B. and Turner, F. (1999) *Biopoetics: Evolutionary Explorations in the Arts*, Lexington, KY: Icus Books.

Cooper, D.E. (1986) *Metaphor*, Oxford: Blackwell.

—— (1992) *A Companion to Aesthetics*, Oxford: Blackwell.

—— (1997) *Aesthetics: The Classic Readings*, Oxford: Blackwell.

Cornforth, M. (1971) *Dialectical Materialism*, London: Lawrence & Wishart.

Corrigan, P. (1997) *The Sociology of Consumption*, London: Sage.

Coser, L.A. (1956) *The Functions of Social Conflict*, New York: Free Press.

Crane, T. (1995) *The Mechanical Mind: A Philosophical Introduction to Minds, Machines and Mental Representation*, London: Penguin.

Cranston, M. (1994) *The Romantic Movement*, Oxford: Blackwell.

Crothers, C. (1996) *Social Structure*, London: Routledge.

Crouch, D. and Ward, C. (1997) *The Allotment: Its Landscape and Culture*, Nottingham: Five Leaves.

Crozier, B. (1987) *Socialism: Dream and Reality*, London: Sherwood Press.

Cudd, A.E. and Andreasen, R.O. (eds) (2005) *Feminist Theory: A Philosophical Anthology*, Oxford: Blackwell.

Culler, J. (1975) *Structuralist Poetics: Structuralism, Linguistics and the Study of Literature*, London: Routledge & Kegan Paul.

—— (1983) *Roland Barthes*, New York: Oxford University Press.

—— (1986) *Ferdinand de Saussure*, Ithaca, NY: Cornell University Press.

Cunningham-Wood, J. (ed.) (1988) *Karl Marx's Economics: Critical Assessments*, volume 2, *Marx's Capital*, London: Croom Helm.

Cupitt, D. (1979) *Explorations in Theology*, London: SCM Press.

—— (1988) *The New Christian Ethics*, London: SCM Press.

Curtis, W.J.R. (1992) *Le Corbusier: Ideas and Forms*, London: Phaidon Press.

Cutler, A., Hindess, B., Hirst, P.Q. and Hussain, A. (1977) *Marx's Capital and Capitalism Today*, Volume 1, London: Routledge & Kegan Paul.

Dahl, R.A. (1956) *A Preface to Democratic Theory*, Chicago, IL: University of Chicago Press.

Dahrendorf, R. (1979) *Life Chances*, London: Weidenfeld & Nicolson.

Dallmayr, F.R. (1981) *Twilight of Subjectivity: Contributions to a Post-Individualist Theory of Politics*, Amherst, MA: University of Massachusetts Press.

Dancy, J. (1985) *An Introduction to Contemporary Epistemology*, Oxford: Blackwell.

Dancy, J. and Sosa, E. (1992) *A Companion to Epistemology*, Oxford: Blackwell.

Dant, T. (1996) 'Fetishism and the Social Value of Objects', *Sociological Review*, 44(3): 495–516.

Danto, A.C. (1964) 'The Artworld', *Journal of Philosophy*, 61:571–84.

—— (1981) *The Transfiguration of the Commonplace*, Cambridge, MA: Harvard University Press.

Darwin, C. (1976) *(1859)* *The Origin of Species*, ed. J.W. Burrow, Harmondsworth: Penguin.

David, H. (1997) *On Queer Street: A Social History of British Homosexuality 1895–1995*, London: HarperCollins.

Davidson, D. (1984a) *(1977)* *Inquiries into Truth and Interpretation*, Oxford: Clarendon Press.

—— (1984b) *(1973)* 'Radical Interpretation', in *Inquiries into Truth and Interpretation*, Oxford: Clarendon Press.

—— (1984c) 'Belief as the Basis of Meaning', in *Inquiries into Truth and Interpretation*, Oxford: Clarendon Press.

—— (1991) 'Truth and Meaning', in *Inquiries into Truth and Interpretation*, Oxford: Clarendon Press.

—— (1993) 'A Coherence Theory of Truth and Knowledge', in E. Lepore (ed.), *Truth and Interpretation*, Oxford: Blackwell, pp. 307–19.

Davies, T. (1997) *Humanism*, London and New York: Routledge.

Davis, J.C. (1981) *Utopia and the Ideal Society: A Study of English Utopian Writing, 1516–1700*, Cambridge: Cambridge University Press.

Dawkins, R. (1976) *The Selfish Gene*, Oxford: Oxford University Press.

—— (1991) *The Blind Watchmaker*, London: Penguin.

Day, G. (1996) *Re-reading Leavis: Culture and Literary Criticism*, Basingstoke: Macmillan.

De Certeau, M. (1984) *The Practice of Everyday Life*, Berkeley, CA: University of California Press.

Delbo, Charlotte (1995) *(1965)* *Auschwitz and After*, tr. R. Lamont, New Haven, CT: Yale University Press.

Deleuze, G. (1983) *(1962)* *Nietzsche and Philosophy*, tr. Hugh Tomlinson, London: Athlone Press.

—— (1990a) *(1969)* *The Logic of Sense*, tr. Mark Lester with Charles Stivale, London: Athlone Press.

—— (1990b) 'The Simulacrum and Ancient Philosophy', in *The Logic of Sense*, London: Athlone Press.

—— (1991) *Cinema*, 2 volumes, Minneapolis, MN: University of Minnesota Press.

Deleuze, G. and Guattari, F. (1977) *(1972)* *Anti-Oedipus: Capitalism and Schizophrenia*, tr. Robert Hurley, Mark Seem and Helen R. Lane, New York: Viking Press.

—— (1987) *(1980)* *A Thousand Plateaus: Capitalism and Schizophrenia*, tr. Brian Massumi, Minneapolis, MN: University of Minnesota Press.

De Man, P. (1979) *Allegories of Reading: Figural Language in Rousseau, Nietzsche, Rilke, and Proust,* New Haven, CT: Yale University Press.

—— (1989) *Blindness and Insight: Essays on the Rhetoric of Contemporary Criticism,* London: Routledge.

Dennett, D. (1996) *Darwin's Dangerous Idea,* London: Penguin.

Denzin, N.K. (1992) *Symbolic Interactionism and Cultural Studies,* Oxford: Blackwell.

Derrida, J. (1973) *'Speech and Phenomena' and Other Essays on Husserl's Theory of Signs,* tr. David B. Allison, Evanston, IL: Northwestern University Press.

—— (1976) *(1967) Of Grammatology,* tr. G. Spivak, Baltimore, MD: Johns Hopkins University Press.

—— (1978) *(1967) Writing and Difference,* tr. Alan Bass, London: Routledge & Kegan Paul.

—— (1979) *Spurs: Nietzsche's Styles,* tr. Barbara Harlow, Chicago, IL: University of Chicago Press.

—— (1981) *Dissemination,* tr. Barbara Johnson, Chicago, IL: University of Chicago Press.

—— (1982) *Margins of Philosophy,* tr. Alan Bass, Chicago, IL: University of Chicago Press.

—— (1987) *The Truth in Painting,* Chicago, IL: University of Chicago Press.

—— (1988a) *The Ear of the Other: Otobiography, Transference, Translation Texts and Discussions with Jacques Derrida,* ed. C. McDonald, tr. Peggy Kamuf, Lincoln, NE, and London: University of Nebraska Press.

—— (1988b) *Limited Inc.,* Evanston, IL: Northwestern University Press.

—— (1992) *Given Time. I. Counterfeit Money,* tr. Peggy Kamuf, Chicago, IL and London: University of Chicago Press.

—— (1994) *Specters of Marx: The State of Debt, the Work of Mourning, and the New International,* tr. Peggy Kamuf, New York and London: Routledge.

—— (1996) *Archive Fever: A Freudian Impression,* tr. Eric Prenowitz, Chicago, IL, and London: University of Chicago Press.

—— (2002) 'The Aforementioned So-called Human Genome', ed. E. Rottenberg, in *Negotiations,* Stanford, CA: Stanford University Press.

Descartes, R. (1968) *(1637 and 1641) Discourse on Method and the Meditations,* Harmondsworth: Penguin.

—— (1986) *(1641) Meditations on First Philosophy,* tr. J. Cottingham, Cambridge: Cambridge University Press.

Devitt, M. and Sterelny, K. (1987) *Language and Reality,* Oxford: Blackwell.

Dewey, J. (1974) *John Dewey on Education: Selected Writings,* ed. R.D. Archambault, Chicago, IL: Chicago University Press.

——, (1997) *(1910) The Influence of Darwin in Philosophy,* New York: Prometheus Books.

Dews, P. (1988) 'Nietzsche and the Critique of *Ursprungsphilosophie*', in D.F. Krell and D. Wood (eds), *Exceedingly Nietzsche,* London: Routledge.

Dickie, G. (1974) *Art and the Aesthetic: An Institutional Analysis,* Ithaca, NY: Cornell University Press.

—— (1984) *The Art Circle: A Theory of Art,* New York: Havens.

Dijck, Hose van (1998) *Imagenation. Popular Images of Genetics,* London: Macmillan.

Diprose, R. (1994) *The Bodies of Women: Ethics, Embodiment and Sexual Difference*, London: Routledge.

Doty, A. (ed.) (1993) *Making Things Perfectly Queer: Interpreting Mass Culture*, Minneapolis, MN: University of Minnesota Press.

Douglas, M. (1969) *Purity and Danger*, London: Routledge & Kegan Paul.

—— (1973) *Natural Symbols: Explorations in Cosmology*, Harmondsworth: Penguin.

—— (1985) *Risk Acceptability According to the Social Sciences*, New York: Sage.

—— (1992) *Risk and Blame*. London: Routledge.

Douglas, M. and Wildavsky, A. (1982) *Risk and Culture*. Berkeley, CA: University of California Press.

Downes, D. and Rock, P. (1982) *Understanding Deviance*, Oxford: Clarendon Press.

Draper, H. (1987) *The 'Dictatorship of the Proletariat' from Marx to Lenin*, New York: Monthly Review Press.

Dreyfus, H. and Hall, H. (eds) (1992) *Heidegger: A Critical Reader*, Oxford: Blackwell.

Dror, Y. (1983) *(1968) Public Policymaking Reexamined*, New Brunswick, NJ: Transaction Books

Du Gay, P., Hall, S., Janes, L., Mackay, H. and Negus, K. (1997) *Doing Cultural Studies: The Story of the Sony Walkman*, London: Sage.

Dube, W.D. (ed.) (1997) *German Expressionism: Art and Society 1909–1923*, London: Thames & Hudson.

Duhem, P. (1962) *The Aim and Structure of Physical Theory*, tr. Philip P. Wiener, New York: Atheneum.

Dummett, M. (1973) *Frege: Philosophy of Language*, London: Duckworth.

Dunning, E. (1999) *Sport Matters: Sociological Studies of Sport, Violence and Civilization*, London: Routledge.

Dunning, E. and Rojek, C. (eds) (1992) *Sport and Leisure in the Civilising Process: Critique and Counter-critique*, Basingstoke: Macmillan.

Dunning, E. and Sheard, K. (1979) *Barbarians, Gentlemen and Players: A Sociological Study of the Development of Rugby Football*, Oxford: Martin Robertson.

Durkheim, E. (1952) *(1897) Suicide: A Study in Sociology*, tr. John A. Spaulding and George Simpson, London: Routledge & Kegan Paul.

—— (1975) *Emile Durkheim on Religion*, ed. W.S.F. Pickering, London: Routledge & Kegan Paul.

—— (1976) *(1912) The Elementary Forms of the Religious Life: A Study in Religious Sociology*, London: Allen & Unwin.

—— (1982) *(1895) The Rules of Sociological Method*, London: Macmillan.

—— (1984) *(1893) The Division of Labour in Society*, tr. W.D. Halls, Basingstoke: Macmillan.

Durkheim, E. and Mauss, M. (1963) *(1903) Primitive Classification*, Chicago, IL: University of Chicago Press.

Dworkin, R. (2005) 'Terror and the Attack on Civil Liberties', in *The Philosophical Challenge of September 11*, ed. T. Rockmore, J. Margolis and A.T. Marsoonian, Oxford: Blackwell.

Dyer, R. (1979) *Stars*, London: British Film Institute.

—— (1985) 'Entertainment and Utopia', in B. Nichols (ed.), *Movies and Methods*, volume 2, Berkeley, Los Angeles, CA and London: University of California Press.

Eagleton, T. (1983) *Literary Theory: An Introduction*, Oxford: Blackwell.

—— (1984) *The Function of Criticism*, London: Verso.

—— (ed.) (1989) *Raymond Williams: Critical Perspectives*, Cambridge: Polity Press.

—— (1991) *Ideology: An Introduction*, London: Verso.

—— (1999) *The Ideology of the Aesthetic*, Oxford: Blackwell.

Eatwell, R. (1996) *Fascism: A History*, London: Vintage.

Eco, U. (1976) *A Theory of Semiotics*, Bloomington, IN: Indiana University Press.

—— (1986) *Faith in Fakes: Travels in Hyperreality*, London: Minerva.

Edgell, S. (1993) *Class*, London: Routledge.

Ehrenberg, J. (1992) *The Dictatorship of the Proletariat: Marxism's Theory of Socialist Democracy*, New York: Routledge.

Elders, F. (ed.) (1974) *Reflexive Water: Basic Concerns of Mankind*, London: Souvenir Press.

Eldridge, J. and Eldridge, L. (1994) *Raymond Williams: Making Connections*, London: Routledge.

Elias, N. (1970) *What is Sociology?*, London: Hutchinson.

Elias, N and Dunning, E. (1986) *Quest for Excitement: Sport and Leisure in the Civilizing Process*, Oxford: Basil Blackwell.

Elkins, J. (2003) *Visual Studies: A Skeptical Introduction*, London: Routledge.

Ellenberger, H. (1970) *The Discovery of the Unconscious: The History and Evolution of Dynamic Psychiatry*, London: Allen Lane, The Penguin Press.

Elshtain, J. (2003) *Just War Against Terrorism*, New York: Basic Books.

Elton, G.R. (1991) *Return to Essentials*, Cambridge: Cambridge University Press.

Empson, William, (1951) *The Structure of Complex Words*, London: Chatto & Windus.

—— (1953) *(1930) Seven Types of Ambiguity*, London: Chatto & Windus.

Engels, F. (1947) *(1876–1878) Anti-Dühring*, Moscow: Progress Publishers.

—— (1973) *(1873–1883) Dialectics of Nature*, tr. C. Dutt, New York: International Publishers.

Erikson, E. (1968) *Identity: Youth and Crisis*, London: Faber & Faber.

Ericson, R. and Haggerty, K. (2002) 'The Policing of Risk', in T. Baker and J. Simons (eds), *Embracing Risk*, Chicago, IL: University of Chicago Press.

Escobar, A. (1994) 'Welcome to Cyberia: Notes towards an Anthropology of Cyberculture', *Current Anthropology*, 35(3): 211–31.

Ettinger, R.C.W. (1972) *Man into Superman: The Startling Potential of Human Evolution–and How to Be Part of It*, New York: St Martin's Press.

Evans, G. (1973) 'The Causal Theory of Names', *Proceedings of the Aristotelian Society*, 47:187–208.

Evans-Pritchard, E.E. (1951) *Kinship and Marriage Among the Nuer*, Oxford: Clarendon Press.

Falk, P. and Campbell, C. (eds) (1997) *The Shopping Experience*, London: Sage.

Fanon, F. (1989) *(1952) Black Skin, White Masks*, tr. Charles Lamm Markmann, New York: Grove Press.

Farrell, F.B. (1994) *Subjectivity, Realism, and Postmodernism: The Recovery of the World*, Cambridge and New York: Cambridge University Press.

Featherstone, M. (ed.) (1990) *Global Culture: Nationalism, Globalisation and Modernity*, London: Sage.

Feldstein, R., Fink, B. and Jaanus, M. (eds) (1995) *Reading Seminar XI: Lacan's Four Fundamental Concepts of Psychoanalysis*, Albany, NY: SUNY Press.

Feyerabend, P. (1975) *Against Method*, London: Verso.

Fine, B. (1977) 'Labelling Theory: An Investigation into the Sociological Critique of Deviance', *Economy and Society*, 6(2): 166–93.

Fink, B. (1995) 'The Real Cause of Repetition', in R. Feldstein, B. Fink and M. Jaanus (eds), *Reading Seminar XI: Lacan's Four Fundamental Concepts of Psychoanalysis*, Albany, NY: SUNY Press.

Finnegan, R. (1989) *Hidden Musicians*, Cambridge: Cambridge University Press.

Fiske, J. (1987) *Television Culture*, London: Methuen.

—— (1989) *Understanding Popular Culture*, Boston, MA: Unwin Hyman.

Fiske, J. and Hartley, J. (1978) *Reading Television*, London: Methuen.

Fleming, R. and Duckworth, W. (eds) (1989) *John Cage at Seventy-Five*, Lewisburg, PA: Bucknell University Press.

Fletcher, J. (1966) *Situational Ethics*, London: SCM Press.

Flynn, R. (2002) 'Clinical Governance and Governmentality', *Health, Risk and Society*, 4(2): 155–73.

FM 2030 (1989) *Are You a Transhuman: Monitoring and Stimulating your Personal Rate of Growth in a Rapidly Changing World*, New York, NY: Warner Books.

Fodor, J. and LePore, E. (1991) *Holism: A Shopper's Guide*, Oxford: Blackwell.

Fontana, B. (1993) *Hegemony and Power*, Minneapolis, MN: University of Minnesota Press.

Forman, J.D. (1973) *Socialism: Its Theoretical Roots and Present Day Development*, New York: New Viewpoints.

Forrester, J. (1990) *The Seductions of Psychoanalysis: Freud, Lacan and Derrida*, Cambridge: Cambridge University Press.

Forte, A. (1973) *The Structure of Atonal Music*, New Haven, CT: Yale University Press.

Foster, G. (1960) *Culture and Conquest*, New York: Wener-Gren Foundation for Anthropological Research.

Foster, S.L. (ed.) (1996) *Corporealities: Dancing Knowledge, Culture and Power*, London: Routledge,

Foucault, M. (1970) *(1966) The Order of Things: An Archaeology of the Human Sciences*, London: Tavistock.

—— (1971) *(1961) Madness and Civilization: A History of Insanity in the Age of Reason*, London: Tavistock.

—— (1972) *(1969) The Archaeology of Knowledge*, tr. A.M. Sheridan Smith, New York: Pantheon Books.

—— (1976) *(1963) The Birth of the Clinic*, London: Tavistock.

—— (1977a) *(1975) Discipline and Punish: The Birth of the Prison*, Harmondsworth: Penguin.

—— (1977b) 'Nietzsche, Genealogy, History', in D.F. Bouchard (ed.), *Language, Counter-Memory, Practice*, Oxford: Blackwell.

—— (1980) *Power-Knowledge: Selected Interviews and Other Writings 1972–1977*, ed. Colin Gordon, Hassocks: Harvester Wheatsheaf.

—— (1981) *(1976) The History of Sexuality*, volume 1, *An Introduction*, Harmondsworth: Penguin.

—— (1991) 'Governmentality', in G. Burchell *et al.* (eds), *The Foucault Effect*, London: Harvester Wheatsheaf.

Foulkes, A.P. (1983) *Literature and Propaganda*, London: Methuen.

Fox, M. (1983) *Original Blessing*, London: Bear/Mountain.

Frank, A.W. (1995) *The Wounded Story Teller*, Chicago, IL: Chicago University Press.

Frankenburg, R. (1957) *Village on the Border*, London: Cohen and West.

Franklin, S. 1993. 'Essentialism, Which Essentialism? Some Implications of Reproductive and Genetic Technoscience', in J. Dececco (ed.), *Issues in Biological Essentialism Versus Social Constructionism in Gay and Lesbian Identities*, London: Harrington Park Press.

—— (1995) 'Science as Culture, Cultures of Science', *Annual Review of Anthropology*, 24: 163–84.

—— (2003) 'Re-thinking Nature-Culture. Anthropology and the New Genetics', *Anthropological Theory*, 3(1): 68.

Frege, G. (1953) *(1884) The Foundations of Arithmetic*, second revised edn, tr. J.L. Austin, Oxford: Blackwell.

—— (1984) *Collected Papers on Mathematics, Logic and Philosophy*, ed. B. McGuinness, Oxford: Clarendon Press.

—— (1993) *(1892)* 'On Sense and Reference', in A.W. Moore (ed.), *Meaning and Reference*, tr. Max Black, Oxford: Blackwell.

Freidson, E. (1970) *The Profession of Medicine: A Study of the Sociology of Applied Knowledge*, New York: Dodd, Mead & Co.

Freud, S. (1908) 'On the Sexual Theories of Children', in *The Standard Edition of the Complete Psychological Works of Sigmund Freud*, Volume 9, tr. J. Strachey, London: Hogarth Press and Institute of Psychoanalysis.

—— (1910) 'A Special Type of Choice of Object Made by Men', in *The Standard Edition of the Complete Psychological Works of Sigmund Freud*, Volume 11, tr. J. Strachey, London: Hogarth Press and Institute of Psychoanalysis.

—— (1924) 'The Dissolution of the Oedipus Complex', in *The Standard Edition of the Complete Psychological Works of Sigmund Freud*, Volume 19, tr. J. Strachey, London: Hogarth Press and Institute of Psychoanalysis.

—— (1955) 'Beyond the Pleasure Principle', in *The Standard Edition of the Complete Psychological Works of Sigmund Freud*, Volume 18, tr. J. Strachey, London: Hogarth Press.

—— (1966) *The Standard Edition of the Complete Psychological Works of Sigmund Freud*, ed. J. Strachey, London: Hogarth Press.

—— (1977) *(1905) On Sexuality: Three Essays on the Theory of Sexuality and Other Works*, ed. A. Richards, tr. James Strachey, London: Penguin.

—— (1979) *(1909)* 'My Views on the Part Played by Sexuality in the Aetiology of the Neuroses', in *On Psychopathology*, ed. A. Richards, tr. James Strachey, Harmondsworth: Pelican Books.

—— (1984) (1920) 'Beyond the Pleasure Principle', in *On Metapsychology*, ed. A. Richards, tr. J. Strachey, London: Penguin.

—— (1991a) *(1900) The Interpretation of Dreams*, ed. A. Richards, tr. James Strachey, London: Penguin.

—— (1991b) *(1915)* 'Instincts and their vicissitudes', in *On Metapsychology: The Theory of Psychoanalysis*, ed. A. Richards, tr. James Strachey, London: Penguin.

—— (2001) *(1919)* 'Lines of Advance in Psycho-Analytic Therapy', in his *An Infantile Neurosis and Other Works*, (The Standard Edition of the Complete Psychological Works of Sigmund Freud, Volume XVII (1917–1919)), London: Vintage.

Fried, M. (1992) *(1965)* 'Three American Painters', in C. Harrison and P. Wood (eds), *Art in Theory 1900–1990: An Anthology of Changing Ideas*, Oxford: Blackwell.

Friedman, M. (1953) *Essays in Positive Economics*, Chicago, IL: University of Chicago Press.

Frisby, D. (1988) *Fragments of Modernity*, Cambridge: Polity Press.

—— (ed.) (1994) *Georg Simmel: Critical Assessments*, London: Routledge.

Frisby, D. and Sayer, D. (1985) *Society*, London: Tavistock Publications.

Frith, S. (1981) *Sound Effects*, New York: Pantheon.

—— (1984) *Sociology of Youth*, County of Lancashire: Causeway Books.

—— (1992) 'The Cultural Study of Popular Music', in L. Grossberg, C. Nelson and S. Frith (eds), *Performing Rites: On the Value of Popular Music*, Oxford: Oxford University Press.

Fukuyama, F. (1992) *The End of History*, London: Hamish Hamilton.

—— (2002) *Our Posthuman Future: Consequences of the Biotechnology Revolution*, London: Profile Books.

Gabbard, K. (ed.) (1995) *Jazz Among the Discourses*, London: Duke University Press.

Gadamer, H.-G. (1975) *(1962) Truth and Method*, tr. Garrett Barden and John Cumming, London: Sheed & Ward.

Gallie, W.B. (1975) *Peirce and Pragmatism*, Westport, CT: Greenwood Press.

Galton, F. (1907) *(1883) Enquiries into Human Faculty and its Development*, New York: Dutton.

Gans, H.J. (1968) 'Urbanism and Suburbanism as Ways of Life', in R. Pahl (ed.), *Readings in Urban Sociology*, Oxford: Pergamon.

Gardiner, M. (1992) *The Dialogics of Critique: M.M. Bakhtin and the Theory of Ideology*, London: Routledge.

Garfinkel, H. (1967) *Studies in Ethnomethodology*, Englewood Cliffs, NJ: Prentice-Hall.

Gay, P. (1984) *The Bourgeois Experience: Victoria to Freud*, Volume 1, *Education of the Senses*, Oxford: Oxford University Press.

—— (1986) *The Bourgeois Experience: Victoria to Freud*, Volume 2, *The Tender Passion*, Oxford: Oxford University Press.

—— (1988a) *The Enlightenment: An Interpretation*, 2 volumes, London: Weidenfeld & Nicolson.

—— (1988b) *Freud: A Life for Our Time*, London: Macmillan.

Geertz, C. (1973) *The Interpretation of Cultures*, New York: Basic Books.

—— (1976) *The Religion of Java*, Chicago, IL: University of Chicago Press.

Gefter, A. (2006) 'This is Your Space', *New Scientist*, 16 September, 46–8.

Gelb, I.J. (1963) *The Study of Writing*, second edn, Chicago, IL: University of Chicago Press.

Gellner, E. (1983) *Nations and Nationalism*, Oxford: Blackwell.

Genette, G. (1980) *Narrative Discourse: An Essay on Method*, Oxford: Blackwell.

Gettier, E.L. (1963) 'Is Justified True Belief Knowledge?', *Analysis*, Vol. 23.

Gibson, W. (1984) *Neuromancer*, London: Grafton.

—— (1986) *Burning Chrome*, London: Gollancz.

Giddens, A. (1973) *The Class Structure of the Advanced Societies*, London: Hutchinson.

—— (1977) *Studies in Social and Political Theory*, London: Hutchinson.

—— (1978) *Durkheim*, London: Fontana.

—— (1979) 'Agency, Structure', in *Central Problems in Social Theory*, London: Macmillan.

—— (1984) *The Constitution of Society: Outline of the Theory of Structuration*, Cambridge: Polity Press.

—— (1990) *The Consequences of Modernity*, Cambridge: Polity Press.

—— (1991) *Modernity and Self-Identity*, Cambridge: Polity Press.

—— (1997) *Sociology*, third edn, Cambridge: Polity Press.

—— (1998) *The Third Way*. Cambridge: Polity Press.

Giddens, A. and Held, D. (eds) (1982) *Classes, Power and Conflict: Classical and Contemporary Debates*, Basingstoke: Macmillan.

Gillian, H., Gillis, S. and Munford, R. (eds) (2004) *Third Wave Feminism: A Critical Exploration*, Basingstoke: Palgrave Macmillan.

Gillies, D. (1993) *Philosophy of Science in the Twentieth Century: Four Central Themes*, Oxford: Blackwell.

Gilligan, C. (1982) *In a Different Voice: Psychological Theory and Women's Development*, Cambridge, MA: Harvard University Press.

Gillis, J.R. (1974) *Youth and History*, New York: Academic Press.

Gilloch, G. (1996) *Myth and Metropolis: Walter Benjamin and the City*, Cambridge: Polity Press.

Giner, S. (1976) *Mass Society*, London: Martin Robertson.

Giroux, H. (1983) *Theory and Resistance in Education*, London: Heinemann.

Giulianotti, R. (2005) *Sport: A Critical Sociology*, Oxford: Polity.

Gruneau, R. (1983) *Class, Sports, and Social Development*, Amherst, MA: University of Massachusetts Press.

Gjertsen, D. (1989) *Science and Philosophy: Past and Present*, Harmondsworth: Penguin.

Glasgow University Media Group (1976) *Bad News*, London: Routledge & Kegan Paul.

Glover, J. (1990a) *Causing Death and Saving Lives*, Harmondsworth: Penguin.

Glover, J. (ed.) (1990b) *Utilitarianism and its Critics*, New York and London: Macmillan.

Goffman, E. (1956) 'Embarrassment and Social Organization', *American Journal of Sociology*, 62: 264–71.

—— (1959) *The Presentation of Self in Everyday Life*, Harmondsworth: Penguin.

—— (1961) *Asylums: Essays on the Social Situation of Mental Patients and Other Inmates*, New York: Doubleday.

—— (1963) *Stigma: Notes on the Management of Spoiled Identity*, New York: Prentice Hall.

—— (1974) *Frame Analysis*, New York: Harper & Row.

Golding, P. and Murdock, G. (1991) 'Culture, Communications and Political Economy', in J. Curran and M. Gurevitch (eds), *Mass Media and Society*, London: Arnold.

Goldman, A. (1986) *Epistemology and Cognition*, Cambridge, MA: Harvard University Press.

Goodman, N. (1976) *Languages of Art*, second edn, Indianapolis, IN: Hackett.

—— (1978) *Ways of Worldmaking*, Indianapolis, IN: Hackett.

Goodwin, R. (2006) *What's Wrong with Terrorism?*, Cambridge: Polity Press.

Gorz, A. (ed.) (1973) *The Division of Labour: The Labour Process and Class Struggle in Modern Capitalism*, Hassocks: Harvester.

Gorz, A. (1980) *Ecology as Politics*, London: Pluto.

Gould, S.J. (1991) *Wonderful Life*, London: Penguin.

—— (1980) *Ever Since Darwin*, Harmondsworth: Penguin.

Goux, J.-J. (1993) *Oedipus, Philosopher*, tr. Catharine Porter, Stanford, CA: Stanford University Press.

Gove, W. (1980) *The Labelling of Deviance*, Beverly Hills, CA: Sage.

Graham, G. (1997) *Philosophy of the Arts: An Introduction to Aesthetics*, London: Routledge.

—— (2002) *Genes: A Philosophical Inquiry*, London: Routledge.

Gramsci, A. (1971) *(1929–1935) Selections from Prison Notebooks*, London: Lawrence & Wishart.

Grant, R.W. (1987) *John Locke's Liberalism*, Chicago, IL: University of Chicago Press.

Gravett, P. (2006) *Great British Comics*, London: Aurum Press.

Gray, J. (1990) *Liberalisms: Essays in Political Philosophy*, London: Routledge.

Gray, R.M. (1996) *Archetypal Explorations: Towards an Archetypal Sociology*, London: Routledge.

Grayling, A.C. (1988) *Wittgenstein*, Oxford: Oxford University Press.

Green, D. and Shapiro, I. (1994) *Pathologies of Rational Choice Theory*, New Haven, CT: Yale University Press.

Greenberg, C. (1992) *(1961)* 'Modernist Painting', in C. Harrison and P. Wood (eds), *Art in Theory 1900–1990: An Anthology of Changing Ideas*, Oxford: Blackwell.

Greenblatt, S. (1980) *The Forms of Power and the Power of Forms in the Renaissance*, Norman, OK: University of Oklahoma Press.

Grossberg, L., Cary, N. and Treichler, P.A. (eds) (1992) *Cultural Studies*, New York: Routledge.

Grossmann, R. (1992) *The Existence of the World: An Introduction to Ontology*, London: Routledge.

Grosz, E. (1989) *Sexual Subversions. Three French Feminists: Julia Kristeva, Luce Irigaray, Michele Le Doeuff*, Sydney: Allen & Unwin.

—— (1994) *Volatile Bodies: Toward a Corporeal Feminism*, Bloomington and Indianapolis, IN: Indiana University Press.

Grunbaum, A. (1984) *The Foundations of Psychoanalysis: A Philosophical Critique*, Berkeley, CA: University of California Press.

Gueguen, P.-G. (1995) 'Transference as Deception', in R. Feldstein *et al.* (eds), *Reading Seminar XI: Lacan's Four Fundamental Concepts of Psychoanalysis*, Albany, NY: SUNY Press.

Gutman, Y. and Berenbaum, M. (eds) (1994) *Anatomy of the Auschwitz Death Camp*, Bloomington and Indianapolis, IN: Indiana University Press.

Habermas, J. (1970a) 'On Systematically Distorted Communication', *Inquiry*, 13: 205–18.

—— (1970b) 'Towards a Theory of Communicative Competence', *Inquiry*, 13: 360–75.

—— (1971) *(1968) Knowledge and Human Interests*, Boston, MA: Beacon Press.

—— (1976a) *(1971) Theory and Practice*, Boston, MA: Beacon Press.

—— (1976b) *(1973) Legitimation Crisis*, London: Heinemann.

—— (1979) *(1976) Communication and the Evolution of Society*, Boston, MA: Beacon Press.

—— (1983) 'Modernity—An Incomplete Project', in H. Foster (ed.), *Postmodern Culture*, London: Pluto Press.

—— (1984) *(1981) Reason and the Rationalisation of Society*, Volume 1 of *The Theory of Communicative Action*, Cambridge: Polity Press.

—— (1987) *(1981) Lifeworld and System: A Critique of Functionalist Reason*, Volume 2 of *The Theory of Communicative Action*, Cambridge: Polity Press.

—— (1988) *(1985) The Philosophical Discourse of Modernity*, Cambridge, MA: MIT Press.

—— (1989a) *(1962) The Structural Transformation of the Public Sphere: An Inquiry into a Category of Bourgeois Society*, Cambridge: Polity Press.

—— (1989b) *(1985) The New Conservatism: Cultural Criticism and the Historians' Debate*, Cambridge, MA: MIT Press.

—— (1990) *Moral Consciousness and Communicative Action*, Cambridge, MA: MIT Press.

—— (2003) *The Future of Human Nature*, Oxford: Polity.

—— (2007) *The Dialectic of Secularism: On Reason and Religion*, San Francisco, CA: Ignatius Press.

Hahn, L.E. (ed.) (1990) *The Philosophy of Paul Ricoeur*, Oxford: Blackwell.

Haldane, J. and Wright, C. (eds) (1993) *Reality, Representation, and Projection*, New York: Oxford University Press.

Haldane, J.B.S. (1924) *Daedalus: or, Science and the Future*, London: Kegan Paul, Trench, Trubner.

Hall, S. (1973) 'Encoding and Decoding in Television Discourse', *CCCS* stencilled paper (see Hall (1980)).

—— (1975) 'Television as a Medium and Its Relation to Culture', *CCCS* stencilled paper no. 34.

—— (1980) 'Encoding/Decoding', in S. Hall, D. Hobson, A. Lowe and P. Willis (eds), *Culture, Media, Language*, London: Hutchinson.

—— (1982) 'The Rediscovery of "Ideology": The Return of the "Repressed" in Media Studies', in M. Gurevitch, T. Bennett, J. Curran and J. Woollacott (eds), *Culture, Society and the Media*, London: Methuen.

—— (1985) 'The Toad in the Garden: Thatcherism amongst the Theorists', in C. Nelson and L. Grossberg (eds), *Marxism and the Interpretation of Culture*, Urbana, IL: University of Illinois Press.

—— (1990) 'Cultural Identity and Diaspora', in J. Rutherford (ed.), *Identity, Community, Culture, Difference*, London: Lawrence & Wishart.

—— (1996) *Critical Dialogues in Cultural Studies*, London: Routledge.

Hall, S. and Jefferson, T. (eds) (1976) *Resistance Through Rituals: Youth Subcultures in Post-war Britain*, London: Hutchinson.

Hall, S. and Whannel, P. (1964) *The Popular Arts*, London: Hutchinson.

Hall, S., Critcher, C., Jefferson, T., Clarke, J. and Roberts, B. (eds) (1978) *Policing the Crisis: Mugging, the State and Law and Order*, London: Macmillan.

Hall, S., Hobson, D., Lowe, A. and Willis, P. (eds) (1992) *Culture, Media, Language: Working Papers in Cultural Studies, 1972–79*, London: Hutchinson.

Halsey, A.H., Heath, S. and Ridge, J.M. (1980) *Origins and Destinations: Family, Class and Education in Modern Britain*, Oxford: Clarendon Press.

Hamilton, P. (1996) *Historicism*, New York: Routledge.

Hamilton, P. and Turner, B.S. (eds) (1994) *Citizenship: Critical Concepts*, London: Routledge.

Hamilton, W.D. (1964) 'The Genetic Evolution of Social Behaviour', *Journal of Theoretical Biology*, 7:1–52.

Hampton, J. (1997) *Political Philosophy*, Boulder, CO: Westview Press.

Hanfling, O. (ed.) (1981) *Essential Readings in Logical Positivism*, Oxford: Blackwell.

Haralambos, M. (1985) *Sociology: Themes and Perspectives*, second edn, London: Bell & Hyman.

Harari, J.V. (ed.) (1980) *Textual Strategies: Perspectives in Post-Structuralist Criticism*, London: Methuen.

Haraway, D. (1991) 'A Cyborg Manifesto: Science, Technology, and Socialist-Feminism in the Late Twentieth Century', in *Simians, Cyborgs and Women: The Reinvention of Nature*, New York: Routledge, 149–81.

—— (1997) *Modest_Witness@Second_Millennium. FemaleMan_Meets_Oncomouse. Feminism and Technoscience*, New York: Routledge.

Harding, S. (1992) *Whose Science? Whose Knowledge? Thinking from Women's Lives*. Ithaca, NY: Cornell University Press.

—— (2003) 'A World of Sciences', in S. Harding and R. Figueroa (eds) *Science and Other Cultures: Issues in Philosophies of Science and Technology*, London: Routledge.

Hargreaves, J. (1994) *Sporting Females: Critical Issues in the History and Sociology of Women's Sport*, London: Routledge.

—— (2000) *Heroines of Sport: The Politics of Difference and Identity*, London: Routledge.

—— (2006) *Physical Culture, Power and the Body*, London: Routledge.

Hargreaves, J. and MacDonald, I. (2002) 'Cultural Studies and the Sociology of Sport', in J. Coakley and E. Dunning (eds), *Handbook of Sports Studies*, London: Sage.

Harker, D. (1985) *Fakesong: The Manufacture of British Folksong, 1700 to the Present Day*, Milton Keynes: Open University Press.

Harland, R. (1987) *Superstructuralism*, London: Methuen.

Harré, R. (1970) *The Principle of Scientific Thinking*, London: Macmillan.

Harrington, J. (1992) *(1656) Commonwealth of Oceana*, ed. J.G.A. Pocock, Cambridge: Cambridge University Press.

Harris, R. (1987) *Reading Saussure: A Critical Commentary on the Cours de Linguistique Générale*, London: Duckworth.

—— (1988) *Language, Saussure and Wittgenstein: How to Play Games with Words*, London: Routledge.

—— (1995) *Signs of Writing*, London: Routledge.

Harrison, C. (1991) *Essays on Art and Language*, Oxford: Blackwell.

Hartmann, P. and Husband, C. (1974) *Racism and the Mass Media*, London: Davis-Poynter.

Harvey, D. (1989) *The Condition of Postmodernity: An Enquiry into the Origins of Cultural Change*, Oxford: Blackwell.

Hassan, I. (1987) *The Postmodern Turn: Essays in Postmodern Theory and Culture*, Colombus, OH: Ohio State University Press.

Hauser, A. (1962) *A Social History of Art*, volume 2, *Renaissance, Mannerism and Baroque*, London: Routledge & Kegan Paul.

Hayes, F.A. (1973) *Law Legislation and Liberty – Rules and Order*, Chicago, IL: University of Chicago Press.

Hayles, N.K. (1999) *How We Became Posthuman: Virtual Bodies in Cybernetics, Literature, and Informatics*, Chicago, IL: Chicago University Press.

Heath, A. (1981) *Social Mobility*, London: Fontana.

Heath, A. (1981) *Social Mobility*, London: Fontana.

Hebdige, D. (1979) *Subculture: The Meaning of Style*, London: Methuen.

Hechter, M., Nedel, L. and Michael, R. (eds) (1993) *The Origin of Values*, New York: de Gruyter.

Hedgecoe, A. (1998) 'Geneticization, Medicalisation and Polemics', *Medicine, Health Care and Philosophy*, 1(3): 235–43.

Hedges, I. (1983) *Language of Revolt: Dada and Surrealist Literature and Film*, Durham, NC: Duke University Press.

Hegel, G.W.F. (1931) *(1807) The Phenomenology of Mind*, tr. J.B. Bailley, London: Allen & Unwin.

—— (1942) *(1821) The Philosophy of Right*, tr. T.M. Knox, Oxford: Clarendon Press.

—— (1948) *Early Theological Writings*, tr. T.M. Knox, Chicago, IL: University of Chicago Press.

—— (1970) *(1817) Philosophy of Nature*, tr. A.V. Miller, Oxford: Clarendon Press.

—— (1971) *(1817) Philosophy of Mind*, tr. W. Wallace and A.V. Miller, Oxford: Clarendon Press.

—— (1975a) *(1817) Hegel's Logic*, tr. W. Wallace, Oxford: Clarendon Press.

—— (1975b) *Hegel's Aesthetics*, 2 volumes, tr. T.M. Knox, Oxford: Clarendon Press.

—— (1977) *(1807) The Phenomenology of Spirit*, tr. A.V. Miller, Oxford: Clarendon Press.

—— (1988a) *Introduction to the Philosophy of History*, tr. L. Rauch, Indianapolis, IN: Hackett.

—— (1988b) *(1827) Lectures on the Philosophy of Religion*, Berkeley, CA: University of California Press.

—— (1991) *(1821) Elements of the Philosophy of Right*, ed. Allen Wood, tr. H.B. Nisbett, Cambridge: Cambridge University Press.

Heidegger, M. (1962) *(1927) Being and Time*, tr. John MacQuarrie and Edward Robinson, Oxford: Blackwell.

—— (1993) *(1951)* 'Building, Dwelling, Thinking', in D.F. Krell (ed.), *Basic Writings,* London: Routledge.

—— (1996) *Basic Writings: Martin Heidegger,* ed. David Farrell Krell, London: Routledge.

Held, D. (1980) *Introduction to Critical Theory: Horkheimer to Habermas,* London: Hutchinson.

Held, D. and Thompson, J. (eds) (1990) *Social Theory of Modern Societies: Anthony Giddens and his Critics,* Cambridge: Cambridge University Press.

Henri, M. (1993) *(1985) The Genealogy of Psychoanalysis,* tr. Douglas Brick, Stanford, CA: Stanford University Press.

Heritage, J. (1984) *Garfinkel and Ethnomethodology,* Cambridge: Polity Press.

Hernadi, P. (1995) *Cultural Transactions: Nature, Self, Society,* Ithaca, NY and London: Cornell University Press.

Hilbert, R.A. and Collins, R. (1992) *The Classical Roots of Ethnomethodology: Durkheim, Weber and Garfinkel,* Chapel Hill, NC: University of North Carolina Press.

Hilferding, R. (1981) *(1910) Finance Capital: A Study of the Latest Phase of Capitalist Development,* London: Verso.

Hill, C. (1975) *The World Turned Upside Down: Radical Ideas During the English Revolution,* Harmondsworth: Penguin.

Hindess, B. and Hirst, P.Q. (1975) *Pre-Capitalist Modes of Production,* London: Routledge & Kegan Paul.

Hirsch, E.D. (1967) *Validity in Interpretation,* New Haven, CT, Yale University Press.

Hirschkop, K. (1986) 'A Response to the Forum on Mikhail Bakhtin', in G.S. Morson (ed.), *Bakhtin: Essays and Dialogues on His Work,* Chicago, IL: University of Chicago Press.

Hitchcock, H.-R. and Johnson, P. (1966) *The International Style,* New York: W.W. Norton.

Hobbes, T. (1994) *(1651) Leviathan,* ed. R.Tuck, Cambridge: Cambridge University Press.

Hobsbawm, Eric (1995) *Age of Extremes,* London: Abacus.

Hodder, I. (1986) *Reading the Past: Current Approaches to Interpretation in Archaeology,* Cambridge: Cambridge University Press.

—— (1992) *Theory and Practice in Archaeology,* London: Routledge.

Hoggart, R. (1957) *Uses of Literacy,* London: Chatto & Windus.

—— (1988) *Life and Times,* 3 volumes, London: Chatto & Windus.

Holdcraft, D. (1991) *Saussure: Signs, System and Arbitrariness,* Cambridge: Cambridge University Press.

Hollingdale, R.J. (1973) *Nietzsche,* London: Routledge & Kegan Paul.

Hollis, M. and Lukes, S. (eds) (1982) *Rationality and Relativism,* Oxford: Blackwell.

Holly, M.A., Moxey, K., and Bryson, N. (eds) (1994) *Visual Culture: Images and Interpretations,* Middletown, CT: Wesleyan University Press.

Holquist, M. (1990) *Dialogism: Bakhtin and His World,* London: Routledge.

Holub, R.C. (1992) *Crossing Borders: Reception Theory, Poststructuralism, Deconstruction,* Madison, WI: University of Wisconsin Press.

Honderich, T. (1993) *How Free Are You?: The Determinism Problem,* Oxford: Oxford University Press.

Honour, H. (1979) *Romanticism*, London: Allen Lane.

Hookway, C. (1985) *Peirce*, London: Routledge & Kegan Paul.

Horkheimer, M. (1972a) *(1937)* 'Traditional and Critical Theory', in *Critical Theory: Selected Essays,* New York: Herder & Herder.

—— (1972b) *(1941)* 'Art and Mass Culture', in *Critical Theory: Selected Essays,* New York: Herder & Herder.

—— (1992) *(1947) Eclipse of Reason*, New York: Continuum.

Horkheimer, M. and Adorno, T.W. (1972) *(1947) Dialectic of Enlightenment*, London: Allen Lane.

—— (2002) *(1947) Dialectic of Enlightenment: Philosophical Fragments*, tr. E. Jephcott, Stanford, CA: Stanford University Press.

Hobsbawm, E. (1987) *The Age of Empire, 1875–1914*, London: Weidenfeld and Nicolson.

Hosek, C. and Parker, P. (eds) (1985) *Lyric Poetry: Beyond New Criticism*, Ithaca, NY: Cornell University Press.

Howie G., Gillis, S. and Munford, R. (eds) (2004) *Third Wave Feminism: a Critical Exploration*, Basingstoke: Palgrave Macmillan.

Hughes, J. (2004) *Citizen Cyborg: Why Democratic Societies Must Respond to the Redesigned Human of the Future*, Cambridge, MA: Westview Press.

Hume, D. (1978) *Enquiries Concerning Human Understanding and Concerning the Principles of Morals*, Oxford: Clarendon Press.

—— (1985) *(1757)* 'Of the Standard of Taste', in *Essays: Moral, Political and Literary,* ed. E.F. Miller, Indianapolis, IN: Liberty Press.

—— (1990) *(1739) A Treatise of Human Nature*, ed. P.H. Nidditch, Oxford: Clarendon Press.

Hunnicutt, B.K. (1988) *Work without End: Abandoning Shorter Hours for the Right to Work*, Philadelphia, PA: Temple University Press.

Hunt, J.D. (1976) *The Figure in the Landscape: Poetry, Painting and Gardening during the Eighteenth Century*, Baltimore, MD: Johns Hopkins University Press.

Hunt J.D. and Willis, P. (eds) (1988) *The Genius of the Place: The English Landscape Garden 1620–1820*, Cambridge, MA: MIT Press.

Huntington, S. (1998) *The Clash of Civilizations and the Remaking of World Order*, New York: Touchstone.

Husserl, E. (1954) *(1938) The Crisis of European Sciences and Transcendental Phenomenology*, Evanston, IL: Northwestern University Press.

—— (1962) *(1913) Ideas*, New York: Collier.

Hylton, P. (1990) *Russell, Idealism, and the Emergence of Analytic Philosophy*, Oxford: Clarendon Press.

Illich, I. (1971) *Deschooling Society*, London: Calder & Boyars.

—— (1976) *Limits to Medicine: Medical Nemesis, the Expropriation of Health*, London: Calder & Boyars.

Ingarden, R. (1973) *The Literary Work of Art*, Evanston, IL: Northwestern University Press.

Inglis, F. (1993) *Cultural Studies*, Oxford: Blackwell.

Ingold, T. (ed.) (1996) *Key Debates in Anthropology*, London: Routledge.

Innis, H.A. (1950) *Empire and Communications*, Oxford: Oxford University Press.

—— (1951) *The Bias of Communication*, Toronto: Toronto University Press.

Innis, R.E. (ed.) (1986) *Semiotics: An Introductory Reader*, London: Hutchinson.

Inwood, M. (1992) *A Hegel Dictionary*, Oxford: Blackwell.

Irigaray, L. (1985a) *(1974) Speculum of the Other Woman*, Ithaca, NY: Cornell University Press.

—— (1985b) *(1977) This Sex Which is Not One*, Ithaca, NY: Cornell University Press.

—— (1986) *Divine Women*, Sydney: Local Consumption.

—— (1991) *(1980) Marine Lover of Friedrich Nietzsche*, New York: Columbia University Press.

—— (1992) *(1990) Culture of Difference*, New York: Routledge.

—— (1993a) *(1984) An Ethics of Sexual Difference*, Ithaca, NY: Cornell University Press.

—— (1993b) *(1990) Je, tu, nous. Towards a Culture of Difference*, London: Routledge.

Jaanus, M. (1995) 'The *Démontage* of the drive', in R. Feldstein, B. Fink and M. Jaanus (eds), *Reading Seminar XI: Lacan's Four Fundamental Concepts of Psychoanalysis*, Albany, NY: SUNY Press.

Jakobson, R. (1971–1985) *Selected Writings*, Volumes 1–6, The Hague and Berlin: Mouton.

—— (1987) 'Linguistics and Poetics', in *Language and Literature,* ed. K.Pomorska and S.Rudy, Cambridge, MA: Harvard University Press.

—— (1990) *On Language*, Cambridge, MA: Harvard University Press.

James, A., Hockey, J.L. and Dawson, A.H. (eds) (1997) *After Writing Culture: Epistemology and Praxis in Contemporary Anthropology*, London: Routledge.

James, C.L.R. (1987) *(1963) Beyond a Boundary*, London: Serpent's Tail.

Jameson, F. (1971) *Marxism and Form*, Princeton, NJ: Princeton University Press.

—— (1972) *The Prison-House of Language: A Critical Account of Structuralism and Russian Formalism*, Princeton, NJ: Princeton University Press.

—— (1991) *Postmodernism, or, The Cultural Logic of Late Capitalism*, London: Verso.

Jarvie, G. (1991) *Sport, Racism and Ethnicity*, Sussex: Falmer Press.

—— (2000) 'Highland Games', in G. Jarvie and J. Burnett (eds), *Sport, Scotland and the Scots*, East Linton: Tuckwell Press.

Jarvie, G. and Burnett, J. (eds) (2000) *Sport, Scotland and the Scots*, East Linton: Tuckwell Press.

Jay, M. (1973) *The Dialectical Imagination*, Boston, MA: Little Brown and Company.

—— (1984) *Adorno*, London: Fontana.

Jekyll, G. (1937) *A Gardener's Testament. A Selection of Articles and Notes*, London: Country Life.

Jenger, J. (1996) *Le Corbusier: Architect of a New Age*, London: Thames & Hudson.

Jenkins, K. (1995) *On "What is History?": from Carr and Elton to Rorty and White*, sixth edn, London: Academy Editions.

Jenks, C. (1991) *The Language of Postmodern Architecture*, sixth edn, London: Academy Editions.

—— (1993a) *Culture*, London: Routledge.

—— (ed.) (1993b) *Cultural Reproduction*, London: Routledge.

Joas, H. (1996) *The Creativity of Action*, Cambridge: Polity Press.

Johnson, B. (1980) *The Critical Difference: Essays in the Contemporary Rhetoric of Reading*, Baltimore, MD: Johns Hopkins University Press.

Johnson, L. (1979) *The Cultural Critics: From Matthew Arnold to Raymond Williams*, London, Boston, MA, and Henley: Routledge & Kegan Paul.

Jones, E. (1964) *The Life and Work of Sigmund Freud*, London: Penguin.

Jones, L. (Baraka, A.) (1965) *Blues People: Negro Music in White America*, London: MacGibbon & Lee.

Jost, E. (1981) *Free Jazz*, New York: Da Capo Press.

Jung, C.G. (1959) *The Collected Works of C.G. Jung*, volume 91, *Archetypes and the Collective Unconscious*, London: Routledge & Kegan Paul.

—— (1993) *(1917) Psychology of the Unconscious: A Study of the Transformations and Symbolism of the Libido*, London: Routledge.

Kac, E. (ed.) (2007) *Signs of Life: Bio Art and Beyond*, Cambridge, MA: MIT Press.

Kant, I. (1964) *(1781) Critique of Pure Reason*, tr. Norman Kemp Smith, London: Macmillan.

—— (1970) *Political Writings*, ed. H. Reiss, Cambridge: Cambridge University Press.

—— (1976) *(1788) Critique of Practical Reason, and Other Writings in Moral Philosophy*, ed. and tr. Lewis White Beck, New York: Garland.

—— (1983) *(1786)* 'Speculative Beginning of Human History', in *Perpetual Peace and Other Essays*, tr. T. Humphrey, Indianapolis, IN: Hackett.

—— (1987) *(1790) The Critique of Judgement*, tr. W.S. Pluhar, Indianapolis, IN: Hackett; (1952) Oxford: Oxford University Press.

Kaplan, E. Ann and Sprinker, M. (1993) *The Althusserian Legacy*, London: Verso.

Kaufmann, W. (1974) *Nietzsche: Philosopher, Psychologist, Antichrist*, Princeton, NJ: Princeton University Press.

Keane, J. (ed.) (1988) *Civil Society and the State: New European Perspectives*, London: Verso.

Kearney, R. and Rainwater, M. (eds) (1996) *The Continental Philosophy Reader*, London: Routledge.

Keller, E. Fox (2000) *The Century of the Gene*, Cambridge, MA: Harvard University Press.

Kelley, T.M. (1997) *Reinventing Allegory*, Cambridge: Cambridge University Press.

Kellner, D. (1989) *Jean Baudrillard: From Marxism to Postmodernism and Beyond*, Cambridge: Polity Press.

Kelly, A. (1982) *Mikhail Bakunin: A Study in the Psychology and Politics of Utopianism*, Oxford: Clarendon Press.

Kennedy, B. (1999) 'Post-feminist Futures in Film Noir', in M. Aaron (ed.), *The Body's Perilous Pleasures: Dangerous Desires and Contemporary Culture*, Edinburgh: Edinburgh University Press.

Kenny, A. (ed.) (1994) *The Wittgenstein Reader*, Oxford: Blackwell.

Kermode, F. (1975) *The Classic*, London: Faber & Faber.

Kevles, D.J. (1985) *In the Name of Genetics: Genetics and the Use of Human Heredity*, New York: Knopf.

Kierkegaard, S. (1966) *(1841) The Concept of Irony*, London: Collins.

Kim, J. and Sosa, E. (1994) *A Companion to Metaphysics*, Oxford: Blackwell.

Klein, R. (1992/3) 'Notes on the Foundations', *Journal of the Centre for Freudian Analysis and Research*, Winter.

Klotz, J.-P. (1995) 'The Passionate Dimensions of Difference', in R. Feldstein *et al.* (eds), *Reading Seminar XI: Lacan's Four Fundamental Concepts of Psychoanalysis*, Albany, NY: SUNY Press.

Knight, F.H. (1921) *Risk, Uncertainty, and Profit*, New York: Houghton Mifflin.

Kolakowski, L. (1972) *Positivist Philosophy*, London: Penguin.

—— (1978) *Main Currents of Marxism*, 3 volumes, Oxford: Oxford University Press.

Kolb, D. (1990) *Postmodern Sophistications: Philosophy, Architecture and Tradition*, Chicago, IL: University of Chicago Press.

Korner, S. (1955) *Kant*, Harmondsworth: Penguin.

Kracauer, S. (1947) *From Caligari to Hitler*, Princeton, NJ: Princeton University Press.

Kracauer, S. (1960) *Theory of Film: The Redemption of Physical Reality*, London: Oxford University Press.

Kraus, R. (1996) 'Welcome to the Cultural Revolution', *October*, 77: 83–96.

Krell, D.F. and Wood, D. (1988) *Exceedingly Nietzsche: Aspects of Contemporary Nietzschean Interpretation*, London: Routledge.

Kripke, S. (1980) *Naming and Necessity*, Oxford: Blackwell.

Kristeva, J. (1969) *Séméiotiké: Recherches pour une sémanalyse*, Paris: Seuil.

—— (1982) *(1980) Powers of Horror: An Essay on Abjection*, New York: Columbia University Press.

—— (1984) *(1974) Revolution in Poetic Language*, New York: Columbia University Press.

—— (1986a) 'Word, Dialogue and Novel', in T. Moi (ed.), *The Kristeva Reader*, Oxford: Blackwell.

—— (1986b) 'The System and the Speaking Subject', in T. Moi (ed.), *The Kristeva Reader*, Oxford: Blackwell.

—— (1987) *(1983) Tales of Love*, New York: Columbia University Press.

—— (1989) *Black Sun*, New York: Columbia University Press.

—— (1991) *(1988) Strangers to Ourselves*, New York: Columbia University Press.

Kristol, I. (1999) *Neoconservatism: The Autobiography of an Idea*, Chicago, IL: Ivan R. Dee Inc.

——(2003) 'The Neoconservative Persuasion', in *The Weekly Standard*, Volume 008, Issue 47, 2003.

Kuhn, T.S. (1970) *(1962) The Structure of Scientific Revolutions*, second edn, London and Chicago, IL: The University of Chicago Press.

Kukathas, C. (1989) *Hayek and Modern Liberalism*, Oxford: Clarendon Press.

Kumar, K. (1978) *Prophecy and Progress*, Harmondsworth: Penguin.

—— (1991) *Utopianism*, Milton Keynes: Open University Press.

Kurzweil, E. (1980) *The Age of Structuralism: Lévi-Strauss to Foucault*, New York: Columbia University Press.

Kymlicka, W. (1989) *Liberalism, Community and Culture*, Oxford: Clarendon Press.

Lacan, J. (1977a) *(1973) Four Fundamental Concepts of Psychoanalysis*, London: Hogarth.

—— (1977b) *(1966) Écrits: A Selection*, tr. Alan Sheridan, ed. Jacques-Alain Miller, London: Routledge.

—— (1979) 'Tuché and Automation', in *The Four Fundamental Concepts of Psychoanalysis*, ed. Jacques-Alain Miller, tr. A. Strachey, London: Penguin.

Laclau, E. and Mouffe, C. (1985) *Hegemony and Socialist Strategy*, London: Verso.

Ladurie, E. Le Roy (1980) *(1978) Montaillou: Cathars and Catholics in a French Village 1294–1324*, Harmondsworth: Penguin.

Laing, D. (1985) *One Chord Wonders: The Power and Meaning in Punk Rock*, Milton Keynes: Open University Press.

Langer, S.K. (1942) *Philosophy in a New Key: A Study of the Symbolism of Reason, Rite and Art*, Cambridge, MA: Harvard University Press.

Laplanche, J. and Pontalis, J.-B. (1973) 'Instinct (or drive)', in *The Language of Psychoanalysis*, tr. Donald Nicholson-Smith, London: Karnac Books and the Institute of Psychoanalysis, pp. 214–17.

—— (1988) *(1967) The Language of Psychoanalysis*, tr. Donald Nicholson-Smith, London: Karnac Books and the Institute of Psychoanalysis.

Laqueur, W. (ed.) (1988) *Fascism: A Reader's Guide*, London: Wildwood House.

Lareau, A. and Shultz, J. (eds) (1996) *Journeys through Ethnography: Realistic Accounts of Fieldwork*, Boulder, CO: Westview Press.

Larrain, J. (1979) *The Concept of Ideology*, London: Hutchinson.

Lasdun, S. (1991) *The English Park: Royal, Private and Public*, London: Deutsch.

Lash, S. and Urry, J. (1987) *The End of Organised Capitalism*, Cambridge: Polity.

Laszlo, E. (1987) *Evolution: The Grand Synthesis*, London: New Science Library.

de Laszlo, V.S. (ed.) (1992) *The Basic Writings of C.G.Jung*, London: Routledge.

Lavers, A. (1982) *Roland Barthes: Structuralism and After*, London: Methuen.

Lavie, S. and Swedenburg, T. (eds) (1996) *Displacement, Diaspora, and Geographies of Identity*, Durham, NC: Duke University Press.

Leach, E. (1970) *Lévi-Strauss*, London: Fontana.

—— (1982) *Social Anthropology*, Glasgow: Fontana.

Leach, N. (ed.) (1997) *Rethinking Architecture: A Reader in Cultural Theory*, London: Routledge.

Leavis, F.R. (1972) *Nor Shall My Sword: Discourses on Pluralism, Compassion and Social Hope*, London: Chatto & Windus.

—— (1977) *The Living Principle: 'English' as a Discipline of Thought*, London: Chatto & Windus.

—— (1979) *(1933) For Continuity*, London: Norwood Editions.

—— (1986) *Valuation and Criticism and Other Essays*, ed. G. Singh, Cambridge: Cambridge University Press.

Leavis, F.R. and Thompson, D. (1933) *Culture and Environment*, London: Chatto & Windus.

Lebovici, S. and Widlocher, D. (eds) (1990) *Psychoanalysis in France*, New York: International Universities Press.

Lechner, F.J. and Boli, J. (eds) (2004) *The Globalization Reader*, second edn, Oxford: Blackwell.

Lechte, J. (1990) *Julia Kristeva*, London: Routledge.

Le Corbusier (1954) *(1948) The Modulor: A Harmonious Measure to the Human Scale Universally Applicable to Architecture and Mechanics*, London: Faber & Faber.

—— (1958) *(1955) Modulor II*, London: Faber & Faber.

—— (1967) *(1933) The Radiant City: Elements of a Doctrine of Urbanism to be used as the Basis of our Machine-Age Civilization*, London: Faber & Faber.

—— (1987a) *(1923) Towards a New Architecture*, London: Architectural Press.

—— (1987b) *(1924) The City of Tomorrow and Its Planning*, London: Architectural Press.

Lecourt, D. (1975) *(1969) Marxism and Epistemology: Bachelard, Canguilhem and Foucault*, London: New Left Books.

Le Doeuff, M. (1982) 'Utopias: Scholarly', *Social Research,* 49(2).

—— (1986) *(1980) The Philosophical Imaginary*, Stanford, CA: Stanford University Press.

—— (1989) *Hipparchia's Choice: An Essay Concerning Women, Philosophy etc.*, Oxford: Blackwell.

Lee, D. (1992) *Competing Discourses: Perspective and Ideology in Language*, London: Longman.

Leech, K. (1973) *Youth-Quake: The Growth of a Counter-Culture Through Two Decades*, London: Sheldon Press.

Lefebvre, H. (1982) *The Sociology of Marx*, New York: Columbia University Press.

Le Huray, P. and Day, J. (eds) (1987) *Music and Aesthetics in the Eighteenth and Early-Nineteenth Centuries*, Cambridge: Cambridge University Press.

Leibniz, G.W. (1973) *Philosophical Writings*, London: Dent.

Lemert, E. (1951) *Social Psychology*, New York: McGraw-Hill.

Lenin, V.I. (1992) *(1917) The State and Revolution*, Harmondsworth: Penguin.

Lentricchia, F. (1980) *After the New Criticism*, London: Athlone Press.

Leupin, A. (ed.) (1991) *Lacan and the Human Sciences*, Lincoln, NE and London: University of Nebraska Press.

LeVay, S. (1996) *Queer Science: The Use and Abuse of Research into Homosexuality*, Cambridge, MA: MIT Press.

Levi, P. (1988) *The Drowned and the Saved*, trans. by Raymond Rosenthal, London: Abacus

Lévi-Strauss, C. (1966) *(1962) The Savage Mind*, London: Weidenfeld & Nicolson.

—— (1968a) *(1958) Structural Anthropology*, Harmondsworth: Penguin.

—— (1968b) 'The Structural Study of Myth', in *Structural Anthropology*, Harmondsworth: Penguin.

—— (1969) *(1949) The Elementary Structures of Kinship*, London: Eyre and Spottiswoode.

—— (1970) *(1964)* The Raw and the Cooked: Introduction to a Science of Mythology, Volume 1, London: Jonathan Cape.

—— (1973) *(1967)* From Honey to Ashes: Introduction to a Science of Mythology, Volume 2, London: Jonathan Cape.

—— (1975) *(1955)* Tristes Tropiques, New York: Atheneum.

—— (1977) *(1973)* Structural Anthropology, volume 2, Harmondsworth: Penguin.

—— (1978) *(1968)* The Origin of Table Manners: Introduction to a Science of Mythology, volume 3, London: Jonathan Cape.

—— (1981) *(1971)* The Naked Man: Introduction to a Science of Mythology, volume 4, London: Jonathan Cape.

Lévy, P. (2001) *Cyberculture*, Minneapolis, MN: University of Minnesota Press.

Lipietz, A. (1987) *Mirages and Miracles: The Crises of Global Fordism*, London: Verso.

Lippman, A. (1993) 'Prenatal Genetic Testing and Geneticization: Mother Matters for All', in *Fetal Diagnosis and Therapy*, 8: 175–88.

Lipton, P. (1991) *Inference to the Best Explanation*, London: Routledge.

Litz, W.A., Menand, L. and Rainey, L. (2000) *The Cambridge History of Literary Criticism*, volume 7, *Modernism and New Criticism*, Cambridge: Cambridge University Press.

Livingstone, M. (ed.) (1991) *Pop Art*, London: Royal Academy of the Arts.

Llewelyn, J. (1985) *Beyond Metaphysics? The Hermeneutic Circle in Contemporary Continental Philosophy*, Atlantic Highlands, NJ: Humanities Press.

Lloyd, A.L. (1967) *Folk Song in England*, London: Lawrence & Wishart.

Loades, A. (1990) *Feminist Theology: A Reader*, London: SPCK.

Locke, J. (1964) *(1693)* John Locke on Education, ed. P. Gay, New York: Teachers' College Press.

—— (1975) *(1690)* An Essay Concerning Human Understanding, Oxford: Clarendon Press.

—— (1980) *(1690)* Second Treatise of Government, ed. C.B. Macpherson, Indianapolis, IN: Hackett.

—— (1988) *(1690)* Two Treatises of Government, ed. P. Laslett, Cambridge: Cambridge University Press.

Lodge, D. (ed.) (1972) *20th Century Literary Criticism: A Reader*, London: Longman.

—— (1990) *After Bakhtin: Essays on Fiction and Criticism*, London: Routledge.

Loos, A. (1966) *(1908)* 'Ornament and Crime', in L. Münz and G. Künstler, *Adolf Loos: Pioneer of Modern Architecture*, London: Thames & Hudson.

Lovejoy, O.A. (1948) *Essays in the History of Ideas*, Baltimore, MD: Johns Hopkins University Press.

Lowenthal, L. (1978) *(1937)* 'Knut Hamsun', in A. Arato and E. Gebhardt (eds), *The Essential Frankfurt School Reader,* Oxford: Blackwell.

—— (1989) *(1932)* 'On Sociology of Literature', in S.E. Bronner and D.M Kellner (eds), *Critical Theory and Society: A Reader*, London: Routledge.

Lucie-Smith, E. (1995) *Artoday*, London: Phaidon.

Luhmann, N. (1982) *The Differentiation of Society*, New York: Columbia University Press.

Lukács, G. (1963) *(1958)* *The Meaning of Contemporary Realism*, London: Merlin Press.

—— (1971) *(1923)* *History and Class Consciousness: Studies in Marxist Dialectics*, tr. R. Livingstone, London: Merlin Press.

——(1978) *(1916)* *The Theory of the Novel*, London: Merlin Press.

—— (1983) *(1937)* *The Historical Novel*, Lincoln, NE and London: University of Nebraska Press.

Lukes, S. (1969) 'Alienation and Anomie', in P. Laslett and W.G. Runciman (eds), *Philosophy, Politics and Society*, Oxford: Blackwell.

—— (1973a) *Emile Durkheim*, London: Allen Lane.

—— (1973b) *Individualism*, Oxford: Blackwell.

Lunn, E. (1982) *Marxism and Modernism: An Historical Study of Lukács, Brecht, Benjamin and Adorno*, Berkeley, CA: University of California Press.

Lupton, D. (1999) *Risk*, London: Routledge and Kegan Paul.

—— (2003) *Medicine as Culture: Illness, Disease and the Body in Western Societies* (2nd ed.), London: Sage Publications

Lynon, H. (1980) *The Story of Modern Art*, London: Phaidon.

Lyons, J. (1977) *Chomsky*, London: Fontana.

Lyotard, J.-F. (1988) *(1983)* *The Differend: Phrases in Dispute*, tr. Georges Van Den Abeele, Manchester: Manchester University Press.

—— (1989) *(1979)* *The Postmodern Condition: A Report on Knowledge*, tr. Geoff Bennington, Manchester: Manchester University Press.

—— (1991) *The Inhuman: Reflections on Time*, tr. Geoffrey Bennington and Rachel Bowlby, Cambridge: Polity Press.

—— (1993) *Political Writings*, tr. Bill Readings and Kevin Paul Geiman, London: UCL Press.

—— (1994) *Lessons on the Analytic of the Sublime: Kant's Critique of Judgment*, [sections] 23–29, tr. Elizabeth Rottenberg, Stanford, CA: Stanford University Press.

Macherey, P. (1978) *(1966)* *A Theory of Literary Production*, London: Routledge.

—— (1995) *The Object of Literature*, Cambridge: Cambridge University Press.

Machiavelli, N. (1983) *(1531)* *The Discourses*, ed. B. Crick, tr. Leslie J.Walker with revisions by Brian Richardson, Harmondsworth: Penguin.

MacIntyre, A. (1981) *After Virtue*, London: Duckworth.

—— (1988) *Whose Justice? Which Rationality?*, London: Duckworth.

MacPherson, C.B. (1962) *The Political Theory of Possessive Individualism: Hobbes to Locke*, Oxford: Oxford University Press.

Macrae, C.N., Stanger, C. and Hewstone, M. (eds) (1996) *Stereotypes and Stereotyping*, London: Guilford Press.

Magnus, B. and Higgins, K.M. (eds) (1996) *The Cambridge Companion to Nietzsche*, Cambridge: Cambridge University Press.

Malinowski, B. (1922) *Argonauts of the Western Pacific*, London: Routledge & Kegan Paul.

Mandel, E. (1972) *Marxist Economic Theory*, London: Merlin.

Mannheim, K. (1960) *(1929)* *Ideology and Utopia: An Introduction to the Sociology of Knowledge*, London: Routledge & Kegan Paul.

—— (1972) *(1924)* 'Historicism', in *Essays on the Sociology of Knowledge*, tr. Paul Kecskemeti, London: Routledge & Kegan Paul.

Marcuse, H. (1972) *An Essay on Liberation*, Harmondsworth: Penguin.

Margolis, J. (1991) *The Truth About Relativism*, Oxford: Blackwell.

Margolis, J., Marsoobian, A. T. and Rockmore, T. (eds) (2005) *The Philosophical Challenge of September 11*, Oxford: Blackwell.

Marini, M. (1992) *Jacques Lacan: The French Context*, tr. Anne Tomiche, New Brunswick, NJ: Rutgers University Press.

Marshall, T.H. (1950) *Citizenship and Social Class, and Other Essays*, Cambridge: Cambridge University Press.

Marx, K. (1968) *(1852)* 'The Eighteenth Brumaire of Louis Bonaparte', in *Karl Marx and Frederick Engels: Selected Works*, London: Lawrence & Wishart.

—— (1971) *(1859) A Contribution to the Critique of Political Economy*, London: Lawrence & Wishart.

——(1973) *(1857–1858) Grundrisse*, Harmondsworth: Penguin.

—— (1975) *Early Writings*, tr. R. Livingstone and G. Benton, introduction by L.Colletti, Harmondsworth: Penguin.

—— (1976) *(1867) Capital: A Critique of Political Economy*, volume 1, tr. B. Fowkes, Harmondsworth: Penguin.

Marx K. and Engels, F. (1970) *(1845–1846) The German Ideology*, London: Lawrence & Wishart.

—— (1985) *(1848) The Communist Manifesto*, Harmondsworth, Penguin.

Mauss, M. (1966) *(1925) The Gift: Forms and Functions of Exchange in Archaic Societies*, London: Routledge & Kegan Paul.

Maynard, P. and Feagin, S. (eds) (1997) *Aesthetics: An Oxford Reader*, Oxford: Oxford University Press.

McCarthy, Timothy (1978) *Marx and the Proletariat: A Study in Social Theory*, Westport, CT: Greenwood Press.

McCarthy, Thomas (1978) *The Critical Theory of Jürgen Habermas*, London: Hutchinson.

McCloud, S. (1993) *Understanding Comics*, Northampton, MA: Tundra Publishing.

McCulloch, G. (1989) *The Game of the Name: Introducing Logic, Language and Mind*, Oxford: Clarendon Press.

—— (1995) *The Mind and its World*, London: Routledge.

McLellan, D. (1973) *Karl Marx: His Life and Works*, New York: Harper & Row.

—— (1975) *Karl Marx*, New York: Viking.

McLuhan, M. (1994) *Understanding Media: The Extension of Man*, London: Routledge.

McQuail, D. (1994) *Mass Communication Theory: An Introduction*, third edn, London: Sage.

McRobbie, A. (1981) 'Settling Accounts with Subcultures: A Feminist Critique', in T. Bennett, G. Martin, C. Mercer and J. Woollacott (eds), *Culture, Ideology and Social Process: A Reader*, London: Open University Press.

—— (1989) *'Jackie:* An Ideology of Adolescent Femininity', in B. Waites, T. Bennett and G. Martin (eds), *Popular Culture: Past and Present*, London: Routledge.

—— (1991) *Feminism and Youth Culture from Jackie to Just Seventeen*, London: Macmillan.

—— (1994) *Postmodernism and Popular Culture*, London: Routledge.

Mead, G.H. (1934) *Mind, Self and Society*, Chicago, IL: Chicago University Press.

Mead, L. (1986) *Beyond Entitlement: The Social Obligations of Citizenship*, New York: Free Press.

Mead, M. (1928) *Coming of Age in Samoa: A Psychological Study of Primitive Youth for Western Civilization*, New York: Morrow.

Meadows, D.H. *et al.* (1972) *The Limits to Growth: A Report for the Club of Rome's Project on the Predicament of Mankind*, London: Earth Island

Meek, R.L. (1973) *Studies in the Labour Theory of Value*, second edn, London: Lawrence & Wishart.

Mehlman, J. (ed.) (1972) *French Freud: Structural Studies in Psychoanalysis*, YFS no. 48.

Meja, V. and Stehr, N. (eds) (1990) *Knowledge and Politics: The Sociology of Knowledge Dispute*, London: Routledge.

Meltzer, D. (ed.) (1993) *Reading Jazz*, San Francisco, CA: Mercury House.

Meltzer, F. (1987) *The Trials of Psychoanalysis*, Chicago, IL and London: The University of Chicago Press.

Mepham, J. and Ruben, D.-K. (eds) (1979) *Issues in Marxist Philosophy*, volume 1, *Dialectics and Method*, Brighton, Harvester.

Merleau-Ponty, M. (1962) *(1945) Phenomenology of Perception*, London, Routledge & Kegan Paul.

Merrell, F. (1993) *Sign, Intertextuality, World*, Bloomington and Indianapolis, IN: Indiana University Press.

Merton, R.K. (1968) *(1949) Social Theory and Social Structure*, New York: Free Press.

Messner, M. (1992) *Power at Play: Sport and the Problem of Masculinity*, Boston MA: Beacon Press.

Mészáros, I. (1986) *Marx's Theory of Alienation*, fourth edn, London: Merlin Press.

Metz, C. (1974) *(1971/1972) Film Language: A Semiotics of the Cinema*, New York: Oxford University Press.

—— (1982) *Psychoanalysis and the Cinema: The Imaginary Signifier*, London: Macmillan.

Meynell, H. (1975) 'Science, the Truth, and Thomas Kuhn', *Mind*, 84: 79–93.

Mies, M. (1986) *Patriarchy and Accumulation on a World Scale: Women in the International Division of Labour*, London: Zed Books.

Milbank, J. (1990) *Theology and Social Theory: Beyond Secular Reason*, Oxford: Basil Blackwell.

Miles, R. (1989) *Racism*, London: Routledge.

Mill, J.S. (1984) *(1859) On Liberty*, Harmondsworth: Penguin.

—— (1988) *The Subjection of Women*, ed. S.M. Okuri, Indianapolis, IN: Hackett.

Miller, D. (ed.) (1995) *Acknowledging Consumption: A Review of New Studies*, London: Routledge.

Miller, F. (1986) *Batman: The Dark Knight Returns*, London: Titan Books.

Miller, J.-A. (1988) 'Another Lacan', tr. Ralph Chipman, *Lacan Study Notes: Hystoria 6/9*, Paris/New York, Published by the New York Lacan Study Group.

Miller, S.M. (1965) 'The "New" Working Class', in A.B. Shostak and W. Gomberg (eds), *Blue-Collar World*, Englewood Cliffs, NJ: Prentice-Hall.

Miller, W. (1958) 'Lower Class Culture as a Generating Milieu of Gang Delinquency', *Journal of Social Issues*, 14: 5–19.

Mills, C.W. (1956) *The Power Elite*, London: Oxford University Press.

Milner, A. (1994) *Contemporary Cultural Theory*, London: UCL Press.

Minson, G. (1985) *Genealogies of Morals: Nietzsche, Foucault, Donzelot and the Eccentricity of Ethics*, Basingstoke: Macmillan.

Mirzoeff, N. (1999) *An Introduction to Visual Culture*, London: Routledge.

Moerman, M. (1988) *Talking Culture: Ethnography and Conversation Analysis*, Philadelphia, PA: University of Pennsylvania Press.

Moi, T. (ed.) (1986) *The Kristeva Reader*, Oxford: Blackwell.

Mommsen, W.J. (1974) *The Age of Bureaucracy: Perspectives on the Political Sociology of Max Weber*, Oxford: Blackwell.

More, M. (2003) *Principles of Extropy, Version 3.11* (http://www.extropy.org/principles.htm)

Moore, A. and Gibbons, D. (1987) *Watchmen*, London: Titan Books.

Moore, M. (1993) *Foundations of Liberalism*, Oxford: Clarendon Press.

Moore, R. (2004) *Education and Society: Issues and Explanations in the Sociology of Education*, Oxford: Polity.

Moreno, A.O.P. (1974) *Jung, Gods and Modern Man*, London: Sheldon Press.

Morgan, W.J. (1994) *Leftist Theories of Sport*, Urban, IL: University of Illinois Press.

—— (1988) 'Adorno on Sport: The Case of the Fractured Dialectic', *Theory and Society*, 17(6): 813–38.

Morgan, W.J. and Meier, K.V. (1995) *Philosophic Inquiry in Sport*, Campaign, IL: Stripes.

Moriarty, M. (1991) *Roland Barthes*, Cambridge: Polity Press.

Morley, D. (1980) *The 'Nationwide' Audience*, London: British Film Institute.

—— (1992) *Television, Audiences and Cultural Studies*, London: Routledge.

Morris, B. (1991) *Western Conceptions of the Individual*, New York: St Martin's Press.

Morris, M. (1988) 'Feminism, Reading, Postmodernism', in J. Storey (ed.), *Cultural Theory and Popular Culture*, Hemel Hempstead: Prentice-Hall.

—— (1993) 'Things to do with Shopping Centres', in S. During (ed.), *The Cultural Studies Reader*, London: Routledge.

Morrow, G.R. (1973) *The Ethical and Economic Theories of Adam Smith*, Clifton, NJ: A.M. Kelly.

Morson, G.S. (1986) 'Dialogue, Monologue, and the Social: A Reply to Ken Hirschkop', ed., G.S. Morson, in *Bakhtin: Essays and Dialogues on His Work*, Chicago, IL: University of Chicago Press.

Morson, G.S. and Emerson, C. (1990) *Mikhail Bakhtin: Creation of a Prosaics*, Stanford, CA: Stanford University Press.

Morton, D. (ed.) (1997) *A LesBiGay Cultural Studies Reader*, London: Westview Press.

Mosca, G. (1939) *The Ruling Class*, New York: McGraw-Hill.

Mosser, M. and Teyssot, G. (eds) (1991) *The History of Garden Design: The Western Tradition from the Renaissance to the Present Day*, London: Thames & Hudson.

Mounce, H.O. (1997) *The Two Pragmatisms: From Peirce to Rorty*, London and New York: Routledge.

Mulhall, S. (1996) *Heidegger and Being and Time*, London: Routledge.

Mulhall, S. and Swift, A. (1996) *Liberals and Communitarians*, Oxford: Blackwell.

Mulhern, F. (1979) *The Moment of Scrutiny*, London: NLB.

—— (1995) 'Culture and Authority', *Critical Quarterly*, 37(1): 77–89.

Mulvey, L. (1975) 'Visual Pleasure and Narrative Cinema', *Screen*, 16(3): 6–18.

—— (1993) 'Afterthoughts on "Visual Pleasure and Narrative Cinema", inspired by King Vidor's *Duel in the Sun* (1946)', in A. Easthope (ed.), *Contemporary Film Theory*, London and New York: Longman.

Mungham, G. and Pearson, G. (eds) (1976) *Working Class Youth Cultures*, London: Routledge & Kegan Paul.

Murdock, G. and Golding, P. (1977) 'Capitalism, Communication and Class Relations', in J. Curran, M. Gurevitch and J. Woolacott (eds), *Mass Communication and Society*, London: Edward Arnold in association with the Open University Press.

Murphey, M.G. (1993) *The Development of Peirce's Philosophy*, Indianapolis, IN: Hackett.

Nǐss, A. (1989) *Ecology, Community and Lifestyle: Outline of an Ecosophy*, translated and revised by David Rothenberg, Cambridge: Cambridge University Press.

Neighbour, O.W., Griffiths, P. and Perle, G. (1983) *The New Grove Second Viennese School: Schoenberg, Webern, Berg*, London: Macmillan.

Nelkin, D. and Lindee, S. (1995) *DNA Mystique. The Gene as a Cultural Icon*, New York: Freeman.

Neocleous, M. (1997) *Fascism*, Philadelphia, PA: Open University Press.

Newby, H. (1988) *The Countryside in Question*, London: Hutchinson.

Newhall, B. (1982) *(1937) The History of Photography*, New York: Museum of Modern Art.

Weber, M. (1946a) Nietzsche, F.W. (1968b) *The Will to Power*, tr. Walter Kaufmann and R.J. Hollingdale, New York: Viking.

Nietzsche, F.W. (1968a) *The Birth of Tragedy (1872), Beyond Good and Evil (1886), On the Geneaology of Morals (1887)*, all in *Basic Writings of Nietzsche*, ed. and tr. Walter Kaufman, New York: Basic Books

—— (1968b) *The Will to Power*, tr. Walter Kaufmann and R.J. Hollingdale, New York: Viking.

—— (1974) *The Gay Science*, tr. Walter Kaufmann, New York: Vintage.

—— (1982) *(1881) Daybreak*, tr. R.J. Hollingdale, Cambridge: Cambridge University Press.

—— (1983) *(1873–1876) Untimely Meditations*, tr. R.J. Hollingdale, Cambridge: Cambridge University Press.

—— (1986) *(1878–1880) Human, All-Too-Human*, tr. R.J. Hollingdale, Cambridge: Cambridge University Press.

—— (1995) *Thus Spoke Zarathustra (1883–92); Twilight of the Idols (1889); The Antichrist (1888/1895)*, all in *The Portable Nietzsche*, ed. and tr. Walter Kaufmann, New York: Penguin.

Nisbet, R. (1980) *History of the Idea of Progress*, London: Heinemann.

Nomberg-Przytyk, S. (1985) *Auschwitz: True Tales from a Grotesque Land*, tr. Rosalyn Hirsch, Chapel Hill, NC: University of North Carolina Press.

Nordau, M. (1894) *Degeneration*, London: Heinemann.

Norman, R. (1980) *Hegel, Marx and Dialectic*, Hassocks, Harvester.

Norris, C. (1985) *The Contest of Faculties: Philosophy and Theory after Deconstruction*, London: Methuen.

—— (1986) *Deconstruction: Theory and Practice*, revised edn, London: Routledge.

—— (1987) *Derrida*, London: Fontana.

—— (1992) *Uncritical Theory: Postmodernism, Intellectuals and the Gulf War*, London: Lawrence & Wishart.

Norton, A. (2004) *Leo Strauss and the Politics of American Empire*, New Haven, CT: Yale University Press.

Nozick, R. (1974) *Anarchy, State and Utopia*, Oxford: Blackwell.

Oakes, P.J., Haslam, S.A. and Turner, J.C. (1994) *Stereotyping and Social Reality*, Oxford: Blackwell.

Oakeshott, M (1975) *On Human Conduct*, Oxford: Blackwell.

—— (1983) *On History and other essays*, Oxford: Blackwell.

Oakley, A. (1984) *The Captured Womb: A History of the Medical Care of Pregnant Women*, Oxford: Blackwell.

O'Connor, A. (1989) *Raymond Williams: Writing, Culture, Politics*, Oxford: Blackwell.

Oelschlager, M. (ed.) (1995) *Postmodern Environmental Ethics*, Albany, NY:, SUNY Press.

Ogden, S. (1979) *Faith and Freedom: Toward a Theology of Liberation*, Belfast, Ontario: Christian Journals Ltd.

—— (1996) *Doing Theology Today*, Valley Forge, PA: Trinity Press International.

Orrù, M. (1987) *Anomie: History and Meanings*, London: Allen & Unwin.

Osborn, F. (1951) *Preface to Eugenics*, New York: Harper.

Outhwaite, W. (1994) *Habermas: A Critical Introduction*, Oxford: Polity.

Page, R.M. (1984) *Stigma*, London: Routledge & Kegan Paul.

Pahl, R. (ed.) (1968) *Readings in Urban Sociology*, Oxford: Pergamon.

Pakenham, Thomas (1997) *The Scramble for Africa: 1876-1912*, London: Weidenfeld & Nicolson.

Palisca, C.V. (1991) *Baroque Music*, third edn, Englewood Cliffs, NJ: Prentice-Hall.

Pareto, V. (1963) *The Mind and Society*, New York: Dover.

Parfitt, T. (2003a) 'Constructing Black Jews: Genetics Tests and the Lemba – the "Black Jews" of South Africa', *Developing World Bioethics* 4 (2): 112–8.

—— (2003b) 'Place, Priestly Status and Purity: The Impact of Genetics Research on an Indian Jewish Community', *Developing World Bioethics* 4 (2): 178–85.

Parsons, T. (1937) *The Structure of Social Action*, New York: McGraw-Hill.

—— (1951) *The Social System*, Glencoe, IL: Free Press.

—— (1975) 'The Sick Role and the Role of the Physician Reconsidered', *The Milbank Memorial Fund Quarterly. Health and Society*, 53(3): 257–78.

Pascal, R. (1973) *From Naturalism to Expressionism: German Literature and Society 1880–1918*, London: Weidenfeld & Nicolson.

Patton, P. (ed.) (1993) *Nietzsche, Feminism and Political Theory*, London and New York: Routledge.

Pearce, F. (1989) *The Radical Durkheim*, London: Unwin Hyman.

Pears, D. (1985) *Wittgenstein*, London: Fontana.

Pearson, R.E. and Uricchio, W. (eds) (1991) *The Many Lives of the Batman*, New York: Routledge.

Peck, J. (ed.) (1987) *The Chomsky Reader*, New York: Pantheon.

Peirce, C.S. (1931–1958) *Collected Papers of Charles Sanders Peirce*, 8 volumes, ed. C. Hartshorn and P. Weiss (volumes 1–6), A.W. Burks (volumes 7–8), Cambridge, MA: Harvard University Press.

—— (1982) 'Definition and Description of Pragmatism' and 'The Fixation of Belief', in H.S. Thayer (ed.), *Pragmatism: The Classic Writings*, Indianapolis, IN: Hackett.

——(1986) 'Logic as Semiotic: The Theory of Signs', in R.E. Innis (ed.), *Semiotics: An Introductory Reader*, London: Hutchinson.

—— (1998) *(1905)* 'What is Pragmatism', in his *The Essential Peirce*, volume 2 (1893–1913), Bloomington and Indianapolis, IN: Indiana University Press.

Perkins, S. (1993) *Marxism and the Proletariat: A Lukácsian Perspective*, London: Pluto.

Pettit, P. (1975) *The Concept of Structuralism: A Critical Analysis*, Dublin: Gill and Macmillan.

Plamenatz, J. (1958) *The English Utilitarians*, Oxford: Blackwell.

Plant, S. (1997) *Zeros and Ones: Digital Women and the New Technoculture*, London: Fourth Estate.

Plato (1975) *Phaedo*, tr. David Gallop, Oxford: Clarendon Press.

—— (1998) *Republic*, Oxford: Oxford University Press.

Plekhanov, G.V. (1974)*(1912) Art and Society, and Other Papers in Historical Materialism*, New York: Oriole.

Pocock, J.G.A. (1975) *The Machiavellian Moment: Florentine Political Thought and the Atlantic Republican Tradition*, Princeton, NJ and London: Princeton University Press.

Poe, E.A. (1982) 'The Man of the Crowd', in *The Complete Tales and Poems of Edgar Allan Poe*, Harmondsworth: Penguin.

Pollack, R.F. (1994) *Signs of Life: the Language and Meaning of DNA*, London: Penguin.

Pollock, John L. (1987) *Contemporary Theories of Knowledge*, London: Hutchinson.

Pommeroy, William J., (1970) *American Neo-colonialism*, New York: International Publishers.

—— (1974) *An American Made Tragedy: Neo-colonialism and Dictatorship in the Philippines*, New York: International Publishers.

Ponzio, A. (1993) *Signs, Dialogue and Ideology*, Amsterdam: John Benjamins.

Popper, K. (1959) *The Logic of Scientific Discovery*, London, Hutchinson.

—— (1963) *Conjectures and Refutations*, New York: Harper & Row.

—— (1972) 'Conjectural Knowledge: My Solution to the Problem of Induction', in *Objective Knowledge*, Oxford: Oxford University Press.

Porter, R. (1996) 'What is Disease?' in his (ed.) *Cambridge Illustrated History of Medicine*, Cambridge: Cambridge University Press.

—— (1997) *The Greatest Benefit to Mankind: A Medical History of Humantiy from Antiquity to the Present*, London: HarperCollins.

Praz, M. (1970) *The Romantic Agony*, London: Oxford University Press.

Priest, S. (1990) *The British Empiricists: Hobbes to Ayer*, London: Penguin.

Primoraz, I. (ed.) (2004) *Terrorism: The Philosophical Issues*, Basingstoke: Macmillan.

Purdy, M. and Banks, D. (eds) (2001) *The Sociology and Politics of Health: a Reader*, London: Routledge.

Putnam, H. (1981) *Reason, Truth and History*, Cambridge: Cambridge University Press.

—— (1995) *Pragmatism: An Open Question*, Oxford and Cambridge, MA: Blackwell.

Qualter, T.H. (1962) *Propaganda and Psychological Warfare*, New York: Random House.

—— (1985) *Opinion Control in the Democracies*, London: Macmillan.

Quine, W.V.O. (1960) *Word and Object*, Cambridge, MA: MIT Press.

—— (1980) *(1953)* 'Two Dogmas of Empiricism', in *From a Logical Point of View*, second edn, Cambridge, MA and London: Harvard University Press, pp. 20–46.

——(1991) 'Two Dogmas in Retrospect', *Canadian Journal of Philosophy*, 21(3): 265–74.

Rabinow, P. (1992) 'Artificiality and Enlightenment: From Sociobiology to Biosociality', in J.C. Kwinter (ed.), *Incorporations*, New York: Zone.

Radcliffe-Brown, A.R. (1952) *Structure and Function in Primitive Society*, New York: Free Press.

—— (1977) *The Social Anthropology of Radcliffe-Brown*, ed. A. Kuper, London: Routledge & Kegan Paul.

Ragland-Sullivan, E. (1986) *Jacques Lacan and the Philosophy of Psychoanalysis*, London and Canberra: Croom Helm.

Rand, E. (1995) *Barbie's Queer Accessories*, London: Duke University Press.

Raphael, D.D. (1985) *Adam Smith*, Oxford: Oxford University Press.

Rawls, J. (1972) *A Theory of Justice*, Oxford: Clarendon Press.

Readings, B. (1991) *Introducing Lyotard: Art and Politics*, London and New York: Routledge.

Renfrew, C. (2003) *Figuring It Out: The Parallel Vision of Artists and Archaeologists*, London: Thames & Hudson.

Renfrew, C. and Bahn, P. (2004) *Archaeology: Theories, Methods and Practice*, fourth edn, London: Thames & Hudson.

Rheinberger, H.-J. (2000) 'Beyond Nature and Culture: Modes of Reasoning in the Age of Molecular Biology and Medicine', in M. Lock, A. Young and A. Cambrosio. (eds), *Living and Working with the New Medical Technologies: Intersection of Enquiry*, Cambridge: Cambridge University Press.

Ricardo, D. (1951) *(1817) Principles of Political Economy*, Cambridge: Cambridge University Press.

Rice, P. and Waugh, P. (1989) *Modern Literary Theory: A Reader*, London: Edward Arnold.

Richards, I.A. (1938) *Interpretation in Teaching*, New York: Harcourt Brace.

Richardson, D. (ed.) (1996) *Theorising Heterosexuality: Telling it Straight*, Buckingham: Open University Press.

Richter, H. (1965) *Dada: Art and Anti-Art*, London, Thames & Hudson.

Ricoeur, P. (1981) *Hermeneutics and the Human Sciences*, ed. and tr. J.B. Thompson, Cambridge: Cambridge University Press.

—— (1984–1988) *(1983–1985) Time and Narrative*, tr. Kathleen McLaughlin and David Pellaner, 3 vols, Chicago, IL and London: University of Chicago Press.

Robbins, D. (2006) *On Bourdieu, Education and Society*, Oxford: Bardwell Press.

Rockmore, T. (1992) *Irrationalism: Lukács and the Marxist View of Reason*, Philadelphia, PA, Temple University Press.

Rojek, C. (1985) *Capitalism and Leisure Theory*, London: Routledge.

—— (ed.) (1995) *Decentring Leisure: Rethinking Leisure Theory*, London: Sage.

—— (1993) 'After Popular Culture: Hyperreality and Leisure', *Leisure Studies* 12: 277–89.

Rorty, R. (1972) 'The World Well Lost', *Journal of Philosophy*, 69:649–65.

—— (1978) 'Philosophy as a Kind of Writing: An Essay on Derrida', *New Literary History*, 10(1): 141–60.

—— (1982) *Consequences of Pragmatism: Essays, 1972–1980*, Brighton: Harvester.

—— (1991) *Objectivity, Relativism and Truth: Philosophical Papers*, Cambridge: Cambridge University Press.

—— (1998) *Truth and Progress*, Cambridge: Cambridge University Press.

Rose, G. (1978) *The Melancholy Science: An Introduction to the Thought of Theodor W. Adorno*, London: Macmillan.

—— (1993) 'Architecture to Philosophy—the Post-Modern Complicity', in *Judaism and Modernity: Philosophical Essays*, Oxford: Blackwell.

Rose, N. (1996) 'Refiguring the Territory of Government', *Economy and Society*, 25(3): 327–56.

—— (2002) 'At Risk of Madness', in T. Baker and J. Simon (eds), *Embracing Risk*, Chicago, IL: University of Chicago Press.

Rosen C. and Zerner, H. (1984) *Romanticism and Realism: The Mythology of Nineteenth Century Art*, London: Faber & Faber.

Rosen, M. (1982) *Hegel's Dialectic and Its Criticism*, Cambridge: Cambridge University Press.

Rosselson, L. (1979) 'Pop Music: Mobilizer or Opiate', in C. Gardner (ed.), *Media, Politics and Culture*, London: Macmillan.

Rossi-Landi, F. (1990) *Marxism and Ideology*, Oxford: Clarendon Press.

Roszak, T. (1971) *(1968) The Making of a Counter Culture: Reflections on the Technocratic Society and its Youthful Opposition*, London: Faber & Faber.

Rotenstreich, N. (1989) *Alienation: The Concept and its Reception*, Leiden: Brill.

Roudinesco, E. (1990) *Jacques Lacan and Co.: A History of Psychoanalysis in France 1925–1985*, tr. Jeffrey Mehlman, Chicago, IL: University of Chicago Press.

Rousseau, J.-J. (1984) *(1754) A Discourse on Inequality*, tr. Maurice Cranston, Harmondsworth: Penguin.

—— (1991) *(1762) Emile, or On Education*, London: Penguin.

Ruben, D. (1979) *Marxism and Materialism*, Brighton: Harvester.

Russell, B. (1905) 'On Denoting', *Mind*, 14: 479–93.

—— (1924) 'Logical Atomism', in R.C. Marsh (ed.) (1988) *Logic and Knowledge*, London: Hyman.

—— (1946) *History of Western Philosophy*, London: Allen & Unwin.

—— (1988) *(1912) The Problems of Philosophy*, Oxford: Oxford University Press.

—— (1988) *(1918)* 'The Philosophy of Logical Atomism', in R.C. Marsh (ed.), *Logic and Knowledge*, London: Hyman.

Russell, B. and Whitehead, A.N. (1910) *Principia Mathematica*, Cambridge: Cambridge University Press.

Ruthven, M. (2004) *Fundamentalism: The Search for Meaning*, Oxford: Oxford University Press.

—— (2002) *A Fury for God*, London: Granta Books.

Ryan, M. (1982) *Marxism and Deconstruction: A Critical Articulation*, Baltimore, MD: Johns Hopkins University Press.

Ryle, G. (1949) *The Concept of Mind*, London: Hutchinson.

Sabin, R. (1993) *Adult Comics: An Introduction*, London: Routledge.

Sacks, H. (1992) *Lectures on Conversation*, 2 volumes, Oxford: Blackwell.

Sadler, T. (1996) *Heidegger and Aristotle: The Question of Being*, London and Atlantic Highlands, NJ:, Athlone.

Said, E. (1978a) *Orientalism*, New York: Random House.

—— (1978b) 'The Problem of Textuality: Two Exemplary Positions', *Critical Inquiry*, 4: 673–714.

Said, E.W. (1993) *Culture and Imperialism*, London: Chatto and Windus.

Sandel, M.J. (1982) *Liberalism and the Limits of Justice*, Cambridge: Cambridge University Press.

—— (ed.) (1984) *Liberalism and its Critics*, Oxford: Blackwell.

Sardar, Z. and Ravetz, J.R. (1996) *Cyberfutures: Culture and Politics on the Information Superhighway*, London: Pluto Press.

Sartre, J.-P. (1958) *(1943) Being and Nothingness*, London: Methuen.

—— (1990) *(1946) Existentialism and Humanism*, tr. Philip Mairet, London: Methuen.

Sassoon, A.S. (1987) *Gramsci's Politics*, second edn, London: Hutchinson.

Saul, J.M. (2003) *Feminism: Issues and Arguments*, Oxford: Oxford University Press.

Saunders, P. (1981) *Social Theory and the Urban Question*, London: Hutchinson.

de Saussure, F. (1983) *(1916) Course in General Linguistics*, ed. C. Bally and A. Sechehaye, tr. Roy Harris, London: Duckworth.

Sayer, D. (1991) *Capitalism and Modernity: An Excursus on Max Weber*, London: Routledge.

Scarre, G. (1996) *Utilitarianism*, London and New York: Routledge.

Scheler, M. (1980) *(1926) Problems of a Sociology of Knowledge*, London: Routledge & Kegan Paul.

Schiffrin, D. (1993) *Approaches to Discourse*, Oxford: Blackwell.

Schmidt, W. (1935) *The Origin and Growth of Religion*, London: Methuen.

Schneiderman, S. (1983) *Jacques Lacan: The Death of an Intellectual Hero*, Cambridge, MA and London: Harvard University Press.

Scholte, J.A. (2000) *Globalisation: A Critical Introduction*, Basingstoke: Macmillan.

Schuller, G. (1968) *Early Jazz: Its Roots and Musical Development*, New York: Oxford University Press.

—— (1989) *The Swing Era: The Development of Jazz 1930–1945*, New York: Oxford University Press.

Schutz, A. (1962) *Collected Papers*, volume 1, The Hague: Martinus Nijhoff.

—— (1964) *Collected Papers*, volume 2, The Hague: Martinus Nijhoff.

—— (1967) *(1932) The Phenomenology of the Social World*, London: Heinemann.

Schutz, A. and Luckmann, T. (1974) *The Structures of the Lifeworld*, London: Heinemann.

Scott, J. (1990) *The Sociology of Elites*, 3 volumes, Aldershot: Edward Elgar.

—— (1996) *Stratification and Power: Structures of Class, Status and Command*, Cambridge: Polity Press.

Scruton, R. (1984) *The Meaning of Conservatism*, London: Macmillan.

Searle, J. (1969) *Speech Acts*, Cambridge: Cambridge University Press.

Sedgwick, E.K. (1994) *Epistemology of the Closet*, London: Penguin.

—— (ed.) (1997) *Novel Gazing: Queer Reading in Fiction*, Durham, NC: Duke University Press.

Sedgwick, P. (ed.) (1995) *Nietzsche: A Critical Reader*, Oxford: Blackwell.

—— (1998) 'Politics as Antagonism and Diversity: Mill and Lyotard', in G. Day (ed.), *Varieties of Victorianism*, Basingstoke: Macmillan.

—— (2001) *Descartes to Derrida: An Introduction to European Philosophy*, Oxford: Blackwell.

—— (2007) *Nietzsche's Economy: Modernity, Normativity and Futurity*, Basingstoke: Macmillan.

Seedhouse, D. (2001) *Health: The Foundation of Achievement*, second edn, Chichester: John Wiley & Sons.

Sen, A. (2005) 'Critical Imprisonments', in *The Philosophical Challenge of September 11*, ed. Margolis, J., Marsoonian A.T. and Rockmore, T., Oxford: Blackwell.

Sen, A. and Williams, B. (eds) (1982) *Utilitarianism and Beyond*, Cambridge: Cambridge University Press.

Shanks, M. and Tilley, C. (1992) *Re-constructing Archaeology: Theory and Practice*, 2nd ed. London: Routledge.

Shepherd, J. (1991) *Music as Social Text*, Cambridge: Polity Press.

Shepherd, J. *et al.* (1977) *Whose Music? A Sociology of Musical Languages*, London: Latimer New Dimensions.

Shiach, M. (1991) *Hélène Cixous: A Politics of Writing*, London: Routledge.

Shope, R.A. (1983) *The Analysis of Knowing*, Princeton, NJ: Princeton University Press.

Silverman, H.J. and Welton, D. (eds) (1988) *Postmodernism and Continental Philosophy*, Albany, NY: State University of New York Press.

Silverman, K. (1983) *The Subject of Semiotics*, Oxford: Oxford University Press.

Simmel, G. (1950a) *The Sociology of Georg Simmel*, ed. and tr. Kurt H. Wolff, Glencoe, IL: Free Press.

—— (1950b) *(1903)* 'The Metropolis and Mental Life', in *The Sociology of Georg Simmel*, Glencoe, IL: Free Press.

—— (1950c) *(1908)* 'The Stranger', in *The Sociology of Georg Simmel,* Glencoe, IL: Free Press.

—— (1957) *(1904)* 'Fashion', *American Journal of Sociology,* 62(6): 541–58.

—— (1959a) *Georg Simmel 1858–1918: A Collection of Essays with Translations and a Bibliography,* ed. Kurt H. Wolff, Columbus, OH: Ohio University Press.

—— (1959b) *(1908)* 'How is Society Possible?', in *Georg Simmel 1858–1918: A Collection of Essays with Translations and a Bibliography,* Columbus, OH: Ohio University Press.

—— (1968) *(1911)* 'On the Concept and Tragedy of Culture', in *Conflict in Modern Culture and Other Essays*, New York: Teachers College.

—— (1978) *(1907)* *The Philosophy of Money,* London: Routledge & Kegan Paul.

—— (1997) *Essays on Culture: Selected Writings*, ed. D. Frisby and M. Featherstone, London: Sage.

Simpson, D. (ed.) (1988) *The Origins of Modern Critical Thought: German Aesthetic and Literary Criticism from Lessing to Hegel*, Cambridge: Cambridge University Press.

Singer, P. (1993) *Practical Ethics*, Cambridge and New York: Cambridge University Press.

Skinner, B.F. (1973) *Beyond Freedom and Dignity,* Harmondsworth: Penguin.

—— (1974) *About Behaviourism*, London: Jonathan Cape.

—— (1976) *Waldon Two*, London: Macmillan.

Skirbekk, G. (1993) *Rationality and Modernity: Essays in Philosophical Pragmatics*, Oslo: Scandinavian University Press.

Smart, B. (1984) *Foucault, Marxism and Critique*, London: Routledge.

Smart, N. (1960) *A Dialogue of Religions*, London: SCM Press.

—— (1971) *The Religious Experience of Mankind*, London: Fontana.

—— (1972) *The Concept of Worship*, London: Macmillan.

—— (1973) *The Phenomenon of Religion*, New York: Herder & Herder.

Smith, A. (1976) *(1776) The Wealth of Nations*, ed. R.H. Campbell, A.S. Skinner and W.B. Todd, Oxford: Clarendon Press.

—— (1986) *The Essential Adam Smith*, ed. Robert L. Heilbroner, Oxford: Oxford University Press.

Smith, G. (ed.) (1988) *On Walter Benjamin: Critical Essays and Recollections*, Cambridge, MA: MIT Press.

Smith, S. (1984) *Reading Althusser: An Essay on Structural Marxism*, Ithaca, NY: Cornell University Press.

Smithson, P. (1975) 'The Slow Growth of Another Sensibility; Architecture as Townbuilding', in J. Gowan (ed.), *A Continuing Experiment: Learning and Teaching at the Architectural Association*, London: Architectural Press.

Soja, E. (1989) *Postmodern Geographies*, London: Verso.

Solomon, R.C. (1983) *In the Spirit of Hegel*, New York, Oxford University Press.

Sontag, S. (1973) *On Photography,* New York: Farrar, Straus & Giroux.

—— (1979) *Illness as Metaphor*, London: Allen Lane.

—— (1989) *AIDS and its Metaphors*, London: Allen Lane.

Sorel, G. (1972) *(1907) Reflections on Violence*, London: Macmillan.

Spanier, B. (1995) *Im/Partial Science: Gender Ideology in Molecular Biology*, Indiana, IN: Indiana University Press.

Spector, J. (1997) *Surrealist Art and Writing 1919–1939: The Gold of Time*, Cambridge: Cambridge University Press.

Spencer, H. (1971) *Structure, Function and Evolution*, ed. Stanislav Andrewski, London: Thomas Nelson & Sons.

Spiegelman, A. (1987) *Maus: A Survivor's Tale*, Harmondsworth: Penguin.

—— (1992) *Maus II: A Survivor's Tale: And Here My Troubles Began*, Harmondsworth: Penguin.

Spivak, G. (1987) *In Other Worlds: Essays in Cultural Politics*, New York: Methuen.

Spradley, J.P. (1980) *Participant Observation*, New York: Holt, Rinehart & Winston.

Sprigge, T.L.S. (1984) *Theories of Existence*, Harmondsworth: Penguin.

Squires, J. (ed.) (1993) *Principled Positions: Postmodernism and the Rediscovery of Value*, London: Lawrence & Wishart.

Stacey, J. (1994) *Star Gazing: Hollywood, Cinema and Female Spectatorship*, London: Routledge.

Stanley, L. and Roland, F. (1988) *Doing Feminist Ethnography in Rochdale*, Manchester: Manchester University Press.

Stanton, E.C. (1990) *The Woman's Bible*, Seattle, WA: Coalition on Women and Religion.

Stanworth, M.D. (1983) *Gender and Schooling: A Study of Sexual Divisions in the Classroom*, London: Hutchinson Education.

Starr, P. (1982) *The Social Transformation of American Medicine*, New York: Basic Books.

Stearns, M.W. (1956) *The Story of Jazz*, London: Oxford University Press.

Sterba, J. (ed.) (2003) *Terrorism and International Justice*, Oxford: Oxford University Press.

Sternhell, Z., Sznajder, M. and Asheri, M. (1994) *The Birth of Fascist Ideology: From Cultural Rebellion to Political Revolution*, tr. David Maisel, Princeton, NJ: Princeton University Press.

Stevens, A. (1994) *Jung*, Oxford: Oxford University Press.

Stevenson, N. (1995) *Understanding Media Cultures: Social Theory and Mass Communication*, London: Sage.

Storey, J. (1996) *Cultural Studies and the Study of Popular Culture: Theories and Methods*, Edinburgh: Edinburgh University Press.

—— (ed.) (1997) *Cultural Theory and Popular Culture: A Reader*, London: Routledge.

Strathern, M. (ed.) (1995) *Shifting Contexts: Transformations in Anthropological Knowledge*, London: Routledge.

Strauss, L. (1965) *(1949) Natural Right and History*, Chicago, IL: University of Chicago Press.

Strawson, P. (1959) *Individuals: An Essay in Descriptive Metaphysics*, London: Methuen.

Strawson, P.F. (1966) *The Bounds of Sense: An Essay on Kant's Critique of Pure Reason*, London: Methuen.

Strianti, D. (1995) *An Introduction to Theories of Popular Culture*, London: Routledge.

Stroud, B. (1984) *The Significance of Philosophical Scepticism*, Oxford: Clarendon Press.

Sturrock, J. (ed.) (1979) *Structuralism and Since: From Lévi-Strauss to Derrida*, Oxford: Oxford University Press.

Suits, B. (1978) *The Grasshopper: Games, Life and Utopia*, Edinburgh: Scottish Academic Press.

Sweezy, P.M. *et al.* (1978) *The Transition from Feudalism to Capitalism*, London, Verso.

Swift, J. (1996) *(1729)* 'A Modest Proposal for Preventing the Children of Ireland from being a Burden to their Parents or Country', in *A Modest Proposal and other Satires*, New York: Dover.

Swiss, T., Sloop, J.M. and Harmon, A. (eds) (1997) *Mapping the Beat*, Malden, MA: Blackwell.

Sztompka, P. (ed.) (1993) *Agency and Structure: Reorienting Social Theory*, Reading: Gordon and Breach.

Tarski, A. (1949) *(1944)* 'The Semantic Conception of Truth and the Foundations of Semantics', in H. Feigl and W. Sellars (eds), *Readings in Philosophical Analysis*, New York: Appleton-Century-Crofts.

Taylor, A.J.P. (1967) *Germany's First Bid for Colonies, 1884–1885: A Move in Bismarck's European Policy*, Hamden, CO: Archon.

Taylor, C. (1975) *Hegel*, Cambridge: Cambridge University Press.

—— (1990) *Sources of the Self*, Cambridge: Cambridge University Press.

—— (1997) *Philosophical Arguments*, Cambridge, MA: Harvard University Press.

Taylor, F.W. (1964) *(1947) Scientific Management*, New York: Harper.

Taylor, T.D. (1997) *Global Pop: World Music, World Markets*, New York: Routledge.

Taylor-Gooby, P. and Zinn, J.O. (2006) 'Current Directions in Risk Research: New Developments in Psychology and Sociology', *Risk Analysis*, 26(2): 397–411.

Thayer, H.S. (1982) *Meaning and Action: a Critical History of Pragmatism*, Indianapolis, IN: Hackett

Thomas, H. (ed.) (1993) *Dance, Gender and Culture*, Basingstoke: Macmillan.

Thomason, B.C. (1982) *Making Sense of Reification: Alfred Schutz and Constructionist Theory*, London: Macmillan.

Thompson, E.P. (1963) *The Making of the English Working Class*, London: Gollancz.

Thomson, P. and Sacks, G. (eds) (1993) *The Cambridge Companion to Brecht*, Cambridge: Cambridge University Press.

Tiles, M. (1984) *Bachelard: Science and Objectivity*, Cambridge: Cambridge University Press.

Tivey, L. (ed.) (1981) *The Nation-State: The Formation of Modern Politics*, Oxford: Martin Robertson.

Tomlinson, G. (1984) 'The Web of Culture: A Context for Musicology', *Nineteenth Century Music*, 7:350–62.

Touraine, A. (1971) *(1968) The Post-Industrial Society*, New York: Random House.

Townsend, P. (ed.) (1982) *Inequalities in Health: the Black Report*, Harmondsworth: Penguin.

Treichler, P. (eds) (1992) *Cultural Studies*, London: Routledge.

Treitler, L. (1989) *Music and the Historical Imagination*, Cambridge, MA: Harvard University Press.

Turkle, S. (1996) *Life on the Screen: Identity in the Age of the Internet*, London: Weiderfeld & Nicolson.

—— (2005) *The Second Self: Computers and the Human Spirit*, Cambridge, MA: MIT Press.

Turner, B.S. (1981) *For Weber: Essays on the Sociology of Fate*, London: Routledge & Kegan Paul.

—— (1984) *The Body and Society: Explorations in Social Theory*, Oxford: Blackwell.

——(1986) *Citizenship and Capitalism: The Debate Over Reformism*, London: Allen & Unwin.

—— (1988) *Status*, Minneapolis, MN: University of Minnesota Press.

Turner, B.S. and Hamilton, P. (eds) (1994) *Citizenship: Critical Concepts*, London: Routledge.

Turner, G. (1996) *British Cultural Studies*, second edn, London: Routledge.

Turner, R. (ed.) (1974) *Ethnomethology*, Harmondsworth: Penguin.

Turner, T. (2005) *Garden History: Philosophy and Design 2000 BC – 2000 AD*, London: Spon.

Turney, J. (1998) *Frankenstein's Footsteps. Science, Genetics and Popular Culture*, New Haven, CT and London: Yale University Press.

Uglow, J. (2004) *A Little History of British Gardening*, London: Chatto and Windus.

Urry, J. (2002) *The Tourist Gaze: Leisure and Travel in Contemporary Societies*, London: Sage.

Van Inwagen, P. (1993) *Metaphysics*, Oxford: Oxford University Press.

Van Pelt, R.J. and Dwork, D. (1996) *Auschwitz: 1210 to the Present*, London and New Haven, CT: Yale University Press.

Vattimo, G. (1988) *The End of Modernity: Nihilism and Hermeneutics in Postmodern Culture*, tr. Jon R. Snyder, Cambridge: Polity Press.

Vaughan Williams, R. (1963) *National Music and Other Essays*, Oxford: Oxford University Press.

Veblen, T. (1953) *(1899) The Theory of the Leisure Class*, New York: Mentor Books.

Veeser, H.A. (ed.) (1989) *The New Historicism*, London and New York: Routledge.

Venturi, R., Scott Brown, D. and Izenour, S. (1977) *Learning from Las Vegas: The Forgotten Symbolism of Architectural Form*, Cambridge, MA: MIT Press.

Voloshinov, V.N. (1973) *Marxism and the Philosophy of Language*, New York and London: Seminar Press.

—— (1976) *Freudianism: A Marxist Critique*, New York: Academic Press.

—— (1988) 'Discourse in Life and Discourse in Poetry', in A. Shukman (ed.), *Bakhtin School Papers*, Oxford: RTP.

Waites, B., Bennett, T. and Martin, G. (eds) (1989) *Popular Culture: Past and Present*, London: Routledge in association with the Open University Press.

Walby, S. (1986) *Patriarchy at Work*, Cambridge: Polity Press.

—— (1990) *Theorising Patriarchy*, Oxford: Blackwell.

Walsh, W.H. (1963) *Metaphysics*, London: Hutchinson.

Walzer, M. (1983) *Spheres of Justice*, New York: Basic Books.

—— (1985) *Spheres of Justice: a Defence of Pluralism and Equality*, Oxford: Basil Blackwell

—— (2004) *Arguing About War*, Yale, CT: Yale University Press.

Watkin, D. (1977) *Morality and Architecture: The Development of a Theme in Architectural History and Theory from the Gothic Revival to the Modern Movement*, Oxford: Clarendon Press.

—— (1992) *A History of Western Architecture*, London: Laurence King.

Waugh, L. (1976) *Roman Jakobson's Science of Language*, Bloomington, IN: P. de Ridder.

Weber, M. (1930) *(1904–1905)* *The Protestant Ethic and the Spirit of Capitalism*, London: George Allen & Unwin.

—— (1946a) *From Max Weber: Essays in Sociology*, ed. H.H. Gerth and C.W. Mills, London: Routledge & Kegan Paul.

—— (1946b) *(1921)* 'Bureaucracy', in *From Max Weber: Essays in Sociology*, London: Routledge & Kegan Paul.

—— (1946c) *(1921)* 'Class, Status, Party', in *From Max Weber: Essays in Sociology*, London: Routledge & Kegan Paul.

—— (1946d) 'India: The Brahman and the Castes', in *From Max Weber: Essays in Sociology*, London: Routledge & Kegan Paul.

—— (1958) *(1922)* 'Three Types of Legitimate Rule', tr. H.H. Gerth, *Berkeley Publications in Society and Institutions*, vol. VI: 1–11.

—— (1964) *(1922)* *The Theory of Social and Economic Organisation*, tr. A.M. Henderson and T. Parsons, New York: Free Press.

—— (1978) *(1921)* *Economy and Society*, ed. Guenther Roth and Claus Wittich, Berkeley, Los Angeles, CA and London: University of California Press.

—— (1979) *(1923)* *General Economic History*, New Brunswick, NJ: Transaction Books.

—— (1994) *(1895)* 'The Freidberg Address', in *Political Writings*, Cambridge: Cambridge University Press.

Weber, R.P. (1990) *Basic Content Analysis*, second edn, Newbury Park, CA: Sage.

Weber, S.M. (1985) 'The Intersection: Marxism and the Philosophy of Language', *Diacritics*, 15(4): 94–112.

Weeks, J. (1989) *Sexuality*, London: Routledge

Weider, D.L. (1974) 'Telling the Code', in R.Turner (ed.), *Ethnomethodology*, Harmondsworth: Penguin.

Welford, A.T. *et al.* (eds) (1967) *Society: Problems and Methods of Study*, London: Routledge & Kegan Paul.

Wellek, R. (1986) *A History of Modern Criticism*, 6 volumes, New Haven, CT: Yale University Press.

West, D. (1996) *An Introduction to Continental Philosophy*, Cambridge: Polity Press.

Whannel, G. (1992) *Fields of Vision: Television Sport and Cultural Formation*, London: Routledge.

White, H. (1987) *The Content of the Form: Narrative Discourse and Historical Representation*, Baltimore, MD and London: Johns Hopkins University Press.

—— (1987) *Tropics of Discourse*, Baltimore, Johns Hopkins University Press.

White, S.K. (1988) *The Recent Work of Jürgen Habermas: Reason, Justice and Modernity*, Cambridge: Cambridge University Press.

Whiteley, S. (ed.) (1997) *Sexing the Groove: Popular Music and Gender*, London: Routledge.

Whitford, F. (1984) *Bauhaus*, London: Thames & Hudson.

Whitford, M. (1991) *Luce Irigaray: Philosophy in the Feminine*, London: Routledge.

Wiggershaus, R. (1994) *(1986) The Frankfurt School: Its History, Theories and Political Significance*, Cambridge: Polity Press.

Wilcox, H. (ed.) (1990) *The Body and the Text: Hélène Cixous, Reading and Teaching*, Hemel Hempstead: Harvester.

Willett, J. (1970) *Expressionism*, London: Weidenfeld & Nicolson.

—— (1984) *Brecht in Context: Comparative Approaches*, London: Methuen.

Williams, R. (1958) *Culture and Society 1780–1950*, London: Chatto & Windus.

—— (1961) *The Long Revolution*, London: Chatto & Windus.

—— (1962) *Communications*, Harmondsworth: Penguin.

—— (1968) *Drama from Ibsen to Brecht*, revised edn, London: Chatto & Windus.

—— (1973) *The Country and the City*, London: Chatto & Windus.

—— (1974) *Television: Technology and Cultural Form*, London: Fontana.

—— (1976) *Keywords*, London: Fontana.

—— (1977) *Marxism and Literature*, Oxford: Oxford University Press.

—— (1983) *Keywords*, second edn, London: Fontana.

—— (1986) *Culture*, London: Fontana.

Willis, P. (1977) *Learning to Labour: How Working Class Kids Get Working Class Jobs*, London: Saxon House.

——(1978) *Profane Culture*, London: Routledge & Kegan Paul.

—— (1990) *Common Culture*, Milton Keynes: Open University Press.

Wilmer, V. (1992) *As Serious as Your Life: The Story of the New Jazz*, London: Serpent's Tail.

Wilson, E. (1991) *The Sphinx in the City*, London: Virago.

Wilson, E.O. (1975) *Sociobiology: The New Synthesis*, Cambridge, MA: Harvard University Press.

—— (1994) *Naturalist*, London: Allen Lane.

Wimbush, E. and Talbot, M. (1988) *Relative Freedoms: Women and Leisure*, Milton Keynes: Open University Press.

Wimsatt, W.K. (1967) *The Verbal Icon: Studies in the Meaning of Poetry*, Lexington, KY: Kentucky University Press.

Winch, P. (1958) *The Idea of a Social Science and Its Relation to Philosophy*, London: Routledge & Kegan Paul.

Winckelmann, J.J. (2001) *Essays on the Philosophy and History of Art*, ed. C. Bowman. Bristol: Thoemmes.

Wirth, L. (1938) 'Urbanism as a Way of Life', *American Journal of Sociology*, 44: 1–24.

Wittgenstein, L. (1961) *(1921) Tractatus Logico-Philosophicus*, tr. D.F. Pears and B.F. McGuinness, London: Routledge & Kegan Paul.

—— (1967) *(1953) Philosophical Investigations*, tr. G.E.M. Anscombe, Oxford: Blackwell.

—— (1956) *Remarks on the Foundations of Mathematics*, tr, G.E.M.Anscombe, Oxford: Blackwell.

—— (1958) *Philosophical Investigations*, second edn, tr. G.E.M. Anscombe, Oxford: Blackwell.

Wolfe, T. (1989) *From Bauhaus to Our House*, London: Cardinal.

Wolff, J. (1981) *The Social Production of Art*, London: Macmillan.

Wollstonecraft, M. (1992) *(1792) Vindication of the Rights of Woman*, ed. M.Brody, Harmondworth: Penguin.

Wood, J.C. (ed.) (1984) *Adam Smith: Critical Assessments*, London: Croom Helm.

Woolhouse, R.S. (1988) *The Empiricists*, Oxford: Oxford University Press.

Wright, E.O. (1985) *Classes*, London: Verso.

Wright, W. (1975) *Six Guns and Society: A Structural Study of the Western*, Berkeley, CA: University of California Press.

Wrong, D (1980) *(1961)* 'The Oversocialised Conception of Man in Modern Sociology', in R. Bocock, P. Hamilton, K. Thompson and A. Walton (eds), *An Introduction to Sociology*, London: Fontana in association with the Open University Press.

Wu, D. (ed.) (1994) *Romanticism: An Anthology*, Oxford: Blackwell.

Yates, F.A. (1975) *Astraea: The Imperial Theme in the Sixteenth Century*, London: Routledge & Kegan Paul.

Yinger, J.M. (1982) *Countercultures: The Promise and Peril of a World Turned Upside Down*, New York: Free Press.

Young, I.M. (1990) *Justice and the Politics of Difference*, Princeton, NJ: Princeton University Press.

Young, M. (1958) *The Rise of Meritocracy*, London: Thames & Hudson.

Young, R.E. (ed.) (1981) *Untying the Text: A Post-Structuralist Reader*, London: Routledge & Kegan Paul.

Young–Eisendrath, P. and Dawson, T. (eds) (1997) *The Cambridge Companion to Jung*, Cambridge: Cambridge University Press.

Zizek, S. (1989) *The Sublime Object of Ideology*, London and New York: Verso.

—— (1992) *Enjoy Your Symptom! Jacques Lacan in Hollywood and Out*, New York and London: Routledge.

Zolloth, L. (2003) 'Yearning for the Long Lost Home: The Lemba and the Jewish Narrative of Genetic Return', *Developing World Bioethics*, 4(2): 127–32.

Zuriff, G.E. (1985) *Behaviourism: A Conceptual Reconstruction*, New York: Columbia University Press.

INDEX OF NAMES

INDEX

Language and Linguistics: The Key Concepts

2nd edition

R.L. Trask

Edited by Peter Stockwel

A comprehensive critical work, *Language and Linguistics: The Key Concepts 2nd edition* is a highly readable A-Z guide to the main terms and concepts used in the study of language and linguistics.

Accessible and clearly presented, definitions include:

- terms used in grammatical analysis
- branches of linguistics from semantics to neuro-linguistics
- approaches used in studying language from critical discourse analysis to systemic linguistics
- linguistic phenomena from code-switching to conversational implicature
- language varieties from pidgin to standard language

Tracing the origin of the concept featured and outlining the key associated individuals, each entry also provides a guide to further reading and is extensively cross-referenced. Engaging and easy to use, this is an essential reference guide for undergraduate and postgraduate students, as well as anyone with an interest in this fascinating field.

ISBN10 0-415-15742-0
ISBN13 978-0-415-15742-1